Material Kenosis

Material Kenosis

A Metaphysical Essay on the Negativity of Death

MARCO STANGO

Foreword by Mark K. Spencer

◥PICKWICK *Publications* · Eugene, Oregon

MATERIAL KENOSIS
A Metaphysical Essay on the Negativity of Death

Copyright © 2025 Marco Stango. All rights reserved. Except for brief quotations in critical publications or reviews, no part of this book may be reproduced in any manner without prior written permission from the publisher. Write: Permissions, Wipf and Stock Publishers, 199 W. 8th Ave., Suite 3, Eugene, OR 97401.

Pickwick Publications
An Imprint of Wipf and Stock Publishers
199 W. 8th Ave., Suite 3
Eugene, OR 97401

www.wipfandstock.com

PAPERBACK ISBN: 978-1-6667-5030-0
HARDCOVER ISBN: 978-1-6667-5031-7
EBOOK ISBN: 978-1-6667-5032-4

Cataloguing-in-Publication data:

Names: Stango, Marco. | Spencer, Mark K., foreword.

Title: Material kenosis : a metaphysical essay on the negativity of death / Marco Stango ; foreword by Mark K. Spencer.

Description: Eugene, OR : Pickwick Publications, 2025 | Includes bibliographical references and index.

Identifiers: ISBN 978-1-6667-5030-0 (paperback) | ISBN 978-1-6667-5031-7 (hardcover) | ISBN 978-1-6667-5032-4 (ebook)

Subjects: LCSH: Death—Religious aspects—Christianity. | Death. | Life—Religious aspects—Christianity.

Classification: BT26 .S75 2025 (paperback) | BT26 .S75 (ebook)

05/23/25

Unless otherwise indicated, Scripture texts in this work are taken from the New American Bible, revised edition © 2010 Confraternity of Christian Doctrine, Washington, D.C. and are used by permission of the copyright owner. All rights reserved. No part of the New American Bible may be reproduced in any form without permission in writing from the copyright owner.

Scripture quotations marked KJV are from the King James or Authorized Version.

Many thanks to the editors and publishers of the following articles who granted permission for them to be reprinted in a significantly revised and expanded form in the present book:

- "Death as Material Kenosis: A Thomistic Proposal," *HeyJ* 61 (2020) 327–46
- "Making Sense of 'Being Dead': A Thomistic Approach," *Studia Neoaristotelica* 18 (2021) 201–24

For Charlie and Joli,
who, from their "master class," may be smiling
at many of the things said in this book

The age is desolate not only because God is dead but also because mortals scarcely know or are capable even of their own mortality. Mortals are still not in the possession of their essence. Death withdraws into the enigmatic. The mystery of suffering is covered over. No one is learning to love.

MARTIN HEIDEGGER, *OFF THE BEATEN TRACK*, 204

We must not follow those who advise us, being men, to think of human things, and, being mortal, of mortal things, but must, so far as we can, make ourselves immortal, and strain every nerve to live in accordance with the best thing in us.

ARISTOTLE, *NICOMACHEAN ETHICS*, 1177B.31–1178A.1

I have set before you life and death, the blessing and the curse. Choose life, then, that you and your descendants may live, by loving the Lord, your God, obeying his voice, and holding fast to him. For that will mean life for you to live on the land which the Lord swore to your ancestors, to Abraham, Isaac, and Jacob, to give to them.

DEUT 30:19–20

Contents

Foreword by Mark K. Spencer	ix
Acknowledgments	xv
Abbreviations	xvii
Introduction	1
Chapter One	
Making Sense of "Death" in Some Analytic Philosophers	20
Chapter Two	
Death as Material Kenosis: A Thomistic Proposal	64
Chapter Three	
The Analogy of Being and the Nonbeing of Death	124
Chapter Four	
The Transhumanist Overcoming of Death and Human Desire: What the Experience of "For a Child Is Born to Us, a Son Is Given to Us" May Tell Us About a Possible Misunderstanding Characterizing Our Technological Civilization	226
Conclusion	295
Bibliography	299
Index	317

Foreword
Mark K. Spencer

ACCORDING TO PLATO, SOCRATES taught that philosophy is the practice of death. The Christian life, St. Paul teaches, requires us to "always bear in the body the dying of the Lord Jesus" (2 Cor 4:10 KJV). On these bases, one might reasonably think, with Friedrich Nietzsche and many after him, that Christianity and classical philosophy are cults of death, resentful of life, in love with suffering and our final demise. When confronted with objections like that, Christians often tend to respond defensively, either by belittling the objection as if it had no grounding at all, or by doubling down on a focus on death, sometimes to the point of confirming the objection. This book is a happy contrast to those tendencies. Marco Stango is able to both take this sort of objection completely seriously, while showing, without defensiveness, that its claims are entirely false. He shows that Christianity involves a complete embrace of *life* and a recognition of the utter nonbeing of death, and that modern views that seem to offer a way to overcome death (for example, through technology or through reorienting one's thinking about death) are actually based on the most obsessive *thanatophilia*.

For all of its problems and internal squabbles, Catholic thought during the last century has undergone a major renaissance. This rebirth of Catholic thinking is found especially in the tradition that runs from Maurice Blondel and Erich Przywara through Hans Urs von Balthasar, Henri de Lubac, Ferdinand Ulrich, Adrienne von Speyr, Josef Pieper, Edith Stein, and others, to many Communio-school and Thomistic thinkers in our own day. My own work is part of this tradition, and Stango works closely with it in this book. This tradition has revitalized Catholic thought in a range of ways. I want to introduce the present volume, and call attention to just how important it is, by considering how it furthers at least five lines of renewal initiated by that tradition.

First, the thinkers in this tradition took on a truly *Catholic* approach to philosophical and theological sources. While remaining solidly rooted in biblical, patristic, and medieval sources, and while endorsing a robustly Christocentric metaphysics, these thinkers displayed an eager openness to what is true in a vast range of sources, from ancient Greeks and Romans to modern German idealists, existentialists, and phenomenologists, to non-Western sources of all sorts. In seeking to synthesize these many sources, they counteracted approaches to Christian thought and religious practice which remain stuck in the resources of only a single philosophical, theological, or spiritual tradition. Those narrower approaches are the ones that have most often fallen into the obsession with death, to which both Christianity's modern detractors and Stango himself are responding. By synthesizing many sources, new ideas were injected into Catholic thought, allowing for a more expansive account of God, being, and the human person, including the place of death in human life. I would contend that Catholic thought, rooted as it is from the New Testament on in a range of Semitic and Greek sources, is *intrinsically* oriented toward synthesizing and learning from many traditions: that is a major part of what it means to be *Catholic*, to think and live *according to the whole (kath'holon)*. By placing his approach to death in the center of this Catholic project, Stango avoids being a slavish adherent of the thinkers in any school, including those in his own tradition. He considers a wide range of views on death and the human person, from analytic philosophers, Epicureans, Platonists, consequentialists, continental philosophers from Hegel through Heidegger to Vattimo, transhumanists and posthumanists, and Christian theologians of all sorts. Most of them come in for pretty severe criticism, but Stango also finds aspects of the truth in each. It seems that nearly everyone has, for all their legitimate insights, to some extent succumbed to a sort of death mysticism or celebration. Stango's goal is a coherent, plausible account, which cuts through all the nonsense and wishful thinking people express about death.

In a second line of renewal, the great Catholic thinkers of the last century embraced the distinction between (to use Martin Heidegger's language) the *ontological* and the *ontic*, or (to use Gabriel Marcel's terms) between *mystery* and mere *problems*. An ontic approach to philosophy and theology merely considers beings, like human persons, as discrete entities with properties and parts, causally interacting with other individual entities. That approach only inquires into how beings are structured and how they interact; philosophy and theology are treated as a series of intellectual puzzles or technical problems, which can be solved if we find the right rationally graspable evidence or technological fixes. That approach fails to ask *ontological questions*, that is, questions about the very meaning of the being of things like the human person or death. On an ontological approach, we recognize that significant aspects of life are *mysteries*, problems that, in Marcel's words, "encroach upon their own data," affecting the very way in which we inquire into them. Existence itself is a mystery: we cannot achieve a vantage point outside of existence from which we can examine it. Rather, we are always already caught up in existence: it affects everything we do, including our inquiries about it. Death, Stango recognizes, can adequately only be approached ontologically and as a mystery. Death is not a mere causal event at the end of biological life, which we can manage by finding the right spiritual or technological techniques. It is, rather, a condition affecting the very mode in which we currently exist, a wound or contradictory condition in our being that is constantly present throughout our earthly lives. Any technical or ontic aspects of death must be understood in the context of inquiring into the very meaning of being.

Too often over the last few centuries, philosophy and theology have become mere ontic or problems-oriented disciplines. But those approaches to philosophy and theology risk a kind of idolatry, substituting concepts and propositions for the living, existential realities to which concepts and propositions are meant to lead us. A third line of renewal brought about by the Catholic thinkers of the last century is that they saw that theology (and, I would add, philosophy), including its most technical sides, must be done, in Balthasar's words, "on one's knees." Genuine intellectual thought is inseparable from spiritual life and prayer. Stango engages in lots of technical metaphysics in this book, but he never loses sight of the spiritual and existential impact of what he is arguing. Indeed, it is because Stango both is rooted in a wide range of source material and is constantly attentive to the spiritual and existential basis of all genuine thought that he is able to move the technical side of the metaphysical tradition forward here in a number of important ways. Let me mention just a few of them. From its origins, philosophy has tried to think through what is distinctive about human death, as opposed to, but also in continuity with other kinds of death and corruption. Stango shows us how to honor the distinctiveness of human death without turning it into something constitutive of human persons as such or into something positive or really existing—all of which, he shows, are tendencies destructive of spiritual and moral life. Death involves "negation without annihilation" and "material kenosis as a mode of being." The nothingness from which creation arises and the nothingness of evil and death are entirely distinct kinds of nothingness, without analogy between them. The Person of the Son can, out of mercy, embrace death, without incorporating death into the analogy of being. These metaphysical developments are precisely what allow him to show how we should freely assume our own death, but never desire it as such. We can hold onto the tradition's rich reflections on the benefits of thinking about death (*ars moriendi*) without falling into the trap of making death something good in itself.

Not only did the great Catholic thinkers of the last century recover an ontological mode of inquiry and couple technical metaphysics with the depths of existential and spiritual life, but, in their fourth significant avenue of renewal, they saw, better than ever before, the centrality of philosophical anthropology and personalism to Catholic thought. At the core of Christianity are the encounters with Christ and the Trinity. These mysteries have direct bearing on how we understand our own personhood and nature: in Christ, human nature is taken up by a divine person, and the Trinity is imaged in us human persons. Building on personalists like Sergius Bulgakov, Max Scheler, and Martin Buber, twentieth-century philosophers like Dietrich von Hildebrand and Karol Wojtyła saw that we must recover a sense for the irreducibility of human persons. It is not the case that human persons are *nothing but* matter or parts of society or anything else other than *whole, mysterious persons*. Even theories from the tradition, like hylomorphism, which explain a great deal about us, are inadequate on their own. They risk reducing us to being *nothing but* soul or body or a substance just like other substances. Even those theories must be taken up into a broader, *personal* context. Just as Stango extends Platonic, Aristotelian, and Thomistic ontology in new and surprising ways, so also he develops a metaphysics of irreducible personhood, and of death's relation to persons. Death is not just something that happens to a soul, a body, or a form-matter composite; rather, it befalls *whole persons*. Likewise, events like birth, parenthood, suffering, and aging must be understood ontologically, as they affect whole persons. Indeed, Stango's most beautiful insights in this book have to do with analogies he draws between fatherhood and resurrection. Just as his development of fundamental metaphysical categories allow him to lay the foundations for a wholly plausible and Catholic spirituality of death, so likewise his developments of philosophical anthropology lay the foundations for significant new insights, many of which are only hinted at in this book. Let me mention two lines of inquiry which would benefit from the anthropological ideas in this book. First, many Catholic philosophers have recently been embroiled in a debate over whether the human person continues to exist when the soul is separated from the body in death, prior to the resurrection. Stango's account of how death is a wound that affects our whole mode of being and of the complex ways that the soul is dramatically affected by death, lay the foundation for moving beyond the impasses that currently plague that debate. Second, that same metaphysics lays the foundation for a new, Catholic metaphysics of disability and impairment.

Finally, the best Catholic thinkers of the last century have offered trenchant critiques of modern thought and technology, while taking the aspirations of modernity seriously. Stango sees technology, including its most death-defying forms, as a genuine expression of our natural desires for immortality and for spiritualizing the natural world. His critique of modern technology is like John Paul II's critique of pornography: it's not that it shows too much of human sexuality, but that it shows too little, not delving into the true personal depths of that mystery. Likewise, Stango shows that the desire to overcome death technologically is not a desire for too much, but a desire for too little. Modern technical attempts to "solve" or "cure" death end up, paradoxically but inevitably, loving and focusing on death more than anything. Stango's critique here is the best account I have ever read of what it means to call our culture a "culture of death": a culture that is entirely focused, in terrified fascination, on our own demise, a focus that affects all of our other approaches to life. Our goal in life should not just be to stave off death for a while, even indefinitely but to overcome the condition death entirely, which can only come from the resurrection. That, in turn, requires us to embrace death, with the crucified Christ, and receive our definitive condition after death. The problem with trying to control death is not that we are "playing God," but that it shows that we do not want to be God seriously enough, that we want to be content with our current death-affected life. Christianity instead offers us the promise of *deification*, of becoming God as God became man. That is the full meaning of the resurrection, the ultimate goal of human life.

Acknowledgments

I COULD HAVE NOT written this book without the encouragement and support of my colleagues at St. Bernard's School of Theology and Ministry, Anthony Coleman, Daniel Drain, Charles Hughes Huff, Matthew Kuhner, Lisa Lickona, and Stephen Loughlin. A special thanks goes to Daniel Drain, Charles Hughes Huff, and Matthew Kuhner, who have read different parts of this book at various points in the writing process and commented on them generously, with that special mixture of attention to details, breadth of vision, and hermeneutical charity that characterize their way of doing philosophy and theology. I owe this group of people much, including the gifts of trust and friendship. A selection of chapter 3 was presented as the inaugural lecture of the St. Bernard's Academic Series in September 2023. I would like to thank all the students who attended and asked questions in that occasion.

I could not forget to thank my colleagues at the school where I served previously, DeSales University. I am indebted to William Hamant, Rodney Howser, Sara Hulse Kirby, Gregory Kerr, and Joshua Schulz for engaging with me in endless conversations about death and other philosophical-theological topics. After my many peregrinations around the world, I had found in the Department of Philosophy and Theology at DeSales University, first, an unexpected academic post, and second, and more deeply, a unique community of life and thought. Part of chapter 2 was presented to a large group of students and faculty in February 2020 as one of the DeSales University Philosophy and Theology Lecture Series. The lecture was well received and sparked an interesting discussion, things for which I am still grateful.

During the time I have spent thinking about the ideas contained in this book I have benefited from the work of and the discussion with

ACKNOWLEDGMENTS

several people. I would like to thank in particular Rebecca Abbott, Maria Barbara Angelucci, Amerigo Barzaghi, John Betz, Martin Bieler, Francesco Botturi, Maria Regina Brioschi, John Brungardt, Rachel Coleman, Peter Colosi, Jason Eberl, Eduardo Fermandois, Christopher Gibson, Savanah Landerholm, Apolonio Latar, Antonio Lizzadri, Giovanni Maddalena, Keith McPartland, James Nolan, Francis Oakley, Matthew Pietropaoli, Federico Ponzoni, Silvano Petrosino, Eric Pommier, Rocco Sacconaghi, D. C. Schindler, Michael Taylor, Angelo Teruzzi, Erik van Versendaal, Luca Valera, and Palle Yourgrau. I am especially thankful to Luca Valera, for his unwavering support and friendship over many years, and Rocco Sacconaghi, not only for his friendship, but also for the many hours spent on the phone and, more rarely, in person, talking about the topic of this book and the mystery of what it means to be a person.

Part of chapter 2 was presented at the 2018 American Catholic Philosophical Association meeting in San Diego. I would like to thank the many people involved with the American Catholic Philosophical Association as well as the American Maritain Association, who continue to be a clear beam of philosophical light as I try to make sense of our world.

I am also deeply grateful to Mark Spencer for accepting to read the manuscript of the book and agreeing to write the foreword. I have experienced a sort of elective affinity for his work, which combines admirably a firm rootedness in the classical and Catholic tradition with a fearless capacity to explore different and even distant philosophical territories. In recent years I have found myself engaged in a similar endeavor, which I have pursued, if not as fearlessly and successfully as he, at least with the same conviction.

Finally, my deepest gratitude goes to my wife, Ursula Roessiger, who not only has read the manuscript and instructed me on how to improve it (instructions which I may have not always followed as diligently as I should have), but who has also lovingly dragged me into her favorite musings on God, kenosis, and death, long before I even thought about writing this book. Her insightfulness is only matched by the patient care, daily compassion, and proverbial irony with which she sustains me and our son. That she means more than I could ever express belongs, as the poet says, to the domain of those *cose che 'l tacere è bello*.

M.S.
Hancock, Massachusetts, August 8, 2024

Abbreviations

Ang	*Angelicum*
Comm	*Communio*
DivThom	*Divus Thomas*
Enarrat. Ps.	*Enarrations on the Psalms*
HeyJ	*Heythrop Journal*
LCL	Loeb Classical Library
NV	*Nova et Vetera*
PL	Patrologia Latina. Edited by J.-P. Migne. 217 vols. Paris, 1844–64
ST	*Summa Theologiae*. By Thomas Aquinas. Translated by Lawrence Shapcote. Latin-English Opera Omnia 13–22. Steubenville, OH: Emmaus Academic, 2012–18
QDP	*Disputed Questions on the Power of God*. By Thomas Aquinas. Translated by Lawrence Shapcote. Latin-English Opera Omnia 25. Steubenville, OH: Emmaus Academic, 2023
QDM	*Quaestiones Disputatae de Malo*. By Thomas Aquinas. Aquinas Institute, n.d. https://aquinas.cc/la/la/~QDeMalo

Introduction

> But you see my aporias here: I would not want to cut off the link between the philosopher and the theologian, moving right away to the discourse of faith as many religious thinkers do, who despise in a certain sense the timid, maybe even shabby, approach of philosophy. I would not want to cut off this link by throwing myself right away into the arms of Christ.
>
> XAVIER TILLIETTE, *MORTE E SOPRAVVIVENZA*, 395–96
> (AUTHOR'S TRANSLATION)

1. VLADIMIR JANKÉLÉVITCH, THE author of a wonderful and voluminous philosophical study on death, once remarked, with a profound taste for paradox, that "there is nothing to say about death." But he was careful enough to justify his position with an important qualification: "In order to say or to explain that there is nothing to say [about death] one needs to spend a lot of words."¹ Another philosopher, Xavier Tilliette, prudentially admonishes the readers of one of his books on death with the following statement: "We should speak about death rarely, but we should think about it often."²

Insofar as death is the negation of life, and thus some form of nonbeing, how could we disagree with Jankélévitch that not much can be said about it? If being and intelligibility are convertible, aren't nonbeing and death precisely that about which there is nothing to say or to think? And insofar as we agree with Tilliette that thoughtful silence may the best attitude toward death, how can we rescue the present book from being yet another pseudo-philosophical chatter about death? How to state,

---

1. Jankélévitch, *Quelque part dans l'inachevé*, 167 (author's translation).
2. Tilliette, *Morte e sopravvivenza*, 418.

in good conscience, that this book is an instance of genuine thinking and not an exercise in idle talk?

At the same time, it should be acknowledged that both Jankélévitch and Tilliette did write many words about death, and rightly so. In fact, how could man abstain from trying to say something about death, even when death remains an unexplainable evil and an unsolvable mystery? And why should the thinking of death be deprived of the hard and slow discipline of the word, even when one agrees that the consummation of the word on this subject may well be thoughtful silence?

2. The aim of this introduction is to spell out the sense in which I take this book to be a work in "Catholic philosophy" and the meaning of the title, "Material Kenosis: A Metaphysical Essay on the Negativity of Death."

Let me start with what I understand by Catholic philosophy. "Catholic philosophy" is of course a variation of the broader label "Christian philosophy" which was at the center of a series of debates in the 1930s regarding whether philosophy could or ought to be "Christian" (and, if yes, what would its nature be) or instead it had to remain noncommittal with respect to revelation in order to remain philosophy.[3] My intent here is neither to reconstruct that complex historical debate nor to try to justify the possibility of Catholic philosophy in general against its detractors, either Christian or otherwise. Rather, I would like to state, in a rather schematic way, the basic outline of the approach to the problem of death that I have followed in this book and why I take it to be an exercise in Catholic philosophy.

As I see it, a book of Catholic philosophy is a book in which whatever reality is under consideration, death in this case, is clarified, i.e., explained and exposed, so that the way in which such reality may be disposed to receive the grace of Christ is made more evident. Theology explores the mysteries of the Triune God, Creator and the Redeemer of the world,[4] while philosophy, and Catholic philosophy especially, explores the mystery of created being vis-à-vis God's creative and redemptive power. Catholic theology and Catholic philosophy are both truly "catholic," that is, they are both concerned with the whole—just as the pope and the emperor in the Middle Ages—and so, in a sense, they do not leave anything out and are concerned with the same, as I said, with the whole—the world

---

3. See Sadler, *Reason Fulfilled by Revelation*.
4. See John Paul II, *Fides et Ratio* §93.

in God and God in the world. But theology sees the world from the point of view of God's creative and redemptive power (because, in the life of faith, we are given a share in the knowledge that God has of himself and of the world), while Catholic philosophy sees God's creative and redemptive power from the vantage of the world. Catholic philosophy must "take care of the world" (with apt concepts, sound arguments, insightful descriptions, etc.) in order to present it as a self-offering to its Creator and Redeemer, in order to be redeemed always again.

As I see it, the guiding question of Catholic philosophy—that which gives Catholic philosophy its unity and defining character—is "What, exactly, is in need of transformation?" (where "transformation" is taken here, based on Scripture, as the mark of the action of grace on nature).[5] A Catholic, adopting for once W. V. O. Quine's amusing insight, could correctly respond: "Everything!"[6] With a little more effort, however, the answer could be further detailed. The advantage of this formulation of the guiding question of Catholic philosophy lies in the fact that it contains all the essential elements that the practice of philosophy in the Catholic tradition seems to favor: the question about the essence of things ("what"); the question about being ("is"); the question about the definitive and yet incipient reality of what is, the "already and not yet" of creation ("need of transformation"). The articulation of this problem and the attempt to provide an answer to it is the task of a philosophy that wants to call itself "Catholic."

This is why in this book the stress falls on death's *negativity*. The "what" of death is that of a specific form of negation, that which classic metaphysics identified as evil and "privation of the due good" (more on this below). As such, the "being" of death is a kind of nonbeing, again, a specific form of negation that goes to the very heart of the human being. This radical negativity at work in our life is at once definitive for our condition without being either original, or constitutive, or even ultimate for us. Accordingly, it is a wound present at the roots of our nature which awaits a corresponding transformation. The concept of "material kenosis" proposed in this book is an attempt to develop a Catholic philosophy of death. While the notion of "kenosis" is obviously of Scriptural

---

5. For the notion of transformation, see Falque, *Metamorphosis of Finitude*, 1–2. I will use "transformation" and "metamorphosis" interchangeably.

6. "A curious thing about the ontological problem is its simplicity. It can be put in three Anglo-Saxon monosyllables: 'What is there?' It can be answered, moreover, in a word—'Everything'—and everyone will accept this answer as true" (Quine, "On What There Is," 1).

derivation,[7] I will explore it philosophically. The reason why I call it "material" will become clear starting with chapter 2.

While from the point of view of Catholic theology death should be seen in the context of faith, and thus, in the context of the ultimate positivity of Christ, who is life and resurrection, from the point of view of philosophy, the life and resurrection that is Christ must be seen in the context of the negativity of death—death understood as material kenosis, as *total negation without annihilation*. And while theology has a certain priority over philosophy—from the Catholic point of view, the very last word on death cannot be but Christological—philosophy has, in turn, a certain relative priority over theology, insofar as it is philosophy that clarifies (explains and exposes) how exactly we should conceive of the world that Christ redeems, the world that receives Christ. In relation to our problem: it is philosophy that explains and exposes what is that death—human death—that Christ assumes and redeems.

Catholic philosophy thus deals in a sense with the "world without God," and especially with "man without God," but only after God has revealed himself in Christ and only after Christ has revealed man to man.[8] What does this mean? On could say, drawing loosely from Blaise Pascal, that Catholic philosophy is concerned with "the misery of man without God" or even with his greatness, but a greatness, however, which is still awaiting to be fulfilled and eschatologically realized. In this sense, philosophy is "Catholic" because what the misery of man truly consists in is definitively and unmistakably revealed only in God's self-revelation in Christ and only in Christ's revelation of man to man. The case of human death is exemplary here, although not exclusive. In fact, history is full of *rumors* (doubts, uncertainties, rationalizations, delusions, coping-mechanisms, etc.) about the meaning of human death (i.e., about death being somehow meaningful) and its role in life: Maybe death is just a part of nature which we can accept once we have understood the role it plays? Perhaps death is the defining fact about human finitude? Or maybe death is a gift which opens our eyes to the beautiful caducity of the world?

---

7. "Have among yourselves the same attitude that is also yours in Christ Jesus, Who, though he was in the form of God, did not regard equality with God something to be grasped. Rather, he emptied himself taking the form of a slave, coming in human likeness; and found in appearance, he humbled himself, becoming obedient to death, even death on a cross" (Phil 2:5–8).

8. Paul VI, *Gaudium et Spes* §22.

INTRODUCTION

It is the *Word of God* who puts a definitive end to the *rumors of man* about God and man. These include the *rumors of man about his own death*. The church teaches that "through one person sin entered the world, and through sin, death" (Rom 5:12). Human death is thus revealed as that total negation without annihilation of man which, despite its being definitive for the human condition as we get to experience it, it is at the same time neither original, nor constitutive of, nor ultimate for us. Hence, it is this death, finally revealed for what it is, that Christ has assumed in his assumption of the fallen human nature and that he has suffered and redeemed in his passion. And it is this death that philosophy has the task of explaining and exposing as best as it can.

It takes Christian revelation (what is "above nature") to discover in a definitive and unmistakable way what belongs to the order of being and what is against it. What belongs to the order of being and what is opposed to it could in principle be discovered apart from Christian revelation, but "only by a few, and that after a long time, and with the admixture of many errors," as Thomas teaches.[9] Philosophy comes into itself only in light of the Christian revelation, that is, it is finally given the guidelines for exploring the natural order of being for what it is—and the resources to avoid fundamental mistakes about what such order is not. Søren Kierkegaard's formula seems to be very precise if we apply it to the "sickness" of death: "To be aware of this sickness [as sickness] is the Christian's advantage over the natural human being [and thus over a philosophy that refuses to be 'Christian' or 'Catholic']; to be cured of this sickness is the Christian's blessedness."[10] As I see it, an account of the "cure" lies more within theology. But account of the awareness of the sickness as sickness lies more within philosophy; thus, while hopefully not itself sick, this book is about a sickness, the total negation without annihilation of human death.

From this perspective, theology remains the queen of the sciences and philosophy the maiden, as in the Middle Ages the pope's authority maintained a primacy over the emperor's (may the historians forgive the simplification of this statement). Nevertheless, just as it was the pope who used to put the crown on the emperor's head, so it was the emperor the one who had to prepare his head in order to receive it. The relation between Catholic theology and Catholic philosophy is never resolved

---

9. *ST* 1, q. 1, a. 1, co.
10. Kierkegaard, *Sickness unto Death*, 21.

once and for all but develops as a mutually enriching polarity: in its concreteness, Catholic thinking is now theological, now philosophical, within a unity which however is not confusion.

Catholic philosophy is one in essence with man's opening himself up to and preparing himself for giving himself to Christ. Analogously to an "examination of conscience" in the moral realm, Catholic philosophy could be called, more broadly, an "examination of being." It accomplishes this examining self-opening and self-preparation by trying to "see" more clearly what is at stake, that is, by attempting an explanation and an exposition of its subject matter. Accordingly, the task of philosophy is not superficially limited to a time "before" Christ. It is the constant self-preparation of the Christian, the self-preparation of the one who has received Christ, of the one who receives Christ always again by exposing his wounded heart to him.

This book then, which aspires to be a work of Catholic philosophy, aims to serve theology and the life of faith precisely by clarifying what human death may be from a philosophical and metaphysical point of view (see below my discussion of the term "metaphysics"; for now, let us take metaphysics to mean, simply, the study of being as being). It thus provides man with some resources to better prepare to receive Christ's life and resurrection. With Hans Urs von Balthasar, we say that Christians are called to be the "guardians of metaphysics."[11] And when it comes to human mortality, metaphysics must "guard" the sheer negativity of death so that its transformation in and by Christ may shine more brightly. To use Adrienne von Speyr's beautiful phrase, death is "the moment when God's word falls silent" and "the waiting for the Son's voice," for the Son of God who is "the complete reinstitution of the divine Word."[12] It is the task of a Catholic metaphysics of death to explain and expose the sheer negativity of this silence. We thus ask: What, exactly, is the negativity of death, and how does it impact, or how is it manifested by, our need of transformation?

3. If I am correct in saying that the precise task of a Catholic metaphysics when it comes to death is to "guard" its sheer negativity against any attempt to turn it into something positive, my proposal in this book is in partial agreement and at the same time (but not under the same respect) in partial disagreement with Françoise Dastur's reading of metaphysics. Dastur, a Heideggerian who has written extensively on

---

11. Balthasar, *Realm of Metaphysics in Modern Age*, 656. See also Schindler, "Guardians of Metaphysics."

12. Speyr, *Mystery of Death*, 50.

death, shares the same concern that I have just outlined—guarding the sheer negativity of death—but she thinks that Western metaphysics and Christianity have done exactly the opposite. For her, metaphysics and Christianity represent the attempt to "conquer," "tame," and "neutralize" the negativity of death: "The conquering of death is the aim not only of metaphysics, which makes claims to a knowledge of the suprasensible and the non-corruptible, but also of religion, in so far as this promises a personal afterlife."[13] Only a non-metaphysical, non-Christian form of thought, then, can responsibly stare at death in its face and treat it for what it is (that is, for what it is *not*).

Plato, Aristotle, and Hegel are the representative figures of this metaphysical strategy aimed at "taming" or "neutralizing" death by turning it into something that "has a place" within a metaphysical framework and thus, we may say, as something that has a meaning.[14] Death is for Dastur, contrary to the metaphysical tradition as she understands it, the simply unthinkable. But metaphysics has turned the unthinkability of death into something thinkable and essential. For Plato, death is the separation of soul and body and thus the very form of the philosophical existence, centered in the pursuit of the suprasensible. The absolute nonbeing of death is thus wrapped in distorting metaphysical garments or, which is the same, Platonic metaphysics does not allow the radical negativity of death to manifest itself for what it is—that is, as that which cannot in any way manifest itself, as what can never be a phenomenon, as what is utterly unthinkable. Platonic metaphysics covers the negativity of death by showing it as a phenomenon—the phenomenon and the task of the truly philosophical life! Also Plato's insistence on the immortality of the soul ends up neutralizing death as negation. The very concept of death as liberation into the immortal, eternal suprasensible seems to undermine the possibility of appreciating the radical negativity of death.

According to Dastur, Aristotle continues in his own way on the same metaphysical path initiated by Plato. Death is thought by Aristotle as symmetrical to generation and thus the nonbeing of death is conceptualized relatively and temporally, that is, as the future no-more of what is at the present time. "In this way non-being—which, however, is the absolute other of being—is provided with a face, an *eidos*—that is, a form, an essence and a concept. Yet it is with this pure non-being of which

---

13. Dastur, *Death*, 1. Tilliette is aware of the problem, but his balanced approach is definitely not dismissive of Western metaphysics (Tilliette, *Morte e sopravvivenza*, 17).

14. Dastur, *Death*, 19–38.

neither 'essence' nor thought is possible that we see ourselves confronted in death."[15]

Finally, according to Dastur, it is Hegel who epitomizes this "covering" tendency present throughout Western metaphysics. For Hegel, in fact, the negativity of death must be integrated into the positivity of being insofar as absolute spirit requires and must pass through the finitude and death of history in order to reconcile itself to itself and therefore "come into itself." Therefore "death, thus raised to the level of the absolute itself, is no more than a preface to resurrection."[16] According to Dastur, the taming of death at work in Western metaphysics is consummated in Christianity, which recapitulates this history through the affirmation of the immortality of the soul and, in particular, of the resurrection of the dead.

The aim of this paragraph is not to assess if and to what extent Dastur's historical account is accurate. The point is, rather, to repeat that, contrary to what she thinks and as I suggested in the previous paragraph, the role of a good metaphysics is precisely that of preserving being from any mark of deathlike negativity (exactly what Dastur pursues through her non-metaphysical philosophy) and thus, by contrast, that of guarding the sheer negativity of death from any wishful taming of it through the stipulation of an original and constitutive relation between being, life, and death. A *Catholic* metaphysics can do so more confidently, precisely in light of what revelation states about death.

This brief sketch of Dastur's position allows me to make another point. Many contemporary thinkers, including Dastur and Jankélévitch, infer from the idea that death is nonbeing the conclusion that death is therefore a "non-phenomenon," the "unthinkable" par excellence, something whose essence cannot be spoken about in any way. For instance, Jankélévitch writes: "We know that death will come. However, since we cannot know *what* death *is* (*quid sit mors*), we do not really know *what* will happen. So, just as we do not know *when*, we also do not know in what that which will happen consists, nor do we know whether it will consist in anything at all."[17] Remarks such as these are very valuable, I

---

15. Dastur, *Death*, 36.

16. Dastur, *Death*, 38. She continues: "From Aristotle to Hegel this absolute negativity [of death], this radical caesura, this purely and simply unthinkable thing death, sees itself converted into 'relative non-being' and 'determinate negativity,' into a 'sublatable' caesura and a simple limit of the thinkable. This testifies ultimately to the inability of metaphysics really to face up to death. Can what is genuinely unthinkable for metaphysics *appear* as such in another kind of discourse?" Emphasis in original.

17. Jankélévitch, *Mort*, 137 (author's translation); emphasis in original.

think, both for the truth they convey and for the mistake they contain. The truth expressed here is that death is a form of negation, a form of nonbeing, and, as such, something that cannot be thought and spoken about by itself or originally. Evil, classically understood as the privation of the due good, is always parasitical on being, and this metaphysical parasitism extends to its relative thinkability. The mistake, however, is to believe that as a consequence death is never a phenomenon for us (how could Dastur and Jankélévitch speak about it if this were true?) or, at least, that it is never a phenomenon that can be brought under the gaze of metaphysical thinking without being tamed and turned into a positive condition of being.[18] Contrary to this tendency, I believe that it is possible to provide an answer to the question, "What, exactly, is the negativity of death, and how does it impact, or how is it manifested by, our need of transformation?" This book attempts to do so while "guarding" the sheer negativity of death against undue attempts to make it something less metaphysically serious and scandalous than it in fact is.[19]

18. Note Dastur's contradiction when she first explains, contra metaphysics, that death is "that which can never become phenomenon" (*Death*, 37), but then she devotes an entire chapter to a Heidegger-inspired "phenomenology of mortal being," as "another kind of discourse" or an "affective" knowledge thanks to which the pure non-being of death can finally appear, that is, become a phenomenon (38). Question: If death is pure non-being, why would it appear through affectivity but not through judgment? What makes affectivity so special to manifest what cannot in principle be manifested? No answer seems to be found in Dastur and in all the authors who belong to the same tradition. The idea that a phenomenology of death does not pretend to reveal death as "present in itself in person" but rather only through a phenomenological analysis of "the manner in which the human being relates to its own death" (40) does not seem coherent: it is obviously the case that there is no other way to reveal the former than by engaging in the latter. A more traditional view, which I follow, seems more on point here: death is of course manifested, but manifested as radical negation—the total negation without annihilation which is the best formula I have found to explain what material kenosis is. This is just another way to say that evil is a phenomenon, but only insofar as its phenomenality is that of a *privatio boni*. Death has the phenomenality of certain accidents of human life (suffering, pain, etc.) once these accidents are metaphysically interpreted as *privationes boni* in themselves and as the trace and partial manifestations of that more radical *privatio boni* which is death. The phenomenality of death is found, *in actu exercito*, in the very experiences of suffering, pain, and illness and, *in actu signato*, in these same experiences as filtered and understood in true metaphysical judgments (similar to the cases discussed by Thomas when he says that we can call something "being" also when this something is a privation in itself but it is expressed in a true judgment, for instance, "Robert is blind." See chs. 1–2 on this).

19. A theme that is not explicitly developed in this book but which would deserve a careful study is the philosophical and metaphysical interpretation of change and becoming, which should also include a reflection on the Catechism of the Catholic Church, § 310. Is becoming, with its alternation of being and nonbeing, necessarily

Material Kenosis

4. Part of the job of a philosopher is to have a sense for the Zeitgeist in which he is called to think. Many recent sociological and cultural studies on death have described the transformation of man's attitude towards death which began in modernity, including its public disappearance due to the development of modern medicine and the transformation of healthcare[20] and the "pornographic" shape that death has acquired today, where the public invisibility of death gives rise to a morbid fascination with the violent representation of death in the media.[21]

What I take to be most relevant to that present situation, however, is the reduction of death to an ontic "problem" to be dealt with technoscientifically and the simultaneous disappearance of death as a metaphysical "mystery." In his *Eschatology: Death and Eternal Life*, Joseph Ratzinger clearly explains this phenomenon. Ratzinger recognizes that, "at first glance, our society's attitude to death seems remarkably contradictory. On the one hand death is placed under a taboo. It is unseemly. So far as possible, it must be hidden away, the thought of it repressed in waking consciousness. On the other hand, one is also aware of a tendency to put

---

interpretable as a series of small deaths? Is the negation of the fact that I am not a child anymore identical or analogous to the negation of death? The child that I was has been destroyed; I still am, but as an adult; the child is gone forever. Isn't this a partial death? After all, my death will only finish the job that all the partial deaths in my life have partially accomplished. We find this idea in Augustine: "By now my evil and wicked youth was dead. I was becoming a grown man" (*Confessions* [Chadwick], 111). But is the negation of death of the same kind as the negation of the nonbeing necessarily implied in the passing of time? What concerns me here is the scandalous, negative aspect of death: death as evil. The classic idea of evil as *privatio boni* is immensely helpful here: the lack of a due good. Is it an evil, a privation of the due good, that, as a thirty-nine-year-old man, I am *not* a child anymore? It does not seem that way. On the contrary, it looks like an evil when I, as an adult, still behave as a child, thus showing the lack of the due good of maturity that becomes a middle-aged man. If one looks at change and becoming through the lens of growth, one can see the negation implied in them not as *negative* and *destructive*, but as *positive* and *fruitful*. To contrast it with the irreversibility of death, Jankélévitch aptly describes change and becoming as an "irreversibility in fullness" (*Mort*, 232). "Be fruitful and multiply" (Gen 1:28) also means: Rejoice in the fact that you are not a child any longer! Thank God that I am not a child anymore, because I have been a child. The Western tradition, for better or worse, tends to interpret the negativity of change and becoming as a metaphysical negation. From here, it is a short step to the claim that the negation implied in change and becoming is either identical or analogous to that of death. It is for this reason that, contrary to the majority of the contemporary discussions on death, I find myself compelled to treat death not primarily as a specific case in the phenomenology of the consciousness of time, but as a case of metaphysical negativity, as an evil.

20. See Morin, *Uomo e la morte*.
21. See Gorer, "Pornography of Death."

death on show, which corresponds to the general pulling down of shame-barriers everywhere. How can this contradiction be accounted for?"[22] To move beyond this seeming contradiction, he identifies the heart of the contemporary transformation of the attitude towards death in the rise and overwhelming presence of the technoscientific framework: "Sickness and death are becoming purely technological problems to be handled by the appropriate institution.... They cease to be physical and metaphysical problems which must be suffered and borne in a communion of life, and become instead technical tasks technically handled by technical people.... Death is to be deprived of its character as a place where the metaphysical breaks through. Death is rendered banal, so as to quell the unsettling question which arises from it.... The repression of death is so much easier when death has been naturalized. Death must become so object-like, so ordinary ... that no remnant of the metaphysical question is left within it."[23] He concludes: "Death becomes the key to the question: What really *is* man? The mounting callousness towards human life which we are experiencing today is intimately bound up with the refusal to confront the question of death. Repression and trivialization can only 'solve' the riddle by dissolving humanity itself."[24]

In this book I take Ratzinger's assessment not only as valid, but also as axiomatic for all I have to say. Some may reject Ratzinger's analysis, stating, for instance, that technology is too complex a phenomenon to take it as the unitary framework that gives shape to most of our beliefs, including our beliefs about mortality. This, I believe, is where philosophical thoroughness risks turning into the incapacity to see the whole picture—it turns into a form of skepticism about the possibility to say anything meaningful about culture, thus excluding itself from any genuine contribution to culture. Expanding on Ratzinger, the formula that I will use throughout the book is that the contemporary approach reduces death to an ontic problem to be dealt with technoscientifically and thus makes it impossible to apprehend death as a metaphysical mystery.

The distinction between "problem" and "mystery" comes from Gabriel Marcel. Marcel laments that "the characteristic feature of our age" is that "the individual tends to appear both to himself and to others as an agglomeration of functions."[25] To this absolutization of functions cor-

22. Ratzinger, *Eschatology*, 69.
23. Ratzinger, *Eschatology*, 70–71.
24. Ratzinger, *Eschatology*, 72; emphasis in original.
25. Marcel, "On the Ontological Mystery," 10. Marcel here touches upon the issue

responds the obliteration of mystery by the problem. As Steven Knepper explains, "A problem is something external to us that can be determinately understood and solved with a generalizable technique. A mystery, on the other hand, is something in which we are inextricably involved. It has roots deep within us, but it also reaches beyond us. While a problem can be solved, a mystery can only be navigated in light of the concrete situation."[26] Mystery is thus the "meta-problematic." As Marcel puts it: "A mystery is a problem which encroaches upon its own data, invading them, as it were, and thereby transcending itself as a simple problem."[27] "I who inquire into the meaning and the possibility of [it], I cannot place myself outside it or before it; I am engaged in this encounter, I depend upon it, I am inside it in a certain sense, it envelops me and it comprehends me—even if it is not comprehended by me."[28]

Thus, this book is a book of metaphysics insofar as it tries to show that death should be understood *primarily* as a metaphysical mystery rather than exclusively as an ontic problem to be dealt with technoscientifically. Not only does the metaphysical mysteriousness of death result from death's meta-problematic character; it is also exacerbated by the fact that death, as I have stated earlier, is definitive for our condition without being original, constitutive of, or ultimate for us. Becoming truly aware of one's mortality means becoming aware of the fact that we are caught into a condition of self-expropriation and that, despite this, it would be unrealistic to think of our condition apart from it. The person who thinks about death metaphysically, as St. Augustine of Hippo did, finds out that death is the radical negation without annihilation of his being, a radical negation which cannot be tamed philosophically and which thus puts the self into question by turning it into a question, a

---

of death: "It is true that certain disorderly elements—sickness, accidents of every sort—will break in on the smooth working of the system. It is therefore natural that the individual should be overhauled at regular intervals like a watch (this is often done in America). The hospital plays the part of the inspection bench or the repair shop.... As for death, it becomes, objectively and functionally, the scrapping of what has ceased to be of use and must be written off as a loss" (11).

26. Steven Knepper, "Gabriel Marcel," 128. He continues: "Death is no longer an inevitable mystery to be confronted but a biomedical problem to be delayed as long as possible and thought about as little as possible." Distinctions similar to that between "problem" and "mystery" have been put forth by other thinkers. With respect to death, Jankélévitch states that "death, seen from a third-person point of view, is problematical but not mysteriological" (*Mort*, 25).

27. Marcel, "On the Ontological Mystery," 19.

28. Marcel, "On the Ontological Mystery," 22.

question which should be given a voice before being given an answer: "Why?"[29] A metaphysics of death is thus the explanation and exposition of such being-put-into-question and being-turned-into-a-question by the mysterious negativity of death. It is the articulation of what Marcel calls "metaphysical uneasiness."[30]

This book is a metaphysical study also in another sense. In the Aristotelian-Thomistic tradition, metaphysics is the science of being qua being. But in this book I deal with death, which is a kind of nonbeing or negation, and I deal with human death, and thus with the human being, who is not being as such. What sense does it make then to still use the term "metaphysics" here? Given that death is a negation (in the sense explained above), the stubborn and undesirable presence of this negation in our lives makes us wonder about its relation with whatever is positive, with being as such. Once we genuinely realize that we are mortal, the negativity of death tends to color all aspects of our life. Does negativity, of which death is such a clear example, play any original and fundamental role in being? Is something analogous to the negation of death an essential ingredient of being qua being? If it is true, as Paul-Louis Landsberg states, that "[human] consciousness imitates the depth of being,"[31] what can we learn from the consciousness of death about being as being? And reversely, what can we learn from a study of being as being about the place that death may occupy in human life? Some issues that I will tackle in this book, especially in chapter 3, can be said to be metaphysical issues in this sense.

29. "Everything on which I set my gaze was death. . . . I had become to myself a vast [question]" (Augustine, *Confessions* [Chadwick], 57).

30. "'Metaphysical uneasiness.—It seems to me probable that metaphysics amounts to nothing else but the activity by which we define an uneasiness.' . . . What are we to understand, then, by this uneasiness? First of all, it is not a form of curiosity. To be curious is to start from a particular fixed centre, it is to strive to grasp or lay hold of an object. . . . To be uneasy, on the contrary, is to be uncertain of one's own centre, it is to be in search of one's own equilibrium. . . . At the same time uneasiness is the more metaphysical the more it concerns anything which cannot be separated from myself without the annihilation of this very self. It is probably true to say that the only metaphysical problem is that of 'What am I?' for all the others lead back to this one" (Marcel, "Value and Immortality," 131). I would suggest that, following this framework, one could even say that the uneasiness becomes maximally metaphysical in the case of death insofar as death is certainly something that cannot be separated from the self (it is definitive for the human condition) while at the same time making the self's center maximally uncertain by being the radical negation without annihilation of the self, which is, nevertheless, neither original, nor constitutive of, nor ultimate for the self.

31. Landsberg, *Experience of Death*, 24.

The adjective "metaphysical" applies to this study yet in another sense. As some have demonstrated,[32] the laborious evolution of the term "metaphysics" and of the corresponding discipline through modern and contemporary philosophy has brought to the fore the tendency to highlight the impossibility to deal with "being qua being" satisfactorily without simultaneously dealing with that being, the human being—one being among beings—who has access to being qua being—who poses the question of being qua being, who is concerned, one way or another, with being qua being, who, therefore, has eyes and heart for being qua being. To put it simply, doing metaphysics always requires an anthropological study, and the study of the human being is never complete, or even aptly centered, apart from a study of being as being understood as the informing energy of man's theoretical and practical concerns.

There is a final sense in which "metaphysical" is an apt descriptor of this study. It seems to me that the best Catholic philosophical literature on death, especially in recent years (Landsberg, Marcel, Tilliette, Melchiorre, Hadjadj, just to name a few), explores the phenomenon of human mortality with great depth, but it fails to make adequate use of the resources provided by Thomas's hylomorphism. The feeling one gets in reading this literature (with some notable exceptions, e.g., Pieper) is that hylomorphism is irrelevant at best, or an obstacle at worst, for thinking the more "existential" or personal dimension of death. In this study I show in what sense a nonstandard reading of hylomorphism provides resources to think about death in its entire breadth. As long as we are willing to consider "hylomorphism" a chapter in Thomistic metaphysics, then this book is a book of metaphysics.

For these reasons, the radical negativity of death that emerges in human life not only raises the question of the role and presence of such radical negativity with respect to being qua being, but also reflects back onto the human being and makes the human being wonder whether there may be any connection between his openness to being as such and that radical negativity which he experiences in death. As one may gather already from what I said earlier, my answer will be that the negativity of death is in no way a positive principle of human experience.

5. One last word on why this book is an "essay." In writing this book, I have often wondered about the issues raised by Jankélévitch and Tilliette. Despite being unsure about the finished result of my thinking and

---

32. See, for instance, Brague, *Anchors in the Heavens*, chs. 1–2.

writing on death, I have always been confident about the felt need to think and write about death, perhaps even against my desire to think and write about some other topic. This felt need to think and write about death has grown stronger and has confirmed itself over the last couple of years. What is most important here is that this need has been governed by a sort of biographical, existential, and intellectual impossibility on my part to think philosophically about death in any other way than in the terms presented in this book—death as that radical negation without annihilation captured by the formula of "material kenosis." Some of the ideas we have become sometimes more tightly related to what we are and the way we truly think than others. When this happens, it becomes harder to separate in one's philosophy the arguments vetted from a detached and impersonal point of view from the deep-seated and tenacious beliefs one has matured. In cases such as this one, biographical and existential self-expression become one, albeit without confusion, with philosophical argumentation.

I am saying this not to prepare the reader to the autobiographical nature of the following chapters. For better or worse, not a single explicit reference to my biography is in fact contained in this book. Rather, I am saying this because I would like to put the reader in the condition of receiving this book in the same philosophical spirit in which it has been written. It is my conviction that philosophers, especially in academia, often sacrifice the glory of expressing their own genuine thought to the false altar of universal and impersonal acceptability. In other words, too often we confuse rational thinking with impersonal philosophizing. Contrary to this attitude, I believe that genuinely rational thinking cannot be but personal, and that "what needs to be thought" is every time entrusted to the particular talents, expressive resources, and situated responsibility of each thinker.

If one must never compromise with the universal requirements of logic and reason, at the same time, one should never neglect the contribution that his inevitably partial and to some extend idiosyncratic perspective may contribute to the manifestation of the truth. If seen in this light, the task of thinking is, to a large extent, not exclusively that of relativizing one's partial perspective to the "objectivity" of universal reason, but more deeply that of understanding, remaining faithful to, and cultivating one's own personal "call to thought." Honesty and self-faithfullness become in this way coessential to the faithfulness to being. While *adaequatio* remains the a priori condition of truth, the "test" of the truth of one's thinking is entrusted to time (which, as the Italian saying goes, "is a gentleman") and to the fruits that such thinking may be capable of bearing for oneself and for other thinkers.[33] Accordingly, the universality to which one's thought may aspire is not that of an impersonal view on being, but rather that of a fruitful dialogue among different and irreducibly personal perspectives coming from and converging toward the same transcendental truth. Hence, I'll let time, my three readers, and my many future selves decide whether the ideas entrusted to this book have in fact been worth pursuing.

It would be false, however, to pretend that I do not believe that the ideas contained in this book are true. At the same time, I also believe that the discovery of truth is essentially and inevitably interpersonal— the multifaceted fruit of the work of many people of good will. The relation between a person and truth resembles Leibniz's monad: each person receives and expresses, i.e., "represents," in his own way the entire universe, that is, the universality of the truth. However, unlike the Leibnizian monad, no personal account of truth is self-sufficient and independent from the account of truth of other monads, of other people. One's thought can only hope to be received, corrected, and completed by other thinkers in order to come into itself, in order to become truly true, in order to become what it is. It is within this ongoing dialogue that also one's blind spots and mistakes can be treated with that mercy of reason that turns even unnecessary errors into opportunities to receive the truth anew, there where fraternal correction and the conversion of the heart meet. Isn't it the case, in fact, that it is precisely in standing corrected by the truth that man most honestly walks his path?

The ideas for which we care, including those contained in this book, deserve our love, despite their and our imperfection. As Charles S. Peirce explains: "Suppose, for example, that I have an idea that interests me. It is my creation. It is my creature; for . . . it is a little person. I love it; and I will sink myself in perfecting it. It is not by dealing out cold justice to the circle of my ideas that I can make them grow, but by cherishing and tending them as I would the flowers in my garden." But if it true, as Peirce suggests, that the ideas that interest us require a form of nurturing analogous to that which we reserve to our children, it will follow that I, who "made" these ideas, am insufficient to give the love that these ideas need to flourish properly, as the experience of any parent testifies. The love

---

33. "Time is a good discoverer" (Aristotle, *Nicomachean Ethics*, 1098a22).

INTRODUCTION

and understanding of others are necessary so that one's ideas and understanding of them may overcome their deficiency and grow into what they aspire to be: "Love, recognizing germs of loveliness in the hateful, gradually warms it into life, and makes it lovely."[34]

While I have tried to be as comprehensive and systematic as possible, I have not attempted to be encyclopedic (a most favorite strategy of many philosophical monographs these days). Instead, I have preferred developing one single argument, taking my cues from different philosophical debates, traditions, and languages. Nor have I tried to build a system. The mirage of the philosophical system often produces the illusion (and the temporary thrill!) of exhaustivity, that is, of having everything under control. Being myself incapable of producing an overarching philosophical system, I take comfort in the thought that a system of thanatology would be even more illusory than any other philosophical system applied to any other subject.

On the one hand, I can only hope to have played the part that was "up to me" to play in the interpersonal "love of wisdom" that is philosophy, and I wait to enjoy a foretaste of exhaustivity through the responses and corrections that my three readers will be so kind to put forth regarding the ideas here contained. On the other hand, in facing the temptation to give up this project due to the many doubts and many mistakes that my thinking on death has not been able to detect or overcome,[35] I have found compelling reasons to write this book anyway in what Charles Péguy, that very dear herald of hope, has to say about philosophy: "A great

---

34. Peirce, "Evolutionary Love," 1:354.

35. Another tempting reason *not* to write this book came to me after reading two books which contain as much scholarship, profundity, and brilliance as a book on death can ever contain. The first book, already a theological classic, is Joseph Ratzinger's above-mentioned *Eschatology*. It exemplifies that very special quality that can be found in Ratzinger's writings, namely, the capacity of venturing into remote territories of scholarship while keeping an almost miraculous balance and an imperviousness to the frivolous, the prideful, and the unnecessary. The second book is Fabrice Hadjadj's *Réussir sa mort*, which I have consulted in the Italian translation, *Farcela con la morte*. Also this book proves the uncommon gifts of its author, who manages to combine in a unique way and, I dare say, sometimes even more sharply than Chesterton, a patient narrative of compelling literary images with a razor-sharp identification and description of the theoretical and cultural problems at stake. I am afraid that my book says much less than what these two masterpieces contain. But if this "less" is said as it ought to be said by its author, this book may have not been written in vain. Three other noteworthy works are Xavier Tilliette's essays on death, which I cite at different points; Journet, *Meaning of Evil*; and esp. Paul-Louis Landsberg's short but exemplary book *The Experience of Death*.

Material Kenosis

philosophy is not one against which there is nothing to say. It is one that has said something. . . . It is not one that has no defects. It is not one that has no empty places. It is one that has full places. . . . The true philosopher knows very well that he is not situated *opposite* an adversary, but *alongside* the adversary, and others, in the face of a reality always greater and more mysterious."[36] While I wish I could state with confidence that my philosophy in this book is a *great* philosophy, I must content myself with the hope that it is philosophy *enough*, that it passes somehow the demanding standard set by Péguy.

5. The outline of the book is straightforward. I do not include here a detailed summary of all the discussions, arguments, and theses proposed in the following four chapters, but I simply provide a sketch of the stages through which, chapter after chapter, the overall argument of the book progresses.

Chapter 1, "Making Sense of 'Death' in Some Analytic Philosophers," introduces the discussion of the negativity of death by contextualizing it within the analytic tradition, with special attention to three approaches: Galen Strawson's "no loss" view of death (taken as representative of a broader linguistic-deflationary approach to death present throughout Western philosophy and epitomized by some analytic philosophers), the application of the digital paradigm to the problem of death, and the materialist view according to which, since human beings are material beings, the death of a human being (the suppression of his life) does not imply the end of his existence. I suggest that these three approaches contribute or are philosophically related to the broader tendency present in our civilization according to which death is an ontic problem to be dealt with technoscientifically rather than a metaphysical mystery. In discussing these three approaches, I conclude that the best way to understand death is to see it as a form of negation of being-life. The need to further clarify how such negation ought to be understood leads to the discussion of chapter 2.

Chapter 2, "Death as Material Kenosis: A Thomistic Proposal," presents a nonstandard interpretation of death in light of St. Thomas Aquinas's hylomorphic doctrine of the human being. According to this reading, death turns out to be the radical (or total) negation of our being which, however, does not amount to the annihilation of who we are. The notion of "material kenosis" is introduced and explained in its most

---

36. Péguy, *Notes on Bergson and Descartes*, 43; emphasis in original.

INTRODUCTION

fundamental traits in this chapter, even though also the following chapters refer back to this notion in order to test further its reach and theoretical fruitfulness. While I take the doctrine contained in this chapter to be a faithful "creative retrieval" and "creative completion"[37] of Thomas's view, I have often wondered whether better Thomists than I would grant it a place in that long and diversified tradition that we call "Thomism." I certainly wish that my interpretation may occupy such a place, but I do not know for sure. Thus, I appeal to such Thomists with the words of Jean of Arc: "If I am not [in the number of the Thomists], may God put me there; and if I am, may God so keep me."

Chapter 3, "The Analogy of Being and the Nonbeing of Death," the longest of the four, addresses from many different points of view the question whether the negativity of death may be representative of and analogous to any fundamental and original trait of life and being. The most basic point in the chapter is that the negation of death is non-analogizable in any way. The materials used in this chapter are mostly drawn from the continental tradition, with a brief (and, alas, very wanting!) discussion of what I see as shortcomings in some kenotic approaches to being and God in Catholic metaphysics and theology. Perhaps the most original and intriguing part of the chapter is the concluding section, in which I provide, in the form of a genealogical argument, reasons to believe that also the continental reflection on death, especially in the Heideggerian and post-Heideggerian tradition, must end up, contrary to its intentions, with the same reduction of death to an ontic technoscientific problem.

Finally, Chapter 4, which has a long title—"The Transhumanist Overcoming of Death and Human Desire: What the Experience of 'For a Child Is Born to Us, a Son Is Given to Us' May Tell Us About a Possible Misunderstanding Characterizing Our Technological Civilization"—tackles the view of trans- and posthumanists according to which death should be overcome technologically. My approach in dealing with transhumanism is to focus on human desire and on how the prospect of a technologically extended and expanded human life compares to what we should rightfully and rationally aspire to. As the title suggests, the chapter develops into a meditation on the desire at work in parenthood as a key to approach the mystery of the resurrection.

---

37. Clarke, *One and the Many*, 1.

CHAPTER ONE

Making Sense of "Death" in Some Analytic Philosophers

A live dog is better off than a dead lion. (Eccl 9:4)

Descartes, I say, was not identical to his body when his body was a corpse.
"Descartes had a serious accident, did he survive?"
"Yes, of course—take a look in his coffin."
The response is absurd.
SAUL A. KRIPKE, "THE FIRST PERSON," 310

"Thy soul will be dead even sooner than thy body;
fear, therefore, nothing any more!"
The man looked up distrustfully.
"If thou speakest the truth," said he, "I lose nothing when I lose my life."
FRIEDRICH NIETZSCHE, *THUS SPOKE ZARATHUSTRA*, 14

1. INTRODUCTION: ANALYTIC PHILOSOPHY AND HUMAN DEATH

1.1. MANY PHILOSOPHICAL DISCUSSIONS on death, especially in the analytic tradition, deal with death as a problem in the domain of *practical philosophy*: Is my death bad for me and, if yes, at what time and under what conditions? Can my death harm me posthumously? Is my death bad for other people? At what time and under what conditions is it prudentially reasonable to die? Do human beings have a duty to die? How is the value of death tied to the broader social and economic conditions of life? Analytic philosophy is at its best here, showing in a compelling way that abstract and even extremely technical discussions are born from and go back to life itself.[1]

Unsurprisingly, the literature presents as many different and nuanced positions as are the philosophers engaging in these debates. It is true that not all of these discussions are concerned directly with the problem of how to *guide* ethical, legal, and political decisions concerning life and death, and that for this reason the classification of these discussions as pertaining to "practical philosophy" may seem arbitrary. Nevertheless, it seems to me that these discussions are conducted in the majority of cases from the point of view of a utilitarian practical reason, i.e., a practical reason concerned with the calculation of costs and benefits of death (utilitarianism or consequentialism). For instance, F. M. Kamm describes "deprivationism," that is, "the standard contemporary view about why death is bad for the person who dies," as a form of consequentialism: "Deprivationism . . . takes a forward-looking, consequentialist view of the badness or goodness of death; death is bad or good depending on whether its consequence is no more good or no more bad life";[2] "the badness (or goodness) of death for a person is discovered by comparing the life he could have had if death did not occur at a certain time to the life he will have if it occurs at that time."[3] An exemplary formulation of this consequentialist approach to the meaning and value of death is provided by Jeff McMahan: "Death is bad for a person (or developing person) at

---

1. Thomas Nagel has identified the interest of analytic philosophy in the "basic questions of life and death" as one of the chief developments of this tradition from its birth up to the beginning of the twenty-first century (*Analytic Philosophy*, 2). He is of course one of the main promoters of this development.

2. Kamm, *Almost Over*, 2.

3. Kamm, *Almost Over*, 1.

any point in his life, provided that the life that is thereby lost would on balance have been worth living. Other things being equal, the badness of death is proportional to the quality and quantity of the goods which the victim is deprived."[4] Even Kamm, herself a critique of standard deprivationism, cannot help propose a different approach which, however, falls within the broader genus of consequentialism—she characterizes it as a "backward consequentialism."[5]

When subjected to the utilitarian calculus, the value of life and death becomes an ever-changing factor. In particular, death could be considered bad because it deprives us of counterfactual future goods; good, if it prevents us from experiencing counterfactual future evils. This kind of discussion must go on forever and its outcome can only be a huge casuistry literature in which real life cases are considered side by side with hypothetical, counterfactual, and often highly unlikely scenarios. In this perspective, death can be considered good or bad in infinitely different ways and can accommodate various degrees of goodness and badness. I will not deal directly with these sorts of problems, even though what I will have to say in this and the following chapters may be indirectly relevant to provide an alternative to the consequentialist framework in which the issue of value of life and death is customarily framed.

In my opinion, however, the interesting point relative to the consequentialist approach to death is that, if it is not taken as fundamental and exclusive of other points of view, it does not exclude the possibility that death may be in itself an intrinsic evil, that is, an evil as such, apart from the circumstances. In fact, as it will become clear in this chapter and then more fully in chapter 2, I support the Thomistic view according to which death is an *evil of privation*. But this does not exclude the possibility that someone in certain circumstances could perceive the evil of death as a lesser evil than (and thus, as an option preferable to) the continuation of life. Bernard N. Schumacher puts it best: "This assertion [death is an evil in itself] does not exclude the possibility that 'N', from his particular point of view, at a given moment and in the particular circumstances of his life, might prefer death to the continuation of his life—even though the price to be paid would be very high, namely, the loss of his very being, as a conscious, free subject. . . . The issue here is not a choice between a good and an evil, but rather a subjective preference: better a greater loss

---

4. McMahan, "Death and the Value," 262.
5. Kamm, *Almost Over*, 2.

that would be easier to endure (death itself, which is without sensation and free of physical and/or psychological suffering) than a smaller loss that is more difficult to endure (the painful sensations accompanying such a life). . . . Therefore, I can very well prefer death while regarding it as an evil, for the evil of death is not dependent on the circumstances; it is an evil in itself, even if at a particular moment I subjectively judge that my life is or is not worth the trouble of living."[6] The capacity that the utilitarian calculus has to turn even the intrinsic evil of death into a good is simply a testimony to the impasse resulting from assuming consequentialism as *the* framework of reference for determining what death is and whether it is as such good or bad.

1.2. Even for thinkers such as Thomas Nagel, for whom the assessment of the badness of death transcends the mere utilitarian calculus, death is bad because it negates counterfactual *future experiences* or, more precisely, the counterfactual capacity to experience in the future (independently, to some extent, from the goods and evils that may be experienced in that future). According to him, human life is characterized by "an essentially open-ended possible future, containing the usual mixture of goods and evils" ("an indeterminate and not essentially limited future")[7] and death is bad precisely because it "abruptly cancels," puts an end to, or *negates*, this possible future.[8] Human life is conceived as a temporal, growing career, and death is taken to mean the negation of the future outmost counterfactual part of this career. To use an image, death is understood as the abrupt cliff that puts a sudden stop to the ride of a vehicle: how smoothly could have the ride continued if instead of a cliff our vehicle had continued its advance on a well-paved road! The question becomes then: What kind of negation is death? When and how is death a concern for the human being? Is death something taking place in a future that I will never encounter? And who is the subject of the negation of death?

Such questions are at the core of Nagel's and other analytic philosophers' discussions of death, and this explains at least partially the omnipresent engagement of these philosophers with Epicurus's and Lucretius's views on how to think about and approach death. As is

---

6. Schumacher, *Death and Mortality*, 206.

7. Nagel, "Death," 10.

8. James Rachels presents a similar position: "If there was anything bad about death, it is because we are able to view a life as in principle open-ended, as always having further possibilities that still might be realized, if only it could go on" (*End of Life*, 51).

well-known, according to Epicurus, death should not be feared because "death is nothing to us, since so long as we exist, death is not with us; but when death comes, then we do not exist."[9] In other words, according to Epicurus, the human being is never really the subject of experience of death and, as a consequence, his fear of death is irrational and unjustified, assuming that one can rationally and justifiably fear only what one can experience at some point. For Epicurus, the fear of death is an "empty evil":[10] whatever kind of negation death may be (annihilation or otherwise), death is never such that may rationally motivate horror and fear. Expanding on the Epicurean tradition, Lucretius advances the additional argument according to which one should not dread one's nonexistence after one's death just as he does not dread his nonexistence before his birth: "Therefore death is nothing to us, it matters not one jot, since the nature of the mind is understood to be mortal. . . . Look back also and see how the ages of everlasting time past before we were born have been to us nothing. This therefore is a mirror which nature holds up to us, showing the time to come after we at length shall die. Is there anything horrible in that? Is there anything gloomy? Is it not more peaceful than any sleep?"[11]

In response to these venerable arguments, analytic philosophers have done what they do best: they have dissected them in all possible ways, looked at them and interpreted them according to their endlessly

---

9. Epicurus, "Letter to Menoeceus," 30–31. Here's the fuller text: "Become accustomed to the belief that death is nothing to us. For all good and evil consists in sensation, but death is deprivation of sensation. And therefore a right understanding that death is nothing to us makes the mortality of life enjoyable, not because it adds to it an infinite span of time, but because it takes away the craving for immortality. For there is nothing terrible in life for the man who has truly comprehended that there is nothing terrible in not living. So that the man speaks but idly who says that he fears death not because it will be painful when it comes, but because it is painful in anticipation. So death, the most terrifying of ills, is nothing to us, since so long as we exist, death is not with us; but when death comes, then we do not exist. It does not then concern either the living or the dead, since for the former it is not, and the latter are no more. . . . But the wise man does not fear the cessation of life, for neither does life offend him nor does the absence of life seem to be any evil."

10. "An empty evil, such as a fear of something that is not actually harmful, can and should be removed by means of reasoning. A non-empty evil, such as physical pain, can (in some cases) be medically treated and will ease over time, but it cannot be removed by reasoning about it. The urgency and the optimism of Epicurean writing about death come from their treating the fear of being dead as an 'empty' evil. . . . Epicurus' point is that after death has occurred, the items for which people feel the most concern—namely, their own body and soul—lack awareness and so are not proper objects of concern" (Long, *Death and Immortality*, 118, 125).

11. Lucretius, *De rerum natura*, 227, 237.

subtle nuances, and pronounced their (often conditional) avowals or disavowals of these arguments.[12]

In this chapter I will refrain from engaging these arguments directly, partly because following them in all their variants would require a different kind of book; partly because I find my own views well represented in the work of other thinkers.[13] In my opinion, however, the technical treatment of Epicurus's and Lucretius's arguments as hard-to-crack puzzles cannot see the forest for the trees. In fact, the appeal of arguments such as Epicurus's and Lucretius's does not lie primarily in their logical soundness; rather, it lies in their *therapeutic value*, that is, in the help they provide in allowing human beings to distract themselves from the thought of death as that on which man has no control and which nevertheless he cannot avoid. While from a certain point of view it may be the case that these arguments are ultimately "an ancient sophism that purports to justify indifference to death,"[14] from a different point of view, their force lies precisely in this: in the magical power of distraction they have on us and on the ensuing, albeit momentary, bliss they bestow on us. Death is not that dreadful evil which we cannot control and which we cannot escape simply because, as Epicurus and Lucretius suggest, death has never been something on which we may want to have control or something which we may want to escape. Thinking otherwise is analogous to committing a category mistake. One may aspire to have control over and escape this or that experience, but not the termination of experience as such. What lies beyond experience constitutes neither a concern for the human capacity for control nor a possible object of avoidance. Doesn't this argument have an *unburdening* effect on us?

Thus, as I understand them, these arguments are supposed to convey just enough logical soundness so that they may be entertained by the mind, but it is once they are entertained by the mind that they disclose their true meaning and purpose, which lies beyond their logical

---

12. See, e.g., Bradley et al., *Oxford Handbook of Philosophy of Death*.

13. For instance, Schumacher sums up convincingly the best criticisms of Epicurus's and Lucretius's views. Epicurus's argument relies upon doubtful premises (what he calls materialism, hedonism, and experientialism) and Lucretius's argument neglects the asymmetry between past and future, the directionality of time, and the fact that, given that death is an evil of privation, the nonexistence of death cannot be likened to the nonexistence prior to birth (a nonexistence which cannot "deprive" anyone of anything, given that the subject is assumed not to be existing) (*Death and Mortality*, chs. 8–10).

14. Mothersill, "Death," 88. The same assessment is found in Landsberg.

soundness: they make death look somewhat "light" and hence bearable. This is no small achievement for a philosophy such as Epicureanism which aims at being therapeutic and at bringing about peace of mind.[15] Obviously, whether such blissful distraction can constitute a successful therapy or whether it is the most desirable philosophical treatment of death are questions that will need to be considered with patience over the course of the entire book. My answer will be negative, but not dismissive.

1.3. When I ask questions such as "What kind of negation is death? When and how is death a concern for the human being? And who is the subject of the negation of death?," I am not interested directly in determining whether there is "life after death," whether the human soul survives death, or whether death is the annihilation of the human being. As will become evident in chapter 2, I will take for granted the conclusions of the arguments presented by Plato, Aristotle, and especially St. Thomas Aquinas and the Catholic philosophical tradition, according to which the intellectual souls of human beings are spiritual and subsistent and therefore indestructible.[16] However, instead of opening up to an investigation on the nature of the so-called "afterlife" and the "separated" condition of the soul after death, these conclusions will constitute the premise for a different kind of inquiry. In particular, the guiding question for my entire inquiry will be: *What kind of negation is the negation of death, given the metaphysical and anthropological framework provided by Thomas's philosophy? In what sense is death "part of" life, and in what sense can we speak of an experience of death? What reasonable attitude shall we entertain concerning death? How are dying and death related? How shall we understand death in light of Thomas's philosophical reception of Christian revelation?* Needless to say, none of these questions will

15. Analogously to what the Epicurean tradition thinks about the theoretical enterprise of physics. "A grave threat impairs human happiness. Can pleasure be perfect if it is disturbed by the fear of death, and by divine decisions in this world and the next? As is shown with great force by Lucretius, it is the fear of death which is, in the last analysis, at the base of all the passions which make people unhappy. It was in order to free people from these terrors that Epicurus proposed his theoretical discourse on physics. Above all, we must not imagine Epicurean physics as a scientific theory, intended to reply to objective, disinterested questions. The ancients knew that the Epicurean were hostile to the idea of a science studied for its own sake. Indeed, philosophical theory is here merely the expression and consequence of the original choice of life, and a means of obtaining peace of mind and pure pleasure" (Hadot, *What Is Ancient Philosophy?*, 117–18).

16. For a contemporary presentation of these arguments, in connection with analytic philosophy and the empirical sciences, see Oderberg, *Real Essentialism*, 241–60; Eberl, *Nature of Human Persons*, 18–58.

be answered in full in the following pages (only a "fool" could aim at "fullness" in this context). However, I hope that what I will have to say will provide some guidance on how to continue to think about issues of life and death. My aim is partly hermeneutical and partly propositional: How can we advance an interpretation of the spirit of Thomas's position in light of some of the more recent developments in philosophy and theology? Can we show that such a "Thomistic" view is compelling and preferable to other views?

1.4. My study of death in this book is *primarily theoretical* rather than practical. This does not mean, however, that this study may not have important implications for how we handle a life deeply marked by the presence of death. In fact, as I will try to show, the negation of death is more radical than what we think when we understand it as the cancellation of a counterfactual future. Death is a *wound of our being* right from the beginning of our existence. We might suggest, without taking this as a definition, that death is less the inevitable eventuality coming to us from the future than the inherited fatal and contradictory condition in which we are born, already "at work" in us during our life and expanding its area of influence more and more as life progresses. This goes against much of the wisdom of the analytic discussion of death and, as we shall see, also significantly redefines positions in the continental philosophical tradition, such as Heidegger's, according to which death is "real" for us now, even "before" the moment of passing.

1.5. I take it as evident that most people today in the so-called "First World" understand death as an ontic problem to be dealt with scientifically and technologically rather than as a metaphysical mystery.[17] The point here, of course, is not that it is impossible to find exceptions to this view, in the First World as anywhere else—exceptions abound. The point is, rather, that this is the mainstream view; the broadly accepted and culturally dominant view; the Aristotelian *endoxon*; the view that even those who disagree with it (such as myself) cannot help but entertain as an almost automatic mental instinct. The background for such belief is a generalized naturalistic framework about life and reality and a related conviction that genuine knowledge of and serious engagement with reality can only be guided by the empirical sciences and their technological infrastructure. This, of course, does not mean that a naturalistic position necessitates such an ontic reduction of the question concerning death

---

17. See the introduction.

or even scientism. It only means that naturalism is a *sine qua non* of the position I am discussing. Nevertheless, it seems fair to say, as Shelly Kagan admits, that "once we become physicalists there is nothing especially deep or mysterious about death."[18]

The very concept of "natural death" does not stand simply for a description of death as an essential principle of biological life; rather, it is already the expression of the modern view in which "nature" is understood as the "object" of a "subject," namely, as something subjected, in principle, to scientific scrutiny and technological intervention.

In taking into consideration the vast analytic literature on death, I have decided to use this axiom of our contemporary age as a criterion of selection of the materials for this chapter, not only in order to avoid writing an encyclopedic book (in which all the minute technical problems concerning death treated by analytic philosophers are discussed and solved) or an overly specialized book (in which one of the technical problems is further complexified and solved); but also in order to show that there exists a strong connection between what nonphilosophers tend to hold as true today—again, the idea that death is an ontic problem to be dealt with scientifically and technologically and not a metaphysical mystery—and some abstract and seemingly abstruse debates in the analytic tradition.

Accordingly, this chapter will be devoted to the discussion of three different positions: first, Galen Strawson's "no loss" view of death, according to which my death is neither a "harm" nor something "crucial" for me because it cannot be conceived of as a "loss" of my future; second, digitalism about death, according to which what is relevant to who I am is the "pattern" of the functions regulating my behavior, a pattern which death does not destroy if the pattern can be saved and reproduced digitally; and third, the "non-terminist" view of death, according to which when I die, I still continue existing as a dead person until my material body is fully disintegrated. I will discuss the third position, the non-terminist view, at much greater length than the other two views simply because I take it to be the philosophically strongest and most interesting view of the three, the discussion of which will allow us to make greater progress in exploring the question of what kind of negation death may be. Discussing non-terminism (but also Strawson's "no loss" view, to some extent) will also allow us to come to terms with the strengths and weaknesses

18. Kagan, *Death*, 184.

of analytic philosophy. If analytic philosophy means anything at all, it means a style of philosophy in which the analysis of language is the preeminent method of inquiry. As we will see, the arguments in support of the "no loss" view of death are based on a somewhat arbitrary fixation with certain ways of speaking about death; similarly, the arguments in favor of non-terminism are usually taken from the analysis of the ordinary language claims about dead people. It will be even more interesting, then, to see the way in which these arguments cannot prove what they expect to prove and thus relativize linguistic analysis as a method for deepening the phenomenon of death (or any other nonlinguistic phenomenon, for that matter).

While I will discuss the arguments relative to these three different positions in their own right, I will advance two main points that suggest a possible unitary interpretation of these positions. The first point is that these positions, despite all their differences, have one main weakness in common: they greatly *underplay the weight of biological life* in defining what we are. This point is even more interesting and, I should say, curious, given the fundamental importance that the philosophers supporting the views under consideration grant the empirical sciences. The second point is that these positions, despite all their differences, have one common reason of appeal: they make the phenomenon of death seems "lighter" than it is, thus rendering the thought of death more bearable. On this score, these three positions in the analytic philosophy of death are not different from the strategies of the great ancient sages Epicurus and Lucretius.

I submit that if there is a value to these three proposals, it is *chiefly therapeutic rather than merely logical*. The formidable naturalism backing them up is, in its deepest meaning, an intellectual palliative against the unbearable thought of death. Thus, I see these arguments as part of that great analytic enterprise, most clearly evident in Ludwig Wittgenstein's later work, which practices linguistic analysis as philosophical therapy or, in other words, which takes philosophy to be aimed at bringing about such a complete clarity in language that tormenting philosophical problems disappear as a consequence.[19] This should not come as a surprise, if it is true, as Blaise Pascal has stated, that human beings find in distraction

---

19. Wittgenstein, *Philosophical Investigations*, 56–58n133. For a reconstruction and critical assessment of Wittgenstein's treatment of death, see Stango, "Wittgenstein, Peirce, and Death."

the only "natural" remedy to the thought of death.[20] Montaigne suggests a strategy equal and opposite to Pascal's insight: not distraction, but the constant thought of death, is that which takes away from death its unbearable sting.[21] Both perspectives have something in common, namely, the attempt to somehow bring under control that which is uncontrollable and the attempt to avoid that which cannot be avoided. As Philippe Ariès has claimed, human beings have always adopted theoretical, social, ritual, and other strategies to "tame" death.[22] The way in which the three strategies discussed in this chapter "make sense of death" results from a mix of linguistic demystification (the "no loss" view and non-terminism) and technoscientific mystification (digitalism) at the service of the aim of taming death. As far as I can tell, then, the most interesting contributions of analytic philosophy with respect to death should be read in continuity with the great ancient Greek tradition of philosophy as spiritual exercises and as an example of that almost inevitable human temptation, which cuts across all epochs, to tame death via a mix of distraction from and familiarization with it.

In relation to the first point, my general strategy will be to argue that biological life is definitory of what we are (even though not exhaustively definitory; necessary, although not sufficient) and that death is (at least) the negation of what we are insofar as it is the negation of our biological life. Conjointly, I will suggest that, at this level, philosophy of nature (together with biology), not linguistic analysis, is the discipline responsible for the study of the nature of death. In relation to the second point, I will argue that, in spite of the appeal they inevitably have for making life humanly bearable, all intellectual strategies that tend to make

---

20. For Pascal's position, see my discussion in ch. 4, sec. 3.

21. "To begin depriving death of its greatest advantage over us, let us adopt a way clear contrary to that common one; let us deprive death of its strangeness; let us frequent it, let us get used to it; let us have nothing more often in mind than death. At every instant let us evoke it in our imagination under all its aspects" (Montaigne, *Complete Essays*, 96).

22. See Ariès: *Western Attitudes Toward Death*, ch. 1; *Hour of Our Death*, pt. 1. Sigmund Freud extends this tendency even to the subconscious: "We showed an unmistakable tendency to put death on one side, to eliminate it from life. We tried to hush it up.... It is indeed impossible to imagine our own death; and whenever we attempt to do so we can perceive that we are in fact still present as spectators. Hence the psychoanalytic school could venture on the assertion that at bottom no one believes in his own death, or, to put the same thing in another way, that in the unconscious every one of us is convinced of his own immortality" ("Thoughts on War and Death," in Freud, *History of Psycho-Analytic Movement*, 289).

the phenomenon of death lighter than it is should be resisted. "Spirit," as G. W. F. Hegel puts it, is what it is "only by looking the negative in the face, and tarrying with it." Thus, the present chapter will cast some serious doubts on the three positions presented above (Strawson's "no loss" view, digitalism, non-terminism), according to which, at least in their implications, death should be understood as something not so burdensome. It will be the job of the following chapters, especially chapters 2–3, to clarify further, this time through the resources of metaphysics broadly understood, what the negation of death truly is (that is, *what it is not . . .*).

1.5. Let me make one final introductory remark to this chapter, which is to some extent relevant to the overall argument developed throughout this book. I do think that there is a connection between the positions in the analytic philosophy of death such as those under examination in this chapter and the default position of our age, that is, the neglect of the metaphysical mysteriousness of death and its reduction to an ontic problem to be dealt with scientifically and technologically. While the connection is explicit only in the case of digitalism, which *is* one of the forms of the technoscientific project to overcome death, I think that something similar could be said also about arguments such as Strawson's and non-terminism. What I am suggesting is *not* that Strawson and all non-terminists do in fact support or are bound to support a technoscientific project to overcome death. Rather, I believe that any *philosophical* strategy aiming more or less explicitly at taming the uncontrollable and yet unavoidable burden of death, tends to create the intellectual, cultural, and, one may even say, "spiritual" space, whether it means it or not, which will sooner or later be occupied by some *technoscientific* project to finally conquer death once and for all. The simple reason for this is that the promises of technoscience for taming death are incomparably superior to the resources of philosophical therapy via linguistic demystification. What seems to me at work here, then, is *philosophy's process of self-undermining*. In refusing to keep the sense of death's metaphysical mystery alive by letting death put the self into question, philosophy condemns *itself* to death, that is, destines itself for being supplemented by the power that is shaping our world without residue into a technoscientific globe.

Once death's "power" of putting the self into question is undermined by reducing the metaphysical dimension of death to a mere problem that philosophical clarification can dissipate and partially overcome (e.g., arguments such as Strawson's), and once the event of death is reduced to a mere accident in the material existence of the human being (e.g., non-terminism), then the space is opened for technoscience to take over any alternative (philosophical and religious) attempts at dealing with death (e.g., digitalism and other forms of the same strategies, often related to trans- and posthumanism, which I discuss in ch. 4).

2. DO I "HAVE" A FUTURE?

2.1. In his book *Things That Bother Me*, Galen Strawson answers the question "Do I have a future?' with a resounding no: "I have no future." In saying this, Strawson does not intend to communicate the idea that we are all doomed to die, which is of course something that he maintains. Rather, his point is that the relationship to "my" future cannot be understood in terms of the "having" relation or, better, as something that I "own," such that calling the future 'mine' is already problematic. His argument is straightforward: since the future is not something that I "own," then the same future is not something that can be taken away from me, insofar as only something that I own can be taken away from me. Along the same lines, it would be a mistake to think that my death brings about a "loss" for me, precisely the loss of the future I would have had, had I not died. Similarly to the case of the taking away of something, the concept of "loss" also presupposes some form of ownership.[23]

Strawson writes: "My future life and experience (the life and experience I will have if I don't die now) don't belong to me in such a way that they're something that can be taken away from me. I am, ploddingly, simply not a thing of such a kind that the life and experience it will have if it doesn't now die can be rightly thought of as a possession of which it can be deprived."[24] The premise of the argument is what Strawson calls the "no ownership (of the future)" view, namely, the idea that my future life and experiences do not belong to me. The ensuing view is, as I have stated, the "no loss (of the future)" view and the related "no worse" view, namely, the idea that dying does not determine a loss for me and that "given that I'm alive *and must die*, my life doesn't go worse for me in any sense if I cease to exist."[25]

---

23. This argument seems to be addressed against positions such as Nagel's, which appeal directly to the notion of "loss": "Any death entails the loss of *some* life that its victim would have had led had he not died at that or any earlier point" ("Death," 7; emphasis in original).

24. Strawson, "I Have No Future," 72.

25. Strawson, "I Have No Future," 75; emphasis in original.

Strawson deepens his argument by introducing the distinction between different ways to experience oneself. One modality of self-experience is that of an "endurer," namely, the experience of oneself as diachronically enduring from birth to death. Another modality is that of a "transient," namely, the experience of oneself as fragmented, as not existing as that specific self at a previous time and as not guaranteed to exist at a later time.[26] In neither of these cases, states Strawson, are we legitimately entitled to believe that the future is something that "belongs" to us: even if I apprehend myself as existing as an enduring subject from birth to death, my experience would not imply that I own my future, and it would thus remain true that death does not take away from me something that is mine.

2.2. This brief reconstruction of Strawson's argument should suffice to make two critical remarks. The first remark is that Strawson relies entirely on linguistic analysis in order to make sense of the phenomenon of death. Does it make sense, he wonders, to think of death in terms of a "loss"? And if not, why? I have selected Strawson's argument for my discussion neither because it is the only argument on the analytic market, nor because it is the most debated, but rather because it is one of the most exemplary, as far as I can tell, of a certain analytic tendency in dealing with the phenomenon of death. Strawson's argument is clear, beautiful, and simple—I am tempted to call it "spotless." It is even sound as far as it goes. Moreover, its logical soundness cannot be separated from the aesthetic appeal that is has, and I am myself captivated by its beauty and cleverness. It relies on a clarification of language which leaves no room for semantic ambiguities. Unfortunately, Strawson's argument is also artificial and methodologically inadequate. It relies on a problematic fixation with certain linguistic expressions, the relation of "having" or "ownership," and suggests the idea that coming to terms with these expressions could help coming to terms with death (albeit not fully, of course). It treats with the method of linguistic analysis something that exceeds the nature of language. It speaks of death while abstracting entirely from the nature of biological life, as if death could be understood, at least minimally, apart from philosophy of nature and biology.

On the contrary, if we think of ourselves primarily as *animals*, as animalists do,[27] then the phenomenon of death is not something that can

---

26. Strawson, "I Have No Future," 77.
27. See the discussion in sec. 4 of this chapter.

be described exclusively, as Strawson does, as a future event which would deny all counterfactual future experiences. Rather, death is something that I need to deal with *in my present* because it is inherited from my past and thus immanent to all my present dealings, i.e., *the past of having been born a human animal*. More explicitly, when I am born, I am constituted as a living organism with a certain internal coherence and functional integrity, but internal coherence and functional integrity are from the very beginning marked by fragility, self-exposure, imperfections, lack-of-guarantee against disruption, etc. So, death is the burden of a life that is given to us in the form of fragility and self-exposure to danger, a fragility and self-exposure which are experienced in every present, if one just pays attention. Every present is shaken from within by this immanent fragility and self-exposure.

The second point is that, connected to the aesthetic value of the argument, the appeal of Strawson's argument lies in its therapeutic power. Now, Strawson is very careful in pointing out that his argument is different from Epicurus's and Lucretius's because, as he explains, there is nothing incompatible between entertaining the "no loss" view and fearing death. For him, one can still fear death, knowing, however, that one cannot fear it rationally on the ground that it constitutes a "loss." At the same time, however, one of the implications of his argument is that it would be a mistake to take death as a "harm" for the human being: my death could be perceived as a "harm" by those who outlive me (with the always-present risk of a "commodification" of my now-gone existence) but not by me, either before I die or after I die.[28] Strawson's conclusion is clear on this point: he says that death is not a "crucial" factor in my life because it is neither a loss nor a harm. As a consequence, contrary to what he indicates, Strawson's argument *does* have crucial therapeutic implications. What I want to suggest is that the force of his argument lies precisely in this palliative function, no matter how small or fleeting. It is for this reason that Strawson, while suspicious of Epicurus and Lucretius, cites Marcus Aurelius approvingly.[29] Strawson thus proposes a sort of *ars moriendi* in the form of a philosophical art of dispelling the linguistic confusions surrounding the concept of death. *Ars* here is aimed not at preparing us to dying, which seems to presuppose that death is represented as a major concern for us, for which we must prepare; rather,

---

28. Strawson, "I Have No Future," 85–86.
29. Strawson, "I Have No Future," 88.

the aim is to amend our ideas through the philosophical demystification of the words we use to speak about death and shape our attitudes accordingly in such a way that death stops being a major concern. The *ars moriendi* is not the work initiated by a self's being put into question by death (whatever this work might be). It is the questioning of the way we speak of death, so that a thin linguistic barrier can be put between our life and death. If seen in this light (as I claim should be done), analytic arguments about death such as Strawson's gain much authority and respectability. They are not linguistic sophisms aimed at entertaining the abstract thinking about death, but rather linguistic tools to appease the uncontrollable and yet unavoidable thought of death.

This is the way in which arguments such as Strawson's aim at "making sense" of death: by dispelling the semantic confusion about death and thus immunizing life, as far as possible, from death's harm and loss. While it remains true, as I shall try to suggest, that this philosophical attitude is partial and unsatisfactory and that a more realistic philosophy of death should rather allow death to put the self into question (the "metaphysical uneasiness" of which Gabriel Marcel speaks),[30] I also think, following Pascal, that arguments such as Strawson's have their place in our facing the problem of death.

3. DIGITALISM AND DEATH

3.1. As we have seen, according to some, we are not justifiably entitled to be troubled by death insofar as we understand death as the event that takes away from us the future that would or could be ours. But the therapeutic strategy which secretly moves, or at least legitimizes *ex post*, the naturalistic approach to death is also found in two other proposals in the contemporary analytic philosophy of death. One proposal, with which I will deal at length in the next section, i.e., non-terminism, takes the physical constitution of the human being seriously but, by underplaying the role of our biology, reduces death to a mere "accident" in the existence of that material being that each one of us is. In so doing, death is represented as a problem which can be in principle treated and even reversed scientifically and technologically. As I will show, non-terminism also suffers from a certain analytic "logolatry" and misses the mark by practicing an insufficient methodology in order to clarify the phenomenon of death. I

---

30. See the introduction.

will show that by limiting oneself to linguistic analysis, one has no reason to prefer non-terminism over terminism.

3.2. The other proposal, to which this brief section is devoted, is digitalism.[31] According to digitalism, each one of us is identical to an informational pattern which in principle can be mapped out and reproduced in artificial supports different from and more efficient and reliable than our present biological bodies. This strategy is one case of that broader attitude according to which being itself is nothing else than information and information is interpreted as a sort of hybrid—both spiritual matter and material spirit.[32] Digitalism, then, takes our physical constitution seriously only insofar as our bodies provide a formal and informational "pattern" that can be mapped out and implemented elsewhere. What matters is not matter.[33] It is, rather, the informational blueprint which structures us at all levels (physical, chemical, biological, behavioral, etc., all read as complementary systems of information) and which has been realized so far in an organic body only because of the blind process of natural evolution.[34] Not only death, then, but also our physical and biological constitution are "accidental" to what we are.

According to this view, death is cast in a twofold, somewhat contradictory light. On the one hand, the naturalism underlying digitalism implies that death is a law of nature, an obvious ingredient of biology, and, as such, it is not a phenomenon which puts the self into question, just as our

---

31. See a definition of digitalism: "*Digitalism* is a philosophical strategy that uses these new computational ways of thinking to develop naturalistic but meaningful approaches to religious problems involving minds, souls, life after death, and the divine" (Steinhart, *Your Digital Afterlives*, xii; emphasis added).

32. For a reconstruction and critical assessment of this attitude, see Stango, "Modern Genealogy of Metaphysics."

33. "Naturalists tend to be materialists about human persons. . . . This materialism is compatible with a metaphysical view known as *patternism*. Patternists affirm that living things, such as human persons, are composed of material parts. However, patternists are mainly concerned with the ways those parts are organized. They are primarily concerned with the *forms* or *structures* of living bodies. Any living thing is a set of material parts (such as atoms), which stand to each other in some system of relations. This system of relations is the pattern of the living thing. Patternists focus on the pattern" (Steinhart, "Naturalistic Theories," 145–46; emphasis in original).

34. "All organisms, by definition, store digital self-descriptions used for self-regulation and self-reproduction. Organisms store these self-descriptions in their genomes. On earth, genomes are realized by RNA and DNA; elsewhere, they may be realized differently. . . . Biologists have argued that the complexity of an organism is the percentage of its genome devoted to genetic self-regulation. Greater genetic self-regulation means greater spirituality" (Steinhart, "Spiritual Naturalism," 319).

daily life is not put into question by the fact that physical events are governed by the laws of physics, say, gravity.[35] On the other hand, however, death is understood merely as a fact, that is, as a factual "accident" in the evolution of life in nature. As a consequence, no metaphysical mysteriousness can be legitimately envisioned in death. Insofar as it is a mere fact of nature (nature is nothing else than a bunch of facts, after all), death carries no metaphysical weight, and the parameters of its intelligibility are established by the logic of science and technology. After all, it would be naïve to take the very notion of "*natural* death" as merely descriptive (i.e., as stating that death is an essential ingredient of biological life). On the contrary, such a notion also performs the function of immunization: insofar as it is "natural," death is as acceptable as any other law of nature, while also being eminently controllable and changeable, at least in principle, as any other fact. If we add to this that digitalism, at least in some of its versions, supports the possibility of a technological, that is, digital, overcoming of death via the informational continuation of the person's life after death, we see clearly that digitalism is a form of trans- and posthumanist project in which death stops being a metaphysical question in favor of becoming an ontic, technoscientific problem.[36]

Now, according to digitalism, life after death is conceivable as the preservation of the pattern that each living being is: "Patternism really takes off with the development of the modern sciences of information. The founder of cybernetics, Norbert Wiener, defines the persistence of living things as pattern preservation. Bodies are no longer thought of as watches; now, they are thought of, in computational terms, as finite state machines. Every body has some finite set of possible biologically distinct *states*, it has some finite set of possible biologically distinct *inputs*, it has some finite set of possible biologically distinct *outputs*, and it has some set of *dispositions*. Each disposition is described by a rule, which looks like this: If the body gets an input when it is in some state, then it produces an output and changes to a new state. The quadruple (inputs, states, outputs, dispositions) is the *program* running on the body. Now, the pattern is the program."[37] Eric Steinhart acknowledges that the trans-

---

35. For an outline of what naturalism means with respect to religious phenomena by the same digitalist thinker I am following here, see Steinhart, "Naturalism."

36. Chapter 4 is devoted to the view of death of trans- and posthumanism, digital or otherwise.

37. Steinhart, "Naturalistic Theories," 146; emphasis in original.

and posthumanist strategies for overcoming death, including digitalism, are at present nothing more than "science fiction."[38]

What I am interested in here is simply trying to understand why, despite this acknowledgment, philosophers such as Steinhart do *not* take digitalism as an exercise in science fiction but rather as genuine philosophy, namely, as a viable metaphysics, anthropology, and even "technological eschatology."[39] Furthermore, analogously to the case of the purely linguistic arguments put forth by Strawson, I think that the logical soundness of digitalism and patternism should be taken only as the entryway to what this overall view is supposed to accomplish, namely, providing human beings with a purely naturalistic, therapeutic hope for facing death. The therapeutic effect is here accomplished not mainly via linguistic demystification, but rather via a mystification of technoscience in conjunction with a radical underplaying of biological life as an essential "ingredient" of what we are.

Now, far be it from me to suggest that one could get away with simply "psychoanalyzing" digitalism. Patternism and digitalism should be understood and discussed in their own right. To this point, I believe that the main internal inconsistency of patternism lies in the fact that it takes the informational pattern with which it identifies the living human being as *indifferent* and *neutral* with respect to the actual organism from which that informational pattern is abstracted and the other artificial supports in which this pattern would be hypothetically implemented. For instance, Steinhart traces the origin of this view back to Aristotle,[40] but he does not seem to recognize that for Aristotle a material substantial form requires a *specific matter* and is not indifferent and neutral with respect to different materials.

The "substantial form" of a material being is *what* the specific matter of that being is insofar as it is apprehended from the point of view of its unitary principle of being. On the contrary, Steinhart's patternism and the ensuing digitalism confuse the Aristotelian form with the *abstract*

---

38. Steinhart, "Naturalistic Theories," 151.

39. "The fourth technological soteriology is *mind uploading*. Scanners will accurately map your brain tissue. But this scanning destroys your brain—it kills you. Nevertheless, mind uploading promises your life after death. After your brain tissue has been mapped, an equivalent brain pattern will be installed in some new robotic or software body. Mind uploading is like having your brain teleported into some robotic or software body" (Steinhart, "Naturalistic Theories," 151; emphasis in original).

40. Steinhart, "Naturalistic Theories," 146.

modelization used to build artifacts.[41] The new technologies, especially computer sciences and robotics, have brought about precisely this: the incredible capacity to realize physical supports for abstract models that *look* and *behave* more and more like the things of which they are models. Seen under this light, the difference between a series of equations written on a sheet of paper and the most advanced humanoid robot built to date is nothing else than this, the *complexification of the physical support exemplifying the abstract modelization*: in the first case, a rudimentary sheet of paper; in the second case, a most advanced piece of hardware. In other words, one of the wonders of contemporary technoscience is the following: an abstract model is *exhibited* not chiefly by way of *displaying* the mathematical information, in the form of symbolic language, on a *rudimentary physical support* to which the mathematical information provided is *extrinsic*; rather, the abstract model is *exhibited* by way of *simulating* the same mathematical information by implementing it in a *complex physical support* capable of looking and behaving in the way in which the thing from which the abstract modelization is taken looks and behaves, thanks to the fact that the mathematical information is *intrinsic* to it (i.e., it *regulates* the way it looks and behaves). In other words, the momentous and wondrous achievements of the computer sciences and robotics on which views such as patternism and digitalism rely are nothing less, but also nothing more, than the transformation of the way in which a modelization is displayed. To use an analogy, the computer simulation of an earthquake is not a "replica" of the physical earthquake; it remains a computer simulation, even if, by hypothesis, one were to create a computer simulation that looks and behaves like a real earthquake. Similarly, the digital or robotic "replicas" of dead people which, according to Steinhart, could guarantee the continuation of these people's lives after their

---

41. One could benefit much from reflecting on the way in which Thomas separates physics, mathematics, and metaphysics by distinguishing among three different kinds or levels of abstraction from matter. See, for instance, Aquinas, *Division and Methods*, q. 5; *ST* 1, q. 85, a. 1, ad. 2. Following this line of thought, it could be said that patternism *replaces* the physical form of a thing with its mathematical modelization and takes the mathematical modelization as *metaphysically sufficient* for guaranteeing the very existence of the thing. Of course, the issue at stake here is much more complex, insofar as the mathematical modelization relevant to patternism and digitalism is already understood in light of modern technoscience and thus, in a certain sense, as always already oriented to the manipulation of the thing. It would be interesting to study the case of Descartes as the precursor of many of these themes, insofar as he was among the first to understand the intelligibility of living bodies starting from the model provided by hydraulic automata. See Brown and Normore, "Automata."

death,[42] would simply be the simulation of certain informational patterns that used to belong to those people, running on and displayed by very complex pieces of hardware.[43] As such, they should be likened to complex and dynamic memorabilia, not different in essence from a photograph or a letter of the departed (and, perhaps, less interesting than the latter).

This said, I still think that, despite the internal inconsistencies of digitalism that I have just sketched out, the main flaw of digitalism with respect to death lies precisely in what constitutes also its main strength, namely, its function as a palliative for facing the uncontrollable and yet unavoidable phenomenon of death. Digitalism makes the negation of death into something "light" insofar as the corpse is just outdated hardware; the immaterial, informational program is what matters and it can be implemented elsewhere, if only technology advances a bit more (as it most likely will). The infinitesimal gap that separates digitalism from science fiction is also what provides the necessary handhold for a purely naturalistic hope against the despair in the face of death. In the case of digitalists such as Steinhart, the *preparatio (viventis) ad mortem* becomes the *preparatio (morituri) ad vitam (technologicam)*.

4. "BEING ALIVE" AND NON-TERMINISM

4.1. In this section I present an argument in defense of the termination thesis, namely, the thesis according to which, since "for living things it is living that is existing,"[44] what we call a "dead organism" is not an organism anymore. The argument is not fully new, as it draws from some doctrines already present in Aristotle, Thomas, and Kant, but it is new as far as the contemporary debate between supporters and deniers of the thesis (respectively, "terminators" and "non-terminators") is concerned. I will develop this argument as a response to non-terminators, who claim that a human being continues to exist as a dead body after he

42. Steinhart, "Naturalistic Theories," 151.

43. It is no surprise, then, that some patternists endorse *simulism*, i.e., the view that states that "our universe runs on some *Great Computer*, which was built by some engineers in some larger universe. Simulism entails that all lives, like all physical processes in our universe, are software processes in the Great Computer" (Steinhart, "Naturalistic Theories," 151; emphasis in original). It may be that the only way to accept as viable the otherwise problematic fact that my postmortem replica is "only" a simulation of me is to state that I, together with the entire universe, have always already been nothing else than a simulation.

44. Aristotle, *On the Soul* 415b12.

dies, at least until his body is decomposed passed a certain vague limit.[45] In short, I will write against the idea, as formulated by Paul Snowdon, that "life processes are not necessary for animal persistence."[46] Despite its implausibility, I devote a lot of space to a discussion of non-terminism in this chapter for two reasons: first, because it shows, even more powerfully than Strawson's argument, that taking linguistic analysis as the chief guide to settle issues of life and death is doomed to sheer inconclusiveness (apart from the therapeutic values of these strategies, which also apply to non-terminism); and second, because the debate between terminism and non-terminism allows us to raise (though not settle) the fundamental question: What kind of negation are we speaking of when we talk about the negation of death? Addressing this question will take us, in chapter 2, beyond linguistic analysis into the field of metaphysics. But let us do one thing at a time and focus on language first.

Insofar as it is a critical assessment of and response to the linguistic strategies of non-terminism, my defense of terminism in this section is also purely *linguistic*. It aims to show that non-terminists are wrong

---

45. The debate concerns not only human beings but all organisms. I take the case of human death as a token representative of the whole debate. Among non-terminators, see Becker, "Human Being"; Carter, "Will I Be a Dead Person?"; Mackie, "Personal Identity and Dead People"; Feldman, "Termination Thesis"; the same points are repeated in Feldman, *Confrontations with the Reaper*, ch. 6; Snowdon, "Animalism"; Baker, *Persons and Bodies*, 207; Francescotti, "Surviving Death." Usually, non-terminators defend their view as the only view fully consistent with materialism: "I believe in a sort of straightforward materialism about people. I think we are our bodies. If this sort of materialism is true, then I am my body. In that case, I must have the same history as my body. Since my body will go on existing for a while after I die (unless I die in a remarkably violent way), I will go on existing after I die. Of course, I will then be dead" (Feldman, "Termination Thesis," 102). The key to the solution of the problem is not materialism or non-materialism, but how to understand "body." I am of course identical to the body that I am, but what are the conditions of persistence of the body that I am? I am an animal, therefore I am identical to this animal body. Hence, again, what are the conditions of persistence of the animal that I am? Is life necessary? Is life an "essential property" (Feldman, "Termination Thesis," 106) for living things? Terminators say yes, non-terminators as Feldman say no. However, the problem cannot be settled by appealing to "materialism," obviously, nor are metaphysical arguments sufficient, as I will try to show.

46. Snowdon, "Animalism," 177. See Kagan: "According to the body view [i.e., physicalism], I will still *exist* during phase C [after biological death]. But I won't be *alive*. And so I won't have what *matters*. That, I take it, is what a body theorist should say" (*Death*, 175; emphasis in original). Kagan's formulation is interesting because, while on the one hand it relies on the non-terminist assumption that "life" and "existence" do not coincide in a physical being, on the other hand it recognizes that what is missing from the lingering existence of a dead organism is precisely what matters, namely, that which made that once-alive physical being what it *was* as such.

when they say that for a terminator "there is no such thing as a dead person"[47] because a terminator cannot take a death claim to be literally true. My strategy relies on two different ways of understanding the predicate "being dead." I shall suggest that "being dead" can be *literally true* of the existing subjects of which it is predicated, but that the truth of the predication is *neutral* with respect to the way we should interpret this claim from the point of view of philosophy of nature and biology. More specifically, I shall claim that the predicate "being dead" can both stand for a real property or state of a being or as the total absence of any possible real property or state of that same thing.[48] I will claim that "being dead" can be interpreted as a real property or state if and only if there is a subject that exists after death. Otherwise, "being dead" does not stand for a real property or state but for the absolute absence of real properties and states.

The position has at least three important implications: (1) Contrary to what non-terminators often claim, terminators can explain why death claims about existing things (i.e., claims containing the predicate "being dead") can be literally true. (2) The literal truth of death claims about existing things is not an argument in favor of non-termination. (3) Treating "being dead" as a real property presupposes the proof, which belongs to philosophy of nature and not to linguistic analysis, of the perdurance of the same being after its death, so that no argument to the existence of a human being after his death and to the interpretation of "being dead" as a real property or state *can be derived* from the fact that some death claims are literally true.

I say that my argument is strictly linguistic because I want to distinguish *linguistic arguments*—i.e., arguments purely based on linguistic analysis—from arguments in *philosophy of nature* and, in this case, more precisely, *philosophy of biology*. Contrary to linguistic arguments, philosophy of biology addresses questions concerning a specific class of beings, biological organisms, their nature, and their properties. When we ask what are the conditions for which a biological organism remains the kind of body it is, we are asking a question in philosophy of biology,

---

47. Mackie, "Personal Identity and Dead People," 222. Interestingly, Mackie equates this to the very different claim that for the terminist "what I call 'dead people' are not really people (or persons).'"

48. Throughout the section, I use *property* not in the Thomistic sense of one of the *propria* of a substance, but in the broader, analytic sense of real feature, trait, or characteristic, as it is commonly done in the analytic literature under scrutiny in this chapter.

not in linguistic analysis. The distinction is important to assess the debate between terminism and non-terminism because, as I see it, there are *two different possible kinds of arguments* which can be raised against the termination thesis: philosophy of biology arguments, such that the identity of a biological organism is not dependent upon its being alive but on other properties; and linguistic arguments, such that the structure of our discourse on "dead people" commits ourselves to believing that existence outlasts life. My argument in this section is strictly linguistic. I take this task to be an important one, as the deniers of the termination thesis rely on linguistic arguments abundantly, either on their own—for instance, when they speak of our ordinary talk—or in order to provide further final evidence to the plausibility of biological arguments. As the linguistic arguments are the pivotal point of the strategy of many non-terminators,[49] it follows that providing an alternative linguistic view would score a strong point in favor of the termination thesis, at least in the sense that the extant arguments against the termination thesis would be proved to be misleading.

My argument can be taken to introduce new elements in the debate between terminism and non-terminism not only in the distinction on which it relies ("being dead" understood as the sign for a real property or state and for the absolute absence of any real property of what the referent of the subject used to be), but also in what it accomplishes compared to the strategies of other terminators. First, the present strategy does not require us to say that our claims about "dead people" belong to a "loose" use of language, or that our claims are not literally true. On my view, our claims about "dead people" are *literally true* and stand in *no need for linguistic emendation*. Rather, they need logical and semantic explication (with possible implications in the domain of philosophy of nature), which I provide in the present section. Accordingly, the linguistic analysis of death claims of a terminist does not require to *explain away* "dead people" talk, but to take it at face value and to *explain* it.

Second, it avoids the limit of a strategy that simply points out that our claims about "dead people" can be true even when their referents do not exist any longer, such as "Socrates is dead," in which case the corpse through which Socrates allegedly outlasted his death is now fully corrupted. The problem is to see whether true claims about dead people

---

49. One notable exception is Francescotti, "Surviving Death."

referred to *existing objects* is sufficient for denying the termination thesis. (The reader could already assume that my answer is negative.)

One last caveat. In this chapter I speak from the point of view of an animalist, more specifically a *Thomistic hylomorphic animalist*.[50] Accordingly, I will appeal at times to notions such as substantial change, material continuity without substantial continuity, indestructibility of the soul, etc. However, my strategy in defense of the termination thesis does not depend on this hylomorphic framework, so I can proceed without having to defend this framework here. Hylomorphic animalists, then, can consider my argument as a way to strengthen their view. Non-hylomorphists can mentally translate my hylomorphist-talk into their favorite linguistic equivalents in other versions of animalism.

As I will show, all the death claims that non-terminators take to be evidence for their position can be given an alternative linguistic reading which allows them to be taken as literally true of the existing bodies to which they refer. Put succinctly, non-terminist arguments are inconclusive because non-terminists have forgotten the linguistic role of what medieval grammarians and, recently, Peter Geach call *alienans*,[51] namely, "an adjective that negates the applicability of what it modifies, like 'decoy' or 'pseudo.'"[52] I shall claim that, if "being dead" is interpreted not as a real property or state, but as the alienans indicating the absolute absence of any real property or state, then death claims can be taken as being literally true of the existent bodies to which they refer, hence providing a linguistic framework compatible with the idea that death is indeed substantial change and thus the end of the existence of the organism. Furthermore, I shall provide an analysis of the major arguments of non-terminators and show that, since what they want to prove cannot be proved by appealing to a realistic reading of "being dead" (i.e., "being dead" being the sign for a real property), their strategy should rely on arguments from the philosophy of nature and biology rather than purely linguistic arguments. With all these elements at hand, I will conclude with some considerations on the possibility of taking "being dead" as meaning a real property or state.

4.2. Let us proceed, then, following the method of the analytic philosophers debating terminism and non-terminism. If Aunt Mary is dead, the statement "This is dead Aunt Mary" is literally true when

50. See Toner, "Hylemorphic Animalism."
51. Geach, "Good and Evil."
52. Thornton, "Disembodied Animals," 204.

referred to Aunt Mary's corpse on her deathbed. (I take this statement as a reliable token-statement exemplifying the problem around which the debate gravitates.) The first point to appreciate is that this statement is *indeterminate* with respect to terminism and non-terminism. In fact, it can be both inferred from it that Aunt Mary still exists as dead in what is left of her on the bed (non-terminism), or that what is left on the bed is just the remaining of what used to be Aunt Mary, a corpse or bodily lump of different substances without real unity which, despite some material continuity with Aunt Mary, has no internal functional integration and therefore no substantial continuity with Aunt Mary (terminism). Non-terminists think that the right inference is the former, while terminists think is the latter. Otherwise put, non-terminists think that the proposition "This is dead Aunt Mary" can be taken to be literally true *only if* it grants the first inference, while terminists, at least in the version of terminism I am defending, believe that it can be *literally true even when* it grants the second inference.

A point that is rarely noted in the debate is that the proposition "This is dead Aunt Mary" is indeterminate, namely, *subjectively vague* with respect to the debate between terminators and non-terminators. Assuming that Aunt Mary is actually dead, the proposition is literally true, and can be grasped as such, without having to commit the utterer to either terminism or non-terminism. It is very common to find in the literature non-terminists claiming that the default position of nonphilosophers is non-terminism. So David Mackie:

> The Termination Thesis strongly conflicts with what ordinary people believe. Non-philosophers think that the Termination Thesis is not only false, but obviously so. . . . Members of other biological species do not necessarily cease to exist when they die. As Feldman has pointed out, the suggestion that a butterfly collector does not really have butterflies in his collection would be greeted with astonishment by any nonphilosopher. The items in the collector's collection are dead; but that does not mean that they are not really butterflies.[53]
>
> Living human beings, then, can become dead human beings. And this too is what we ordinarily believe.[54]

---

53. Mackie, "Personal Identity and Dead People," 234.
54. Mackie, "Personal Identity and Dead People," 234–35.

Non-philosophers, then, regard my view that members of biological species do not necessarily cease to exist when they die as an obvious truth. That means, at least, that those who endorse the Termination Thesis need some very strong grounds for doing so. My view can with fairness be regarded as the default view here.[55]

Such remarks are in no way convincing or conclusive. In my view, it is more reasonable to claim that most nonphilosophers take death claims as *true in their vagueness*, without asking whether non-terminism or terminism is correct. This is so because the intuitions guiding our common-sense judgments on this matter rely on an implicit and unreflective linguistic framework which is *neutral* with respect to the problem of whether life and existence are one and the same for organisms. So, ordinary vague talk, as far as it goes, is fine, and does not need any revision. But it is not the case that the literal truth of "This is dead Aunt Mary" necessarily implies non-terminism. It *could also* imply terminism. Thus, non-terminators are wrong in saying that, if we take ordinary talk at face value, non-terminism is the "default position": the truth of the vague proposition "This is dead Aunt Mary" does not imply in itself either non-terminism or terminism. What philosophy can do is to *unpack the still-implicit metaphysical options* implied in our unscrutinized, ordinary vague talk, and to point in the direction of a further, more complex reflection, a reflection in philosophy of nature and biology, to which the last word on the issue belongs.[56]

However, most terminators would disagree with me that "This is dead Aunt Mary" can be *literally true* from the point of view of terminism. They often say that "This is dead Aunt Mary" corresponds to a loose speech, something that cannot withstand scrutiny without having to be radically revised. Expressions such as "Aunt Mary" must in this case be used in a loose way simply because, according to them, there is no such thing as Aunt Mary any longer. Nor can we say that a body is left behind, only now dead, as the body which was identical to Aunt Mary simply went out of existence.[57]

55. Mackie, "Personal Identity and Dead People," 235.

56. For a clear example of how the problem of death should be addressed from the point of view of philosophy of biology, see the discussion on hylomorphism and the empirical criteria for human death in Carrasco and Valera, "Diagnosing Death."

57. Non-terminators seem to imply that terminators must use language "flexibly" and "loosely" to keep together our linguistic practices and their terminist views: "A visitor to Madam Tussaud's might well ask where David Beckham is. It is surely not the case that

What I want to suggest is that terminators concede too much to the non-terminators. They are misguided when they say that claims such as "This is dead Aunt Mary" cannot be taken as literally true within terminism. Non-terminators are wrong when they say that "This is dead Aunt Mary" can be literally true only if interpreted in the non-terminist sense. It is wrong to say that the truth of "This is dead Aunt Mary" implies non-terminism as a "default position" of ordinary talk. On the contrary, the literal truth of "This is dead Aunt Mary" does not imply non-terminism but is perfectly *compatible with the terminist interpretation*. For this reason, it does not have to be loose talk in order to be true in the terminist sense.

Simply put, the literal truth of "This is dead Aunt Mary" is compatible with the two views, non-terminism and terminism. The argument of the terminists is that the only correct inference from the truth of "This is dead Aunt Mary" is to the non-terminist interpretation. I will spell out their argument in the next section. I call their argument "linguistic" because it hinges upon a certain understanding of notions such as predication, truth, properties, being, and existence merely derived from the linguistic analysis of death claims. However, I will show that their argument is not conclusive because a different linguistic analysis can be given which concludes in terminism without giving up the literal truth of the statement. More strongly, under a certain linguistic interpretation

---

this use implies or indicates that the wax object there *actually* is, as we might say, the real David Beckham. In fact, we clearly use language flexibly, and we rely on the audience to latch on to the reference (or significance) of what we are trying to talk about by using a term which does not strictly apply, but which has a basic meaning that enables the audience to link it to the intended object or feature. . . . The audience naturally regards the word 'Beckham' as picking out the model of Beckham. The idea, then, is that this is what is happening when we talk of a dead animal as 'an animal'" (Snowdon, "Animalism," 182; emphasis in original). Snowdon continues: "One should postulate such an ambiguity (or usage) as is being advocated with the term 'animal' only if there is strong evidence for it, which, as far as I can see, does not exist." Similarly, a terminator "can say that of course there are 'dead people.' But on his view, all talk of dead people is slightly loose, for as he sees it, it would be more accurate to say that there are dead bodies former segments of which were people" (Feldman, "Termination Thesis," 108–9). More strongly, Mackie says that the terminist "ought to be able to explain away this usage" ("Personal Identity and Dead People," 222). Some terminators seem to agree: "We do not have good reasons to believe that there is any such thing as a dead body. . . . While I do not think intuitions can be left out of the mix, pre-theoretical intuitions and their expression in customary linguistic usage should not be given too much weight" (Hershenov, "Do Dead Bodies Pose a Problem," 35, 39). Contrary to this approach, I suggest that propositions containing "being dead" can be *literally true without having to imply that they stand for real properties or states in a subject*: there truly are "dead bodies" without "being dead" meaning any real property or state. Consequently, no linguistic revisionism is needed.

of a death statement, the literal truth of the statement *requires* the truth of terminism.

4.3. The debate on the termination thesis has had until this moment a strange balance. Authors on both sides defend their respective positions by appealing to arguments in philosophy of nature and biology. Terminators have rightly appealed heavily to arguments in philosophy of biology and have left the linguistic arguments on the background, while non-terminators have appealed widely to linguistic analysis and have left the biological arguments in the background.[58] Examples of the argumentative style of non-terminists include the following:

> We give evidence . . . in our predicative practice, of thinking that the living entity is the same as the dead thing. . . . "This (dead) butterfly was caught four days ago."[59]

> In the way we speak, then, we clearly seem to regard being dead as something a previously alive entity can be.[60]

> It's not clear that people do stop being people when they die. We certainly speak of "dead people," as for example when we say that dozens of dead people were found in the rubble after the earthquake.[61]

> Although metaphysics cannot be read straight off language, metaphysics tends to start with language. . . . Once the looseness of relation between language and metaphysics is granted, the task of the [sic] defending metaphysical claims become harder. This indicates that we should be rather cautious about invoking linguistic flexibility.[62]

So, there is a difference in stress in the two approaches. I agree with many of the biological arguments for the termination thesis, as, for instance, developed and presented by David Oderberg, Peter Van Inwagen, David Hershenov, Eric Olson, among others.[63] I have nothing to add to

---

58. Besides Francescotti, "Surviving Death," see also Mackie, "Personal Identity and Dead People," 236–39, as an exception.

59. Snowdon, "Animalism," 182.

60. Snowdon, "Animalism" 178.

61. Feldman, "Termination Thesis," 104.

62. Snowdon, "Animalism," 182.

63. Oderberg, *Real Essentialism*, 69–70; Van Inwagen, *Material Beings*, 146–49; Hershenov, "Do Dead Bodies Pose a Problem"; Sumner, "Matter of Life and Death"; Toner, "Hylemorphic Animalism," 71; Olson, *Human Animal*.

these arguments, and the best I can do here is to repeat a couple of them as they are stated by their authors. For instance, Eric Olson convincingly writes:

> The changes that go on in an animal when it dies are really quite dramatic. All of that frenetic, highly organized, and extremely complex biochemical activity that was going on throughout the organism comes to a rather sudden end, and the chemical machinery begins immediately to decay. If it looks like there isn't all that much difference between a living animal and fresh corpse, that is because the most striking changes take place at the microscopic level and below. Think of it this way: If there is such a thing as your body, it must cease to exist at *some* point (or during some vague period) between now and a million years from now, when there will be nothing left of you but dust. The most salient and most dramatic change that takes place during that history would seem to be your death. Everything that happens between death and dust (assuming that your remains rest peacefully) is only slow, gradual decay. So whatever objects there may be that your atoms now compose, it is plausible to suppose that they cease to exist no later than your death. There is no obvious reason to suppose that any 150-pound object persists through that change.[64]

Similarly, David Oderberg writes:

> Fido goes the way of all doggy flesh, leaving behind a canine corpse. It might be said, pointing at the corpse, "There is Fido," meaning that Fido is still a dog, albeit a dead one. But a dead dog is not a kind of dog any more than the proverbial rubber duck is a kind of duck, or, to change the analogy, than a dead parrot is anything other than an ex-parrot. A substantial form supplies the proper functions and operations of its instances. Since no functions and operations take place in a dead dog—indeed the processes undergone by and taking place in a corpse are in general the very *reverse* of those undergone by and taking place in a functioning dog—clearly a dead dog does not fall under the substantial kind *dog*. . . . We can eliminate the idea that the canine form is the form of a certain kind of corpse. It is tempting to think that a living dog just is a dead dog plus something extra, and one might imagine dead Fido's being miraculously brought back to life and call that the re-addition of canine form to canine matter. But dead flesh is not a formally impoverished

---

64. Olson, *Human Animal*, 151–52; emphasis in original.

kind of living flesh: in dead flesh, from the moment death occurs, not only is the substantial organic canine form absent but it is replaced by the very form of a dead thing, in which new functions of decay and disintegration immediately begin to occur. The reanimation of dead Fido by means of the readdition of the organic canine form would involve not the superaddition of something to a corpse, but the actual *reversal* of disintegrative processes already commenced. In other words, Fido's form *qua* living dog is the form of living flesh, i.e., the living flesh has a formal cause in Fido's substantial form; there simply is no metaphysical space for another kind of flesh to which the organic canine form is added to produce a living, breathing dog.[65]

Arguments such as Olson's and Oderberg's suggest that biological life is not an accident to what we are: we are organisms, i.e., animals essentially characterized by an *integrative unity*, and death is the end of the organisms and animals that we are.[66]

---

65. Oderberg, *Real Essentialism*, 69–70; emphasis in original.

66. The question regarding what exactly in the failing of an organism can be taken as evidence that the end of that organism has occurred (cardiac death, brain death, etc.), including the problem of how to define such evidence (What counts, precisely, as cardiac death? What counts as brain death?), is a strictly empirical, biological question (and thus also a question in philosophy of nature and biology), and should be treated as such. In order to sort this problem out, the appeal to the philosophical definition of death as separation of soul and body cannot decide anything. See John Paul II: "The death of the person is a single event, consisting in the total disintegration of that unitary and integrated whole that is the personal self. It results from the separation of the life-principle (or soul) from the corporeal reality of the person. *The death of the person*, understood in this primary sense, is an event which *no scientific technique or empirical method can identify directly*. Yet human experience shows that once death occurs *certain biological signs inevitably follow*, which medicine has learnt to recognize with increasing precision. In this sense, the 'criteria' for ascertaining death used by medicine today should not be understood as the technical-scientific determination of the *exact moment* of a person's death, but as scientifically secure means of identifying the *biological signs* that a person has indeed died. It is a well-known fact that for some time certain scientific approaches to ascertaining death have shifted the emphasis from the traditional cardio-respiratory signs to the so-called 'neurological' criterion. Specifically, this consists in establishing, according to clearly determined parameters commonly held by the international scientific community, the complete and irreversible cessation of all brain activity (in the cerebrum, cerebellum and brain stem). This is then considered the sign that the individual organism has lost its integrative capacity. With regard to the parameters used today for ascertaining death—weather the 'encephalic' signs or the more traditional cardio-respiratory signs—the Church does not make technical decisions [nor should the metaphysician, I may add]. She limits herself to the Gospel of duty of comparing the data offered by medical science with the Christian understanding of the unity of the person, bringing out the similarities and the possible conflicts capable of endangering respect for human dignity" ("Address," §§4–5; emphasis in original). For

In short, the heart of the issue between terminism and non-terminism must be settled at the biological level, and I think that arguments drawn from philosophy of nature and biology proving the truth of terminism are already available. However, given that most of the non-terminators rely on linguistic arguments, I believe we need a stronger *linguistic argument* for terminators to respond to the non-terminators. I provide this argument here. The terminators who already rely on the biological arguments might consider whether the linguistic argument presented here strengthens their view or if it is just an unnecessary "philosophical overkill" of non-terminism.[67] Non-terminators who tend to give more stock to the linguistic arguments rather than the biological arguments can consider whether this argument shakes their belief, even just a bit. In any case, it seems to me that the present argument is helpful to advance the discussion further.

The linguistic argument for denying the termination thesis can be formulated in the following way:

1. "This is dead Aunt Mary" is literally true (when it refers to the dead body or corpse of Aunt Mary).

2. If "This is dead Aunt Mary" is literally true, then the predicate "being dead" must stand for a real property or state of the something to which it refers, the subject "This = Aunt Mary." (In predicate logic, we should have an indexical existential quantifier quantifying over the conjunction whose conjuncts are the identity x = Mary, the function Ax, and the other function Dx. However, for the purpose of the present argument, there is no need to stick to this complex formulation. We can stipulate to take "This is Aunt Mary" as the subject and "she is dead" as the predicate.)

3. A predicate can stand for a real property or state only if there is an existing something to which the real property or state belongs, "of which" it is a real property or state.

4. Therefore, there is something existing, the organism, to which the real property or state expressed by the predicate "being dead" belongs.

---

a debate internal to the Catholic world, see Spaemann, "Brain Death"; Tonti-Filippini, "Bodily Integration" (response to Spaemann).

67. I take the expression from Mackie, "Personal Identity and Dead People," 239.

5. Therefore, the organism persists also after its death, though it persists as dead.

6. Therefore, the existence of the organism is not the same thing as its life.

7. In conclusion, the termination thesis is false.

Though not formulated in these terms by any of the deniers of the termination thesis, I believe this is a fair, explicit reconstruction of their metaphysical argument. The reconstruction of the argument shows why it is purely linguistic. It makes no reference to problems such as the conditions of substantial continuity for an organism; it simply hinges upon the conditions of possibility under which a statement can be literally true of an existing referent. It relies on a specific understanding of predication and truth. This is the argument I will try to refute. My overall strategy is very simple. It draws in a sense from a Thomist and Kantian approach, although one does not have to be either a Thomist or a Kantian to accept it.[68]

What I want to argue is that "This is my dead aunt" can be *literally true even without taking the predicate "being dead" to stand for a real property or state*, and that therefore it stands in no need of linguistic emendation even from the point of view of terminism. The truth of the proposition does not commit ourselves to the view that the predicate "being dead" stand for a real property or state. It begs the question to believe so, as non-terminators do. An alternative, likely reconstruction of the meaning and truth of the proposition is that "being dead" does not stand for a real property or state, but, elaborating on Kant, it stands for the *absolute absence of any real property or state of the thing to which the subject of the proposition refers*; elaborating on Thomas, it is the alienans of that of which it is truly predicated.

The Kantian part of this argument relies of course on Kant's doctrine that existence is not a real property but the absolute position of real properties. Paraphrasing, one could say that "exists" should not be taken to stand for a real property in the object as, for instance, the properties grasped by predicates such as "being an aunt" or "being tall" do. Kant was using this insight to show in what way the ontological proof for the existence of God cannot be conclusive. More generally, I take his consideration to show that a proposition can be true even when its logical

---

68. Others have noted the similarity between Thomas and Kant on this point, e.g., Gilson, *Christian Philosophy*, 57.

constituents do not refer to real properties in their referent. Extending this intuition to the opposite case of the predicate "being dead," one could say that the literal truth of propositions containing "being dead" does not imply by itself that "being dead" is a predicate standing for a real property or state of the referent of the subject of the propositions. This logical option opens the possibility for a different metaphysical reading of the true propositions containing "being dead." Paraphrasing Kant, one could say that, just as the proposition "Aunt Mary exists" does not imply that Aunt Mary's existence is one of the real properties constituting her essence, such as "being an aunt" and "being tall," but means the "absolute position" of all the real properties constituting Aunt Mary's essence; similarly, the proposition "Aunt Mary is dead" referred to Aunt Mary's corpse does not imply that the predicate "being dead" stands for a real property or state of Aunt Mary, because it *could* be taken to mean the *absolute absence or removal of all the real properties or states* that used to constitute Aunt Mary.

The Thomistic part of the argument relies on the different meanings of "being," as already discussed by Aristotle.[69] In *In Sent* 2, d. 34, q. 1, a. 1, Thomas distinguishes three different meanings of "being."[70] In a first sense, "being" is predicated as it is divided by the ten genera and therefore stands for something existing in the nature of things. In a second sense, "being" signifies the truth of the proposition. He writes: "So whatever is said to be a being in the first sense is a being also in the second sense: for whatever has natural existence in the nature of things can be signified to be an affirmative proposition. . . . But not everything which is a being in the second sense is a being also in the first sense." This last remark leads Thomas to the third and crucial for our discussion meaning of "being." "Being" can also be said of a privation, such as "blindness" is: "But blindness is not something in the nature of things, but it is rather a removal of being: and so even privations and negations are said to be beings in the second sense, but not in the first sense." What I have called the literal truth of a proposition such as "This is dead Aunt Mary" corresponds to the second meaning of "being" pointed out by St. Thomas. Thus, in his terms, what I meant to say is that the being-true of propositions containing "being dead" is noncommittal with respect to non-terminism (which corresponds to the inference from being in the second sense to being in

---

69. Aristotle, *Metaphysics* 5.

70. Cf. also *ST* 1, q. 48, a. 2, ad. 2. See Klima, "Semantic Principles," 91–97.

the first sense) and terminism (which corresponds to the inference from being in the second sense to being in the third sense). The additional point is that the third sense of being is perfectly compatible with the second one. When I say "This is dead Aunt Mary" and the proposition is true, I am not committing myself to the view that there is a real property or state in the referent of the subject corresponding to the predicate "being dead." On the contrary, I am saying that all the real properties and states that used to characterize Aunt Mary are purely and simply absent from that referent—look for them as much as you want, you will never find them *there*. "Being dead," then, does not stand for a real property or state, something existing in that piece of world that is the corpse lying on the bed, but rather for a *negation or a privation*. In this case, the *radical negation and privation of life and existence*.

In simple terms, "being dead" works logically as an alienans, namely, an adjective that negates the applicability of what it modifies, like "decoy" or "pseudo" or "forged."[71] I think that St. Thomas's remarks help us emendate a bit further this characterization of the alienans: in fact, strictly speaking, the alienans "being dead" does not deny the applicability of the subject "Aunt Mary" to its referent (such denial would make sense only by assuming that the first meaning of being is the only possibility available); on the contrary, it *requires* the application of the subject to its referent *in order to state that* all the possible semantic and ontological content of that subject does not find any correspondence whatsoever in it. In other words, the subject *must be applied* to the referent in order to be what it is, an *essentially frustrated* subject in its reference.[72]

---

71. See Thornton, "Disembodied Animals." See also Hershenov: "A *dead body* would then be no more a body than a *dry lake* is a lake, or a toy soldier is a soldier, or *counterfeit money* is money" ("Do Dead Bodies Pose a Problem," 52; emphasis in original). The first two examples are borrowed from Olson, *Human Animal*, while the third is from E. J. Lowe via Mackie, "Personal Identity and Dead People."

72. The terminist reading does not imply that the proposition refers to *nothing*. The referent, the corpse in this case, is clearly *existing*; only, it does not have the existence of a human being, but rather of a lump of matter. Understanding "being dead" as an alienans does not imply what Snowdon suggests: "It does not seem that the predicate 'x is dead' behaves like a predicate that implies that the thing to which it applies does not exist. . . . We seem quite prepared to co-ascribe both being dead and lots of other properties that seem to imply existence. We can say, 'That animal is dead and I shall eat it/throw it in the river/photograph it.' If I am doing these things to it presumably it exists. . . . There is, it appears, no general entailment from 'x is dead' to 'x does not exist'" ("Animalism," 178–79). Similarly, Mackie provides what he takes to be a reductio ad absurdum of the view that "being dead" is an alienans: "So, if 'dead' is an adjective like 'counterfeit,' then just as dead people are not really people, so dead roses will not be roses. . . . Worse still, dead bodies

This framework explains in a different way the stress that non-terminators put on the importance of the reference. They wonder, how do terminators explain that it is *precisely this thing* that is said to be dead? The precision of the reference, in their view, is strong evidence that there is an existent referent of which the predicate "being dead" expresses a real property or state. But this, again, begs the question, as a different linguistic reading is possible. When I say "This is dead Aunt Mary" when referring to Aunt Mary's corpse, I am saying that all the real properties or states which constituted my aunt's reality are absolutely absent *from this body* and not from other bodies. It is in *this* lump of matter and *only in this lump of matter*—with its bodily traits, which *look like* Aunt Mary—that the absence of Aunt Mary's reality is made most evident and grieved. Aunt Mary's corpse, together with the claim referring to it stating that "This is dead Aunt Mary," could be taken then as a complex (i.e., non-purely linguistic) "negative sign," i.e., a presence that signifies an absence.[73]

The *practice of grieving the dead body* is, in fact, another of the main empirical evidence put forth by non-terminators to support their view.[74] The Kantian-Thomistic proposal here presented shows how the terminist point of view explains the attitude of grieving the dead body at least

---

will not really be bodies. This will strike most people as an unacceptable view. . . . It is very doubtful whether anyone could seriously maintain that dead bodies are not really bodies" ("Personal Identity and Dead People," 223). But this is not so. "Body" can in fact be taken in two senses; in one sense, it means "living body," that is, (living) "animal"; in another sense, it means a lump of matter, of whatever kind (or kinds) this lump of matter might be. Now, when we refer to a corpse as a "dead body," we are denying not that what is there is a lump of matter, but that it is a living body and therefore an animal or an organism. Clearly, this reading presupposes terminism. But the only point is to show that, from a metaphysical standpoint, we can hold that "dead" is an alienans and that "these are dead bodies" can be true without also committing ourselves to the claim that what we are referring to are not real lumps of matter.

73. See Melchiorre, *Sul senso della morte*, 29. See also Heidegger: "This interpretation of the transition from Dasein to something merely objectively present, however, misses the phenomenal content in that the being still remaining does not represent a mere corporeal thing. Even the objectively present corpse is, viewed theoretically, still a possible object for pathological anatomy whose understanding is oriented toward the idea of life. Merely-being—objectively-present is 'more' than a *lifeless*, material thing. In it we encounter something *unliving* which has lost its life" (*Being and Time*, 221; emphasis in original).

74. "I have in mind the way humans seem to regard the dead bodies of those they have loved as being the loved one themselves. Thus, parents who lose their children to violent deaths want desperately to keep the child from being buried or cremated *so that they can still see their child*. The emotion here seems to rest on the conviction that the dead entity is their child whom they are still seeing and cannot come to terms with no longer seeing" (Snowdon, "Animalism," 178; emphasis in original).

as adequately as the non-terminists do. In a certain sense, it explains it even better, as the dramatic sense of the total absence of the person from the corpse is better accommodated by the terminist rather than the non-terminist: when faced with the death of a person, we are saying that *all of that person is gone*, not just some essential property. It is the *radical contrast between the material continuity* (painfully brought to our attention by the physical resemblance) and *the substantial discontinuity* between (live) Aunt Mary and her corpse that accounts for the drama of grieving a corpse.[75] Similarly, the indication on a tombstone saying "Here lies [dead] Aunt Mary" is not a lie from the terminist point of view, pace Feldman, if we read it according to the framework just presented: "Here lies [dead] Aunt Mary" is literally true, not a lie, because it is exactly in the corpse buried "here" that the absolute absence of Aunt Mary is made dramatically evident—not in any other corpse buried in any other tomb, but in this one. By taking "being dead" as an alienans, the literal truth of graveyard inscriptions such as "Here lies [dead] Aunt Mary" is saved.[76]

75. Carter wonders, "How is it possible that the head injury inspected in Flan (what is left after death) in an autopsy is taken to be causally responsible for the death of Flam if Flan did not exist before Flam's death?" ("Will I Be a Dead Person?," 169). Clearly the difficulty stems from the *presupposition that substantial change excludes any kind of continuity* between Flan and Flam. Appreciating the *material continuity* between Flan and Flam would allow Carter to solve the puzzling scenario he considers in this passage. The same considerations apply to Feldman: "In a field behind my house there stands a huge old elm tree. It has been dead for many years. I suppose it was a victim of the so-called Dutch Elm Disease. I also suppose that the tree was well over fifty years old at the time of its death. I doubt that anyone would want to say that the large arboreal object currently in the field never lived or that it came into existence just a few years ago when the elm tree died. Virtually everyone would agree . . . that this now-dead tree is more than fifty years old and that it previously lived. Careful study of the annual rings might seem to confirm these estimates of age and former life" ("Termination Thesis," 101–2). General point about organisms: "In every case, if an organism dies, but its remains remain, then it remains. The transition from being alive to being dead is a transition that happens to *some persisting object*. . . . In some cases there is reason to wonder about why a person died. . . . In these cases, a medical examiner might perform an autopsy. By looking closely at details of the corpse, the examiner hopes to learn more about what happened to the person who died. . . . The object that formerly was a living person still exists—now as a corpse—and still contains the bullet. If such a thing could happen, then TT is false" (102; emphasis in original).

76. My position has received the following objection in a number of occasions: "Suppose I state, 'This is Aunt Mary' at time *t* (leaving out the term 'dead'). If I state it at time *t*, it is true if and only if Aunt Mary exists at *t* and I am using 'this' to designate her. If I state, 'This is Aunt Mary' at *t* and I am using this to designate a corpse, then what I say is true if and only if that corpse is Aunt Mary. None of this changes if I add the term 'dead' to my statement: if I say, 'This is dead Aunt Mary' at *t*, and I am using 'this' to designate a corpse, then what I say is true if and only if the corpse is Aunt Mary. Hence the

If we take "being dead" as standing not as a real property or state of somebody, but as the absolute absence of any real property or state of that somebody, then we can take all the "being dead" claims to be literally true of bodies which have no substantial continuity with the persons who were there before. More strongly, if we take Thomas's third meaning of being, we should say that propositions such as "This is dead Aunt Mary" are literally true *only if* the body lying there has no substantial continuity with Aunt Mary. Under this interpretation, the lack of substantial continuity and the nonexistence of the reality meant by the subject is required for the truth of the proposition. In fact, substantial continuity and persistence would make the claim false, as something real of Aunt Mary would still be present in the referent and therefore the condition of the radical negation in the referent of what the subject stands for demanded by the predicate "being dead" would not be satisfied. It would be false that all the real properties or states which constituted my aunt's reality are absent from the body. With reference to the non-terminist argument, this alternative metaphysical framework rejects premises 2 and 3: the literal truth of a proposition containing the predicate "being dead" does not imply

---

opponents of the termination thesis will conclude that the literal truth of 'This (corpse) is Aunt Mary,' and the truth of 'This is dead Aunt Mary,' implies that Aunt Mary continues her existence as a corpse, which she cannot do if the termination thesis is true." This objection is flawed in several ways: First, if I designate Aunt Mary's corpse by saying, "This is Aunt Mary," my statement is either *elliptical*, since what is meant is "This is *dead* Aunt Mary," or flatly *equivocal*, just like for Aristotle and St. Thomas, calling a corpse "man" is an example of equivocity. For this reason, if I say, "This is Aunt Mary" to refer to Aunt Mary's corpse, either the statement is elliptical and true (but again, is it true according to non-terminism or terminism?), or it is equivocal and false. Second, the objection states that adding "dead" to "This is Aunt Mary" changes nothing. In general, this is false, both for non-terminists and terminists. If the statement means that adding "dead" to "This is Aunt Mary" does not change anything in the sense that "this" refers to Aunt Mary's corpse, the statement is correct, but again, the philosophical point that I am making is that the truth of the statement is compatible with both non-terminism and terminism. Third, and most importantly, the objection seems to suggest that the referentiality of indexicals such as "this" depends wholly on the descriptive content of the sentence: Aunt Mary must still be there for "This is (dead) Aunt Mary" to refer to Aunt Mary's corpse successfully. But this understanding of indexicals is false (see Braun, "Indexicals"), and one can still provide a terminist account of the literal truth of the statement. Accordingly, even after Aunt Mary has died, I can refer to the corpse and state, "*This* is dead Aunt Mary," not necessarily because Aunt Mary persists in her existence as dead (non-terminism), but because, alternatively, Aunt Mary has undergone what Aristotle calls a *substantial change*, and the *material and spatiotemporal continuity* between Aunt Mary and her corpse is a sufficient condition to fix the referent of the indexical "this" to the corpse and describe it as "dead Aunt Mary," where "dead" is an alienans (terminism).

that there is a real property or state corresponding to the predicate in the referent to which the subject also refers.

4.4. One should be aware of the limitations of my proposal. In fact, the argument does not prove conclusively that the termination thesis is correct. In fact, my argument just shows that the literal truth of statements such as "This is my dead aunt" does not imply the denial of the termination thesis. It shows that *a different linguistic interpretation of this truth is possible*. That we should prefer this alternative interpretation is something that *linguistic analysis itself cannot decide*. I think that the choice of the best linguistic interpretation depends ultimately on arguments in *philosophy of nature and biology*: if the arguments for biological essentialism are sound, then people should prefer my linguistic reconstruction (or any equivalent reconstruction) and conclude that terminism is the way to go; if the arguments against biological essentialism are not sound, then people should prefer the "real property" reconstruction and conclude that non-terminism is preferable. But terminism and non-terminism are doctrines belonging to philosophy of biology, in the sense that only a philosophical reflection of biological data can tell us what the conditions of identity and persistence of an organism are. By itself, the linguistic analysis of language cannot decide much, not because our linguistic practices and the metaphysical assumptions present in them are not important with respect to the truth of the whole issue, but rather because, upon scrutiny, we find that the philosophical *experimentum crucis* for deciding between terminism and non-terminism must be conducted not at the level of linguistic analysis but at the level of philosophy of biology.

As I charge non-terminators of begging the question by interpreting "being dead" as a real property or state, so they could charge me of begging the question for interpreting it as the absolute absence of any real property or state of a human being. But they would be right *only if I claimed that I can prove the termination thesis simply based on my linguistic argument*. However, this is not my intent. On the contrary, what I claim is that *there is no linguistic reason to prefer one position or the other*. "Being dead" can be construed in different, and equally sound linguistic ways. So, I do not fail where the non-terminators fail, viz. believing that a linguistic argument is sufficient to settle the issue between terminism and non-terminism.

Nevertheless, my argument accomplishes something. First, it shows that the whole discussion *should focus more on philosophy of nature and biology and less on linguistic analysis*. This means that, if non-terminators want to provide conclusive arguments, they should provide conclusive arguments in philosophy of biology and not in the analysis of language. In this sense, the present linguistic argument plays an almost exclusively negative function, removing the elements of confusion and opening the space for the real debate: the conflict lies in philosophy of biology, not in linguistic analysis. It works like Wittgenstein's famous ladder:[77] The argument must be used only in order to be eventually discarded; it "cleans up" the field from linguistic prejudices and reestablishes philosophy of biology in its due place. Second, it shows that, when we deal with the metaphysical implications of true statements such as "This is dead Aunt Mary," there is no reason to prefer non-terminism over terminism, as non-terminators often say. We must appreciate subjective vagueness as a constitutive element of ordinary talk because it allows a genuine grasp of truth that is free from the burden of having to decide previously among competing technical philosophical issues. Third, by providing a different metaphysical reading of the evidence usually used non-terminators, it weakens the plausibility of their view. Since non-terminators seem to imply that a non-terminist linguistic reading of propositions containing "being dead" is the only reading compatible with their truth, proving that a different metaphysical view is possible undermines the strongest metaphysical reason non-terminators have advanced to convince us to endorse their view.

In conclusion, for those who find, as I do, good biological reasons in favor of the idea that a human being cannot continue to be the kind of being that he is after death, my linguistic argument will be an additional contribution in favor of the termination thesis. For those who do not find such biological reasons, my argument shows that they should not find comfort in linguistic analysis. And for those who are noncommittal, my linguistic argument shows that the truth of our linguistic practices is as compatible with terminism as it is with non-terminism.

4.5. Unsurprisingly, I believe that the appeal of the non-terminist position (especially if it is defended only through linguistic arguments) does not result from its logical soundness (which is inconclusive, as I have demonstrated), but by its therapeutic function. As in the cases previously discussed, non-terminism also accomplishes something valuable for man: the sense, the linguistically produced illusion-hope, that death may be not too bad for man (or any other living thing) after all. According

---

77. Wittgenstein, *Tractatus Logico-Philosophicus* 6.54.

to non-terminism, in fact, death is only an "accident" in the existence or "material career" of an organism. "Being dead" is, accordingly, a phase sortal, perhaps indicating a very serious change in the organism, but not a change so radical as to determine the end of the organism. It is thus intriguing to think of how such a seemingly abstruse philosophical position can in fact provide the perfect linguistic underpinnings to the metaphysical view implied in one of the contemporary "technological soteriologies" discussed by Steinhart, namely, "cryonics." As Steinhart explains, cryonics "promises that, when you die, the pattern of your brain or body can be preserved by freezing. After cures for aging and disease have been discovered, your brain or body can be thawed out and revived. It will then be repaired and rejuvenated. The continuity from your dying body to your revived body is informational but not biological. Your soul will be reinstated by your revived flesh. Cryonics is a kind of resurrection. Your career contains two lives: The [f]irst ends when you are frozen; the second begins when you are revived."[78] Note: your career contains *two lives* but only *one existence*, the existence of the material thing that you are, perduring through the states of being alive, dead, frozen, and then alive again once thawed and technologically resurrected.

4.6. Let us move now to a final point. That "being dead" is not a predicate standing for a real property or state when referred to a corpse does not mean that, by hypothesis, "being dead" can *in no case* mean a real property or state. The question becomes, then, on what conditions could "being dead" be predicated as a real property or state? The response is, only if the individual human person could continue to exist, in some way or another, after his own death. The Thomistic tradition seems to provide a good example of this option: as our immaterial soul cannot be reduced to our biological life, our biological death does not destroy fully who we are; our soul survives. How could the surviving soul be defined with respect to death? It could be defined, precisely, as a dead human being, as a dead person. On this view, only the separated soul could be truthfully described as a dead human being, where "being dead" stands for a real property or state. *If we take "being dead" as meaning a real property or state, the truth of a proposition containing the predicate "being dead" can be guaranteed in a robust way only if the proposition is referred to the separated soul.* In this case, "being dead" does not function as an alienans. When I speak of "dead Aunt Mary" referring to Aunt Mary's

---

78. Steinhart, "Naturalistic Theories," 150–51.

separated soul, "being dead" does not mean that all the possible semantic and ontological content of "Aunt Mary" (e.g., being a living human being) is missing from the referent; rather, I am saying that that referent is identical to Aunt Mary, even though Mary is "dead"; even though Mary finds herself in a diminished, weakened, dramatically imperfect and *negated* condition, represented by the loss of the body. In Thomistic terms, one would say that in this case "being dead" does not signify the absence of the substance "Mary" from the referent; it signifies that the substance, expressed by the proper name, is present in the referent in a special state; it has a certain property, that of having been separated from the body and of being therefore in a dramatically imperfect and negated condition.

It is not hard to find in the contemporary literature on death the comment that Christians do not take death seriously because they believe in an afterlife. For instance, Jeffrie G. Murphy writes: "Other-worldly Christians . . . , who counsel that at least certain persons (the saved) should not fear death . . . , argue either that there is no such thing as death or that death is a good thing. In practice, of course, these two claims—insofar as they are intelligible at all—tend to be collapsed together."[79] One could show that this claim is mistaken at many different levels, existential, philosophical, and religious. If one grants that a first level for "taking death seriously" is making explicit in what ways the predicate "being dead" can be true, it follows that only in light of a position such as the Christian and Thomistic one, which preaches the survival of the personal soul after death, the predicate "being dead" can refer to a subsistent reality capable of having "being dead" as one of his most fundamental properties or states. One main question remains open, however, namely, whether in this case "being dead," meaning a real property or state, refers to something "positive" in the subject. I will have a few things to say about this point at the end of this section.

As is well known, according to Thomas our personal soul survives our death. However, a recent debate between corruptionists and survivalists has animated an interesting discussion on whether it is the human being that I am that survives, partially and yet truly, in the separated soul. Survivalists claim it is, corruptionists claim it is not.[80] Reconstructing

---

79. Murphy, "Rationality and Fear," 52.

80. The literature is vast (maybe too vast). For corruptionism, see Toner, "St. Thomas Aquinas on Death"; for survivalism, see Eberl, "Do Human Persons Persist." For further bibliography on the debate, see Toner, "Personhood and Death," 135nn1–2. The debate concerns whether what survives death—the intellectual soul—is sufficient

the debate would be impossible here. The only thing I would like to reflect on is, again, on what conditions our propositions containing "being dead" can be true, and in what way. With respect to the corruptionist and survivalist debate, it seems safe to say that only in case survivalists were right, a proposition such as "Aunt Mary is dead" could be true and "being dead" could mean a real property or state. In fact, even though the corruptionist position would allow us to interpret "being dead" as a real property of something, as the soul *does* survive as separated, arguably as the consequence of the death of the person, it would nevertheless prevent us from saying that it is the same person who is in a dead state, because the soul would fall short of guaranteeing the permanence of the person. In short, corruptionism allows us to take "being dead" to mean a real property or state, but denies that the referent of the predication can be *the person*. In thinking of Aunt Mary's separated soul, the corruptionist could not also think truthfully, "Dead Aunt Mary, pray for us!," simply because the soul the corruptionist is addressing in his prayer can be said to be in a dead state, but cannot be said to be Aunt Mary. Conversely, only if survivalists are right one can take "being dead" as describing a real property or state of the very person of which that predicate is predicated.

There is a tendency in contemporary analytic philosophy of death to deny the survival of the soul and yet to take "being dead" as a real property, not of the subject in question, but of her "story." For instance, Stephen E. Rosenbaum writes: "Being dead is the state in which one finds oneself (so to speak) after one dies. Being dead is clearly not part of a person's life, in the normal sense, though we might say that it is part of a person's history."[81] When we do not believe in the possibility of a personal afterlife, "being dead" can be taken to mean a real property only of a subject-history, i.e., the subject of narrations, books, collective memories and practices, etc. While this fact might have a deep philosophical and religious meaning, I have tried to point out that the Thomistic tradition, under the survivalist interpretation, provides us with a different, arguably complementary, view: believing that a personal survival in one's separated soul is possible

---

to make the statement that the human being survives death true. Corruptionists say no, survivalists say yes. Although born autonomously among Thomists in recent years, the debate echoes the twentieth-century discussions between Catholic and Protestant theologians on how to understand the destructive power of death and the continuity in the interim state. See Remenyi, "Death as the Limit." I find myself closest to the position presented in De Haan and Dahm, "After Survivalism and Corruptionism," according to which the separated soul is an incomplete person.

81. Rosenbaum, "How to Be Dead," 121.

provides us with the only state of affairs capable of grounding the truth of propositions that take "being dead" as a real predicate.

One final question is whether taking "being dead" to mean a real property or state in the separated soul-person implies that being dead is something positive in the soul, or rather a removal of being, as "being blind" is the removal of sight in the human being. The answer must be that, also in this case, "being dead" is a negative property, not something positive "in the nature of things" but a *privation of being*. Yet, it is not easy to have a clear understanding of the "nature" of the negation/privation of death. On the one hand, it is not the mere privation of a power, such as in the case of blindness, because death affects the *whole person* and is therefore a *radical negation* of the being of the person. On the other hand, if we assume survivalism, such radical negation cannot mean the *annihilation of the person*, namely, cannot mean the *absolute removal of all the real properties and states of the person*, as in the case of "being blind," which is the absolute removal of the power of vision, or in the case of "being dead" referred to a corpse. For these reasons, I believe, developing a better account of the negation-privation of death remains an urgent task for the Thomistic hylomorphic understanding of the human being. What kind of negation is the negation of "being dead"? And is death something that affects me only during or after the event of death? Isn't it rather truer to state that, while alive, a certain "being in death" is already true of my condition? And what kind of negation is such "being in death"? I try to answer these and related questions in chapter 2 through a reinterpretation of Thomas's hylomorphic account of the human person.

CHAPTER TWO

Death as Material Kenosis
A Thomistic Proposal

> O young tree of the knowledge of Good and Evil,
> behold how my dissolution begins
> because I have laid my hands upon you,
> and already my soul and body are being divided,
> as the wine in the vat from crushed grape!
>
> PAUL CLAUDEL, *TIDINGS BROUGHT TO MARY*, 32

> What you call dying is merely the conclusion of death;
> what you call living is simply dying alive;
> as for the bones, they are what death leaves of you
> which the tomb cannot devour.
>
> FRANCISCO DE QUEVEDO, *SUEÑOS*, 213 (AUTHOR'S TRANSLATION)

> Is it possible to reverse the superficial Epicurean dialectics of the mutual inaccessibility of I and Death? When I am, death is *not*! The negation implies the abyss of negativity, death is the unknowable and the dread. When death is, I am *not*: under my steps an abyss opens up, the nothing, death annihilates me.
>
> XAVIER TILLIETTE, *MORTE E IMMORTALITÀ*, 77 (AUTHOR'S TRANSLATION); EMPHASIS IN ORIGINAL

DEATH AS MATERIAL KENOSIS

1. DEATH AND HYLOMORPHISM

1.1. WE CONCLUDED CHAPTER 1 acknowledging that, even assuming that death is in fact the substantial change of an organism, as the Thomistic tradition suggests, it is not at all clear what kind of negation "being dead" may be for the subsistent, incorruptible soul. Moreover, we speculated that maybe death is not reducible to the final event of passing and that the intuition that we are somehow always already "in death" may be more than a metaphor. How should we then understand this "being in death" and how is it related to dying and being dead? And is it possible to try to understand these questions without writing off the Thomistic hylomorphic view of the human person? Not only do I think that the Thomistic hylomorphic view of the human person is salvageable; I am convinced that it is the best framework to truly make sense in a unitary way of the questions that I have just raised. According to the Thomistic metaphysical view I shall present in this chapter, death is *material kenosis*, understood as self-negation and self-emptying.[1] This idea is supposed not only to supplement the current debates on hylomorphism and death, but also to respond to some criticisms that St. Thomas Aquinas has received from many sides. As I see it, material kenosis, in all its different aspects, is nothing else than an explication of the idea of death as the separation of soul and body from a Thomistic hylomorphic point of view.[2] Before

---

1. The notion of kenosis, taken from its Greek sense of self-emptying and self-negating, is fit to unpack the unexplored implications of St. Thomas Aquinas's hylomorphism of the human being. Of course, the fact that the same notion is used in Phil 2:7 to describe Christ's incarnation, passion, and death opens interesting scenarios for a theology of death. In brief, explaining why human death is best understood as material kenosis should in turn help explaining God's kenosis in Christ: understanding human death as material kenosis suggests that God's kenosis should be chiefly interpreted in relation to Christ's human death. In this sense, material kenosis could help theology distance itself from classical and contemporary forms of kenotic Christology (i.e., the view that Christ had to give up or hold in check some of his divine prerogatives incompatible with his humanity) without however giving up kenosis completely. The "likeness of the sinful flesh" (Rom 8:3) assumed by Christ is one with his kenosis, that is, his incarnation means immediately a life destined to human suffering and death, which are best understood kenotically according to my proposal. See Weinandy, *In Likeness of Sinful Flesh*, 81. For more on this, see sec. 7.

2. While Thomas does not explicitly explore material kenosis, the view I propose is one that can be developed from the resources he provides. Material kenosis is therefore "Thomistic" in the sense that it is grounded in St. Thomas's ideas. "'True Thomism' surpasses the thought of all Thomists and even that of St. Thomas himself, somewhat in the way that humanity surpasses each of the human beings that instantiate it individually" (Hayen, *Intentionnel selon Saint Thomas*, 18–19).

presenting material kenosis in more detail, I shall provide further context for the problems that underlie the present discussion.

1.2. Philosophers have recently reconsidered Thomas's concept of death, either directly, in the context of the bioethical discussion of the medical criteria for determining death,[3] or indirectly, in the context of the metaphysical debate over corruptionism and survivalism.[4] The idea at work in these debates is that death is a substantial change consisting in the separation of soul and body. As such, death is understood as the event taking place at the end limit of life causing the shift of the human being from worldly presence to worldly absence—we can call this the standard hylomorphic account of death.[5]

In his study on the theology of death, Karl Rahner has not spared the standard hylomorphic account of death from radical criticism.[6] In his view, the "classical theological description of death" has serious metaphysical shortcomings, as it cannot account for what is most specific in the case of the human being, namely, the "personal" dimension of death. Rahner grants the hylomorphic metaphysics of soul and body, and the corresponding description of death as the separation of soul and body, only a secondary and limited value. Accordingly, he offers an alternative metaphysical framework which in his view is better suited to think through death without leaving out any of its essential components. On his proposal, the human being is the "dialectical oneness" of "nature" and "person," i.e., cosmology and subjectivity, passive subjection to metaphysical laws and active phenomenally-pregnant deeds of self-determination. On Rahner's view, death is properly understood only in light of the "natural" and the "personal" principles so understood. In this way, death is shown to be not only the passive event of substantial change lying at the end limit of life, but also the experience of personal self-appropriation of mortality brought about by free acts throughout life.[7] Death is not merely suffered passively from without, but is also the

---

3. See Eberl, "Thomistic Understanding of Human Death"; Spencer, "Reexamination of Hylomorphic Theory"; Jones, *Approaching the End*, chs. 5, 7; Amerini, *Aquinas on Beginning and End*, 238–40; Flannery, "Defining Death with Aristotle and Aquinas." See also Sánchez Sorondo, "Concept of Brain Death."

4. See 61n80.

5. The same description of death, separation of soul and body, is endorsed in the Catechism of the Catholic Church § 366.

6. See Rahner, *Theology of Death*. I will refer to this book time and again throughout this study.

7. Needless to say, the personal self-appropriation of death posited by Rahner is

active consummation of the subject from within. Hylomorphism and the "separation" concept of death accounts only for nature, not for person and subjectivity. Hence, the traditional hylomorphic framework allows only for a limited grasp of the phenomenon of death.

More specifically, Rahner's complaints about the standard description of death as the separation of soul and body are: (1) Such a description does not account for the fact that death is an event affecting the human being as a whole, as it explains only the "natural" or cosmological (one may say "biological") aspect of death. (2) It does not account for the fact that death affects the spiritual-personal dimension of the human being. That is to say, the traditional description cannot explain what happens to the soul through the separation. (3) It remains silent about the nature of the separation.

Now, from a standard hylomorphic perspective, objection 1 seems unfair: insofar as it is a substantial change, the separation of soul and body determines the destruction of the human being as a whole, as the composite of soul and body.[8] However, objections 2 and 3 might be more serious problems for the description of death understood from the point of view of a standard hylomorphism.[9] To these, we might add another difficulty not explicitly raised by Rahner, that is: objection 4. In light of standard hylomorphism, the separation of soul and body is the substantial change occurring at the end limit of life, determining the shift of the human being from worldly presence to worldly absence. But if this is

---

strongly influenced by Heidegger's "being toward death" (Heidegger, *Being and Time*, 219).

8. Balthasar oscillates between objections 1 and 2 in discussing the problem of anxiety in the face of death: "According to Thomas, the threat to nature or substance, which produces natural fear, can apply only to physical death (and thus to the separation of the soul from the body, the dissolution of the 'composite'); it can never threaten the being of the creature as a whole. The soul's consciousness of its immortality and thus of its invulnerability to the *malum corruptivum* of nothingness is so powerful, and medieval man's confidence in being is so great, that an anxiety of the sort that would cast doubt on finite, creaturely being does not come into view at all" (*Christian and Anxiety*, 122).

9. Josef Pieper moves too quickly over Rahner's objections. Pieper rightly points out that the nature of the separation of soul and body depends on how we conceive their union, but then he says that the separation is easily understood as "the abolition of a connection" (*Death and Immortality*, 24) Then, he provides a fairly standard account: the spiritual soul, "although profoundly affected by death, connected with the body by its innermost nature and remaining related to it, nevertheless persists indestructibly and maintains itself, remains in being" (28). The insufficiency of this rejoinder motivates the present paper. In fact, what is left to say about the soul's being affected by death once we have agreed that death does not annihilate it? *Nothing*?

all we can and should say about death, all the New Testament passages claiming that death is a force already at work in our lives can only be given, at best, an exclusively moral interpretation or, at worst, a simply figurative reading. Contextually, if death is only a substantial change occurring at the end limit of life, the rich philosophical and theological meditation on the *ars moriendi* becomes less intelligible, insofar as the very concept and practice of *ars moriendi* seem to imply that death is already "something" in life before we undergo the fatal substantial change at the end of our earthly days. In other words, the tradition of the *ars moriendi* undermines the widespread belief, both inside and outside philosophical circles, that "death is a nonphenomenon, a nonobject of which any experience is *a priori* excluded."[10]

While the present chapter is not organized as a response to Rahner, as it covers more ground, what I will have to say on material kenosis goes in the direction of a *nonstandard hylomorphic proposal* capable of answering Rahner's objections. As a consequence, reading the rest of the chapter against the backdrop of Rahner's objections might be beneficial for a genuine understanding of what material kenosis is supposed to accomplish. The reader should also keep in mind the problems with which we are left in the previous chapter, which resonate with the objections raised by Rahner: What kind of negation is, properly speaking, the negation of death? How does a Thomistic hylomorphism contribute to answer this question?

The notion of death as the separation of soul and body represents an interesting case study for assessing a broader concern, which emerged in the last century, about the extent to which a hylomorphic metaphysics is capable of describing the reality of the human being in all his breadth. Famously, Karol Wojtyła, by relying on the new directions of philosophical inquiry opened by phenomenology, has claimed that Aristotelian-Thomistic hylomorphic metaphysics goes only so far as to grasp the "objective-cosmological" dimension of the human being, therefore leaving the "subjective-personalistic" dimension out.[11] The world of human "consciousness," of the "self-experiencing subject," cannot be reached by the hylomorphic conceptuality of soul and body, which remains within the limits of a purely objective-cosmological approach in anthropology.

---

10. Reichlin, "Experience of Illness," 83.

11. See Wojtyła: "Thomistic Personalism"; "Subjectivity and the Irreducible." For a careful rejoinder from a Thomistic perspective, see Spencer, "Aristotelian Substance and Personalistic Subjectivity."

Wojtyła does not think that Catholic anthropology should dispose of hylomorphism. Nevertheless, he suggests the need for a phenomenological integration of hylomorphism. Such integration would be possible only as an integration "from the outside" of hylomorphism, so to speak, as the conceptual resources of hylomorphism only enable us to think of the human being cosmologically.

If applied to the limited dominion of death, Wojtyła's criticism squares with Rahner's. Hence the question: Is it true that a comprehensive metaphysics of human life and death can be accomplished only by *external integration* of Thomas's hylomorphism, either in the more conciliatory way proposed by Wojtyła, or in the more revisionary way suggested by Rahner?

Finally, commentators have lamented the shortcomings of Thomas's hylomorphism for theology, precisely with respect to the transformative power of grace on the reality and experience of death.[12] The focus of the complaint is the lack of integration between this hylomorphic metaphysics and the theological perspective on death.[13] Since according to Scripture the power of death in the world has been conquered by Christ's death, it would seem ultimately inadequate to view death in purely negative or neutral terms, because "such an 'event' acquires a distinctively positive flavor as the hope of new life out of a situation of death (Rom 4:17, 6:5; Rev 14:13)."[14] According to this critique, the metaphysical categories deployed by Thomas only permit us to think of death as something bad (the destruction of the person) or neutral (the fact that the soul is left unimpaired by death), but are ultimately incompatible with the "good news" cast on human death by the death of Christ. It is

12. That graced death is "transformative" is the thesis of Novello, *Death as Transformation*. Compare to a similar point in Falque, "Suffering Death," 46–47.

13. For instance, Novello, *Death as Transformation*, 4–5; more moderately, Jones, *Approaching the End*, 141–42. Contrary to the objection, Ratzinger claims that St. Thomas's hylomorphism of soul and body providentially provides Christian faith with an adequate philosophical anthropology, able to articulate in metaphysical terms the destiny of immortality to which the person is called despite death (*Eschatology*, 148–50). Although this thesis is illuminating, Ratzinger glosses over the difficulties raised by Rahner, Jones, and Novello. He proposes a conciliatory reading of Thomistic metaphysics and theology which falls short of explaining in what way hylomorphism and the theological transformation of death are not at odds, and in what sense, if any, hylomorphism could be considered more fit than other metaphysical accounts of death for thinking the Christian experience of death. In short, to cope with the objections, one would need to focus more on the relation between hylomorphism and death and less on the relation between hylomorphism and immortality.

14. Novello, *Death as Transformation*, 4.

the same complaint about the irreconcilable hiatus present in Thomas between the "dogmatic" and the "spiritual," and between the "natural" and the "graced" account of death, which has led Rahner to criticize the hylomorphic doctrine and to try to find a better synthesis in the dialectics of nature and person described above.

Contrary to these popular criticisms, I believe that the hylomorphic notion of death has the resources to face the challenges described so far. However, I submit that in order to see this, one has to go beyond the standard interpretation of the hylomorphism of the human being. Hylomorphism is usually left in an *underdeveloped state* and needs robust unpacking, especially when the elaboration of a metaphysics of death is at stake. I take the following comment by Romano Guardini as inspiration and guidance for what I have to say in this and the following chapters, which is, in my view, nothing else than a "creative retrieval" of Thomas's position: "The clear conceptual structures of Thomas Aquinas, not to speak of Bonaventure or the Victorines, reveal their true and full significance and all their energy in tension only when we understand that they are the elaboration of the lived experience, both metaphysical and religious."[15]

1.3. As anticipated, I shall develop a nonstandard hylomorphism of death which gravitates around the notion of kenosis. In the view I shall present, death, from a hylomorphic perspective, is best understood as material kenosis. While this chapter cannot address all the problems raised in this introduction, the rest of the book (chs. 3–4) will provide a picture broad enough to also include an answer to all the problems at stake. Despite some isolated references to phenomenology and theology, the aim of this chapter is only to present the metaphysical groundwork for the project. The corollaries of material kenosis for the lived experience of death will be slowly drawn over the next two chapters. And yet, having a broader sense of all the problems at stake will help us appreciate more deeply in what way, if any, material kenosis can provide a better metaphysical framework for also accommodating the phenomenological and theological perspectives on death.

According to my proposal, the mode of being of the human person *in via* is kenotic, and his death is best characterized as material kenosis. It is true that a kenotic understanding of human life and death is not new. For one, Jean-Yves Lacoste has put forward recently a

---

15. Guardini, *Opposizione polare*, 21.

"kenotic treatment of the question of man," which is supposed to replace the classical Thomistic philosophical framework with the resources of Heidegger's existential analytic of Dasein.[16] While I believe that the phenomenological-hermeneutical perspective on the human being and the Scriptures should be welcomed, I disagree with the background thesis that a kenotic understanding of man's fallen life can be gained only if we leave Aristotelian-Thomistic metaphysics behind. On the contrary, the present proposal aims to show precisely how such a kenotic view is not at odds with but rather follows from a hylomorphic metaphysics adequately understood.[17]

Plato famously claimed that philosophy is nothing other than the caring exercise of death, *meletē thanatou*.[18] Material kenosis shows that this is so, but not for the reasons adduced by Plato. For him, the soul in life must abstract herself as much as possible from the influence of the body: "Doesn't the soul of the philosopher especially hold the body in dishonor and flee it and seek to become a soul herself by herself?"[19] In this practice of self-abstraction, the soul experiences and anticipates the final separation of soul and body in death as something desirable. For an Aristotelian like Thomas, this view must be partial and suspicious, insofar as according to it the body is not only something negative, but also something from which the soul can abstract itself without suffering any negative consequence.[20] On a broadly Thomistic view, philosophy, that is,

---

16. See Lacoste, "Toward a Kenotic Treatment." See also Hinshaw, "Kenosis of the Dying."

17. For this reason, the opposition on which Falque relies between Thomas's concept of death as separation of soul and body and a more modern theological concept of death as transformation of finitude is overcome by material kenosis ("Suffering Death," 46). On the kenotic hylomorphism presented in this paper, the immortality of the soul does not mean that death is "a leap [of the soul] toward another world," as Falque says, but rather a katabasis of the soul through the vicissitudes of the body and therefore a kenotic transfiguration of the entire person through the drama of its substantial form. The present proposal is also decidedly opposed to contemporary continental philosophical-theological readings of human kenosis, for instance, Dubilet, *Self-Emptying Subject*, for which, due to a questionable Deleuzian reading of Meister Eckhart, the desirable outcome of kenosis is the anonymization of the self into a purely impersonal life.

18. *Phaedo* 8a. See also Kalkavage, "Plato's *Phaedo*."

19. *Phaedo* 65d.

20. This is why a Thomist should reject the Platonic idea that the only way to harm the soul is through an immoral behavior. "Socrates, even in *The Apology*, is engaging in metaphysics. He's making, in effect, a type-theoretical or categorial claim: each type or category of entity is (at least partially) defined by its characteristic mode of harm or benefit.... Unlike physical possessions, which are *harmed by destruction*, the soul is

the life of logos, recognizes that the human soul must inevitably witness and withstand its own concrete negation in and through the decay of the body. As I will try to show, for any Christian philosophy that takes Thomas's Aristotelianism seriously, the exercise of death practiced within the philosophical life must be kenosis through the body, not abstraction from the body. The essential movement of logos, that is, philosophy, is ultimately the movement of kenosis, not the Platonic abstractive movement of the soul's gathering in herself away from the body, *synethroismene hautes eis heauten*. The difference between abstractive self-gathering and material kenosis marks the difference between the Platonic and the Aristotelian understanding of philosophy as "care of death."[21]

1.4. The chapter is structured in the following way. After summing up Thomas's theological explanation of death and introducing kenosis as the mode of being of the soul after the fall (sec. 2), I defend the view that our hylomorphic constitution is imperfect (what I shall call "impaired

---

harmed not by destruction or death but only by *immorality* (and we ourselves are the only possible authors of that). Being murdered by a Nazi harms your body. Becoming a Nazi harms your soul" (Yourgrau, *Death and Nonexistence*, 186–87; emphasis in original). Despite this standard Platonism, there are clues of a different view of the relation between soul and body in Plato (especially in *Phaedrus* 246c), but maybe not strong enough to overcome the traditional dualistic reading of Plato.

21. The systematization of Plato's dialogues into "Platonism" is obviously a problem, and I find this shortcoming also in Thomas's standard interpretation of Plato's anthropology. Pieper, for instance, questions at least some aspects of the standard interpretation and points out the importance of the body for Plato in the *Phaedrus*. But also the idea of philosophy as the "care of death" in the *Phaedo* should probably be given a different, richer, and less problematic interpretation than the standard one I am following here. Kalkavage proposes to interpret the whole dialogue (and thus also the claim that philosophy is the "care of death") in light of Socrates's fight against "misology," the hatred of reason and argument: "The exhortation to Phaedo to 'bring the argument back to life' serves to shift the emphasis away from anxiety over one's own personal fate to the concern that the logos, in spite of setbacks and apparent failures, be constantly renewed, like the web of Penelope or like the Phoenix who rises out of her own ashes. This point suggests that the so-called proofs for the immortality of the soul that we find in the dialogue and for which the dialogue is famous, are really subsidiary to the deeper concern for the immortality we approach and enjoy right now when we forget and busy ourselves with arguments. This busying ourselves with argument is itself a form of philosophic music. It is the 'greatest music,' which, by absorbing the philosophically-minded human being in the search for truth and for the strongest possible argument, distracts him from the all-too-human anxiety about his temporal end. It redirects his attention and care to that for the sake of which he lives" ("Plato's *Phaedo*," s.vv. "Part III: The Life and Death of Argument," para. 11). While agreeing with this interpretation, I still think that, if there is an essential difference between Plato's view of the human being and the Thomas's Aristotelian hylomorphic anthropology (as there is), then this difference must bear upon their respective accounts of death.

hylomorphism") against three likely objections (sec. 3). I then explain why death cannot be understood only as substantial change (sec. 4). Then, I move on to explain the central notions of material kenosis (sec. 5) and kenotic change (sec. 6) and to show their centrality for the antecedent discussion. I complete this discussion with some remarks on why human material kenosis expands Thomas's view of God's kenosis (sec. 7). I conclude this chapter by unpacking the notion of material kenosis further in light of Erich Przywara's metaphysics of the analogy of being, with special reference to the two formulations Przywara uses to speak of the intra-creaturely analogy of being: first, creaturely being described as "essence in-and-beyond existence" (secs. 8, 10); and second, creaturely being described as the "oscillating rhythm" of "possibility and actuality" (secs. 9–10).

2. THE SOUL'S KENOTIC MODE OF BEING

2.1. Thomas explains the origin of death theologically.[22] Death is the consequence of the sin of our first parents. In the state of original justice before the fall, human life was made incorruptible by the presence of grace, thus making the hylomorphic union of soul and body perfect. Bodily death was introduced as the just punishment for sinning.[23] On this view, death is in a sense "natural" and in another sense "unnatural."[24] It is natural because the matter of our body is composed of "contraries," which by natural necessity tend to decomposition. At the same time, it is unnatural because the intellectual soul is indestructible. God conferred on the human being the favor of being exempt from the necessity of corruption resulting from his material constitution by making the body perfectly subjected to the organization- and life-giving function of the soul, but this favor was lost with sin.

The theological explanation of the origin of human death provided by Thomas shows why it is crucial to read his hylomorphic metaphysics within the theological context.[25] Doing so helps us to avoid the metaphysical mistake which consists in believing that the hylomorphic unity

---

22. See *ST* 1, q. 76, a. 5, ad. 1; *ST* 1, q. 97, a. 1, co. and ad. 3; *ST* 1–2, q. 42, a. 2, ad. 3; *ST* 1–2, q. 85, a. 5, co.; *ST* 2–2, q. 164, a. 1, co.; *QDM* q. 5, a. 4, co.

23. *ST* 1–2, q. 19, a. 10, ad. 2.

24. *ST* 1–2, q. 85, a. 6, co.; *ST* 2–2, q. 164, a. 1, ad. 1; *QDM* q. 5, a. 5.

25. As sketched, for instance, in Stein, *Finite and Eternal Being*, 195–97.

of soul and body in the person is *perfect*.²⁶ The union, in fact, was made perfect only by grace before original sin. In the present condition, the matter of the body has a rebellious tendency to withdraw from the organization- and life-giving power of the soul, and the soul grows weaker and weaker in its capacity to organize matter into life. The body is not fully subjected to the soul. The soul is not fully capable of configuring the body. The harmony that would ensue from a perfect hylomorphic union—consisting in perfect bodily responsiveness to a holy soul, unshakable health, physical strength and agility, etc.—is not available to us in our fallen condition. Our condition is one of *impaired hylomorphism*.

2.2. While not central to our problem, it is impossible to avoid a discussion, albeit brief, of the claim, put forth by some contemporary Christian theologians and philosophers, that death, in the sense of *biological death*, is not the consequence of the first sin. As explained above, Thomas suggests that death is, from one point of view, natural to man, and, from another point of view, unnatural. In other words, despite the mortality intrinsic to the bodily constitution specific to his essence or nature, man was created immortal according to the original "divine project,"²⁷ that is, he was originally preserved from death through a special gift of grace. Man's first sin removes this special gift and thus exposes man to the intrinsic fragility of his natural constitution. Based on this account, one may say that according to Thomas, it has always been the case that it is "natural" for man to be informed by the "supernatural" power of God to truly be what he is. To use a paradoxical Pascalian language, it belongs to human nature either *to be itself* by participating in what is *more than itself*, or *to be less than itself* by saying no to this participation. As Josef Pieper reminds us, "Homo naturaliter non est humanus sed superhumanus est."²⁸ In short, biological death and the pain and suffering which it implies are truly introduced by sin.

---

26. This mistake seems to me omnipresent in the literature. It is sometimes, if not caused, at least incentivized by contemporary scholarship. Most of the contemporary rediscovery of Thomas's philosophy of mind is guided by a desire to overcome not only forms of naturalistic monism, but especially to free Thomas from any possible trace of soul and body dualism, either Platonic or Cartesian. Despite its indisputable merits, this "anti-dualist" operation, by stressing the deep unity of the human being, has led, I believe, to neglect the relevance of the aspects of imperfection present in the hylomorphic union of soul and body for a more nuanced metaphysical picture of the human being.

27. Ratzinger, *Divine Project*.

28. James V. Shall, "Foreword," in Pieper, *Leisure*, 12.

Now, this view is disputed by dissenting Christian views, both in the Protestant and in the Catholic world. What is more interesting for our purpose is the view of some Catholics, such as Emmanuel Falque, according to whom biological death, pain, and suffering, are wholly natural, that is, they have always already been part of the human condition because they belong to the essence of what it means to be finite and to be animals.[29]

In his dense and profound discussion of this problem, Falque proposes essentially three reasons for his thesis. First, from a scientific point of view, not recognizing that biological death is wholly natural to man makes it impossible to accept the evidence of evolution and other physical laws such as entropy. Second, from a philosophical and theological point of view, not recognizing that biological death is wholly natural to man makes it impossible to appreciate man's finitude and relies on a mythological understanding of Adam's condition "before" the fall as whole and perfect, while on the contrary, Adam's original God-given condition has always been one of perfectibility. Third, from a theological and a philosophical point of view, not recognizing that biological death is wholly natural makes it impossible to appreciate the meaning of God's incarnation in Jesus Christ. On the contrary, admitting that biological death is an essential dimension of the finite human condition makes us appreciate the fact that Jesus's taking death upon himself does not belong to the reparative act of the Redeemer, but to the loving act of a God who wants to enter into the entirety of the human natural experience.

Falque's perspective has some indisputable strengths, the chief of which is the desire to propose a view of death that is faithful to the biblical account while also being respectful of the best theories of biological evolution that we have and avoiding a naïve philosophical and theological conception of the human condition, a condition in which man would be already perfect in all possible ways instead of being perfectible, and a condition in which man's self-enactment would not imply the overcoming of constitutive limits and obstacles. Despite his laudable desiderata, Falque's proposal seems to me to be ultimately not preferable to a view such as Thomas's. Let us consider his three arguments one by one, albeit briefly.

As mentioned, Falque maintains that not recognizing that biological death is wholly natural to man makes it impossible to accept the evidence

---

29. Falque, *Guide to Gethsemane*, 10–25.

of evolutionary history.[30] This thesis has become a common theme in recent debates on the Christian view of death vis-à-vis evolutionary history. For instance, Ian McFarland writes: "It is now beyond dispute that there was no point where human existence was characterized by immunity from death, absence of labour pains, or an ability to acquire food without toil.... The geological record makes it clear that natural disasters, disease, suffering, and death long antedate the emergence of the human species. It follows that such phenomena cannot be interpreted as the consequence of human sin."[31] Some Thomists have addressed this issue, pointing out that, contrary to what Falque and others believe, there is no incompatibility or contradiction between a position such as Thomas's (which is, as far as I can tell, also the official position of the Catholic Church)[32] and evolutionary theory. Following Paul A. Macdonald, we could state, "Although there are indeed no scientific reasons that directly support Thomistic and Catholic teaching about Adam, there is real reason for thinking that what evolutionary science in particular says about the material or empirical origins and nature of the first human beings is compatible with it. It is indeed possible to hold that what Aquinas says about Adam and what evolutionary science says about Adam are *both* true."[33]

To support this conciliatory view, a first point in need of clarification is that Thomas "explicitly denies that no suffering and death occurred before the Fall." Accordingly, "the claim that predating animals did not engage in predative acts before the Fall [is] 'wholly unreasonable' (*ST* I, q. 96, a. 1, ad. 2)."[34] Thomas continues: "For the nature of the animals was not changed through man's sin in such a way that certain animals, e.g., lions and falcons, for whom it is now natural to eat the flesh of other animals, lived off plants at that time.... Therefore, there would have been natural conflict among certain animals."[35] As Macdonald puts it: "Affirm-

---

30. Falque, *Guide to Gethsemane*, 11, 119–20n8.

31. McFarland, "Fall and Sin," 143.

32. "The Church, interpreting the symbolism of biblical language in an authentic way, in the light of the New Testament and Tradition, teaches that our first parents, Adam and Eve, were constituted in an original 'state of holiness and justice.' ... As long as he remained in the divine intimacy, man would not have to suffer or die" (*Catechism of the Catholic Church* §§375–76).

33. Macdonald, "In Defense of Aquinas's Adam," 465. I follow Macdonald's reconstruction and arguments closely in what I have to say on this point.

34. Macdonald, "In Defense of Aquinas's Adam," 457.

35. *ST* 1, q. 96, a. 1, ad. 2.

ing Aquinas's claim that Adam did not suffer and would not have died, had he not sinned, does not require denying the claim that evolutionary history contains lots of suffering and death, or the more specific claim that Adam's evolutionary predecessors in the genus *homo*, and whatever other hominins among whom he lived, did not suffer and die."[36]

Moreover, Adam's unique condition, i.e., the immunity from death deriving from the gift of original justice, would have been in line with the uniqueness of his metaphysical constitution:

> Of course, affirming with Aquinas that Adam did not suffer and would not have died, had he remained sinless, also entails affirming with Aquinas that God specifically distinguished Adam from the rest of the animal creation on a distinctly metaphysical and not merely material or empirical level. . . . Taking on board what evolutionary science says about the gradual emergence of human beings on a material or empirical level, there is no reason why it is not possible to hold instead, in a genuinely Thomistic spirit, that God, at some point in evolutionary history, directly infused a rational soul along with original justice in already existing hominins—even two specific hominins capable of supporting a rational soul (per the teaching of the Catholic Church)—from whom all human beings as rational animals, or soul-body composites, descend. Consequently, as chosen by God to be the first bearer of rational life, Adam alone, among the creatures with whom he lived, was able to avoid having to experience suffering and death in pursuing the distinctly supernatural end that God had assigned him. . . . This also entails . . . that Adam's soul had the power to assist his body in maintaining itself over time, and thereby prevent damage from incurring at the molecular or cellular level, even if (per the "disposable-soma" theory of aging) his body had to expend significant resources on processes such as growth and reproduction. Accordingly, Adam (and his progeny, had they also been endowed with original justice) would not have succumbed to any age-related ailments or undergone the sort of aging that terminates in death (senescence). . . . There is nothing incongruous in claiming that Adam's incorruptible soul, as initially graced by and subject to the ever-living God, was capable of preserving his body from corruption and so prevented him from experiencing any suffering or death.[37]

---

36. Macdonald, "In Defense of Aquinas's Adam," 457.
37. Macdonald, "In Defense of Aquinas's Adam," 457–58.

In short, it seems to me that Falque's "demythologization" of the claim that death entered the world through sin (Rom 5:12), which he aims to accomplish by excluding that "death" may mean "biological death," seems unnecessary—unnecessary precisely because there are no scientific reasons to support it.

Falque's second argument states that not recognizing that biological death is wholly natural to man makes it impossible to appreciate man's finitude and relies on a mythological understanding of Adam's prelapsarian condition as whole and perfect, while on the contrary, Adam's original God-given condition has always been one of perfectibility.[38] One first point is that Falque relies on a notion of finitude, common to many other authors throughout modern and contemporary philosophy, in which finitude is almost a synonym of death, and in which the limit of death is taken as continuous with and as the original archetype of all the limits of human life. On the one hand, Falque is correct in proposing a non-sinful notion of finitude, against a false idea of finitude that sees all finitude as a "less" and as a fall from a condition of infinite plenitude. On the other hand, however, since he wrongly sees death as almost a synonym of finitude, he ends up including biological death, "simply death," within the original notion of the creature. Accordingly, for him death is neither "an accident of Creation" nor "a product of a supposed Fall," and "anxiety" nothing else than "the total and definitive assumption of human finitude given to us by God."[39] The anxiety over death, then, is for Falque "anxiety over finitude" and it has nothing to do with "anxiety over sin."[40] But the fundamental premise of the argument here is the identification of mortality and finitude, such that, once one denies the premise, the conclusion does not follow.

Nor does the connection between death and sin mean the denial of man's original condition of perfectibility. A neat counterexample to Falque's implication is Thomas's discussion of what Genesis means when it is stated that man was put in the garden of Eden "to cultivate and care for it" (Gen 2:15).[41] Both man and the world are created as being perfect-

---

38. Falque, *Guide to Gethsemane*, 12–21.
39. Falque, *Guide to Gethsemane*, 47.
40. Falque, *Guide to Gethsemane*, 46.
41. "As Augustine says . . . these words in Genesis may be understood in two ways. First, in the sense that God placed man in paradise that He might Himself work in man and keep him, by sanctifying him (for if this work cease, man at once lapses into darkness, as the air grows dark when the light ceases to shine); and by keeping man from all corruption and evil. Secondly, that man might dress and keep paradise, which dressing

ible, and so, contra Falque, for Thomas the original, prelapsarian perfection of creation (in which Adam is supernaturally sheltered from death) does not exclude, but rather *implies perfectibility*. That man is perfectible means that he requires cultivation, the cultivation that he receives from God himself and the self-cultivation which he performs by cultivating the world (the immanent effect of his productive activity). Note, with respect to this point, that Thomas insightfully distinguishes between "work" and "labor": man in the prelapsarian condition would have been the subject of work ("subject" in the sense of both the subjective and the objective genitive) but not the subject of labor.

Falque is certainly right in pointing out that the serpent's words put pressure on man's greatest temptation, namely, the desire of being already a perfect whole and the rejection of the condition and work implied in being a perfectible being. But this point has nothing to do per se with the naturalness of death. It has to do with a lack of trust on the part of man in the Giver of being, and in an unjustified perceived contradiction between being given wholly and being given as a limited and perfectible nature.[42] Once again, there is no incompatibility among believing that biological death is the consequence of sin, thinking that man is created as a perfectible being, and maintaining that the serpent tempted man by putting pressure on his ambiguous desire for being a whole.

Falque's final argument maintains that not recognizing that biological death is wholly natural makes it impossible to appreciate the meaning of God's incarnation in Jesus Christ.[43] On the contrary, following Falque, admitting that biological death is an essential dimension of the finite human condition would make us appreciate the fact that Jesus's taking death upon himself does not belong to the reparative act of the Redeemer, but to the loving act of a God who wants to enter into the entirety of the human natural experience. What can be said against this third, formidable objection? One first point is that Jesus's love to man implies that he is willing to lovingly assume with the human condition everything that belongs to it—what is natural, to perfect it; what is fallen, to redeem it; the whole man, to make him participate in divine happiness. Love and reparation are not disjoined in God's desire to enter the human condition and to live it according to all its factors.

---

would not have involved labor, as it did after sin, but would have been pleasant on account of man's practical knowledge of the powers of nature" (*ST* 1, q. 102, a. 3, co.).

42. On this, see below ch. 3, sec. 2.
43. Falque, *Guide to Gethsemane*, 13–16.

Moreover, from a more general point of view, a more traditional and Thomistic approach to the problem of death seems better than Falque's for at least two reasons.[44] First, Falque clearly disjoins the biological dimension of death from its spiritual meaning. According to him, the death that is truly caused by sin is the self-closure of the subject into itself: "A (spiritual) self-confinement of humankind within a finitude [read: death] that is not itself sinful."[45] What one loses here, however, is the *eidetic unity of the moral and the physical* when it comes to man's constitution and his rejection of the gift of being. To put it simply, the moral no has consequences for the entirety of the human person, ensouled body, and not just for what Falque, adapting Heidegger, would call man's "being-in-the-world" (an attitude of closedness with respect to and proud autonomy from God and the others). In other words, the fallen "being-in-the-world" is that attitude of closedness with respect to God and the others which is so radical that is also inscribed in our very bodily condition—we are subject to pain, we suffer, *we die, in a way that* was not meant to be.[46] On the contrary, Falque ends up limiting the consequences of sin to a disembodied "being-in-the-world."

Second, if biological death and thus physical pain and spiritual suffering *as we know them now* were truly essential to our original condition

---

44. For lack of space and competence, I will not address directly the fact that Falque's reading also suffers from a certain unilaterality in interpreting the fall as a mere anthropological archetype and not also as a historical event, not differently from scholars such as André LaCocque, *Trial of Innocence*. A more balanced exegesis seems to be possible, one that takes the mythological style of the narration at face value without discounting the reference to a historical fall and the archetypical value that this historical fall assumes for all the descendants of our first parents. On this, see, e.g., Ratzinger, *Divine Project*; Ratzinger, *Eschatology*, pt. 2.

45. Falque, *Guide to Gethsemane*, 47.

46. This does not mean that an element of natural pain would have been absent in the prelapsarian condition. "It is worth noting that it is entirely consonant with the Thomistic picture that I have offered that human beings always have been susceptible to pain, because pain, whether physical or mental, is part of the normal, healthy functioning of sentient animals, including human beings. . . . By virtue of not experiencing sickness or disease, or any other substantial harm to his physical or mental well-being, Adam would not have experienced pain, or at least, the sort of significant pain associated with sickness and disease, as well as other physical or mental infirmities. And so . . . if Adam experienced any pain at all, it either would not have posed a significant threat to his overall well-being, om a physical or mental level; or, it would have been the sort of minor, fleeting pain that proved useful to him in dealing with real or potential harms within his natural environment, so that he could inhabit and navigate it successfully" (Macdonald, "In Defense of Aquinas's Adam," 459). See also Tabaczek, "Is Pain Metaphysically Evil?"

instead of being the consequence of sin, one could be seriously tempted to agree, following the reflections of David Bentley Hart, who draws from Ivan's objections in Fyodor Dostoevsky's *The Brothers Karamazov*, that the belief in God is in fact impossible.[47] Even if God entered the mortal and suffering condition, why would have he created such a condition in the first place? Maybe for allowing the machinery of evolution to work properly? Maybe as a test for man? How could the belief in God the Creator stand a chance when faced with only one instance of unjust suffering? Only an overly romanticized view of death and suffering can make us take them to be a God-given limit which we are called to overcome in order to find meaning in life.[48]

Let me make one final observation on whether death was already part of man's prelapsarian condition according to the divine project. It may well be that the human being would have ended his earthly days also in the prelapsarian condition. His temporal and historical perfectibility would have been fulfilled in being given the privilege of entering in a definitive way the eternal life of God. However, all these counterfactual musings often lose sight of the fundamental fact that what "death" means within this scenario—*the definitive confirmation of man's temporal life in the eternal being-life-love of God*—is most definitely not what is meant by "death" within the postlapsarian perspective—*the negation of man's being-life-love*. In other words, when it comes to the discussion of this point, the element of continuity between the two meanings of death—the end of the earthly days—tends to obscure the more profound and radical element of discontinuity—death in the first sense is a final confirmation of and in being-life-love, while in the second sense it is the chief antagonism to being-life-love consequent to and coessential with man's rejection of the gift of being.

---

47. Hart, "Devil's March."

48. Falque, following Gustave Martelet, says that human finitude, in its natural condition, includes death and suffering, and thus includes a natural anxiety. In entering this anxiety, this death, and this suffering, God acts not as the "Redeemer" (which would imply that death is a consequence of sin), but nevertheless as someone who comes to "alleviate an intrinsic defect in our finitude." And he continues: "But this was in order to involve us in the ultimate Glory of his Life." According to this view, God creates out of love an intrinsically deficient nature, which can die and suffer; but does so only "in order to involve us in the ultimate Glory of his Life" (*Guide to Gethsemane*, 18). Are thus human death and suffering just a carefully planned ploy for preparing the grand finale? Who could believe in such a God? Hart's reflections on this point become truly haunting—and rightly so.

2.3. Let us go back to the suggestion that our present condition is one of impaired hylomorphism. The idea that human hylomorphism is impaired has two fundamental implications. First, it implies that the "separation of soul and body" is not just an event, but rather an after-the-fall *connotation of the hylomorphic relationship between soul and body*. Second, it also means that death cannot be considered only as substantial change, that is, only as the event taking place at the end limit of life marking the shift from worldly presence to worldly absence. Rather, death must also be understood as a *definitive condition of the soul-body composite*. To put the two points differently, after the fall, life and death are intertwined, and the "mode of being" of the soul reflects such intertwinement.[49] The corruption that puts an end to our earthly life is only the last act of a phenomenon of separation-corruption that begins much earlier. While we are living, we are also already dying, as many thinkers, both before and after the birth of existentialism, have clearly recognized.

As St. Augustine of Hippo says, what we are born into is, quite literally, a "life-in-death" or a "death-in-life."[50] Augustine's insight is further developed in a meticulous linguistic scrutiny, which analytic philosophers would love, of the meanings of expressions such as "dying" and "death," "living," "before death," "after death," and "in death."[51] One of his points is particularly relevant for our discussion. He writes: "In fact, from the moment a man begins to exist in this body which is destined to die, he is involved all the time in a process whose end is death. . . . Now

---

49. The language of the "modes of being" of the soul is taken from *ST* 1, q. 89, a. 1, co. I will appeal to this language of the "modes" at various crucial points in this study.

50. Augustine, *Confessions* (Outler), 5. I usually refer to the Chadwick translation, but the Outler translation expresses the mutual immanence of life and death more sharply. We might welcome Przywara's suggestion that the two formulas are not equivalent: death-in-life is more descriptive of the condition of sin, while life-in-death of the life of the condition of redemption. As anticipated (but this will become clearer in the following pages), I suggest to supplement the standard interpretation on which for Thomas death is only the substantial change decreeing the end limit of the person's worldly presence, as presented, for instance, in Rousseau, "Thomistic Philosophy of Death"; Velde, "Thomas Aquinas on Original Sin"; and Brook, "Effects of Original Sin." The integration is not extrinsic to Thomas's theological perspective. He considers the following objection: "If death were a punishment of sin, it would have followed sin immediately. But this is not true, for our first parents lived a long time after their sin (Gn. 5:5). Therefore, seemingly, death is not a punishment of sin" (*ST* 2-2, q. 164, a. 1, ob. 8). In his response, his agreement with St. Augustine is explicit: "According to Augustine, although our first parents lived thereafter many years, they began to die on the day when they heard the death-decree, condemning them to decline to old age." See also *QDM* q. 7, a. 7, ad. 14.

51. Augustine, *City of God* 13.1-11.

if each man begins to die, that is to be 'in death,' from the moment when death—that is, the taking away of life—begins to happen in him (and we may assume this, since when this taking away is completed he will not be in death, but after death) then everyone is in death from the moment that he begins his bodily existence. For what else is going on, every day, every hour, every minute, but this process of death?"[52] It seems to me that a Thomistic hylomorphic understanding of the human being, understood according to its entire breadth, can provide the metaphysical underpinnings for the meaning of this being "in death."

The first point—that "separation of soul and body" is not just an event, but rather an after-the-fall *connotation of the hylomorphic relationship between soul and body*—is fairly straightforward. The hylomorphism of the person is impaired by a metaphysical "wound";[53] it is imperfect.[54] However, I would like to push this metaphysical view forward and suggest, beyond Thomas but not against him, that the condition so described should be understood as a *new mode of being of the soul*, an essentially kenotic mode of being. More precisely, our soul has a kenotic mode of realization that strikes midway between the natural-supernatural mode of realization of our original condition (in which the "natural" unity of soul and body is brought to perfection by "supernatural" grace), on the one hand, and the unnatural condition of disembodied existence after the separation from the body, on the other hand.[55] As both the soul's perfect hylomorphic presence in the body and its absence from it are modes of being of the soul, I submit that also the present condition of the soul should be considered as a special mode of being of the soul in its own right. I suggest to call this mode of being of the soul *kenotic* because, as I will explain later in this chapter, it is essentially a mode of being of self-negation, destined to a process of self-emptying.

Supplementing our understanding of the person by bringing into the picture the kenotic mode of being of the soul is important because usually, when speaking of metaphysical death as the consequence of sin,

---

52. Augustine, *City of God* 13.10. It seems to me that Augustine ends up preferring a different use of the expression "in death." At the same time, the expressions taken from the *Confessions* quoted above seem to converge toward this use of the expression "in death."

53. *Vulneratio naturae* (ST 1–2, q. 5, a. 3, co.).

54. A notable acknowledgment of this point is found in Eberl, "Thomistic Understanding of Human Death," 32–33.

55. See Aquinas, *Disputed Questions on Truth*, q. 19, a. 1, co.; ST 1, q. 89, a. 1, co.

the stress falls almost exclusively on the body.[56] Standardly, it is said that the loss of the original graced condition, originating in the rebellious act, causes the contraries in the body "to be left free" to back out of the life-giving function of the soul. What ensues is death. But this new condition, I think, is not simply one that affects the soul only at the end of life, when it is forced by the corruption of the body into the unnatural mode of being of separation; nor does it affect the soul "only from the outside," extrinsically, so to speak, as a carpenter is unhindered in his intrinsic capacity to build tables when he has no access to materials and tools. On the contrary, the shift from the natural-supernatural to the fallen condition not only inaugurates a new space of destructive freedom in the body, but also a new mode of being for the soul, in which the formal movement of configuration is, right from the beginning, counteracted by a self-emptying and self-negating movement forced upon it by the body, what St. Paul calls the "principle at war with the law of mind" (Rom 7:22–25). The soul, contracting sin-death through the body,[57] is therefore created, against the intentions of the Creator, into a mode of being in which life is already affected by death, positivity by negativity, configuration by self-emptying and self-negation.[58] The radical imperfection that Thomas sees in the separate soul after death-as-substantial-change[59] is

---

56. Unfortunately, we find misleading formulations in Thomas, for instance: "That the soul remains after the body, is due to a defect of the body, namely, death. Which defects was not due when the soul was first created" (ST 1, q. 90, a. 4, ad. 3). Consistent with this framework would be to think of the effect of sin on the soul only in moral terms, as a "disorder among the powers" (ST 1, q. 85, a. 3). However, other times Thomas puts the stress on the soul, for instance: "Death inasmuch as it is a punishment of original sin is caused from this that the soul has lost the power by which it could preserve its body from corruption; and even this punishment pertains principally to the soul" (QDM q. 4, a. 3, ad. 4).

57. QDM q. 16, a. 4, ad. 21. See also Johnson, "Augustine and Aquinas on Original Sin."

58. Since for Thomas the transmission of the original sin consists in the defects on the side of the body redounding immediately to the soul (ST 1–2, q. 81, a. 1, co.), I suggest to see the kenotic mode of being of the soul as such redounding effect. See in sec. 5 the notion of Ur-kenosis.

59. As Anton Pegis has rightly pointed out, there is a significant development of Thomas's doctrine on the separated soul, from early texts, which make the separated soul like an angel and endowed with knowledge and volition superior to what it had while embodied, to the more mature texts, in which the separate soul is portrayed as having a radically imperfect and unnatural mode of existing and acting (Pegis, "Separated Soul"). This development in St. Thomas is now standardly recognized in the scholarship; see, for instance, Pasnau, *Thomas Aquinas on Human Nature*. So, when I speak of the soul's radical imperfection I assume the later view as the most representative of Thomas's mature thought.

an imperfection that already affects the soul long before the substantial change occurs, and precisely right from its conception, as the soul is born into death-as-kenotic-mode-of-being.

I shall explain at length in section 5 why I find the label "kenotic" suited to describe this mode of being of the soul, especially with respect to its being self-emptying and self-negating. Before getting there, however, I turn now to some likely objections against impaired hylomorphism.

3. WHY IMPAIRED HYLOMORPHISM

3.1. On the proposal of this chapter, the soul is born into a kenotic mode of being because of sin, which determines an intrinsic impairment in the hylomorphic union. The guiding idea here is that the hylomorphic union of soul and body is identical in the natural-supernatural condition before sin and in the present fallen condition only in nature but not in the mode of realization. In fact, while the nature of the relation remains unchanged (it remains hylomorphic), the mode of its realization is not neutral with respect to grace or sin, and this *change in mode* is something intrinsic, not extrinsic, to the relation. One might say that the hylomorphic relation (and thus the "being" and "oneness" of the human being) is always either "superior" or "inferior" to itself: either hyper-realized through grace or impaired due to the fall. If sin determines a change in the mode of being of the soul, it must also determine an intrinsic change in the union—from the perfect union made such by the presence of God's grace to the impaired union of the fallen condition.

Some might want to resist the claim that the hylomorphism of the person is intrinsically impaired. That is, some might want to argue that, even given our mortal condition after the fall, the relation of soul and body, the hylomorphic union, is not impaired in itself. According to this first alternative to impaired hylomorphism, some could say that from a hylomorphic point of view it is absurd to claim that the soul is not perfectly present in the body. If this were true, the objection continues, some of the parts that I take to belong to my body (say, the parts mostly affected by the signs of illness and decay) would actually not be parts of my body because, upon impaired hylomorphism, the soul, imperfectly present in the body, would not "reach" and inform them. But this seems absurd. As a consequence, impaired hylomorphism should be rejected.

I believe that this difficulty can be easily dismissed by saying that the imperfection of the presence of the soul in the body is not to be understood with respect to extension, but with respect to *intensity*. While present in the entirety of the body, the soul is nevertheless imperfectly present in it because its organization- and life-giving function is not consequential enough to counter, over time, the tendency to dissolution inscribed in the body.

A second alternative to impaired hylomorphism is theological. It consists in identifying the cause of our mortality simply with the loss of God's grace.[60] On this view, the impairment in our nature should be predicated not of hylomorphism, but of the absence of God's grace in us. However, this second view also has serious shortcomings. In fact, this view overlooks that the presence of God's original grace in us sheltered us from death only by making our nature perfect. As our nature is that of being a hylomorphic composite of soul and body, it follows that God's original grace worked on us by making this hylomorphic union perfect. Thus, the loss of God's grace amounts to the loss of the perfection of the union, if the presence or absence of God's grace in us has to have any real effect on our nature.

Nor will it do to say, finally, that the cause of our mortality is not the impaired hylomorphism, but rather the tendency present in the contraries of our body to break free from the life-giving function of the soul.[61] In fact, hylomorphism simply means that the body is being informed by the soul and is therefore subjected to its organization- and life-giving function. Thus, a limited subjection to this function, manifested in the "rebellious" tendencies of the body, is ipso facto a limitation in the actualization of the hylomorphic union. The very organizing- and life-giving function of the soul is weakened after sin, because the fullness of its realization is only possible by dwelling in God's grace.

Those who want to retain the idea of an unimpaired hylomorphic union of soul and body might do this by interpreting it as something like a hylomorphic phase sortal of a person.[62] A healthy baby might be considered to be in such a stage of unimpaired hylomorphic union. The imperfection of the hylomorphic unity could be relegated to the decaying,

---

60. This second view might be taken to be suggested by statements such as: "The death of the soul is the privation of grace, by which the soul was united to God" (*QDM* q. 2, a. 9, ad. 2).

61. This third view might be taken to be suggested by statements such as: "The very necessity of dying, to which man was immediately subject, is called a kind of death of man, according to that passage in Rom (8:10) 'The body, it is true, is dead by reason of sin'" (*QDM* q. 7, a. 7, ad. 14).

62. As an application of Wiggins, *Identity and Spatio-Temporal Continuity*.

ill, and suffering person, and not to the healthy newborn or growing child. St. Thomas sees different phases in the process of the weakening of the organization- and life-giving function of the soul: at first, the soul is strong enough not only to counteract the destructive effects of constant external forces on the body, but also to guarantee growth. Later on, the soul can only transform enough material for the renewal of what is lost. At last, the organization- and life-giving function becomes so weak that the decline of the organism begins until the end comes.[63] And yet, the reading based on phase sortals overlooks the theological tenet that, by being born in sin, we are also born in death. There is no phase sortal in the career of a human being in which we are not infected by sin and death. If any metaphysical, and not purely figurative or moral, meaning should be given to this tenet, it should be claimed that the separation of soul and body that is accomplished and fulfilled in the moment of passing away is somehow already present in the newly born life. Simply put, the hylomorphic union of soul and body in the healthy newborn is as impaired, although not as evidently so, as in the decaying, ill, and suffering person: it is the same imperfection in essence, although not in degree of realization and manifestation. What manifests later in life as decay, illness, and suffering, is nothing other than, on one side, the unfolding, in the form of events and processes of the "separation" of soul and body, of the impaired mode of being of the union, and on the other side, the anticipation of the final separation.

Moreover, the phase sortal solution does not answer the fundamental metaphysical question: Apart from the different stages in the life of a person, is the unity of soul and body perfect in that person? Is the unity destined to hold, or is it rather destined to weaken and eventually fall apart? As we already know, the answer is that after the fall we are destined to die, as the soul's informing effect grows weaker and weaker. This implies that since the moment a human being is conceived, her life is wounded: the hylomorphic unity is already destined to fall apart and, in this sense, is already impaired.

4. WHY DEATH IS NOT ONLY SUBSTANTIAL CHANGE

4.1. If the hylomorphism of the human being is truly imperfect, it follows that death is not simply the future event that will fall upon us in the

---

63. *ST* 1, q. 119, a. 1, ad. 4.

form of a substantial change, turning our worldly presence into worldly absence. Rather, it is "something" our being deals with every day, the Pauline "law of sin dwelling in [our] members." It is the metaphysical "wound of nature" present at the heart of our very being. As hylomorphism is intrinsically impaired, "separation of soul and body" is not only the event of substantial change occurring at the end limit of life, but is, in essence, the negative dimension characterizing the way the very union of soul and body is realized in us since conception. It is death-as-kenotic-mode-of-being of the soul. However, the negativity of death is neither reducible to the *mode of being* of the soul, nor to the *final event of substantial change*. In fact, it includes other dimensions, that is, *intermediate events and processes of corruption* leading to the end.

Thomas recovers the different meanings of death, which go well beyond the idea of the substantial change putting an end to our worldly presence.[64] He certainly intends death as the final substantial change of a human being.[65] However, he also speaks of death as the phenomenon of corruption taking place in decaying, becoming ill, and suffering. All these are variations internal to the idea that death is an evil of privation. The former is characterized as "privation as a result," while the latter as "privation in process."[66] Sometimes St. Thomas refers to them also as "pure and simple privation," consisting in "being corrupted," and "becoming corrupted," as in the case of sickness.[67] Other times Thomas distinguishes between "death in fact" and "death in becoming."[68] He even postulates the possibility of an "everlasting death" as the metaphysical condition of the damned.[69] So, Thomas intends death to be understood as a substantial change, as a process, and as a process without a substantial change. This last case is particularly telling. The bodies of the damned in the afterlife are "incorruptible" in the sense that the process of corruption

---

64. See Leget, *Living with God*, 20.

65. *ST* 1, q. 4, a. 5, co.

66. *ST* 1-2, q. 18, a. 8, ad. 1. See the analogous distinction between "actual loss" and "gradual loss of being" in *QDM* q. 1, a. 1, ad. 2.

67. *ST* 1-2, q. 73, a. 2, co.

68. *ST* 3, q. 50, a. 6, co. Thomas explains that "death is said to be 'in becoming' when anyone from natural or enforced suffering is tending towards death: and in this way it is the same thing to speak of Christ's death as of His Passion: so that in this sense Christ's death is the cause of our salvation." The theological centrality of death in becoming might imply that death in becoming should be read also in an anthropological context, as the *analogatum princeps* of the various analogical meanings of death.

69. *ST*, Supplementum, q. 86, a. 2, ad. 3.

to which they are subject—i.e., the pains of hell—has no end: the lot of the damned is an endless corruptibility without final corruption. It is evident that if death simply meant substantial change, the notion of an endless death would make no sense.

The implication of this broad understanding of death is clear: if death also means that "privation in process" corresponding to decaying, getting ill, and suffering, these experiences are, quite literally, *experiences of death*. In other words, only a flawed metaphysical view that forced us to limit our understanding of death to the moment of substantial change would prevent us from interpreting experiences of decay, illness, and suffering as experiences *of death*. Contrary to what most people believe (either professional philosophers or not), the question whether an experience of death is even possible must receive a frank and resounding yes. And contrary to what most people are inclined to think, this question should not be limited to the problem of whether we will be able to experience (and if yes, how, and for how long, etc.) the moment of the substantial change taking place at the end limit of our lives.

Through these different cases, then, Thomas provides us with something like an *eidetic variation* on the phenomenon of death. What this quasi-phenomenological analysis shows is that we should understand death in light of the essential phenomenon of corruption. It is *corruption* that allows for an *analogical understanding of the different phenomena of death* in their essential relation. If seen from the point of view of metaphysical anthropology and phenomenology, life, from its very beginning, is intertwined with its own corruption. Becoming ill, suffering, and decaying are corruption in-the-making, and as such they do not exclude life, but require it in order to take it away.[70] Passing away is the moment in which the process of corruption is finally consummated, made perfect;

---

70. On this view, then, the presence of death in life is neither limited to, nor primarily represented by, the human being's self-appropriation of death in the free "acts by which he freely disposes of his whole person," as it seems to be in Rahner, *Theology of Death*, 51. The reality and experience of decaying, becoming ill, and suffering, also in their radical passivity, constitutes the presence of death throughout life. In all fairness to Rahner, he acknowledges the point I am making when he writes: "Suffering . . . is nothing else than the *prolixitas mortis*, the extension of death, which St. Gregory the Great calls life which, through suffering, is lost unto death" (83). However, it is hard to see how Rahner can coherently understand suffering as the upwards extension of death given his framework. At most, suffering could be seen as the precondition for the upwards extension of death, which should be identified, in Rahner's terms, with the personal acts of self-appropriation.

Material Kenosis

it is the substantial change of the organism.[71] And the condition of the damned is that of a process of corruption which has no end, an everlasting corruption-in-the-making.

As one can see, the privation of death is not chiefly the privation of a counterfactual future, but rather the *privation of the perfect hylomorphic oneness of the origin*. It is a legacy, not a destiny; or, better, it is a destiny because it is a legacy. It is the loss of an original condition of metaphysical wholeness, fullness, and consistency, which unfolds—degenerates—until it has fully negated our being.

Going back to our original point, this analogical approach to corruption shows that, if death is literally, and not simply figuratively or morally, already part of our life, an adequate hylomorphic metaphysics cannot take death to be merely a substantial change. In order to make sense of death, substantial change might still have *analogical priority*, but *not literal and metaphysical exclusivity*.[72] Death is, in its most inclusive and therefore most adequate meaning, nothing else than the dramatic unfolding of the intrinsically impaired hylomorphism of the human being through intermediate events and processes of corruption leading to a final substantial change. We should acknowledge that all those stages in the life of a person that lead to the final separation of soul and body, especially decaying, becoming ill, and suffering, are moments in which the separation of death is not just prepared figuratively, but is *actually anticipated*, that is, *partially realized*.[73] Therefore, these moments must also share in, although partially, the same metaphysical characterization that death has: that of a separation of soul and body. What does material kenosis have to do with this? I shall now turn to explain why this hylomorphic view of death is best understood as material kenosis.

---

71. On this use of "perfect," see Aquinas, *Commentary on Metaphysics*, bk. 5, lec. 18.

72. Paul Ricoeur writes that "the figures of evil do not form a system, like one can do in thinking of the good" (*Living Up to Death*, 39). Does this principle undermine the possibility of thinking illness, suffering, and passing analogically in the unity of death? I think not, even though one would have to explain how the analogy of evil differs essentially from the analogy of being.

73. In relation to this point, Mark K. Spencer writes: "Human death, the loss of all matter, is a *sui generis* change, neither substantial nor accidental, in which the soul ceases communicating human nature and *esse* to matter. This is an immense loss to the human substance—in Marco Stango's words, it is a 'material kenosis,' an emptying out of what we are, a 'radical negation without annihilation,' in which we are stripped to our roots (though not without some gain)—but it is not substantial corruption" (*Irreducibility of Human Person*, 319). I would remark that I do believe that death is substantial change and substantial corruption. But I would add that death as substantial change is not sufficient to grasp the broader phenomenon of mortality.

5. MATERIAL KENOSIS

5.1. As anticipated, I take the mode of being of the soul to be essentially kenotic. In a sense, calling our hylomorphic constitution "impaired" falls short of elucidating in what way the imperfection of the hylomorphic union affects the soul. This characterization is still too abstract. This is why I appeal to the notion of kenosis, essentially understood as *self-emptying* and *self-negation*. (The importance of stressing the fact that the soul's self-emptying and self-negating is always mediated by the body, is always *material*, will become clear shortly.)

Two tenets of hylomorphism are especially helpful to elucidate and justify this view. First, the idea of kenosis follows from the Thomistic and already-Aristotelian tenet that it is more correct to say that the soul contains the body rather than the body contains the soul.[74] The relation of containment should of course be understood hylomorphically, not topologically.[75] The soul contains (*cum-tinet*, holds together) the body by configuring it as the body that it is. The configuration- and life-giving function of the soul is a containing function, in the sense just described. In contrast to this containing function, the tendency of the vital energies to withdraw from the containing function of the soul is an emptying movement. Obviously, not even this emptying movement is topological. Rather, it is the metaphysical dynamic opposing the natural containing function of the soul and the subjection to containment of the body. Death, on this view, is therefore an emptying, i.e., *kenotic*, metaphysical phenomenon. To stress the kenotic essence of death even further, one might say that what the soul contains, i.e., the body, has a tendency to withdraw from the soul and therefore to empty the soul of the bodily material through which and in which it performs its containing function.[76]

But we should push this line of reasoning further. In fact, describing death as the soul's being emptied of the body still implies an excessively dualistic picture of the phenomenon. In fact, what the soul is emptied

---

74. "Although corporeal things are said to be in another as in that which contains them, nevertheless, spiritual things contain those things in which they are; as the soul contains the body" (*ST* 1, q. 8, a. 1, ad. 2). See also *ST* 1, q. 76, a. 3, co.

75. This does not mean that hylomorphism has no implications for the topology of the human body. On the contrary, the human body has the topology that it has only because of the configuring function of the soul.

76. This view accords with the idea present in Adolf Faller, that death is better understood as the body "leaving" the soul, "withdrawing" from it, rather than the soul leaving the body ("Biologisches von Sterben und Tod" [1956], quoted in Pieper, *Death and Immortality*, 24).

of is not the body as something external to it, but *the body as something intrinsic to its very being*. On Thomas's view, the soul is "essentially" the form of a human body: despite some of its powers exceeding the receptive capacity of matter, its nature remains that of being the form—the intellectual subsistent form, and yet substantial form—of a *material being*.⁷⁷

A second tenet essential to hylomorphism, this time distinctly Thomistic, can complete the picture. The idea is here *that the being of the body of the person is the same being of the soul*. The person has one unitary act of being, participated by the soul to the body and the entire composite. Thomas says that even after death, the separated soul retains the being of the composite and therefore also the bodily being that it had before death in its embodied condition: "The human soul retains the being of the composite (*esse compositi*) after the destruction of the body: and this because the being of the form is the same as that of its matter, and this is the being of the composite."⁷⁸ The rationale is that the being of the person is unitary, at once spiritual and bodily. (Note: the fact that the soul's being is not only bodily because it is intellectual does not exclude that it is also *essentially* bodily.) To clarify this notion, one might draw the distinction between two considerations of the bodily being of the person. The distinction would be between the bodily being as participating in the organic body through the soul's act of configuration, and the same bodily being as present in the separated soul. The latter is unremovable from the soul's being because it is nothing else than the very being of the soul. On the contrary, the former is removable—and this removal is what we call death. The problem is of course understanding how the two dimensions are related, that is, how the removable dimension (the participation of the soul to the body) affects the unremovable dimension (the bodily being irremovably present in the soul). I suggest that the loss of the participating bodily being occurring in death suffered by the bodily being irremovably present in the soul should not be understood as the loss of something external to the soul. It is rather the scandalous

---

77. "The soul is essentially [*secundum suam essentiam*] the form of the body" (*ST* 1, q. 76, a. 1, ad. 4). See *ST* 1, q. 75, a. 7, ad. 3; q. 75, a. 5, co. (*de ratione animae*). Other times, Thomas adopts the language of "being" (rather than the language of "essence") for making a similar point. For instance: "The intellectual soul is united by its very being [*per suum esse*] to the body as a form" (*ST* 1, q. 76, a. 6, ad. 3). Other times, he speaks in a way that seems neutral between "essence" and "being," such as: "To be united to the body belongs to the soul by reason of itself [*secundum se*]" (*ST* 1, q. 76, a. 1, ad. 6).

78. *ST* 1–2, q. 4, a. 5, ad. 2. See *ST* 1, q. 76, a. 1, ad. 5.

loss of the soul's *own being*—*scandalous* because the soul, while losing its being, retains it all the same; it is not annihilated by this loss while being radically negated by it. In death, the soul "pours out" its being completely without however becoming naught.[79] It becomes clear then why, on this metaphysical perspective, I call the mode of being of the soul *kenotic*. In losing the body's participation with the being of the soul, the soul also loses its being, not in the sense of a substantial, annihilating change, but in the sense of a radically self-negating, and in this sense kenotic, modification.

Thomas seems to draw a different conclusion from the idea that the being of the body is the same as the being of the soul, a conclusion that seems incompatible with the kenotic picture I have just sketched. He says that even after being separated from the body the soul has "perfect being" (*perfectum esse*), even though it does not have the "perfect specific nature" (*perfectam naturam specie*).[80] The whole crux consists in interpreting the "perfection" of being St. Thomas ascribes to the separated soul. Thomas describes what happens to the separated soul by comparing it to what happens in other cases to the parts of a whole when the whole is destroyed: the parts can either cease to be altogether (e.g., when a human being dies, the eye as eye ceases to be altogether) or the parts can turn into different kinds of things, things with a different actuality (e.g., a part of a line has another being when it is cut off from the entire line). Thus, Thomas opposes the "perfection" of the soul after the separation from the body to what happens in the case of two other kinds of change, annihilation and substantial change. That the soul still has "perfect being" after death means: the soul has not been annihilated; the soul has not become some other kind of being.

It becomes evident, then, that my kenotic proposal does not contradict in any way Thomas's view, as in fact, according to the kenotic reading, the soul is neither annihilated nor transformed in death. Nevertheless, the kenotic reading can supplement Thomas's view when he remains silent about *how* we should understand the deep loss the soul undergoes in death despite its unshakable perfection.[81] In other words,

---

79. The image is chosen of course to stress again the isomorphism with the scriptural accounts of Christ's kenosis: "He poured out his soul to death" (Isa 53:12).

80. *ST* 1–2, q. 4, a. 5, ad. 2.

81. Thomas's most explicit attempt to account for the loss that the soul undergoes in death concerns the loss of the natural conditions for intellectual knowledge, as described, for instance, in *ST* 1, q. 89 (on this, see the cited works by Pegis and Pasnau).

the kenotic reading is an attempt to read *conjointly* the two theses advanced by Thomas, namely, that the soul after death has "perfect being" and yet has lost the "perfection of its specific nature."

In its dramatic intertwinement with death, life is a self-emptying and self-negating metaphysical phenomenon. The body, which the soul contains, has a tendency to withdraw from the soul and therefore to empty the soul of the bodily material through which and in which it performs its containing function. This is what occurs in decaying, becoming ill, and suffering, and what is finally brought to conclusion in the event of passing away. Upon hylomorphism, the soul's being-emptied of the body turns out to be a phenomenon of self-emptying: it is the soul's being that is negated, self-negated, due to the mediation of the body.

It is in this sense, then, that the various processes and events of corruption affecting our life, i.e., decay, illness, and suffering, can be considered instances of material kenosis. They are events, processes, and experiences of self-negation and self-emptying without annihilation. However, the notion of material kenosis does not cover only these processes and events. To appreciate this point, we have to go back to what I have called the "kenotic mode of being" of the soul after the fall. As I have anticipated in section 2, the mode of being of the soul is immediately, that is, upon creation, although not originally, kenotic. The idea here is

---

In its disembodied condition, the separated soul thinks without the support of sense-perception and imagination through to the intellectual species that God provides it directly. But the natural condition for the human being's intellectual knowledge requires the body, as human intellectual knowledge naturally occurs through abstraction of the intellectual species from the phantasms and application of the species to the phantasms. Thus, the separated soul finds itself in an unnatural condition due to the loss of the body. The point that I would like to raise is that accounting for the soul's loss of the body by simply appealing to the unnatural conditions of intellectual knowledge in the separate state does not seem satisfactory given Thomas's own hylomorphism. In fact, one should ask: Is the unnatural condition of intellectual knowledge an *exemplification* of the loss of the body undergone by the soul, or should it rather be considered the *essential description* of such a loss? It seems hard to say that the soul's loss of the body can be satisfactorily described by appealing to the unnatural conditions of intellectual knowledge of the separated soul, and this is for one fundamental reason. The reason is that the soul is hylomorphically related to the body, while the intellect is not hylomorphically related to imagination and brain processes (on this see my "Understanding Hylomorphic Dualism"); the relation of the body to the intellect is instrumental (even though it is a natural, and not merely accidental, instrumental relation), while the relation of the body to the soul is not instrumental because the relation between soul and body is hylomorphic. As a consequence, saying that the human intellect loses its natural yet instrumental relation to the body when the soul is separated falls short of grasping the essence of the loss of the body undergone by the soul in death. Once again, the idea of material kenosis is supposed to supplement Thomas on this point.

that the creation of the soul in the body carries within itself an original kenotic event, an Ur-kenosis, which is again dialectical: the soul is immediately (upon creation but not by origin) subject to a radical negation of its natural inclination, as it has to give up the perfection of its organization- and life-giving function by receiving in itself the effects of the evil present in the body it informs (a mediated self-negation again); in turn, the body, by being subjected to the consequently imperfect informing power of the soul, begins its Calvary of corruption, whose effects will be manifested in decaying, becoming ill, and suffering.[82] Ur-kenosis, then, is the way the soul is infected by the original sin. It corresponds to the establishment of the soul in its kenotic mode of being; it unfolds in decaying, becoming ill, and suffering; and is brought to completion in passing away, when the emptying of the soul, due to the withdrawing of the body (the soul's mediated self-emptying), is finally completed.

4.2. It should be clear at this point in what sense death, viewed from the point of view of hylomorphism, is kenotic. Material kenosis is nothing else than an analysis of what the "separation" of death means.[83] Soul and body are, at the same time, *one* and *two*. They are "one" because they share the same act of being, and they are "two" because they are, despite their unity, irreducible to each other.[84] Only in light of this unitary-yet-dual hylomorphism of soul and body can we appreciate the possibility of material kenosis: if soul and body were just "two," the separation would simply amount to the positivity of the liberation of the one (the soul-angel of Platonism) from the other (the body-prison); and if soul and body were just "one," the separation would be, upon metaphysical scrutiny, only decomposition, annihilation (the outcome of any purely immanentist view of the human being). Again, the material kenosis of the person's being is only possible in light of the unitary-yet-dual framework of hylomorphism: since soul and body are "one," the corruption of the body is the self-negation of the soul; and yet, since soul and body are "two," such self-negation does not result in annihilation.

82. Balthasar describes the intra-Trinitarian life as Ur-kenosis (*Action*, 331). I use this notion here only in the anthropological sense described, but the possible theological implications of the framework can be already intuited. The notion is originally taken from Sergei Bulgakov.

83. Material kenosis is thus a response to Rahner's objection 3 (see sec. 1).

84. "The soul is indeed very distant from the body, if we consider the condition of each separately.... But inasmuch as the soul is the form of the body, it has not an existence apart from the existence of the body [*inquantum anima est forma corporis, non habet esse seorsum ab esse corporis*]" (*ST* 1, q. 76, a. 8, ad. 3). See *ST* 1, q. 76, a. 2, ad. 1.

Material Kenosis

4.3. I would like to conclude this section with a couple of further remarks on the importance of understanding this kenosis as *material*. The material nature of the kenotic phenomenon of death follows from the fact that the kenosis of the human being, hylomorphically understood, is *rooted in the decay of the body*. It is in decaying, becoming ill, suffering, and passing away in the body, that the soul is emptied of its essential material being. Whatever additional "spiritual" meaning one might give to the kenotic experience of the soul, one should be clear about the fact that such an experience is *structurally centered in our experience of the body*. The kenosis is the decay of the ensouled body that I am.

However, it is also true that the kenosis of the human being is first and foremost an affair of the soul. Since I am a subsistent soul essentially informing a body, it is the soul itself that undergoes the process of self-emptying and self-negation, of having its own being withdrawn from itself. If my soul did not in some sense "transcend" the body, the withdrawing of the body from the soul would also, in the very same process, diminish the soul to the point of annihilation. But by being subsistent, the soul withstands and witnesses its own emptying and negation. In this second sense, then, the experience of kenosis is *structurally centered in the soul*.

But this focus on the soul does not change the fact that the soul's kenosis is only realized through the decay of the body. So, the decay of the body causes the self-emptying of the soul, but this self-emptying in the soul and of the soul is only possible in and through the body (I would be tempted to say, *as a body*), as it is the movement of the body withdrawing from the soul.[85] Any "spiritual" kenosis in the human being must pass through a "material" kenosis, and any episode of "material" kenosis is the occasion for a "spiritual" kenosis. It is worth quoting at length here José Granados's profound reflections on suffering and the body, which elucidate what the idea of material kenosis also tries to capture:

> Let us recall, indeed, that the body is the proper place of suffering, in the etymological sense of "being passive" (suffering as pathos). Thus, we speak of suffering as bodily not because we equate suffering with pain, but rather because human suffering is rooted in the body and is possible because of the body.[86]

---

85. This is certainly the case if we take material kenosis to be, at least partially (if not primarily), a "passion." See *ST* 1–2, q. 22, a. 1, co.

86. Granados, "Theology of Suffering Body," 552–53.

> [There is] an analogical continuity between the experience of disease or of physical suffering in general, and other forms of suffering caused by wounds in man's ties with others or by the anxiety experienced by those who find no meaning in their journey.[87]

A radical separation between physical pain and "spiritual" suffering is inadequate. Rather, we can assume that these different ways of suffering retain the same analogical structure. In other words, because all suffering is rooted in our bodily condition (as a rapture of the harmony of our participation in the world, in others, and in God), the organism's disease is symbolic of any other kind of "spiritual" suffering. As Levinas puts it, referring to Nemo's reading of Job, suffering consists in "a gnawing away of human identity, which is not an inviolable spirit burdened with a perishable body, but *incarnation*, in all the gravity of an identity which mutates in itself.... Despair despairs like pain in the flesh. Physical evil is the very depth of anxiety, whence ... anxiety, in its carnal acuity, is the root of all social miseries, of all human dereliction: of humiliation, of solitude, of persecution."[88]

6. KENOTIC CHANGE

6.1. Material kenosis affects the soul deeply. On the kenotic view, the soul undergoes a *kenotic change*. Acknowledging the kenotic change to which the soul is subject in decaying, becoming ill, suffering, and passing away, might help us to fill in a gap in the account of death given by standard hylomorphism.[89] What kind of change is undergone by the soul in death? The response of standard hylomorphism is usually that when death comes, the human being, the ensouled body, does not exist anymore; he has undergone a substantial change and has become a corpse. However, his soul survives death in a separate mode of being. While the substantial change of death has intervened on the ensouled body directly, by producing in it the substantial change, its intervention on the soul is only indirect, as no formal change has occurred in the soul. It should not surprise us that, if death is conceptualized only as substantial

---

87. Granados, "Suffering Body, Hope," 655.
88. Granados, "Suffering Body, Hope," 659–60.
89. Rahner's objection 2 (see sec. 1) is the consequence of this gap. What I say in this section should be taken as a response to the objection.

change—something I have suggested we should not do but that standard hylomorphism tends to do—then it is natural to see the soul as not being touched directly by death because it is only indirectly touched by the substantial change. So, according to standard hylomorphism, the soul is only indirectly touched by death; it is indirectly touched by death only when it is separated from the body when or after death-as-substantial-change takes place. It is also not clear what kind of change the soul undergoes: If it is neither a substantial change nor a Cambridge change, what kind of change is it? Is it satisfactory to just call it accidental?

We have two metaphysical options at this point. The first option is to deny that we need to characterize the change undergone by the soul in any robustly metaphysical way. On this view, at worst, one does not need anything more than to characterize the change negatively by saying that the soul enters a new mode of being, the *unnatural* mode of being of its separated condition. At best, one simply contents himself with characterizing the change as accidental: if the change undergone by the soul is not substantial (an intellectual soul cannot in principle undergo such change), it must be accidental. *Tertium non datur*.

The second option consists in looking for new concepts to understand what change is undergone by the soul if not a substantial change. This second option seems more adequate than the first one. In fact, saying that the soul enters a new mode of being still leaves open the question of what kind of change accounts for this passage to a new mode of being. Similarly, simply claiming that the change in the soul is accidental seems to fall short of the radical nature of the change undergone by the soul in its material self-emptying. Finally, since we are working within a hylomorphic framework, the lack of a clear account of what happens to the soul in being abandoned by the body might give the impression, more fitting of a dualistic anthropology, that the soul is somehow untouched by this loss, that the soul does not "die" in any serious sense (which excludes, however, annihilation), that all the stress is on the dying animal and not on the separating soul.

It is for these reasons that I consider the idea of material kenosis suited to fill in the gap. On this view, the change that the soul undergoes in dying is a *kenotic change*, and more specifically the material kenosis described. The soul is dramatically emptied of a whole essential dimension of its being, i.e., the body, while nevertheless remaining what it is, as it does not become any other sort of thing; it is neither annihilated nor transformed. In short, material kenosis is a *radical negation without annihilation* of the soul's being, where "radical" means that what is negated in the person's being is not one of its "parts," but its entirety, its "root," its *actus*, in such a way, however, that annihilation does not follow. The difficulty in thinking of these two aspects of death conjointly—that negation is entire and radical and yet is not annihilating—is precisely what calls for the introduction of the category of kenosis.[90]

Remember that Thomas claims that the separated soul retains the bodily being that it had before death. The bodily being's "presence" in the separate soul is precisely this: the *presence of an absence*, that is, a radical negation without annihilation. The body "survives" death by becoming present in the separate soul in the form of a radical negation immanent to the soul. The meaning of Thomas's claim that the separated soul retains the whole being of the person after death, including her bodily being, cannot be simply explained by saying that the person, surviving in the separated soul, has lost its natural completeness but not its substantial identity. Nor can it be explained by saying that for St. Thomas the soul, despite its capacity to exist as separated, does not become a purely intellectual substance, but remains the substantial form of a bodily substance, or the bare minimum of a bodily substance. These two formulations do not convey the power of Thomas's position. Affirming the scandalous existence of a bodily substance without a body means affirming the existence of a radically negated, i.e., self-negated and self-emptied, being. In other words, it means affirming a being who has been subjected to a negative change that is neither substantial nor merely accidental but, I suggest, *kenotic*.

6.2. A couple of images may be helpful to clarify what I mean by negation without annihilation. Let us think of an artist who is not an artist only accidentally (i.e., a human being with an artistic talent), but,

---

90. What accounts for the fact that negation is entire and yet non-annihilating is precisely the idea of kenosis. In death, the person's being is *wholly* negated, though not annihilated. Edward Feser speaks of death as "full body amputation" ("Aquinas on the Human Soul," 95). Analogies between amputation and handicap and the disembodied state are also found in Purtill, "Intelligibility of Disembodied Survival"; and Gorman, "Personhood, Potentiality, and Normativity." That "full" makes all the difference in the world, as I am sure Feser would concur. It marks the essential difference between amputation proper (which can be only of a part of the soul-body composite) and some more radical form of negation of the person's being, which I have suggested understanding as kenotic. It is precisely this totalizing negation that leads Bernhard Welte to speak of death as the "most serious of all serious cases": "What is this everything? What do we have to give death? Precisely nothing less than everything.... This is its [death's] seriousness" (*Morire*, 37–38).

per impossibile, who is an artist essentially. This artist would still be a subsistent being, someone whose being can be described as "artistic" according to the entire breadth of its essence. Now, imagine that this artist is deprived of all his works of art as well as the material with which he produces works of art: the clay becomes recalcitrant to receive the form of his art. It seems fair to say that in this case this artist, while still not annihilated—reduced to a pure nothing—would be nevertheless totally negated as artist, that is, totally negated in his very being. This, I submit, is the radical or total negation without annihilation of man's being which is death and, accordingly, the true meaning, speculatively unpacked, of the Aristotelian formula "separation of soul and body."

Or, to use a different image, one should say that the soul "losing" the body is not comparable to a tea spoon raised up from the liquid in which it was submerged (corresponding to the body), thus presenting itself in its purified fullness, in its silvery, shiny essence. Rather, the soul "losing" the body is like the lover losing his beloved with whom he has identified himself.

6.3. From what I have said earlier, it follows that the radical negation without annihilation of the soul is not restricted to the substantial change. Substantial change only brings this kenotic change to completion. The introduction of kenotic change into life is as immediate as conception. The "absence" of the body is already "present" in the kenotic mode of being of the soul and in the processes, events, and experiences of corruption that the human being undergoes throughout life. Of course, the "absence" of the body in the embodied and in the separate soul is not identical in quantity, but it is in essence, if the essence of this scandalous absent-presence or present-absence of the body is understood as the radical negation without annihilation of the soul. In being born into death and in being subject to decay, illness, and suffering, a human being is already exposed to the essential kenosis of death, to the self-emptying and self-negating process leading to the end.[91] He experiences in life the "absence" of his present body (the body does not respond as I wish, the

---

91. With respect to the difference between illness and pain, see Agazzi and Tymieniecka: "A pain, even an acute one, is usually 'localized,' it does not affect our self-identity, it can make our normal operating difficult, but does not alter our attitude toward ourselves and our life, while illness, even a non-serious one, has the effect of making us feel dependent on the other people's help, of transforming our body into an obstacle, a hostile presence that blocks our projects, desires, intentions, an obscure threat to our survival or to our 'quality of life.' In such a situation we feel wounded 'as a whole,' it is our whole life that is affected" ("Complex Phenomenon of Illness," xii).

body hurts against my will), or the "presence" of an absent body (this unresponsive and suffering body of mine imposes itself on me, this body of mine in which I am stuck and which I am).[92]

6.4. From my point of view, the theoretical value of this formal characterization of death—death as "radical" or "total negation without annihilation"—cannot be overestimated. This "radical negation without annihilation" is precisely the "what" of that phenomenon we call human death. It explains what this phenomenon is—that is, *what it is not*, its nonbeing, its specific form of negation. Heidegger, among others, has pointed out that, properly speaking, only human beings "die," that is, that only human beings are faced with the *phenomenon* of death *as death*.[93] Adapting this Heideggerian and traditional view, one could say that only human beings are aware of death as death. In other words, only in the case of the human being the awareness of one's mortality prepares and is perfected in the *knowledge of the whatness of death*, its being a radical negation without annihilation. (Since Heidegger's view is often charged of the "anthropocentric bias" that is allegedly typical of the Western tradition, I would like to point out, in my defense, that there does not seem to be anything particularly anthropocentric about my view, insofar as it seems fair to say that no nonhuman animal entertains the intelligible notion of radical negation without annihilation. This is so a fortiori, given that it is likely that even most *human animals* will not agree with the proposal I am articulating in these pages.[94]) The metaphysical insight, reserved to those who practice this discipline, brings to light that which is already confusedly apprehended in the common experience of death and dying, i.e., in the experience of decay, illness, and suffering: that decay, illness, suffering, and death are essentially tied;[95] that death is no joke, no

---

92. This conclusion opens the possibility, which however I will not explore here, of a phenomenology of illness conducted in hylomorphic spirit. More specifically, material kenosis removes the metaphysical prejudices that prevent a phenomenology of decay, illness, and suffering, from being interpreted as a phenomenology of death, prejudices which are very widespread in contemporary philosophy, as well described in Schumacher, *Death and Mortality*. Interesting phenomenological analyses are developed in Carel, *Phenomenology of Illness*, even though without any reference to hylomorphism. In general, the possibility of a phenomenology of death would constitute a response to Rahner's objection 4 (sec. 1).

93. Heidegger, *Being and Time*, 223–24.

94. For a book that challenges this alleged anthropocentric bias, see Susana Monsó, *Playing Possum: How Animals Understand Death*.

95. Accordingly, the often-exploited distinction between "dying" and "death" (e.g., we experience the process of "dying," but we do not have evidence to state that we

event touching us partially; that it is radical and totalizing; and yet, that our life, strangely, sustains and undergoes its own demise, thus allowing for the difficult-to-square thought that it may somehow withstand death while being radically destroyed by it.

This of course does not mean that human beings have the same experience of mortality as other animals do *plus* some additional knowledge of the essence of the phenomenon. We forget too easily that *genuine knowledge* implies a mutual *participation*: a participation of the object known in the nature of the knowing subject (the "spiritualization" of the known object); and a participation of the knowing subject in the nature of the known object. In the case of death, the knowing subject participates in a nonbeing, that is, in the total negation without annihilation of death. (Insofar as what is known is a kind of nonbeing, it is of course a linguistic approximation to speak of "participation." Perhaps it would be more fitting to say that the knowledge of death implies for the knowing subject a *de*-participation.) This is why, as Leo Tolstoy's *The Death of Ivan Ilyitch* shows most iconically,[96] the genuine knowledge of one's death is

---

experience "death" as such) is untenable if it is taken to imply that we can never experience death. Death is already "present" in the very fallen constitution of our being, and it is anticipatorily and analogically taking place in the many instances of decay we experience daily. Even Schumacher in his otherwise excellent study takes this highly questionable distinction for granted and applies it, for instance, to the clarification of "death as the object of experience" (*Death and Mortality*, ch. 7).

96. "At the bottom of his heart Ivan Ilyitch knew that he was dying, and was in continual despair. At the bottom of his heart Ivan Ilyitch knew that he was dying; but so far from growing use to this idea, he simply did not grasp it—he was utterly unable to grasp it. The example of the syllogism that he had learned in Kiseveter's logic—Caius is a man, men are mortal, therefore Caius is mortal—had seemed to him all his life correct only as regards Caius, but not at all as regards himself. In that case it was a question of Caius, a man, an abstract man; he had always been a creature quite, quite different from all others; he had been little Vanya with a mamma and papa, and Mitya and Volodya, with playthings and a coachman and a nurse; afterwards with Katenka, with all the joys and griefs and ecstasies of childhood, boyhood, and youth. What did Caius know of the smell of the leathern ball Vanya had been so fond of? Had Caius kissed his mother's hand like that? Caius had not heard the silk rustle of his mother's skirts. He had not made a riot at school over the pudding. Had Caius been in love like that? Could Caius preside over the sittings of the court? And Caius certainly was mortal, and it was right for him to die; but for me, little Vanya, Ivan Ilyitch, with all my feelings and ideas—for me it's a different matter. And it cannot be that I ought to die. That would be too awful. That was his feeling. . . . 'It can't be! It can't be, but it is! How is it? How's one to understand it?' And he could not conceive it, and tried to drive away this idea as false, incorrect, and morbid, and to supplant it by other, correct, healthy ideas. But this idea, not as an idea merely, but as it were an actual fact, came back again and stood confronting him" (Tolstoy, *Death of Ivan Ilyitch*, 43–44).

almost inevitably prompted by and dependent upon the *actual experience* of decay, sickness, and suffering. And this is why it is important to distinguish between two forms of knowledge of death: an abstract, impersonal, notional knowledge of death, in which the participatory structure of knowledge is realized only in one direction; and a concrete, personal, and lived knowledge of death, in which the participatory structure of knowledge is realized in both directions. In the former case, the known object participates in the nature of the knowing subject and is thus spiritualized, i.e., revealed in its universal essence. According to this first form of knowledge, death is known as that essential radical negation without annihilation to which all human beings are subject. I can thus know that "All human beings are mortal" in the sense encapsulated in the notion of material kenosis apprehended abstractly and impersonally. From here, given the additional premise that "I am a human being," I must derive the inescapable conclusion that "I am mortal." But this conclusion 'does not touch me' because the knowing subject is not truly participating, as far as his knowledge goes, in that radical negation without annihilation that is death. Based on this merely notional form of knowledge of death, to use the remarkable expression by Vladimir Jankélévitch, "I will die in general, but never in particular."[97] For the second participation to occur (the genuine participation of the knowing subject in the known object), the radical negation without annihilation of death must impose itself upon the knowing subject through the *actual experience* of decay, illness, and suffering (either one's decay, illness, and suffering, or the decay, illness, and suffering of those one loves). It is only at this point that the knowledge of death reaches my haecceity; it is only at this point that I truly know that I will die "in particular" or, better, that *I am already dying "in particular."*[98] It is at this point that I am truly given to know the meaning of what Gabriel Marcel calls "metaphysical uneasiness."[99] It is

---

97. Jankélévitch, *Mort*, 151. Freud's often-quoted and often-misconstrued remark that "at bottom no one believes in his own death" could be taken to mean exactly what Jankélévitch is stating here. See 30n22.

98. The participatory nature of knowledge which I have adopted to sketch the two different kinds of knowledge of death (one abstract, impersonal, and notional, the other concrete, personal, and lived) explains what almost everybody acknowledges without explaining. Jankélévitch, for instance, rightly claims that the syllogistic knowledge of my own death never reaches the depth of my being. The lived knowledge of my own death is always an "event" irreducible to a reasoning; it is an "intuition"; it requires a "salto mortale." But, I believe, only the participatory nature of knowledge explains why this is so.

99. Marcel, "Value and Immortality," 131.

only at this point that the knowledge of death puts the self into question. Thus, a genuine knowledge of material kenosis requires participating in the radical negation without annihilation of death (it requires a cognitive de-participation) *at least* through the experience of decay, illness, and suffering, which bring to consciousness the negativity of the impaired hylomorphism that always already defines our fallen, broken, wounded condition.

7. MATERIAL KENOSIS AND GOD'S KENOSIS

7.1. Before concluding, it might be helpful to provide a sketch of a possible theological implication of the Thomistic view of death presented in this chapter. Death as material kenosis can in fact cast some light on how to understand the Pauline characterization of God as kenotic. In his Commentary to St. Paul's Epistle to the Philippians, Thomas explains that God, by emptying himself, did not for this reason give up his divine nature. Just as the fact that God descended from heaven does not mean that he ceased to exist in heaven, but that he began to exist in a new way on earth, so the fact that he emptied himself does not mean that he gave up his divinity, but that he assumed what he did not have, namely, the human nature. The crucial point in Thomas's interpretation is his explanation of why St. Paul appeals to the concept of emptiness: "How beautiful to say that *He emptied himself*, for the empty is opposed to the full! For the divine nature is sufficiently full, because every perfection of goodness is there. But human nature and the soul are not full, but capable of fullness, because it was made as a slate not written upon. Therefore, human nature is empty. Hence he says, *He emptied himself*, because He assumed a human nature."[100]

Thomas's position on God's self-emptying can be summed up in two claims: (1) God empties himself not in the sense that he gives up or holds in check some of his divine prerogatives, but that he assumes human nature in incarnation. (2) Such assumption is characterized as an "emptying" of himself because human nature is empty, i.e., the human soul is potentially open to receive all the forms through knowledge but is not originally filled with any of them. While Thomas is speaking of the "human nature and soul," the analogy with the unwritten slate makes us think of the human intellect almost immediately. Although it is not

---

100 Aquinas, *Commentary on Philippians*, 2.2.57.

explicit, the passage echoes the doctrine of the human intellect which is capable of receiving all of the forms because it is in itself deprived of any form in particular—because it is empty. By extension, we can read Thomas saying here that the intellectual nature of the human being is, as such, capable of acquiring knowledge and developing the virtues while having at the beginning only a potentiality for knowledge and virtue.

Thomas's position is interesting not only for the two points just stressed, but also because, more broadly, it establishes a methodological principle: whatever God's self-emptying might signify, its meaning should be sought by looking at the human nature. It is by sticking to this Thomistic principle that I would like to go beyond Thomas's letter. In my view, God's incarnation and death is described as a kenosis, as a phenomenon of self-emptying, because human death is itself a kenosis, the self-emptying and self-negation of material kenosis. God's kenosis has been of course interpreted in the light of Jesus's death on the cross. What I would like to add to this view is that it is a Thomistic hylomorphic framework adequately understood that allows us to see clearly why death must be, in rigorous metaphysical terms, a phenomenon of self-emptying and self-negation. *It is because human death is material kenosis that God's incarnation and death in Christ is rightly described as kenotic.* A confirmation of this is that the emptying of incarnation of Christ is immediately tied by the apostle to the cross.[101] Of course, to accept this understanding of kenosis we have to grant the Thomistic principle that St. Paul's words should be made sense of by appealing to a certain view of human nature (the "emptiness" of the soul, which can be in a sense all things) or the human condition (the "emptiness" of a soul whose being is fully negated without being annihilated). But if we are willing to do so, I believe that my proposal manages to advance the Thomistic interpretation of God's kenosis a bit further.

In short, understanding human death as material kenosis explains in what way God's assumption of human nature is an emptying: neither because God gives up or holds in check his divinity; nor simply because the human soul is created as an unfilled tabula rasa; but, more deeply, because the assumption of the human nature means for God to willingly accept the destiny of self-emptying and self-negation which coincides with man's death.

---

101. "And being found in the human form he humbled himself and because obedient unto death, even death on the cross" (Phil 2:8).

7.2. To conclude, according to material kenosis, the substantial change of the ensouled body is the final act of radical negation in the kenotic drama of the informing soul, which spans from the first moment of its experiencing illness, suffering, and decay, to the moment of passing away, and which, at a more fundamental level, is inscribed in the very mode of being of the soul since the human being's conception. This kenotic movement, the kenotic change of the soul, is not confined to the final moment of substantial change. The material-kenotic change of the soul is, in fact, coessential to its kenotic mode of being, and as such affects life in all its stages. Each stage in life characterizable as decaying, becoming ill, and suffering, is an episode in the drama of material kenosis. Despite the fact that material kenosis is ultimately accomplished only in passing away, its reality affects life as a whole. And as this material kenosis is part of our life, so is death. This Thomistic hylomorphism can open up the possibility for interpreting any phenomenology of decaying, becoming ill, and suffering as a genuine phenomenology of death.

8. MATERIAL KENOSIS AND PRZYWARA'S ANALOGY OF BEING: ESSENCE IN-AND-BEYOND EXISTENCE

8.1. Erich Przywara has developed a creaturely metaphysics organized around the principle of the analogy of being. Przywara is crucial because his metaphysics of the *analogia entis* puts the problem of nonbeing at the center, insofar as for him the span of the analogy is precisely between the "nothing" of creation and "Creator out of nothing." His conceptuality allows us to unpack new aspects of the notion of material kenosis which would otherwise remain hidden.

According to Przywara, the analogy of being has a cruciform shape in which the intra-creaturely, horizontal dimension of the analogy of being is inscribed in and opens up to the vertical analogy of the relation between creatures and God (the "metaphysical analogy" from below) and of God and creatures (the "theological analogy" from above). It is in the vertical dimension of the analogy that the horizontal dimension is fulfilled.

In this section I will draw the consequences of Przywara's Thomistic metaphysics for a deeper understanding of the concept of material kenosis. In so doing, I will rely primarily on two different formulations of the intra-creaturely analogy of being: first, creaturely being described as "essence in-and-beyond existence"; and second, creaturely being described as the "oscillating rhythm" of "possibility and actuality," which Balthasar calls "Przywara's dialectical interpretation of Thomas's real distinction."[102] However, our confrontation with Przywara's thought will not be over until we will come to terms with his conclusive and comprehensive formulation of the analogy of being, in which the problem of *non-being* becomes crucial. In fact, as Przywara states, "analogy in the strictest sense" is "between being (God) and nothingness (the creature)."[103] He writes: "Analogy... is what is ultimately fundamental... the ultimate structure, encompassing and thoroughly shaping everything. Within the intra-creaturely it spans the abyss between being and nothingness that lies perpetually open within all becoming: *enti et non-enti aliquid secundum analogiam convenit, quia ipsum non-ens ens dicitur analogice*. But it also spans the even greater distance between the divine Is, which alone, as such, is 'true being' (*germanum Est*), and the creaturely 'is,' which in comparison with God (*secundum commensurationem*) looks like nothing (*Deo comparata, invenitur quasi nihil*)."[104]

That death, the ultimate consequence of man's original sin, reduces us to "nothing" is a claim that some recent Catholic theologians, such as Romano Guardini and Hans Urs von Balthasar, are willing to put forth. Part of the reasons for doing so must be found in the fact that only by appreciating the utter negation of our condition in sin-death can one truly acknowledge the superabundant positivity of the gift poured forth on us in Christ's kenosis (incarnation, passion, and death) and resurrection. In Guardini's words: "What is death as the Christian sees it?... He [the Christian] accepts death as the provision of the Living God for his redemption.... Death is the entrance into new life.... In Christ the arch reaches out to the side of God for each of us. Death is the darkness which the arch has to span.... Death guarantees the gravity of this deliverance and of this re-creation, for without death the message of the Gospel would be sheer fantasy."[105] Or according to Fabrice Hadjadj's pithy formulation: "In order to be a good resurrected person, it is necessary first to have died [truly and fully] (by a death that is still scandalous)."[106]

---

102. Cited in Oster, "Thinking Love," 664.

103. Przywara, *Analogia Entis*, 236. See also Gonzales, *Reimagining the* Analogia Entis, 168–202.

104. Przywara, *Analogia Entis*, 236.

105. Guardini, *Last Things*, 27–28.

106. Hadjadj, *Resurrection*, 57. The published English translation may be

Material Kenosis

In a similar vein, Leonard J. DeLorenzo has convincingly spoken of the nothingness of man in his condition of sin-death. It is by descending into this condition, which DeLorenzo characterizes as a "state of nonexistence—that is, existence without life," that Christ reaches "creation's extreme distance from its Creator" and therefore manages to reestablish from within the "true nothing" of a fallen creation—that metaphysical dialogue of love between creation and the Father that was lost as a consequence of man's sin of pride.[107] What is interesting here for us is his metaphysical characterization of death as nothing: "The notion of death with which Christianity reckons . . . is the view of death that approaches creation's absolute zero in self-contradictory nonexistence."[108] He goes as far as describing man's condition as one of annihilation: "On Holy Saturday, the Son's ultimate Word is his silence—the silence of obediently accepting the will of the Father even unto the absolute limit of creaturely existence: its annihilation."[109] For these reasons, redemption becomes "God's 'second gift' unto nothing."[110]

Developing a suggestion by Brian D. Robinette,[111] DeLorenzo correctly sees a connection between creation and redemption in the fact that God's power manifests itself in both cases as a power over nothing: "In the light of the Resurrection of Christ, we discern that the doctrine of creation and the doctrine of resurrection of the dead have at least one essential feature in common: they both have to do with the power of God's love over nothing."[112]

While DeLorenzo makes here a crucial point, his proposal is weakened, it seems to me, by the fact that no metaphysical account is provided of such "true nothingness" of man and creation. Moreover, by not distinguishing carefully the two senses of nonbeing—the negation of death and the *nihil* of *creatio ex nihilo*—DeLorenzo cannot provide an account

---

misleading. Following the original French ("Pour être un bon ressuscité, il faut d'abord être un bon mort"), the best translation of "être un bon mort" may be not "to die well" but "to be truly dead."

107. DeLorenzo, *Work of Love*, 87. See also Balthasar, quoted in DeLorenzo, *Work of Love*, 93.
108. DeLorenzo, *Work of Love*, 88.
109. DeLorenzo, *Work of Love*, 91.
110. DeLorenzo, *Work of Love*, 94.
111. Robinette, *Grammars of Resurrection*, 361.
112. DeLorenzo, *Work of Love*, 96. He significantly quotes Rom 4:17, according to which God's word "gives life to the dead and calls into existence things that do not exist."

DEATH AS MATERIAL KENOSIS

of why their connection in man's experience of death and redemption is scandalous. In short, precisely because it is essential, with DeLorenzo and others, to speak of man as reduced to "nothing" by death in order to appreciate the superabundant positivity of the gift of redemption, it is also essential to give an *adequate metaphysical account* of what such "nothing" looks like. This can be done, on the one hand, by steering away from a reduction of man and creation to utter annihilation (which would ensue in the purest of metaphysical contradictions) or to a condition of utter lack of relation with God (which would result in the Barthian post-lapsarian view of the world criticized by Przywara as "theopanism,"[113] what Maritain called the "annihilation of man before God"[114]). On the other hand, however, such a metaphysical account must take the total negation of death seriously and avoid understanding this "nothing" as purely metaphorical.

Additionally, the notion of the "dereliction of the absence of God" developed by Hans Urs von Balthasar makes metaphysical sense only if something like the figure used to describe death in these pages—total negation without annihilation—can be used. In fact, if the negation of the presence of God is not total, then the dereliction of the God-forsaken man is not real; but in order to be real and not a pure nothing, dereliction and God-forsakenness cannot annihilate God's presence, God's providential indwelling. Once again, we must think the dereliction and the God-forsakenness as a presence preserved in its total absence—the presence of an absence. Thus, metaphysically, the "dereliction of the absence of God" is plain and simple the presence of Being in creation, preserved, however, as total absence. And this is human death, understood as material kenosis, namely, as the total negation without annihilation of the human being. As such, "nothingness" (not absolute nothing, but precisely, the nothing of evil, of complete solitude and loneliness, of utter dereliction, which can be "real," i.e., present, only in its total parasitical dependence on what exists) is chiefly present in the world through man, namely, through man's death. Although spread out throughout the cosmos, only in the human being, in virtue of his subsistence, nothingness presents itself *as nothingness*, "in the flesh." It is only in light of the understanding of death as material kenosis that this metaphysical account can be given.

113. Przywara, *Analogia Entis*, 19–20.
114. Maritain, *Integral Humanism*, 70.

Przywara adopts the notion of "nothing" to refer to the creature by placing it in the context of his reflection on the analogy of being. It is precisely this richly metaphysical idea of nonbeing that will come to our help to clarify the questions left open by theologians such as DeLorenzo and Balthasar regarding the meaning of nonbeing (when attributed to the creature), as well as to provide a better vantage for appreciating the meaning of material kenosis. As I have already said, on the one hand, Przywara's treatment of "nothing" in the context of the analogy of being provides deeper tools to unpack the metaphysics of material kenosis. On the other hand, however, my claim is also that the "nothing" included within the analogy of being in its entire "span" is not treated in a concrete and adequate way unless it deals with the problem of the negation of death in its difference-relation with the *nihil* of *creatio ex nihilo*. For this reason, the metaphysics of material kenosis can shed some further light on the analogy of being itself.

8.2. In the Thomistic tradition, finite being is "finite" because of the real distinction in it between "essence" and "existence" or "act of being." In Przywara's execution of this idea, we find one first variation of the analogy of being, the formulation of which is "essence in-and-beyond existence." This idea expresses a "metaphysics of creaturely being."[115] In the analogical tension between essence and existence, in fact, the particular form of creatureliness is found in the "suspended correlation" of existence and essence.[116] While in God essence and existence coincide, so that one can think of God as the *Ipsum Esse Subsistens*, in creatures the relation between these two principles or polarities is never settled in a perfect equation. Moreover, such a correlation is suspended because it is concretely realized every time according to an oscillating "back-and-forth" that refuses any form of a priori determination and ensues different modalities of the composition of essence and existence.

Within and through the spectrum of all these different modalities, however, analogy remains the abiding form of creaturely being, according to the formulation "essence in-and-beyond existence." For instance, in dealing with the problem of philosophy in light of the transcendentals true, good, and beautiful, Przywara exemplifies the principle just stated (i.e., different modalities of composition of essence and existence within the same abiding form of creaturely being) by describing the theoretical

---

115. Przywara, *Analogia Entis*, 407.
116. Przywara, *Analogia Entis*, 406–7.

life, primarily relative to the true, as falling on the side of a "relatively pure essence," i.e., in the activity of men whose existences "get lost" in the revelation of the pure essence of what is true. Similarly, Przywara describes the ethical life, which is defined by its relation to the good, as the "tension of becoming between existence and essence" ("become what you are"), in the sense of a constant negotiation in the attempt to realize what is essentially good within the existing conditions of life, in order to achieve one's destined form. He characterizes the esthetic or artistic life, defined by its relation to the beautiful, as a "relatively ideal existence," namely, as life in which the existent becomes an icon of the ideal form of the beautiful.[117] We can see in these examples the ways in which the polarity of "essence" and "existence" is jointly and differently realized while keeping the fundamental structure ("essence in-and-beyond existence") analogously identical.

What is interesting here for our purpose is that framing the metaphysics of creatures according to the polarity of essence and existence allows us to bring to light essential aspects of the Thomistic metaphysics of form and matter which would remain otherwise hidden, with special reference to the problem of death. What specific modality does the back and forth tension between essence and existence take when man faces death understood as material kenosis? The formula "essence in-and-beyond existence" means that the act of being of each creature is, every time, the "already" of a determinate being with its own substantial form and actual accidents (essence-in-existence), but also the "not yet" of the imperfect participation in the exemplar cause which resides in God (essence-beyond-existence)[118]—the same rhythm of *grandeur* and *misère* reflected upon by Pascal. Moreover, as Przywara explains, this creaturely metaphysics of the analogy of being "comes to completion [only, we should add] when it envisions God, since the tension of the correlation of existence and essence (essence in-and-beyond existence) proper to the realm of the creaturely points beyond itself to an *absolutum* of existence-and-essence: to God, that is, understood as the essential identity of existence and essence, as the pure Is (*ipsum Est*, as Augustine puts it; *ipsum*

---

117. Przywara, *Analogia Entis*, 407.

118. "Formae rerum in mente divina existentes sunt, ex quibus fluit esse rerum quod est commune formae et materiae" (Aquinas, *Disputed Questions on Truth*, q. 10, a. 4, co.). Thomistic metaphysics cannot be understood without this exemplarist dimension, which is stressed particularly in St. Bonaventure. See also the idea that each creature is "suspended" in the *proportio* of existence and essence (Balthasar, *Realm of Metaphysics in Antiquity*, 409).

esse, as Thomas Aquinas puts it)."[119] The two fundamental orientations of the analogy of being—the one horizontal, the other vertical—spring from each other according to the analogical ("bottom *up*") fundamental movement of philosophy. How does this principle help us understand more deeply material kenosis?

As we said, material kenosis means the total negation without annihilation of the person. By unpacking hylomorphism according to the correlation of essence and existence, the meaning of this "total negation without annihilation" becomes even clearer, precisely in the form of the essence in-and-beyond existence. One should remember here what has been established earlier in this chapter, namely, the reinterpretation of the doctrine of the "subsistence" of the "intellectual soul" and of death as "separation of soul and body," the result of which was precisely the dynamic figure of material kenosis. In bringing the notion of material kenosis to a new fruition in light of Przywara's creaturely metaphysics, one should say that in material kenosis the essence "in" existence is *totally negated* (without however being annihilated), to the point that *nothing* of such essence is left in the still-abiding existence, or, more precisely, to the point that such essence is precisely still *present* in the abiding existence of the person as *totally negated*. Only in this way we take seriously the radicality of the negation of death from a Christian point of view without falling into the fatal (Protestant?) error of embracing annihilation in the hope of a "more robust," i.e., more Christian and less Greek, resurrection.[120]

Material kenosis, as we have seen, navigates the narrow course which steers away from the Scylla of a monolithic understanding of the so-called immortality of the soul (which does not take the total negation of death seriously) and the Charybdis of nihilism (which neglects the subsistence of the soul). But Przywara helps us recognize an even deeper truth essentially related to the point just made. In fact, in the "back-and-forth" of the correlation of essence and existence, the negated "in"-dimension of the essence remains, insofar as the person is not annihilated, not only in the form of its immanent total negation, but also, and more profoundly, in the form of its "beyond" within the transcendence of God. In dying, my essence is still "in" the abiding existence that I am but only as if it were *totally stretched towards the "beyond" me* (where this "totally"

---

119. Przywara, *Analogia Entis*, 407.
120. See Cullman, *Immortality of the Soul*.

corresponds to the "total" of the "total negation" of death), in the hands of God, who "gives it" and only could "give it back."[121]

In this sense, one could talk of an *experiential intensification in death of man's sense of the exemplar cause*, in such a way that nothing is left "in" me other than an intensified presence of such a cause which, however, being identical with God, transcends me totally.

8.2.1. Let us elucidate this view more carefully. While the notion of the "subsistence of the soul" is usually established through a meditation on those human capacities that transcend that of which bodies are capable, namely, the intellectual capacities, the phenomenon of death and a creaturely metaphysics put it under a light that allows to see what such subsistence ultimately implies. One could see this by comparing the Thomistic view here developed with Heidegger's radical philosophy of finitude.[122] It is in fact in the light of the temptation of the Heideggerian "embrace of finitude" in death (Dasein is "being-towards-death") that one can see what the "subsistence" of the human soul means. Contrary to being the place of any univocal resemblance with God,[123] the *subsistence of our being in the figure of the "subsistence of the intellectual soul"* is the point from which the "back" of the movement of analogy is faced with the impossibility of an ultimate "self-enclosure" into absolute non-being—it is the principle of an *unsurpassable relation to and dependence on* God that shines even through the deepest negation of being and life, namely, death.[124] In this sense, following Przywara's interpretation, the

---

121. We find in Ludwig Feuerbach an unexpected confirmation of this, which of course he criticizes: "But he [man] desires to be nothing in himself, because what he takes from himself is not lost to him, since it is preserved in God. Man has his being in God; why then should he have it in himself?" (*Essence of Christianity*, 22).

122. See Przywara, *Analogia Entis*, 218–19, even though my analysis goes beyond what Przywara says.

123. Claude Bruaire calls such illusion of univocity a "theomorphic delirium." I recall that he once said, "The substance's subsistence [and the subsistence of the spiritual soul] does not liberate from anguish before death nor from the groundless suffering of the other's death." See also López, *Spirit's Gift*. Przywara actually suggests that it is in created spiritual being that the "negative potentiality" of being (i.e., the complete dependence of created being on God) "is reinforced" precisely due to its (conditional) "necessity" (i.e., the fact that spiritual being is not destined by nature to 'fall apart'), insofar as "it becomes clear that the expression 'necessity' is really still intra-creaturely—that is, that God remains beyond even the opposition between 'possible' and 'necessary'" (*Analogia Entis*, 225). See also *ST* 1, q. 75, a. 5, ad. 5.

124. "Being for oneself, in the active return of oneself to the ultimate source, indicates the type of subsistence proper to the substance.... Subsistence (*hupokeimenon*) is rooted in the gift's incapacity to be called back" (López, *Gift and the Unity*, 91).

Heideggerian "running towards death" (*Vorlaufen*, anticipation) embracing finitude is not a mark of metaphysical humility, but rather the creature's ultimate but desperate attempt to affirm a closure upon itself; it is existential titanism; or maybe, if lack of humility and titanism are too much, Heidegger's attitude is at least an a priori (and thus, dogmatic) decision for immanence.[125]

Nevertheless, one learns much from the Heideggerian position due its uncompromising honesty. Such honesty consists in the fact that, as Heidegger has correctly seen, this ultimate self-closure could only be realized, logically speaking, as a self-closure *into nonbeing as annihilation*, which is the precise meaning of "being-toward-death."[126] Heidegger therefore, coherently with his view on death, identifies the horizon of emergence of all beings with "Nothing," just as nonbeing is the ultimate destiny of beings.[127] But this possibility is precisely what the subsistence of the soul rules out: the subsistence of the soul in the face of death is what prevents the ultimate active self-closure (into absolute nonbeing) of the human creature and therefore opens up, in the "back-and-forth" of the movement of analogy, to the acknowledgment of the constitutive relation with God as the ultimate positivity of existence.[128]

125. See "Husserl and Heidegger," in Przywara, *Analogia Entis*, 613–22. Przywara seems to interpret Heidegger in a straightforward metaphysical way without paying too much attention to Heidegger's methodological limitations to the domain of phenomenology, which leave theological and metaphysical issues out. Despite this interpretative attitude may have some flaws, I think that it highlights where the real issue lies. For this reason, I follow Przywara.

126. The Heideggerian position is therefore more rigorous and honest than any form of radical immanentism that sees perfect self-mediation as possible, like in all the philosophies criticized by Desmond. The destiny of a mirage of perfect self-mediation as self-closure is ultimately proven to be impossible not only because its logical result would be self-closure into annihilation, as Heidegger admits and is willing to pursue, but also for the reasons adduced here, namely, that any attempt to establish a perfect ontological self-closure has to face the ultimate obstacle of a self-subsistence whose life and dynamism is that of an unsurpassable relation to God.

127. Przywara here brings together, correctly in my view, the Heideggerian "productive Nothing" (*Analogia Entis*, 229) that we find, for instance, in "What Is Metaphysics?" and "nonbeing" as the destiny of being understood as radical self-enclosure (*Analogia Entis*, 218) exemplified by "being-towards-death" in *Being and Time*.

128. We find in Przywara an interesting parallel between the affirmation of the priority of the positivity of being over the nonbeing of nihilistic self-enclosure and the impossibility of the pursuit of evil *as evil*: "In that creaturely 'of itself' is 'nothing,' it contains within itself the possibility of that suicidal plunge into nothing which is the nihilistic characteristic of the innermost tendency of evil. But precisely here the 'positive,' which is stronger, triumphs: for the nihilistic itself, as such, can be willed only under a *ratio boni*, and is thus itself still sustained by the positive 'is' of the Is. . . . Even

DEATH AS MATERIAL KENOSIS

In other words, man cannot close "back" in himself, not even in the face of death and not even in the seemingly heroic acceptance of his embracing "radical finitude" in "running towards death." On the contrary, in virtue of the subsistence of his being which is totally negated in death, man is brought "forward" to the "Is" who prevents his self-closure into absolute nonbeing by indwelling him as the "beyond" of his totally-negated essence. Entering into the mysterious reality of the subsistence of the soul means therefore, as Przywara says, to put oneself on the threshold of the "redemptive de-absolutization of a fallen 'absolute.'"[129]

One can discover here an unexpected implication of the Neoplatonic metaphysical figure of the *reditio completa* taken up by Thomas which is traditionally used to describe the nature of spirit in its essential difference from the body and therefore also by extension the subsistence of the soul of man.[130] The *reditio completa* of the intellectual soul, far from being that self-closure into nothing of the perfect circle of autonomy up to the extreme risk of death, is on the contrary a radical "always-already-being-kept-in-relation to" God and, therefore, "being-kept-open-by" God "to" God.[131] But we must be precise and acknowledge that the concrete modality of relation to God is precisely the one described by the horizontal-cum-vertical analogy of essence in-and-beyond-existence. The dying person is "stretched" out of himself in the total negation of his being toward that "Other" in which his essence is *realized as promised*, as the "not yet" of the "already"—an already that is reduced to an almost pure existence without essence ("total negation").

This seems to suggest that there is no fundamental contradiction, but rather mutual enrichment, between a substance-centered and a relation-centered understanding of the human being. Instead of coinciding with a fundamental, self-authentifying solitariness (i.e., the solitariness of Heidegger's being-towards-death), dying coincides with

---

nothingness itself, as nothingness, must bear the stamp of the Is, and therefore must be subject—of service—to it" (*Analogia Entis*, 226). In this claim we could read a Przywarian critique of the Heideggerian *Vorlaufen* as a sort of performative contradiction.

129. Przywara, *Analogia Entis*, 406.

130. See Brand, *Book of Causes*, prop. 6 (7); Aquinas, *Commentary on Book of Causes*, prop. 7.

131. "This implicit experience [the experience of the entirety of being as gift] can be had only by a being that is spirit in the kernel of its subjectivity, a being that carries out what Thomas Aquinas calls *reflexio completa*: the total taking possession of itself in the total transcending of itself to a 'Thou' that is recognized as the other who loves" (Balthasar, "Movement Toward God," 3:17).

the manifestation of an unsurpassable relationality that is the vertical foundation of all horizontal sociality.

8.2.2. What we have just explained has a further, crucial implication. The fact that the subsistence of the soul is metaphysically revealed as a *nothing* (the total negation of the essence "in" the abiding existence) prevents us from believing that the insuppressible relation in which we are constituted could be symmetrical. That our subsistence is revealed as nothing means that in our being everything is received and, compared to God, we are precisely *like* nothing.[132] In other words, the nothing at the core of our subsistence corresponds to our *radical and permanent contingency*. However, while our nothing is *evidenced precisely in the negation of death*, it is *in no way identifiable with the nonbeing of death*.[133] The suggestion to be explored is that the negation of death opens up for us, though dramatically and through radical suffering, the possibility of the joy of the *nihil* of *creatio ex nihilo*.[134]

To go back to the Neoplatonic notion, the *reditio completa* of our being is not the affirmation of oneself as one's origin, but rather the active savoring one's being given to oneself completely *out of nothing*; the fundamental experiential texture of our act of being, therefore, is not the "self-affirmation" of a *conatus essendi* that has in itself its origin and goal (Spinoza's *conatus*), but the prayerful "memory" of a radically transcendent origin that, while dwelling in our deepest roots, remains infinitely beyond our nothing (St. Augustine's *memoria*).

It is because of this constitutive and insuppressible relation to God that human death may even be considered a *factor of liberation*. Dying, explained through the metaphysics just proposed (i.e., the essence "in" the existence is preserved as totally negated, which intensively points to the "beyond" of the preservation of this essence in God) means not only that the dying person is nothing compared to God. It means also that no other creature and no other power can make a definitive claim on the (dying) person. Any other creature's power on me is, in the end,

---

132. See Aquinas, *Disputed Questions on Truth*, q. 2, a. 3, ad. 18; q. 2, a. 11, ad. 5.

133. "Creation is to be understood as the reception of a good not due in any way, so that there cannot be even a subject of that reception. It is absolute reception; there is not something which receives, but sheer receiving" (Schmitz, *Gift*, 32).

134. "The 'Is' indwelling us is therefore the utterly beyond us, just like nonbeing is utterly different from being; but our relation to the Is, however, is not that of a mere dialectic of being and nonbeing, but precisely that of an analogy that bears within itself the presence of nonbeing through which the presence of God indwelling his creature shines as infinite transcending the creature himself" (Przywara, *Analogia Entis*, 217–18).

nothing—is annihilated in the total negation of my essence. No matter how tightly any power holds me captive, such power is eventually denied its object in my death. (It is the case of Cato in Dante.)[135] The metaphysical structure described, then, reveals God's providential work in man even in the face of death: in the very fact of dying, man is liberated from any power that wants to make a definitive claim on him and is liberated to the "hope" (metaphysical, natural, rational "hope") that this "Beyond" in whom my essence is preserved and by whom my being-negated is still given may manifest his generosity once again, in ways that cannot be imagined apart from revelation.

In conclusion, the creaturely, analogical metaphysics of essence in-and-beyond existence, in conjunction with material kenosis, shows at least four things: first, that in dying, a totalizing stretching out to God essentially corresponds to the total negation without annihilation of our being. Second, that this corresponds in turn to an intensification in man of the sense of his exemplar cause that resides in God (man's "essence" realized as promise, as the imposing "not yet" of a disappearing "already"). Third, that the stretching out to God in our being totally negated reveals the insuppressibility of God's creative faithfulness to us and therefore the impossibility of an ultimate position of self-closure into annihilation on man's part. And fourth, that the stretching out to God and the intensification of the sense of the exemplar cause happen precisely in our becoming nothing—that is, never without embracing the material kenosis of death.

9. MATERIAL KENOSIS AND PRZYWARA'S ANALOGY OF BEING: THE RHYTHM OF POSSIBILITY AND ACTUALITY

9.1. According to the second version of the intra-creaturely analogy, the creature is a dynamic, growing synthesis ("oscillating rhythm" of "back-and-forth") of "possibility and actuality."[136] In order to understand the Przywarian interpretation of this piece of Aristotelian-Thomistic metaphysics, one must be aware that Przywara proposes a (controversial yet fully correct, in my view) reading of the Aristotelian notion of "essence" as a continuum of specific possibilities on the way to actualization.[137]

---

135. Dante, *Purgatorio*, canto 1.
136. Przywara, *Analogia Entis*, 208.
137. This does not mean that "possibility" has priority over "actuality"; on the

Material Kenosis

In its back-and-forth movement, the creature oscillates back to the essence-bound womb of undifferentiated possibilities from which its actual existence has taken its concrete shape, therefore delimiting the vast horizon of possibilities by "enacting" some of them into actuality.[138] But this movement would not be complete without the movement forward of the possibilities pushing forth toward their actualization in the direction of a total fulfillment (the entelechy as the "rest in motion" of the creature). This back-and-forth of the horizontal analogy of creaturely being powerfully accounts for the temporal ontological career of a creature, whose coming out of its essence-bound womb of possibilities through its various actualizations is, in the very same movement, its being called to its entelechy, to the fullness of its "is."

By bringing together the language of the first and the second version of the intra-creaturely analogy of being, one could say that the essence "in" existence coincides with this movement backwards, in which the enacted-actualized possibilities of the creature are seen on the backdrop of its essence-bound horizon of unactualized possibilities. And yet, as we have said, this backwards movement points beyond itself (Przywara calls it the "dynamic," "charged possibility" that "presses" beyond itself "towards actualization"), in the direction of a horizontal transcendence of yet-to-come enactments. The essence which lies "beyond" the existence of the creature is the horizontal transcendence of unactualized possibilities. Ultimately, however, this movement forward is not simply that of an entelechy specific to the creature, where the creature would finally "be" in fullness according to its nature, but is a movement toward that ultimate "Is" that transcends all limitations and possibilities, that *Ipsum Esse Subsistens* in whom creatures and their specific entelechies find their ultimate foundation: analogy as a "participatory being-related-above-and-beyond."[139]

Based on this framework complementary to the analogy of essence in-and-beyond existence, one can see that the "beyond" is that of a yet-to-be-achieved full creaturely actuality which is ultimately guaranteed

---

contrary, as Przywara clearly states (e.g., *Analogia Entis*, 208–9), actuality has priority over possibility, both in generation and in the being of the creature itself. In fact, in order to have an essence with its specific yet infinite array of possibilities on the way to actualization, some of these possibilities must be already enacted-actualized in the creature's actual existence (there is no "free-floating" essence that is not the essence *of* an existent).

138. Przywara, *Analogia Entis*, 209.
139. Przywara, *Analogia Entis*, 213.

only in its self-transcendence into the Pure Act of God, into the fullness of a union without confusion with the Origin of all being.[140] Just like the unbridgeable "gap" in the creature between essence and existence opens up to the vertical dimension of the analogy of being toward God, so here the same vertical dimension is indicated by the "gap" between possibility and actuality in finite being.[141]

9.2. One can test here once again the fruitfulness of Przywara's analogy of being in order to clarify more deeply the concept of material kenosis. Since material kenosis is the total negation without annihilation of the human being, in dying the total negation of the yet-to-come of possibilities coincides with the *total negation of the human essence* and therefore with the *total negation of the existing creature*. But since death is not annihilation, the negation of the horizon of possibilities is *not simply its removal*, together with the existent, but rather *its permanence in the existent as an impossibility*; it is the *impossibility of possibility*.[142] One can see here how Heidegger's definition of death as the "*possibility of the impossibility of existence in general*"[143] is lacking (due to its lack of metaphysics) and should in fact be reversed. Heidegger, in conceiving death as the possibility of the impossibility of Dasein, is still thinking of death within the horizon of Dasein's self-project. Thus, Heidegger, by privileging possibility over actuality, loses the genuine sense of death understood as negation of actuality (and thus, as impossibility of possibility). On the contrary, according to the Przywarian unpacking of material kenosis just proposed, the possibility is already present in its being negated—it is the *given* impossibility of the possibility.

---

140. Przywara, *Analogia Entis*, 217.

141. "Thus the sphere of creatureliness . . . 'has' (ontically) being and (noetically) truth (goodness, beauty) in such measure as it is related, beyond itself, to this latter, superordinated sphere. That is to say: analogy is established as a participatory being-related-above-and-beyond. . . . Here we have the notion that finds its classical formulation in Augustine: the principle of non-contradiction designates, both ontically and noetically, a 'ground' that 'trembles above the nothing,' and thus shows that those standing upon it are of themselves 'nothing,' rather than that they of themselves (ontically and noetically) 'are.' . . . This Aristotelian notion is further clarified, however, by Thomas Aquinas's profounder notion that the 'is (valid)' 'is (valid) in the Is (Truth, etc.)' (*dicuntur omnia esse in Deo, in quantum continentur ab ipso*) because, fundamentally, the 'is (valid)' signifies the 'being of the Is (Truth, etc.) in all things' (*Deus est in rebus sicut continens res*)" (Przywara, *Analogia Entis*, 212–14; emphasis in original).

142. This phrase is actually used by Levinas, *Totality and Infinity*, 235.

143. Heidegger, *Being and Time*, 251; emphasis in original.

And yet, that the soul is subsistent means that the horizon of possibility, while totally negated, is not utterly removed and annihilated. It is precisely this abiding, insuppressible possibility in us (i.e., the subsistent soul), in the midst of its very impossibility (i.e., the total negation of our being), that allows us to open ourselves to God as the One in whom such insuppressible possibility is kept alive, not in the midst of a creaturely impossibility (horizontal dimension), but in the fullness of the Pure Actuality from whom all possible created being originates (vertical dimension).

Thus, integrating this point with what was said in the previous section, one should conclude that this abiding possibility "in" us manifests its ultimate consistency only in the "beyond" of the Purely Actual. It is for these metaphysical reasons—an insuppressible possibility of life even in the most radical givenness of the impossibility of life—that it is deeply reasonable to entertain the thought of and desire for a fullness of life even when all hope seems lost and must in fact face the ultimate trial of the total negation without annihilation of death.

10. FROM THE POINT OF VIEW OF THE THEOLOGICAL ANALOGY OF BEING

10.1. It is at this point that the *reversal* that Przywara sees in the analogy of being becomes relevant for our inquiry. In fact, the creaturely analogy of being, "as a participatory being-related-above-and-beyond, has as its profounder premise as analogy of the self-imparting-relation-from-above of the divine identity of the Is."[144] In other words, understanding being analogously means seeing that created being's foundational aspiration to God reveals God's free gift of being as its more fundamental indwelling origin, and this gives to this analogy (the analogy between *God* and creatures, i.e., God's "self-impartation" "from-above" to the creatures) "objective priority" over the other dimension of the analogy (the analogy between *creatures* and God):[145] "Analogy is, at its highest point, analogy as a dynamic back-and-forth between the above-and-beyond (of a transcending immanence) and the from-above-into (of an indwelling transcendence)."[146]

---

144. Przywara, *Analogia Entis*, 214.
145. Przywara, *Analogia Entis*, 213–14.
146. Przywara, *Analogia Entis*, 216.

DEATH AS MATERIAL KENOSIS

If this essential reversal accounts for the fact that any creaturely metaphysics of the analogy of being, in its movement upwards, should place at the heart of any contemplation of being the original "movement downwards from above" of God's free act of creation, it also puts into correct perspective what occurs in material kenosis. In material kenosis, in fact, the movement upwards towards God as the ground of the abiding possibility that is totally negated "in" us must bear within itself the *more original* movement downwards of God from above, which is the fully gratuitous movement through which God can reinstate and fulfill such possibility into its final transfiguration into an ultimate perfect actualization. As the original gift of being in creation is received as grace, so too the insuppressible possibility abiding "in" us (as our being is fully negated without being annihilated) allows us to "hope against all hope" (death is a total negation) and yet not irrationally (it is not annihilation) in the gratuitous fore-giving and perfecting gift of being of a new creation. God remains, in both cases, the ultimate "measure from above"[147] of the gift of being, the horizon which has priority even in the unfolding of material kenosis, so that this movement from above (which is in no way guaranteed or necessitated, and yet corresponds to the deepest aspiration of human reason) remains the heart of our movement upwards.

This whole discussion belongs to what Przywara calls the "theological analogy of being," namely, the analogical understanding of being "from the point of view" of God's intervention into history. One could push the question of creation and material kenosis further by adopting precisely this vantage: How does material kenosis help us understand the analogy of being from the point of view of God's relation to creation—the theological analogy of being? Still in other terms: What has our meditation on the metaphysics of human death revealed regarding the connection between God and a fallen creation?

I have already addressed these questions in part in the previous section. As I have explained, by reflecting on the implications of material kenosis we get a better grasp of the sense in which we say that death has reduced the ties between creation and God to *nothing*. Such a "nothing" is neither the absolute absence of relation that Barth envisions; nor is it merely the "nothing" of the creature in its mere creatureliness vis-à-vis God. And yet, as material kenosis tries to show, it is a genuine nothing. Przywara's account of the analogy of being seems sometimes, at least in

---

147. Przywara, *Analogia Entis*, 209.

its most frequent formulations, to stop here, at the level of creatureliness. On the contrary, the *concrete analogy of being* must take into account the effective condition of the human being in his "nothing," which cannot be understood without the negation of death. Such "nothing" is the nonbeing of the totally negated but not annihilated existence, or act of being, of the human person. It is the nonbeing of the negation of being by embracing which we are assimilated to the *nihil* of *creatio ex nihilo* and out of which we are created and re-created and deified by God's grace in Christ.[148]

Hence, any treatment of the actual span or "arch" of the metaphysical analogy of being in its concreteness must take this meaning of the "nothing" of man into account. It must also take into account the fact that God in his unconditional love has always already welcomed within himself precisely that ultimate negation introduced by man's free act of rebellion (that which is conceivably the most foreign and contrary to himself and being, the *id quo minus cogitari nequit*), a love which has reached its fulfilling realization in Christ's cross, death, and descent into hell. This is the sense, I think, of Przywara's claim that the heart of the theological analogy of being is a "blessed contradiction": "The original analogy between *imago Dei* and the *consortium Dei* appears 'restored' in the 'blessed contradiction' of a '*consortium Dei a Deo derelicti*,' i.e., of an impartation of a participation in God as (so to speak) not-God."[149]

By assuming the human nature in Christ through the yes of Mary, God has emptied himself in the sense that his divinity, the fullness of being, has been hypostatically united, without confusion, to the "nothing" of the human being, so that by embracing and bearing the negation of human death he could "destroy" it. But how do we make sense, in metaphysical terms, of our *experience* of the "victory" of Christ over death? According to the metaphysics that I have proposed, we experience Christ's victory over death in perceiving that by fully surrendering to the

---

148. "Thus, logically, the practical Christian life is the living out of this descent.... And therefore it is a life that is fulfilled in the knowledge of one's own nothingness. Just as the entire greatness of God appears in the "nothingness" of Christ (Phil. 2:7ff), and just as the full holiness of God appears in Christ as the 'lamb . . . bearing the sins of the world,' the proper Christian face of 'deification' and 'spiritualization' is seen in the opposition between the nothingness of the human being and the All of God, between the sin of man and the mercy of God: 'such is . . . the greatest knowledge, that man should know that he is *per se* nothing; and, whatever he is, he is of God and on account of God'" (Przywara, *Analogia Entis*, 368).

149. Przywara, *Analogia Entis*, 568.

negation of death we are assimilated once again to the *nihil* of *creatio ex nihilo*. This experience is a movement of resurfacing, if one can speak this way, from the less-than-nonbeing of the total negation without annihilation of death to the *nihil* of *creatio ex nihilo*, into which the fore-giving re-creation of the grace of Christ is poured as the superabundant gift of new being-life stemming from the cross.

Thus, following Przywara, we should say that our *imago Dei* is "restored," but only in a new "form," which is the form of Christ on the cross, the *Christus deformis* who has willingly become slave, sin, and curse. The human being is redeemed not "through Christ" but "into" him, as a "member" of Christ and therefore "into being 'crucified with Christ.'"[150] Przywara states that the "complete form of the *imago Dei*" is the following: "The human being as the 'image of God,' inasmuch as he is the '*ad imaginem*,' the likeness to the *one* 'image of God in Christ in Mary,' as to an 'image of glory in deformity and lowliness.' The *imago Dei*, in the full sense of this term, is the human being in the symbol of the 'crucified' and the 'mother of seven sorrows.'"[151] In line with his suggestion, one could sketch out the formula more concretely by introducing the acquisition resulting from our treatment of material kenosis. Accordingly, the entire span of the concrete analogy of being goes from "nonbeing" to God, that is, from "nonbeing" (the negation of material kenosis in the nonbeing of the creature) to God in Christ (who assumed the nonbeing of material kenosis in the nonbeing of the creature) in Mary.

Establishing what kind of negation the negation of death is—material kenosis, understood as a radical negation without annihilation of man's being—still does not say anything about the "role" or "place" of such negation in life. Death seems to be certainly inescapable. But is it constitutive of the human condition? Is it definitive? Or even ultimate? What becomes of death when many thinkers start understanding it as original to the human condition and even synonymous with man's finitude? Unpacking and addressing such questions is the goal of chapter 3.

---

150. Przywara, *Analogia Entis*, 567.
151. Przywara, *Analogia Entis*, 569.

CHAPTER THREE

The Analogy of Being and the Nonbeing of Death

> Evil... has greater nonexistence and otherness from the Good than nonbeing has.
>
> PSEUDO-DIONYSIUS, *COMPLETE WORKS*, 2.19

> The divorce between man and reality is preceded by a scission internal to man's unity. It is through the wound of this scission that the soul, principle of life, power of relation, origin of the communion among the components of the human being and among the human being and the world, escapes bit by bit. It is for this reason that the majority of the human beings die before having lived, and the earth is populated more by ghosts than by the living. Modern philosophy's banishment of the concept of the soul, which has not become the prerogative of preachers, is explained in light of an obscure resentment against the impotence to live, balanced out by the mechanisms of intelligence that go around in circles, and in light of the frenzy of action.
>
> MARCEL DE CORTE, *FENOMENOLOGIA DELL'AUTODISTRUTTORE*, 40

The irreducible character of suffering which makes it impossible for us not to have a horror of it at the moment when we are undergoing it is destined to bring the will to a standstill, just as absurdity brings the intelligence to a standstill, and absence of love, so that man, having come to the end of his human faculties, may stretch out his arms, stop, look up and wait.

SIMONE WEIL, *GRAVITY AND GRACE*, 112

1. INTRODUCTION

1.1. THE PRESENT CHAPTER addresses many different issues linked by a common theme, that is, *the need to avoid turning the negativity of death into something positive*, either metaphysically (i.e., death is originally and dialectically tied to life), theologically (i.e., a certain analogous, non-metaphorical meaning of "death" is an essential trait of the very Life of God), or experientially (i.e., "death" is a personal act epitomizing human freedom).[1] As we have seen in the previous chapter, the entire span of positivity, of being, is faithfully described by the *metaphysical notion of analogy*. We must try to see now that the negativity of death has no place and plays no role at all in being analogically understood—no matter how willing we are to stretch the notion of metaphysical analogy. Death is *unanalogizable*.

Something similar should be said about the understanding of being as *gift* and *self-gift*. It is my conviction, in fact, that being as gift does not carry *originally* within itself any trace of the negativity of death. "Being" understood as gift to the other is not, in fact, self-negation, but rather self-affirmation, precisely in the sense of the self-affirmation of a gift, which cannot be but self-giving to the other.[2] The "self-negation" that Catholic metaphysics sometimes tends to read into the original notion of the gift is self-negation only in a metaphorical sense and thus has nothing to do with the literal form of negation of being which is the essence

---

1. See Cunningham, *Genealogy of Nihilism*, for a philosophical and theological study of the "logic of nihilism" ("a sundering of the something, rendering it nothing, and then having the nothing be after all as something" [xiii]).

2. Rémi Brague comes close to this point when he reflects on the fact that, for man, the apprehension of his being-life as transcendentally good (that which is explicitly denied, in his interpretation, by Nietzsche's nihilism) means not only "love of living" (i.e., an egotistical form of self-affirmation, thus a perverted form of love, a mere *desire of living*) but "love of life" (i.e., the affirmation of life's goodness in the form of an aspiration to share and communicate such goodness, a *desire of giving* life). See his *Anchors in the Heavens*, ch. 6.

of death.³ While gift is the affirmation of being's profound nature, death is its radical negation. Thus, metaphysically speaking, it is impossible to turn the negativity of death into something positive.

1.2.1. Preserving the analogy of being from any original involvement with the negativity of death is even more important given that there exists in the so-called continental philosophical tradition a tendency to turn death into something positive and constitutive of being in general and of the human condition in particular. In its different versions, death, for some of the philosophers in this tradition, becomes an essential and positive metaphysical condition for being to be what it is, and for others the necessary horizon of meaning within which Dasein can constitute itself as such. In both cases, the common trait of these positions is having turned the negation of death into something positive and, consequently, having lost the negativity of death in its specificity.

This tendency present in continental philosophy may be only one specific reflection of a much broader tendency that Romano Guardini finds at work "everywhere" in European modern culture: "It is present everywhere the idea of gnostic origin that contradictions are polarities: Goethe, Gide, C. G. Jung, Th. Mann, H. Hesse.... They all take evil, the negative... to be dialectical elements in the totality of life and nature."⁴ For Guardini, such an attitude "is manifested in all that can be called gnosis, in alchemy, in theosophy. It is found in a programmatic form in Goethe, for whom the satanic even enters God, evil is the original force of the universe, as necessary as the good, and death is just another element of this totality, whose opposite pole is called life."⁵

---

3. There remains nevertheless a certain ambiguity in Thomas's most interesting comments on the nature of love as ecstasy implying the lover's "division" with himself: "But because nothing can be transformed into another without withdrawing, in a way ("quodammodo"), from its own form, since of a single thing there is a single form, therefore preceding this division of penetration [of the lover into the beloved] is another division by which the lover, in tending toward the beloved, is separated from himself.... Further still, because nothing withdraws from itself unless it is unbound from what was containing it within itself, as a natural thing does not lose its form unless the dispositions retaining this form in the matter are unbound, it is therefore necessary that that boundedness by which the lover was contained within his own bounds be taken away from him" (Aquinas, *Sentences Commentary*, sent. 3, d. 27, q. 1, a. 1, ad. 4). Thomas perpetrates here the same ambiguity that is already present in Augustine: "*As strong as death is love. And since charity itself destroys what we were, so that we may become what we were not, love makes in us a kind of [quamdam] death*" (Augustine, *Enarrat. Ps.* 121.12 [author's translation]).

4. Guardini, *Diario*, 245.

5. Guardini, *Lettere teologiche*, 63.

1.2. The theological discourse is in one sense simpler and in another sense much more complex and scandalous than the philosophical discourse. Given the nature of the present study, I will refrain from a proper theological discussion. Nevertheless, I should make few remarks here in order to provide some further context to the argument developed in this chapter.

The Catholic discourse on death and negativity is "simple" insofar as Catholics believe that "death has been swallowed up in victory" (1 Cor 15:54–55). St. Paul continues in triumphant terms: "Where, O death, is your victory? Where, O death, is your sting?" The history of the church itself is full of saints, old and recent, who have died in the peace of the Lord and who have endured even the most cruel and painful deaths in the hope of the Risen Christ. For our purposes, suffice it here to remember that St. Francis of Assisi goes as far as calling "bodily death" "our sister."[6] It seems impossible to deny that Christ has transformed from within the meaning of death.

At the same time, however, the Catholic experience of death remains more ambiguous and paradoxical. Has all the drama and sense of contradiction of death been eliminated by Christ? It does not seem to be so. Jesus at various points weeps because of human death (e.g., John 11:35). Moreover, as Hans Urs von Balthasar has stressed, Jesus experiences on the cross the condition of utter forsakenness of death.[7] Furthermore the Second Vatican Council has repeated that death remains a contradiction: "It is in the face of death that the riddle of human existence grows most acute. Not only is man tormented by pain and by the advancing deterioration of his body, but even more so by a dread of perpetual extinction.

---

6. Francis of Assisi, "Canticle of the Sun," esp. the lines "Praise be You, my Lord,/ Through our Sister Bodily Death."

7. See Balthasar: "If Jesus has suffered on the Cross the sin of the world to the very last truth of this sin-godforsakenness—then he must experience, in solidarity with the sinners who have gone to the underworld, their—ultimately hopeless—separation from God, otherwise he would not have known all the phases and conditions of what it means for man to be unredeemed yet awaiting redemption" ("Descent into Hell," 4:408). See also Jacques Servais's commentary: "In an extreme position justified by nine of the scriptural witnesses, Luther went so far as to declare Christ 'damned.' Careful not to cross such a line himself, von Balthasar nevertheless tries to transcend the extrinsicism of the traditional Thomist solution, in which the offense and reparation for the offense remain exterior to each other ... demanding that [Christ] freely assume the inner condition of the sinner. In order to join the latter in his own freedom, the undertaking in his favor must in fact take place, according to [Balthasar], there in the very place where the refusal and curse took place" ("Postscript," in Balthasar and Speyr, *To the Heart of Mystery*, 100–101).

He rightly follows the intuition of his heart when he abhors and repudiates the utter ruin and total disappearance of his own person."[8] It seems fair to say then that the Christian experience of death, no matter how hopeful, does not get rid of death's dramatic element of negativity, of *death's meaninglessness*. How do we account for Christ's transformation of death without avoiding the abiding negativity present in it?

It seems to me that in order to answer this difficult question honestly we must have the courage to hold on to the permanent and essential element of negativity present in death. Put differently, one must have the courage not to close the gap between being and nonbeing, between love and its negation. In other words, when contemplating death, faithfulness to being, which is the greatest aspiration of the metaphysician, means precisely the intellectual courage to leave the gap between being and nonbeing open, to acknowledge that the gap is unbridgeable. Against any temptation to read something positive into the negation of death, *metaphysics must guard the unbridgeable gap between being and nonbeing*. In so doing, it seems to me that metaphysics pays its due service to theology.

The person who believes in Christ approaches death knowing that the negation of death, no matter how radical and totalizing, is not the last word on existence. He approaches death so not only, and not primarily, because he knows that his soul is immaterial and thus indestructible, but because he knows that Christ himself, true man and true God, has experienced the scandal, the anguish, the contradiction, the meaninglessness, and the forsakenness of death before him and that Christ therefore is "there" when it is his turn to experience the same scandal. The task of metaphysics is to *unveil this scandal for what it is*, thus resisting the temptation of behaving as a wannabe theology. The light of the resurrection is so bright because the negation of death is so dark. The knowledge of

---

8. Paul VI, *Gaudium et Spes* §18. See also Rahner: "Death is absolutely universal in human life. Everyone accepts it as natural and obvious that he must die. At the same time, a secret protest and an inextinguishable horror before this end abides in every man. A metaphysical anthropology cannot explain this fact. If one is convinced that man as a spiritual being is immortal, it is impossible for him to understand why he should be so afraid to die. The only escape from this dilemma would seem to be to degrade this anxiety before death to a mere expression of the purely vital, bodily urge of self-preservation. This would, however, be no real answer; it would simply conceal and disguise the problem. Dogma and theology enter at this point. Man is, rightly, afraid of death. Actually, he should not die, for he still possesses within himself, if not the reality, then the due demand, at least, for that vitality of divine life, which if it could assert itself, pure and unveiled, in this earthly life would completely eliminate death" (*Theology of Death*, 61–63; see also 78–80).

the indestructibility of the soul only exacerbates the scandal of death. In short, death has been won and overcome by Christ, but not removed or turned into something positive. It would be a mistake to think that death's negativity has been removed by Christ.

1.2.1. The metaphysics of the *hypostatic union* may be relevant at this juncture.[9] As we know, the perfect union between the divine and human natures in the one person of Christ does not amount to a confusion between the two natures, nor does it deny their abiding distinction. I think that something similar could and should be said about the way in which human death is assumed in Christ. In being assumed and redeemed, human death is not for this reason brought into a confusion with being; it remains the negation of being that it is; it does not stop being forever distinct in its essence from being, life, and love. Nevertheless, in virtue of being freely taken on and suffered by God in Christ, it is, as the apostle says, "swallowed up"—"for by His death He freed man from death."[10]

That human death is assumed and thus redeemed means that human death is united to the person of Christ in the hypostatic union of the divine and human natures. In this sense, human death is transformed from within and human beings know by faith that after Christ not even the experience of God's forsakenness in death is a good reason to curse God and life. We are, in this sense, free from death. Nevertheless, the God who became company to us in Christ "to the point of death, even death on the cross," does not remove the negativity of death. Death remains a total negation of human life, a dramatic narrow path through which each man has to go.[11] One could invoke St. Augustine's authority here: "It is not that death has turned into a good thing, when it was formerly an

---

9. "Salvation clearly implies for Balthasar that God must, via the Hypostatic Union, identify himself, in Christ's human soul, with the very evil and Godforsakenness he is seeking to redeem the human race from" (Oakes, "Internal Logic of Holy Saturday, 193).

10. Paul VI, *Gaudium et Spes* §18.

11. Guardini already explains how the theological discussion of the simplicity of God's nature and the multiplicity of his attributes is instructive in order to understand how the judgments about God allow for the simultaneous affirmation of the simplicity of God and the qualitative irreducibility of the different attributes found in him (*Opposizione polare*, 84). One may say that this approach explodes in considering the metaphysics of the hypostatic union. For instance, John Paul II makes explicit use of this principle when he states: "The simultaneous presence of these two seemingly irreconcilable aspects is rooted in the fathomless depths of the hypostatic union" (*Novo Millennio Ineunte* §26).

evil. What has happened is that God has granted to faith so great a gift of grace that death, which all agree to be the contrary of life, has become the means by which men pass into life."[12]

1.2.3. It is not hard to spot a certain tendency to treat the negativity of death as something positive among deep and influential Catholic thinkers. Just to give a few examples, I would say that in the following cases "death" is turned into something positive, into a positive condition for being to be what it is.[13] Cyril O'Regan speaks of death as the putting of the self "out" in order to make room for God and others in oneself.[14] Caitlin Smith Gilson speaks of the lover's total self-abnegation to the beloved as "death," as well as of "death" as the "distance" or the "letting go" necessarily present within any loving relation to the world.[15] The examples could be multiplied. However, all these examples name something essential to the positivity of being understood as love-gift. Consequently, if death is taken as negativity, none of these examples actually imply a genuine form of death.

For instance, giving oneself in love does not imply necessarily negating oneself. It is, on the contrary, the free and active overflow of one's being-love and it is, in this sense, the most profound affirmation of who one is. On the contrary, all those human practices that express an attitude of proud and selfish "self-affirmation" are actually, when metaphysically filtered, forms of self-negation, as Boethius has taught us once and for all.[16]

Considering O'Regan's example, one should say that the claim that "prayer is letting God in and the self out" is misleading if taken literally (as certainly O'Regan knows), even more so if read in the Augustinian context of O'Regan's discussion. In fact, the only way to "let God in" is, to follow O'Regan's spatial metaphor, to make the self "stay in." God indwells being. In fact, St. Augustine fights against the "dispersion" of the self into the many pleasures and immoral practices of the world and calls for the return of the self into itself (his famous *redire in seimpsum*) as a way to find God, who dwells in there. So, the true affirmation of the self (against the "false" self-affirmation in the dispersion of the world, which is actually

---

12. Augustine, *City of God* 13.4.

13. I am suggesting of course that the word "death" is used by the authors that I am going to mention literally and not simply metaphorically.

14. O'Regan, "Changing the Subject to Christ."

15. Smith Gilson, "Heaven and Transcendental Meaning."

16. Boethius, *Consolation of Philosophy*, 75–76.

a self-negation) is the privileged way to also "let God in" and thus affirm him.

The lesson to be learned from these brief remarks, I think, is that the metaphorical use of death, which is not only legitimate, but also instructive at so many levels, becomes harmful when illegitimately turned into a literal metaphysical truth. However, one may still wonder whether the appeal to the metaphorical use of language is sufficient to account for the infinite distance between being-life-love and death. Shouldn't we admit a more radical equivocity? How should we interpret G. K. Chesterton's words, that "All creation is separation" and that "Birth is as solemn a parting as death"[17]? Doesn't this kind of talk run the risk of assimilating, albeit analogically, the negativity of death to the positivity of creation and being?

1.2.3.1. I would like to dwell on this difficulty a little longer and exemplify the idea that Catholic thinkers run sometimes the risk of turning death into something positive with another example drawn from Adrienne von Speyr's profound meditation on death. In many ways, Speyr's treatment of the problem of death is illuminating. As she explains, death is the consequence of and punishment for sin as well as God's way to shake man from his postlapsarian indifference, so that he may be brought back to him ("tribulation, suffering and death . . . are there to replace man's attempts at avoidance").[18] In death, man comes to realize that the world he builds almost inevitably self-referentially is vanity. In facing death, man experiences that God's Higher Judgment displaces and relativizes man's judgment. This self-referential world falls apart when in death man discovers his helplessness (the experience of being crumbled and crashed "signifies the death of everything that is man's own possession, and above all of his own judgment. It is man's confrontation with a greater judgment").[19] In death, fallen man is reintroduced, albeit through the negativity of death, to that eternity for which he is made (death as "unknown eternity operating from within transitory time").[20]

The center of her discussion is the death of Christ, because by being incorporated into his death the "bitterness" of death becomes for us "blessedness." Her meditation on this point is particularly illuminating as she states that Christ's victory over death does not mean that the faithful

17. Chesterton, *Orthodoxy*, 48.
18. Speyr, *Mystery of Death*, 27.
19. Speyr, *Mystery of Death*, 32.
20. Speyr, *Mystery of Death*, 53.

is spared the negativity of death: "The bitter side is not simply identical with the blissful side; the two are not confused. There remain two ways of looking at this, corresponding to two experiences which every human being has to undergo in some way or another."[21]

Speyr's profound view of death can hardly be summed up in these few remarks, especially because her treatment is eminently theological. Nevertheless, one of her fundamental philosophical and metaphysical tenets seems to me, once again, a mistake which ends up turning death into something positive. One can see this especially in her metaphysical account of the "now" of human life understood as a "critical moment," the moment of man's dramatic self-decision vis-à-vis God. It seems that the *dramatic dimension of the now*, the now as intrinsically dramatic, has according to Speyr its condition of possibility, precisely, in death, which she understands here as the fact that man's life comes to a temporal end. As she says, death "gives birth to the moment." She writes:

> Once the first sin has taken place, death becomes an inner necessity. If God had not instituted death, man could have imagined that, each time he offended God, he could subsequently make it good, supply what he had failed to do, obliterate his turning away from God by turning toward him. . . . In other words, he would have imagined that he was basically able to redeem himself. But by death and the finite time which leads up to it, God has shown man that his turning away is far more serious than he had thought, so grave that of himself he cannot make it good. . . . The destruction of the relationship of repose between God and man gives birth to the *moment*, that is, the uniqueness of a "now" within a time that is running out. . . . Previously there was no irretrievable "now" cutting into temporal duration. There were changes in this duration, but they were full of the promise of future and recurrence. . . . Now [because

---

21. Speyr, *Mystery of Death*, 58. See in particular what she says on the death of the saints: "Whatever the death of the individual saint may look like, it must serve to interpret the Lord's death. The mystery of loneliness, forsakenness and rejection in the Lord's death is so fruitful that God cannot do otherwise than allow his saints to taste something of it. . . . And now the saint is about to die as a man. . . . In the process of dying, he may experience fear and pain to such an extent that the Yes of his consent may be inaudible, and he may cease to understand. But that is not essential, for supernature has so enveloped his nature that God does not cease to hear the response of his Yes to his mission (which is equivalent to his holiness). He is completely taken up to God's plane, even in cases where a human observer, and perhaps the saint himself, can no longer discern anything of the divine." It is hard not to think here of Bernanos, "Dialogues of the Carmelites."

of death and the ensuing finitude of time] there is a "here and now" in complete uniqueness.[22]

What is at stake here is not the validity of her theological approach to death—death has been allowed by God so that man could be prevented from believing he could save himself, etc.—but the philosophical and metaphysical value that is given to death, which is, moreover, unnecessary to her broader and more urgent theological point. Contrary to what Speyr suggests, it seems to me that the "now" and the "moment" are dramatic not because of death but rather because they are entrusted to a human freedom which is aware of the fact that time is relative to and embraced by the eternity of God. So, let us consider the arguments implicit in Speyr's passage, which can also be found in other thinkers, especially Christian existentialists.

The arguments are essentially two. First, without the finitude of time, each action would not have the dramatic definitiveness that it has; it would just be an irrelevant drop lost in an infinite ocean of possibilities. Thus, the "now" and the "moment" would not be the place in which the person decides dramatically of his definitive destiny. Second, supposing the availability of an indefinitely prolonged time, the result would be the realization of all possibilities, including their repetition. As a consequence, human choices would be devoid of that dramatic uniqueness that they otherwise have given a finite time.

The first argument seems to stress more the character of definitiveness of the choice-now, made possible by death (as opposed to the lack of definitiveness in the case of an indefinitely prolonged time), while the second argument stresses more the character of uniqueness of the now and its choice (as opposed to the lack of uniqueness in the case of an indefinitely prolonged time, for the reason that an indefinitely prolonged time would seem to imply necessarily the recurrence of events). Simply

---

22. Speyr, *Mystery of Death*, 9–10; emphasis in original. I would note here, in passing, that Max Scheler has an interesting insight contrary to Speyr. For him, in fact, it is the "universal and normal" phenomenon of "removal" or "undoing" of death which allows us to take our endeavors "seriously" and to give "importance" to them: "Only a general undoing of the evident idea of death by the vital instinct makes the phenomenon that I would call 'metaphysical lightness' possible: that state of mysterious calm and 'joy' in the face of the weight and the evidence of the thought of death. . . . A being who had in front of him constantly the evidence of that same death of which he nevertheless has experience intimately would live and behave in a very different way from the normal man" (*Morte e sopravvivenza*, 59).

put, each moment truly "counts" if and only if one does not have an infinite number of such moments at his disposal.

To the first argument, one can say that the "now" and the "moment," in order to be dramatic and definitive, do not require per se the *demise of time*; rather, they simply require that the temporal order of history is *not absolutized* or, which is the same, that time is lived in the light of the eternal. For a historical being who lives his free choices in history with the consciousness of the eternal—as certainly man did in his prelapsarian condition, as Speyr stresses—each action is dramatically definitive even assuming an indefinitely prolonged time, because *factum infectum fieri nequit*. Not only what one has done remains in one's memory and determines one's personal makeup, but that very action is eternally inscribed in the eternity of God. In the absence of death, understood here as the end of one's time, the "now" and the "moment" could be devoid of their dramatic definitiveness only under the condition that either history was explicitly absolutized or that eternity was implicitly forgotten. Human life and its "moments" are dramatic and definitive not because they are imbued with the limit of death, but because they are open to and they are lived in the light of the eternity of God.

The same point could be put differently. Any "now" in history is essentially a decision for or against the good. Any decision against the good is the irrevocable loss of a *unique opportunity to do the good* and for that particular good to shape history in a unique way. If that opportunity is missed, that opportunity is lost forever and the evil perpetrated is eternal in God's eternal knowledge of the temporal. The fact that an indefinitely prolonged time still lies ahead would not change the fact that a unique opportunity to do the good has been lost *forever*. Only superficiality and forgetfulness would turn the dramatic dimension which is essential to history into a non-drama, a non-risky business. Consequently, the now and the moment would have been dramatic and definitive also for the man in that "primal state" in which "time was always fresh, never to run out." Death does not institute the dramatic dimension of the moment. On the contrary, it narrows down what would otherwise be an indefinitely prolonged drama.[23]

---

23. Note that what I am saying here does not imply that without sin man's temporal existence would have been indefinitely prolonged. Man's temporal life was destined to be mysteriously fulfilled and confirmed into eternity: consummation without negation or destruction.

With respect to the second argument, one could say that the view that death is required for the now and its choice to be truly unique and unrepeatable presupposes the idea that an indefinitely prolonged time would necessarily imply recurrence. In turn, the idea of a necessary recurrence of events given an indefinitely prolonged time presupposes an undue isomorphism between first act and second act. Contrary to this latter assumption, an indefinitely prolonged time and the series of ("second") acts which could populate it are only a potential infinite, while the first act of a being is, in a certain sense, an actual infinite. The first act of a being is a participated actual infinite because it is the continuous origin of all the discrete second acts that do flow and could flow from it. Given the non-isomorphism between first act and second acts, even an infinite time and the infinite series of discrete second acts that would populate it would never exhaust the possibilities virtually present in an infinite continuum, nor would repetition be necessary, because a potential infinite (an indefinite series of second acts unfolded over an indefinitely prolonged time) could never equate an actual infinite (the continuous infinite of a first act).

1.3. Jacques Lacan has denounced that the religious discourse in general, and the Christian discourse in particular, suffer from the vice of wanting to turn everything into "meaning." In his view, only psychoanalysis would be left to give us the courage to face the negativity present in life without mystifying it or taming it.[24] Others, for instance, Hans-

---

24. "And they [Christians] know quite a bit about meaning. They can give meaning to absolutely anything whatsoever. A meaning to human life, for example. They are trained to do that. . . . Psychoanalysis is a symptom. But we have to understand what it is a symptom of. It is clearly part of the discontents of civilization Freud spoke about. What is most likely is that people won't confine themselves to perceiving that the symptom is what is most real. People are going to secrete as much meaning as anyone could possibly wish for, and that will nourish not only the true religion but a pile of vile ones. . . . There is *one* true religion and that is the Christian religion. The question is simply whether this truth will stand up—namely, if will be able to secrete meaning to such an extent that we will truly drown in it. . . . It will find correspondences between everything and everything else. That's its very function" (Lacan, *Triumph of Religion*, 64–66). In the same spirit, Edgar Morin calls the association of joy and death in Christianity a "frenzy of death" (*Uomo e la morte*, 208). As it is in the case of Lacan, also with respect to Morin, one should take his observation *cum grano salis*. In fact, what he says should be taken as a widespread misinterpretation of the Christian mystery and not as a genuine insight. For instance, when, following Marx, Morin interprets religion in general and Christianity in particular as the "effort to make the pathological situation of the mortal individual normal" (317–18), his reading could not be further from the truth. The contemporary source of Lacan's and Morin's line of reasoning is found in Nietzsche, *On the Genealogy of morality*: "Man, the bravest animal and the one most

Georg Gadamer, have voiced similar concerns.[25] In the terms that I have adopted here, the religious Catholic discourse would suffer, according to Lacan, from the vice of not having the courage to keep the gap between being and nonbeing open, of turning death into being and meaning. While Lacan's critique is certainly untrue if taken as a universal claim about Catholic doctrine, theology, and philosophy, it is nevertheless true that Catholic thinkers and believers run the risk of overlooking the negativity of death, thus removing the dramatic dimension of mortality from human experience. What follows in this chapter is an attempt to take Lacan's challenge at face value and to face the negativity of death for what it truly is, that is, for what it is not.

1.4. A helpful way to frame my proposal in this chapter is to state that, according to the Catholic view which I am trying to probe philosophically, death is *definitive* negativity for the human condition without being either *original*, or *constitutive*, or even *ultimate*.

Virtually all the possible positions that one can take on the role that death plays in human life boil down to a certain decision with respect to these four features. For instance, from a religious and metaphysical point of view, death could be considered *original*—this is the case of Hegel, Kojève, and some of their descendants, such as Simmel, Jonas, Tillich, and Jankélévitch, as I will show in section 3 of this chapter. Similarly, from a phenomenological point of view, death could be considered as *constitutive* of the human condition, as it is for Heidegger, Sartre, Gadamer, and Vattimo, although these authors vary greatly in the details of their doctrines.[26] From the point of view of a historically-informed metaphysics—and a Catholic metaphysics must be so informed—death ought to be considered *definitive* for the human condition. However, despite

---

accustomed to suffering, does *not* negate suffering in itself: he *wants* it, he even seeks it out, provided one shows him a *meaning* for it, a *to-this-end* of suffering. The meaninglessness of suffering, not the suffering itself, was the curse that thus far lay stretched out over humanity—*and the ascetic ideal offered it a meaning!*" (117, emphasis in original).

25. "And lo and behold we have the Christian idea of paradise or of heaven, which is the heaven of the seeing again. Are all these eventually ways of not wanting to think non-being? . . . Now we ask: how did philosophy receive this promise of overcoming death that is contained in Christian teaching, and how did it understand this transformation of death into life? Should we not say the following: any attempt that philosophical thought makes to think the transformation of death into life does not really think death?" (Gadamer, "Death as a Question," 1:61, 64).

26. I limit myself here to the tradition marked by the explicit reference to Heidegger's thought on death, for the simple reason that it is this tradition that has become synonymous with the continental engagement with death.

being one of the "last things," death is not *ultimate* for Catholics, insofar as through his cross and resurrection Christ has won death. As we shall see in the following chapter, one could say that for transhumanism death becomes ultimate precisely because it is not taken as definitive.

1.5. The structure of this chapter is the following. After providing the sketch for a metaphysical interpretation of the fall by showing in what way death should be considered as the meontic wound in man's constitution resulting from man's rejection of the gift of being (sec. 2), I take into consideration certain contemporary philosophical and theological approaches which seem to grant death a more positive role than necessary. Thus, I provide a critical assessment of the positions of Georg Simmel, Hans Jonas, Paul Tillich, and Vladimir Jankélévitch, showing that their different views share a common principle, i.e., the ontologization of death, and that such principle is the consequence of their neglect of the original meaning of the notion of creation (sec. 3). Then I provide some provisory notes for a critical assessment of Ferdinand Ulrich's kenotic metaphysics of *esse commune* and Hans Urs von Balthasar kenotic Trinitarian theology (sec. 4). The engagement with the analogical positivity granted to death is further developed through a critical analysis of the ways in which death is understood as "the personal act" par excellence in human life (sec. 5). I conclude the chapter by providing a unitary reading of the Heideggerian tradition on death (with special reference, besides Heidegger, to Hans-Georg Gadamer, Jean-Paul Sartre, Gianni Vattimo, and other late Heideggerians), and I put forth the conclusion that this tradition, which begins its course by taking death as a transcendental condition of possibility of human existence, must end up undermining itself and thus reducing death to an ontic problem (sec. 6).

2. DEATH AS THE REJECTION OF THE GIFT OF BEING: AN ATTEMPT AT A METAPHYSICAL INTERPRETATION OF THE FALL

2.1. Scripture teaches that death as we know it—that is, in my language, death as negation—entered the world through man's sin: "Through one person sin entered the world, and through sin, death" (Rom 5:12). That the origin of death may be traced back to a free and radical self-determination of man against God and against himself is certainly mysterious, although some have convincingly suggested that human beings can experience the intrinsic correlation, the overlapping eidetic, of moral and physical evil.[27] What I aim to do in this section is attempt to delineate the outline for a metaphysical interpretation of the fall as the "cause" of death. In doing so, I have found most helpful to adopt and develop independently the two notions of "having" and "being" which Gabriel Marcel has introduced in his existential diary.[28] More specifically, I have found that the Thomistic interpretation of being as gift, exemplified in the work of authors such as Ferdinand Ulrich, Kenneth L. Schmitz, Antonio López, and David C. Schindler,[29] and Marcel's analysis of the logic of having vis-à-vis the logic of being, provide conjointly a sufficient framework for trying to see more clearly what the negation of death might be and how it became part of our condition. The goal of this discussion is to further wrestle with the question concerning the true nature of death's negation, a question which has been at the center of this study since chapter 1. This time, the overall concern is to show that there is no analogical original commonality between the negation of death and the positivity of being because death is the *meontic wound corresponding to man's rejection of the gift of being*.

2.2. As the metaphysicians of being as gift explain, the act of being is, at one and the same time, the total gift of God and the fundamental act of the substance. This paradoxical union of "receiving" and "doing" the gift of being explains that God donates being *ex nihilo* (nothing is presupposed to God's creative act) and, at the same time, that participated being subsists in the creature, is the creature's being and not God's. God "gives" being, that is, he gives it away, and in so doing he makes the substance be the "subject" of its own act of being. It remains of course true that the creature would be nothing without God's creative act. And yet, the creature unequivocally *is*. According to this account of creation, *agere sequitur esse*, but *esse* is itself a kind of fundamental *agere*: the substance's fundamental enactment of the act of being. Thus, the primacy of *esse* does not conflict with the idea that, in a sense, there is nothing more fundamental than the substance's *agere*.

---

27. See, e.g., Pieper: it is part of our experience that there is a connection between sin and death because there are "misdeeds after which one no longer wished to go on living" (*Death and Immortality*, 58–59). See also his *Concept of Sin*.

28. Marcel, *Being and Having*, esp. "Outlines of a Phenomenology of Having," 154–74.

29. Ulrich, *Homo Abyssus*; Schmitz, *Gift*; Antonio López, *Gift and the Unity*; Schindler, "Metaphysics as Prayer."

THE ANALOGY OF BEING AND THE NONBEING OF DEATH

Insofar as I am created, it is true that "I am my life" or that "I am my being."[30] In other words, there is an identity between me and my act of being. Of course, this statement neither denies that I am given to myself by God ("I = my being" does not imply that I am the origin of myself), nor does it imply that I am being as such, or that my essence implies my act of being.[31] It does, however, exclude that the relationship between "I" and "my life" is anything short of a relationship of identity.[32]

This rudimentary summary of the Thomistic metaphysics of being as gift is already sufficient to clarify in what way death may have come about and why we say that it is a negation of life and being. At the origin of man's fall there is the *disbelief* about the gift, about the gift *as gift*, about being-life as gift. Man fails to believe that being-life has been truly given away or donated to him. Such a disbelief is paired with man's *distrust* toward God, the Giver of the gift of being. Man cannot trust that God actually gives being away. As such, in the postlapsarian condition, man's fundamental act—what I have called the fundamental enactment of the act of being—falls short of *being*, and becomes an *act searching for* being, an acting in order to be, as if what man had received needed to be "secured" through his action in order to "be" and in order to be made his own. Here, in a certain sense, the logic of the *agere sequitur esse* is reversed: *esse sequitur agere*, that is, *esse* is understood and lived as a "thing"

---

30. "Every excellence of anything whatsoever is ascribed to it in respect of its being [*suum esse*]" (Aquinas, *Summa Contra Gentiles* 1.28).

31. Accordingly, it is of course still true that *ens* is not *esse* and that *ens* is that which "has being"; see Aquinas, *Commentary on Metaphysics*, 12.1.2419. St. Thomas explicitly states the contradictory of what I am suggesting, that is, that "a created form . . . has being, and yet is not its own being" (*ST* 1, q. 7, a. 2 co.). Yet, the contradiction between Thomas's view and what I am saying is only superficial and nominal. The present point and the following analyses can be read in connection with Stein, *Finite and Eternal Being*, 54–57.

32. Marcel claims that the idea that "I am my life" is a metaphysical mistake. He continues in the same direction when he affirms that man misunderstands his being when he does not live in light of the "disposability" of his own self. Marcel explains that the "love of one's-self regarded as disposable" means "love of what God may make of me" (*Being and Having*, 69). One may wonder why this radical openness to God's will should be rendered through the idea of a metaphysical disposability of one's self. It is not its disposability, but rather its preservation as a gift from and for that keeps it open to God's will. It is hard to reconcile the idea of a metaphysical disposability of created being with the words of a God who claims that "even the hairs of [our] head have all been counted" (Luke 12:7). He also writes: "Being non-disposable; being occupied with self" (73). Note how, on this point, his analysis is strikingly different from mine: being occupied with self is that attitude of acedia that flows from one's perceiving oneself as disposable, as less than being and gift, as a thing that must be secured into being against disposability.

that man's activity must secure, must treat possessively and guardedly, in order to be made his own, in order to be turned into "being."

We find here the seeds of that attitude toward existence which was made canonical by Arthur Schopenhauer's metaphysical pessimism. As Blondel explains the pessimist position, "All the immense oppression of hearts come, not from the fact that those who suffer are, but from the fact that, not being, they think they are and will to be."[33] The pessimist solution would be, then, "to kill in ourselves not the being that is not, but the chimerical will to be." And yet, as Blondel proves, act we must, and the illusion of a perfect *noluntas* always underlies a "will to nothing" that is nothing other than the most perfectly disordered version of an insuppressible love of being.[34] Suicide, which Schopenhauer refused insofar as he saw in it the extreme affirmation of a frustrated desire for life (as also Pascal saw well), is not the only phenomenon in which the subtle contradiction of the pessimist emerges; also Schopenhauer's "encratism" reveals the same contradiction; to force one's "will to be" to wither is just another way to deal with the fact that one's will to be has not been given the right conditions to flourish, the conditions in which suffering is not the rule. Thus, the logical option of metaphysical pessimism proves to be only chimerical. As such, it turns into one of the different forms of practical utopianism, as the history of the twentieth century seems to have proven.

According to this reading, the fall coincides with the loss of that condition in which man's self-awareness is grounded in the claim "I am my life" or "I am my being." "Being" is lost insofar as it is represented and lived as *not-truly-given*; the relationship between me and my being is not one of identity; what is given is something less than being—let us call it, following Marcel, "life as a thing"—and the relationship that the I entertains with it is less than the relationship of identity—a relationship of mere "having." *Action* becomes the mediation through which the I tries to secure into *being* that life that the I only *has*. In short, I am saying the very opposite of what Weil maintains when she writes: "Being and having. Being does not belong to man, only having."[35]

---

33. Blondel, *Action*, 41.

34. Emil M. Cioran makes a very similar point in *Un apolide metafisico*, 38: "Although I have a gloomy concept of life, I have always had a big love for existence, a love so big that it turned into the negation of life, because I did not have the means to satisfy my desire to live" (author's translation).

35. Weil, *Gravity and Grace*, 38.

THE ANALOGY OF BEING AND THE NONBEING OF DEATH

In creating the world, God is in relation to the world by indwelling his gift of being.[36] God draws participated being "from his heart" (*creatio ex nihilo*), as Ulrich beautifully puts it,[37] and is thus present in his gift of being. We are closer to God, that is, we acknowledge God's presence in us, to be in us, only when we are "at our fullest," only when we *are*, that is, when we receive *being as a gift* and therefore we allow ourselves simply *to be* and to act accordingly—in the unity of being and act, of being that is already act and act that flows from being—instead of taking being as a "thing" that we only *have* and which, for this reason, must be secured through a jealous, distrustful, frenzied, and fearful action.[38] When the gift of being is not received as such, life becomes restless activity.

It is true that, insofar as I am given to myself by God, the relation of identity that I have with myself or with my being is always inhabited by God as the ultimate Giver of being and thus it can never turn into a *relation of possession*.[39] However, what I have said—i.e., that the I entertains

---

36. E.g., "He is in all things giving them being" (*ST* 1, q. 8, a. 1–a. 2, co.). This of course does not imply that the relation between the creature and God is symmetrical as in the case of the relations among creatures. See *ST* 1, q. 13, a. 7.

37. Ferdinand Ulrich, *Gebet als geschöpflicher Grundakt*, quoted in Schindler, "Metaphysics as Prayer," 185.

38. These features of the postlapsarian enactment of the act of being constitute the different facets of the same fall, that is, of the replacement of the logic of being with the logic of having. In acting, we are "jealous" because we must become possessive of life insofar as it has been reduced to something that we only "have" and thus can escape us at any moment; we are "distrustful" in the sense that in distrusting God as the Giver of being-life we identify our jealous action as our own origin; we act and live in a "frenzy" because our action comes "always too late" and we feel that we constantly need to "do more" and "catch up" in order to be what we can never be—the very origin of our being—and in order to bring about what can never be brought about—the securing of our life into "being"; we are "fearful" because we know and feel that our life is never secure.

39. Ulrich develops this point by reading the "ontological difference" into what he calls "dialogical difference": "Here, I am for 'myself' a given 'I' (-Thou), without ever being able to sublate the difference between the gift (= I) and myself as the recipient (= I), to extinguish this dialogical difference, through which my self is structured, or 'to mediate' it reflexively from my existential standpoint. In this center, I am not present to myself as the Other who is 'thought,' but entrusted to myself as a 'gratuitous,' given friend. I cannot trap the life given to me in a 'concept'; I cannot make the transferred gift available to myself as something known and administer it however I may think best. I cannot withdraw myself from the movement originating in the Giver, in which he expresses himself to me. To do so would mean (or in any event only appear to mean) that I had succeeded in absorbing the gift into myself, separated it from its source, and then subsequently, by abstraction, isolated the essence of my life as an object of thought" (Ferdinand Ulrich, *Gebet als geschöpflicher Grundakt*, quoted in Schindler, "Metaphysics as Prayer," 184).

originally a relation of identity with his being—is quite the opposite of a relation of possession. A relation of possession is nothing more than a violent intensification of a relation of mere having. If the I is in a relation of identity with his being, the relation of having is ipso facto excluded, and the relation of possession is excluded a fortiori. Metaphysicians sometimes confuse the fact that the creature's *being is participated* with the idea that the creature simply *has its being*, but this confusion should be avoided at all costs. That the creature is identical to its participated being is a metaphysical insight into the genuine nature of creation; that the creature is understood as simply having its being is the beginning of the disaster.

As we can see, the fall could be interpreted as the substitution, through a free act of disbelief and distrust against God and against oneself, of a logic of being ("I am my life") with a logic of having ("I have my life").[40] This act, accompanied by the disbelief and the distrust I have mentioned above, introduces into life a *self-negation*, a twisting of the logic of being and an *internal distance of being from itself*, precisely because "my life" is not apprehended anymore as "who I am" but only as some "thing" that I have. To follow Pieper's suggestion, this condition might be described as a fundamental form of "acedia."[41] Its result is that *meontic wound* at the heart of the creature which in the previous chapter I have characterized as a radical negation without annihilation.

If life is something that I only have, it becomes rational (a rationality, however, which relies on a fundamental mistake, as when one draws conclusions correctly, but from wrong premises) to try to secure it against everything and everybody else—or by instrumentalizing everything and everybody else. Our life becomes dominated by a gloomy hope animated by a frenzy of achievement: "So we never live, but we hope to live."[42]

---

40. See Schmitz, *Gift*, 73–74.

41. Pieper opposes "leisure" to "acedia" in the following terms: "Leisure is only possible when a man is at one with himself, when he acquiesces in his own being, whereas the essence of *acedia* is the refusal to acquiesce in one's own being" (*Leisure*, 46). Pieper continues describing leisure as an "attitude of non-activity, of inward calm, of silence; it means not being 'busy,' but letting things happen. Leisure is a form of silence, of that silence which is the prerequisite of the apprehension of reality.... For leisure is a receptive attitude of mind, a contemplative attitude, and it is not only the occasion but also the capacity for steeping oneself in the whole of creation" (46–47).

42. Pascal, *Thoughts*, 65n172. Another symptom of radical metaphysical insufficiency which we perceive of our being is that, as Pascal remarks, "we desire to live an imaginary life in the mind of the others, and for this purpose we endeavor to shine. We labour unceasingly to adorn and preserve this imaginary existence, and neglect the

2.2. If this is true, we should be careful not to misinterpret the statements of a theologian as great as Joseph Ratzinger. Speaking of Mary, he writes: "To magnify the Lord means not to want to magnify ourselves, our own name, our own ego; not to spread ourselves and take up more space, but to give him room so that he may be more present in the world."[43] This statement is of course true if we take it according to the intention of its author. It means to exclude self-idolatry and egotism, to point out that the idolatry of the self is incompatible with a genuine relation with God. Nevertheless, statements such as this one are easily misunderstood. In fact, if we read it with a modern eye, we end up believing that in order for God to be present in the world and in ourselves we need to displace ourselves, to undermine ourselves. We have to become small, little, so that he can be. One has to become insignificant in order for God to manifest his meaning. Modernity has struggled with this insoluble problem since it started to conceive of God as one being among others. The rightful conclusion of *modernity's prejudice about the metaphysical competition between Creator and creature* thus becomes manifest in Nietzsche and Sartre: in order for us to be, God must be killed, removed. But is this true? Or isn't this rather a complete misunderstanding of the logic of creation?

To follow Ratzinger's terminology here: What does it mean to "give God more room"? Or even more precisely: In what "room" does God dwell? The answer is simple: he indwells being, that is, the gift of being that he gives to his creation out of love. It follows that God can be with us only if he is in us, and he can be in us only if we *are*. Where would God, the *Ipsum Esse Subsistens*, be if not in being?[44] As a consequence, it is not by withdrawing from being, but rather by putting ourselves forward in being, by actively acquiescing in our own being, as it were, that we can make room for God in ourselves and in the world.

---

real. And if we possess calmness, or generosity, or truthfulness, we are eager to make it known, so as to attach these virtues to that imaginary existence. We would rather separate them from ourselves to join them to it; and we would willingly be cowards in order to acquire the reputation of being brave. A great proof of the nothingness of our being, not to be satisfied with the one without the other, and to renounce the one for the other!" (Pascal, *Thoughts*, 59–60n147). True subjective idealism is nothing but this: I do not exist unless I am constantly recognized, unless I exist as "an imaginary life in the mind of others." It is too easy to point out how this reverse subjective idealism permeates our society, social media, the development of virtual reality, etc.

43. Joseph Ratzinger, in Balthasar and Ratzinger, *Mary*, 75.
44. One could remember here bk. 1 of St. Augustine's *Confessions*.

It follows that the sin of the first man was in fact not a putting himself forward in being, but rather a *withdrawing from being*. As I have suggested, this withdrawal corresponds to the substitution of the relation of being with the relation of having. This is very difficult to understand—how was this even possible? Without expecting to remove the opacity, the unintelligibility, of this original sinful act, one could try to use the distinction proposed at the outset of this section to explain, to clarify at least the dynamic of what must remain opaque and unintelligible. Understanding being as *gift* is helpful. By receiving life as his own being, which is the intention of God's creative act, man *could have been*, simply. He could have just lived, securely and leisurely, relying on the stable ground of the Giver,[45] and he could have put his work into making this gift bear its fruit for himself and for the others. On the contrary, by choosing to receive life as a thing that he only had, that is, by distrusting the Giver as the giver of a *gift*, man proceeded to treat it like something that had to be "secured into being" through his action. In this sense, and only in this sense, man started to understand and enact his life-being as the product of his own action. As we were saying, from *agere sequitur esse* to *esse sequitur agere*.

2.3. In so doing, by "delaying" being as the product of his action, man accomplished three goals, that is, he undermined himself in three complementarily destructive ways, corresponding roughly to what is traditionally called the loss of the grace of "original justice": (1) He "deprived" God of his natural dwelling place in him by distrusting the gift of being and by taking life as a thing to protect-produce rather than as *his own* being. (2) He "delayed" in a certain sense his relation with God and "forced" God to appear on the scene of the world less as the reliable ground of being-life and more as the God who is put in the condition to have to call us forward into being and out of that condition of fear and distrust that we have chosen for ourselves (the Pascalian theology of the *pari*).[46] (3) He ipso facto established himself—that is, his action—as his own origin by distrusting God as the Original Giver of being.

---

45. See Matt 6:25–34.

46. "The world exists for the exercise of mercy and judgment, not as if men were placed in it out of the hands of God, but as hostile to God; and to them He grants by grace sufficient light, that they may return to Him, if they desire to seek and follow Him; and also that they may be punished, if they refuse to seek or follow him" (Pascal, *Thoughts*, 191n584). Incidentally, the existential "thrownness" that Heidegger ascribes to Dasein picks upon the first point—a certain loss of God as ground—but does not convey the whole story, the second point, that God insistently appears as a calling. Of

The underlying point here is that by establishing with himself a relation of having rather than of being, man has reduced himself, belittled himself, rather than having "magnified" himself. He should have magnified himself by welcoming the fact that his being was a gift, that he simply was, and instead he feared it. He has not made himself too big and thus subtracted all space to God. He has subtracted all space to God because he has made himself too small—he has delayed his own being-life by putting an unbridgeable distance between himself and his being-life; by taking his being-life as something he only has and by anxiously chasing it as the effect of his producing, a product which always arrives too late for him to truly be.[47]

We are not wrong when we say that in sinning man wanted and still wants to put himself in the place of God—the sin of "pride," or pride as sinfulness itself. Man wanted and still wants to be God, that is, the origin of his being-life. But we easily misunderstand this statement if we do not understand also that, at the bottom of this fatal move, there is not the courage—or maybe, the *hybris*, the temerity, the modern titanism, etc.—to magnify ourselves, but rather the fearful decision to belittle ourselves by turning our life-being into a thing that we only have and we must

course Heidegger's existential analytic of Dasein aims at being methodologically neutral with respect to theology. Nevertheless, nobody denies today the clear theological inspiration of his early thought, based especially on the study of St. Paul, St. Augustine, and Martin Luther, which gives us to right to point out the shortcoming that I just mentioned. Despite bracketing phenomenologically the problem of God, Heidegger still puts forth something like a vocational structure of existence when he speaks of the call of conscience, but some interpreters, notably Martin Buber, deny that Heidegger's conscience can ever amount to something more than the monological voice of Dasein. See Buber, *Problema dell'uomo*.

47. The so-called primacy of the practical typical of certain modern philosophy and culture and the disappearance of the theoretical and the contemplative might as well be considered the thematization in this philosophy and in this culture of the essential trait of the fall. This logic becomes very explicit with Marx, for whom, as it is well known, the true face of reality is what lies ahead of us as the product of philosophy understood as revolutionary transformation of the world; with Sartre, who claims that "existence" precedes "essence"; and with Butler more recently, for whom (gender) identity is the result of performative practices. An interesting fact is that contemporary philosophy has acknowledged the inevitable "arriving too late" of the action that aims at securing life into "being," especially in the form of utopian thought. For Ernst Bloch, for instance, "being" exists only in the mode of the "not yet" (*Principle of Hope*, esp. vol. 1). Bloch's utopianism is the monstrous transformation of classical teleological metaphysics. Far from me to suggest the interpretation that these philosophies are somehow "philosophies of the fall." Nevertheless, it seems to me that these philosophies reveal in clear terms the consequences of the substitution of the logic of being with the logic of having, and the ensuing reversal of *agere sequitur esse* with *esse sequitur agere*.

safeguard jealously and produce into being to make it truly our own, in an endless search for what can never be. Pride feeds off fear and distrust, just as they all feed off false humility. As someone said, true humility for man would be to accept having been made like God—more simply here, accepting *being given to be*.[48] Man should have humbly embraced the unsurpassable glory of being[49]—the glory for which he is made: What glory could be superior to that of being?—instead of fearfully diminishing himself to the *vulgar* condition of someone who merely has and therefore proudly chasing his own being as the product of a self-originating action. Man could have *humbly* accepted that *he truly was* rather than *proudly* affirming that *he was not truly*. As St. Bonaventure has correctly pointed out, sinfulness always has "despair" built into it.[50]

Man's idolatrous decision in the first sin and in every sin which has followed the first one is not just that of diminishing God by elevating a thing to the status of God, but also and contextually that of diminishing his own being-life by turning it into a thing which he has to worship with and through his hopeless *agere*. Any idolatrous gesture, as we learn from Scripture and from our own experience, always produces around itself a scene of death.

2.3. The present analysis could be deepened by suggesting that the shift from "being" to "having" is at the same time the pernicious introduction into being of a *quantitative logic* which is foreign to being understood as gift. As Étienne Gilson has remarked, "In the order of actual existence at least, a thing either is, or is not, and there is no half-way house between these two positions."[51] There is unquestionably a link between the quantitative and the qualitative in being and life. In fact, what Hegel thought about the relationship between quantitative and qualitative applies also here.[52] A change in quantity may cause a change in quality (e.g., the progressive losing of more and more diopters will eventually result in blindness) or even of substance (e.g., if I lose a drop of blood I am fine, but if I lose too much I die).

---

48. See Hadjadj, *Réussir sa mort*.
49. See Hadjadj, *A moi la gloire*.
50. Bonaventure, *Breviloquium*, cited in Falque, *Guide to Gethsemani*, 24, 130.
51. Gilson, *Being and Some Philosophers*, 16. This view of course does not exclude that the same simple positivity of being is shared across the universe according to the various essential "measures" of the different creatures.
52. Hegel, *Science of Logic*, 288–91.

Nevertheless, it is also true that, in a sense, when it comes to the metaphysics of being understood as gift, the logic of quality should be considered independent from the logic of quantity. If what is given is truly being (and not less than being, some "thing") and if the given is truly a gift, then being is given wholly, integrally, even if my being does not exhaust the transcendental totality of being. In other words, when I am given the gift of being, nothing is held back. If nothing is held back, that means that everything is given.[53] As long as I am, everything is given because being is given wholly, as Gilson implies. Of course this does not mean that I am the whole, that I am everything. And yet, if everything is given to me—if nothing is held back in the gift of being—that means that I am *a whole*. As Aristotle would put it (with reference to substances in general), I am a whole without being the whole.

The wholeness or totality which is at the center of the Heideggerian concern motivating his reflections on death[54] is not, pace Heidegger, what is given by death, but, on the contrary, what is given in the gift of being. *Being is given in its totality*, that is, without holding anything back, and thus it is given as gift (not as some "thing" that one only "has").[55] It is because the gift is given *totally* that I am *a totus*. This totalizing gift of being is realized as a personal history that grows and, by growing, unfolds the virtualities already present in the original gift of being[56] (nothing is "added" to being "from the outside," as it were), as if what is "new" realized in unexpected ways what had "already" happened in the original gift of being and at the same time pointed in the direction of what "yet" awaits to happen for that original gift to become what it is. Life is an origin that always re-totalizes itself by growing in new, contingent, event-like, and freely chosen ways. Finitude and totality, or totality as finitude, has nothing to do *originally* with the negativity of death (contra Heidegger).

This means that being as gift is, in a limited and qualified sense, "immune" to the quantitative diminishment that a human being undergoes

---

53. "When we say that substance does not admit of more or less, we do not mean that one species of substance is more perfect than another; but that one and the same individual does not participate in its specific nature at one time more than at another; nor do we mean that a species of substance is shared among different individuals in a greater or lesser degree" (*ST* 1, q. 93, a. 3, ad. 3).

54. See sec. 6 of this chapter.

55. Of course, we are not *being itself* (only in God act of being and essence coincide), and nevertheless, we *are*—to which of course one should always add, "in God."

56. Compare to the difference between virtuality and potentiality.

when he ages and gets sick. Despite the indisputable connection between quality and quantity that being manifests at a certain level of analysis, at a deeper level, the logic of quality and the logic of quantity do not intersect, do not overlap: it is essential to the gift of being to be given wholly, so that until a creature is, it is wholly. Even in the midst of a fragile, weak condition, having awareness of being as gift means having awareness that being has been and is given in its integrality. Qualitatively, being refers to the pure simplicity of the positive, which is irreducible to a "thing," and its giftedness means that nothing is held back by God.

Based on the well-known distinction between *anitas* and *quidditas*, we sometimes tend to think that the response to the question *An sit?* can only be factual. However, the metaphysics of the gift of being implies that *anitas* does not refer only to the factual existence of a creature, but also, and more deeply, to what such *anitas* is beyond the whatness of the nature or essence of the creature.[57] In other words, *anitas*, thought as gift, has a certain eidetic, which is that being is *given wholly*, in its complete and simple positivity.

That a creature "is" means that it "is." As Jacques Maritain explains, this claim is not a pure tautology, but is the application of the principle of identity to the problem of the act of being.[58] What does it mean for a creature to be? It means that the act of being that the creature receives is not a "thing" that it simply "has" (i.e., that the logic of having is not sufficient to account for the nature of the gift of being); it means that the gift of being is subject to a qualitative logic (the pure simplicity of the positive opposed to the pure negativity of nonbeing) which is, albeit in the limited and qualified sense explained, immune and irreducible to a quantitative logic. This confirms once again that the original relation that I entertain with my being or my life is one of identity.

2.4. The concept of material kenosis provides a way into this logic of totality. As I have stressed at length, the negation of death is total and totalizing. It cannot be fully understood if we stick to a mereological perspective (one "part" of the human being is negated, say, the body, while another, the soul, is not). Apprehending death as death means becoming

---

57. Clarke points out the importance of grasping the meaning of the act of being beyond the mere fact of existing (*One and the Many*, 79–80). However, his proposal that the act of being means for everything that is "an act of standing out from nothing and actively presenting itself to the community of real beings" (51) is not the one relevant for my discussion.

58. See Maritain, *Preface to Metaphysics*, 92–94.

aware that within any seemingly partial negation—I get a cold, I cut my finger, my head hurts—the total and totalizing negation of death is manifesting itself, and this is what the concept of death as material kenosis is supposed bring to light. We see here that the logic of death mirrors the logic of the gift of being: if being is given wholly, totally, in the gift of creation, so the corruption of such gift on the part of the creature means a totalizing self-negation.

2.5. In the apprehension of oneself as mortal, the totalizing negation of death brings to light the *nihil* of *creatio ex nihilo*. From this vantage, by opposition to this *nihil* that the creature "is" without God, one is put in the condition to experience once again the gift of life-being in its simple positivity, in such a way that we come to see that the logic of quantity and that of having are derivative, secondary and, in this sense, fallen logics.[59] St. Thomas and some metaphysicians after him have said that the meaning of "being" is gained, at least partially, by opposition to nonbeing. So, when we see our being-life by opposition to the nonbeing which has a "priority of nature" within us (the *nihil* of *creatio ex nihilo*),[60] we rediscover the meaning of being in its pure simplicity, in its qualitative logic immune and irreducible to any quantitative logic.

It is part of the very same rediscovery when we see that framing the life-being that is gifted to us in quantitative terms is akin to adopting a logic of "having" (life is some "thing" that we only "have," etc.) as opposed to a logic of "being." In fact, if life is "something" that we only have, this means that life-being has been given only partially, that is has been *half-given*, namely, that what has been given is a "thing" and not being, and that the given is not truly a gift because something has been held back (that "something" which is missing for the given to be a true gift of being). Contrary to this, if what is taken away in death is everything, that means that we are brought back to the vantage of the *nihil* that we are *sine Deo*; and this means that what is given in the gift of life-being is in fact everything.

---

59. See Chesterton, *Orthodoxy*, 38.

60. "Further, let us even suppose that the preposition 'out of' imports some affirmative order of non-being to being, as if the proposition that the creature is made out of nothing meant that the creature is made after nothing. Then this expression 'after' certainly implies order, but order is of two kinds: order of time and order of nature. If, therefore, the proper and particular does not follow from the common and the universal, it will not necessarily follow that, because the creature is made after nothing, non-being is temporally prior to the being of the creature. Rather, it suffices that non-being be prior to being by nature" (Aquinas, "On the Eternity," para. 16).

Material Kenosis

It is crucial to note here that, according to this proposal, the nonbeing that plays the admittedly *paradoxical positive role* in allowing us to rediscover the depth of our creatureliness is not the negation of death, but rather the *nihil* of *creatio ex nihilo*. Man could have appreciated the depth of his creatureliness, the nothing that lies at the bottom of his constitution and thus the gift of life-being in its totalizing nature, even "before" or "without" undergoing the total negation of death. Accordingly, one must say that *it just so happens* that man must go through the negation of death in order to rediscover the *nihil* of *creatio ex nihilo*. It is the brute force of a fact rather than the rational necessity of a metaphysical law rooted in being. As such, this "having to go through the negation of death" remains, in a sense, without reason. It is the "lack of reason" of evil.

Strictly speaking, then, one should not claim that the negation of death is "functional to" the rediscovery of the *nihil* of *creatio ex nihilo*. This would mean giving the negation of death a positive role, as when we read in William Desmond, for instance, that death plays the function of bringing about the "desirization" of life.[61] In my view, this claim is imprecise and runs the risk of providing a vitalistic (!) interpretation of death and of reading a pseudo-Heideggerian position into the Christian view.[62] Contrary to Desmond's proposal, what intensifies life is the rediscovery

---

61. Desmond, *Desire, Dialectic, and Otherness*.

62. Some philosophers try to interpret Heidegger's stress on death in continuity with the humanistic and Christian tradition of the memento mori. For instance, George Pattison, *Heidegger on Death*, places Heidegger's reflection on death in the wake of Luther's and Kierkegaard's thought. Now, there is no question that Luther and Kierkegaard (and Augustine, Pascal, etc.) lie in the background of Heidegger's formation. Nevertheless, the biographical and intellectual influence cannot be interpreted as theoretical continuity insofar as Heidegger radically transforms their view, as proven by the fact that he jettisons both the humanistic and the Christian meaning of the memento mori and the "humanistic" metaphysical tradition in general. Niederhauser writes: "Heidegger stands in the tradition of, among others, Socrates, Augustine, Luther, Hegel, and Kierkegaard. For them, our mortality is so fundamentally human that one has to wonder whether our current ignorance of our mortality, the attempts to eradicate mortality scientifically, might not itself be of a great inhumaneness" (*Heidegger on Death and Being*, xviii). Just to take the clear case of St. Augustine, it is hard to see how for him death could be considered "fundamentally human." Even Sartre's assessment that Heidegger was the one to give "philosophical form" to the "humanization of death" is misleading in this regard, as the polemic on the meaning of "humanism" seems to show. See Sartre, *Being and Nothingness*, 553. Bernhard Welte's words at Heidegger's eulogy seem the most balanced on this issue: "Nor did he [Heidegger] ever break off his ties with the community of the faithful. True, he went on his way, and had to do so, following his command, and it is unlikely that one could call this way a Christian one in the accepted sense of the word. But it was the way of perhaps the greatest seeker of this century" ("Search and Find," 303–4).

of the *nihil* of *creatio ex nihilo*, not death per se. To speak paradoxically, we could say that God's providence has always already relativized the negation of death to the *nihil* of *creatio ex nihilo*. This "relativization to" is not a "functionalization of." The metaphysical courage needed here is that of not closing the unbridgeable gap between the two nonbeings; it is the courage to not see death as a factor of meaning, as a positive ingredient of being. A good test for a good metaphysics of death is whether it is capable of dealing with it without turning it into something positive.

Thus, in confronting death, we are called to embrace the two nonbeings of our condition in very different ways (despite the fact that they are in our experience one within each other, one inscribed within the other): we embrace the *nihil* of *creatio ex nihilo because it is not a negation*, but because it is the mark of God's totalizing generosity; and we embrace the nonbeing of death *despite its being a negation* of God's generosity, because it is always already relativized to the *nihil* of *creatio ex nihilo*. Overlooking this distinction, as it is often done, brings about all those misunderstandings that end up turning death into a positive constitutive principle of being or into a positive horizon of meaning, either in philosophy or theology.

Moreover, learning that being is either given or not given, and thus that the being that we are given is a totalizing gift irreducible to something that we only have, defuses the metaphysical *contradiction* at work in the fall. In fact, the quantitative logic of the "half-given" also generates the metaphysical contradiction of thinking one's "I" as in a sense coming before one's being: "I" must secure into "being" the life that has been given to me as something that I only "have" and thus make it "my own." The perceived halfness of the "gift" translates into an I standing in a relation of pure "having" to its life—an I with a ghostly consistency; an I that is not truly; an I who believes that being has not been given away as a gift and who is forever suspended between *resentment* (the resentment for having been given life only as a thing to have, for having been cheated out of "being" proper) and *utopia* (the utopia of securing one's life into being). Such "I" conceives of itself as something that "is," while at the same time apprehending its consistency as reduced to the action through which life must be secured into "being" and made "its own." The I "is" and at the same time "is not": a half-living contradiction.[63]

---

63. One is reminded here of the beautiful opening remarks of Blondel: "I act, but without even knowing what action is, without having wished to live, without knowing exactly either who I am or even if I am. This appearance of being which flutters about

On the contrary, experiencing being as a true gift in its absolute positivity from the vantage of *nihil* frees the I from this self-imposed enslavement to resentment and utopia—it frees the I from Hegel's unhappy consciousness that can never realize what it prospects—and from the metaphysical contradiction of a half-given being (the "I") that precedes being ("life" produced as "one's own," made into one's "being," through the I's action).

It is in this sense true—but in a way that escaped Plato—that the meditation on being typical of philosophy and the meditation on death belong together. Thus, by embodying the *nihil* of *creatio ex nihilo* in our self-negating flesh, we are put in a condition to see from a *definitive* vantage that what we receive is not a thing that we have, but rather our very being. I call this vantage "definitive" because there is no more radical vantage from which one can place himself in order to have access to the qualitative, nonquantitative, absolute positivity of being: when we become aware that death is a totalizing negation, we become, in thought and body, as it were, a subsistent *nihil*.[64]

On the one hand, insofar as we are totally negated by death, we become "less than nonbeing," the *id quo minor cogitari nequit*.[65] On the other hand, insofar as we still are, the positivity of being manifests its qualitative simplicity incompatible with any logic of mere having and half-givenness—nothing is withheld in the gift of being. Whether and how this metaphysical evidence also becomes effective existentially, spiritually, or psychologically, is a mystery to which there is no answer.

In short: if the total negation without annihilation of death reduces us to *nothing* (in the sense of the paradoxical figure of the subsistent *nihil*), what is lost in this negation is precisely *being*; and if what is lost is being, what is *still* given (for us to still be, although totally negated) is *everything*, that is, being in its qualitative purity, being in its wholeness. The gift of being is at its root incompatible with the giving of a thing that

---

within me, these light and evanescent actions of a shadow, bear in them, I am told, an eternally weighty responsibility, and that, even at the price of blood, I cannot buy nothingness because for me it is no longer. . . . Perhaps I will learn whether or not this phantom I am to myself, with this universe I bear in my gaze, with science and its magic, with the strange dream of consciousness, has any solidity" (*Action*, 3).

64. A similar idea, expressed by the notion of "void [*nichtig*] being," is found in Stein, *Finite and Eternal Being*, 321; see also: "Nature or essence is not suspended by evil but is 'inverted,' transformed [*umwandeln*] into its negative counterpart" (322).

65. Compare to Pseudo-Dionysius: "Evil . . . has greater nonexistence and otherness from the Good than nonbeing has" ("Divine Names" 2.19, in *Complete Works*, 85).

is simply had and therefore is also at odds with the logic of "half-giving" which accompanies the being given a thing to which I stand in a pure relation of having. If what is given is truly being, being is given away as a gift—as Ulrich says, "given for nothing." Donated being has always already been secured in the unconditional and thus unwavering nature of the original act of donation of being. If what is given is being, being must be given away and received as a gift: true "giving" and "being" imply each other.[66]

2.6. This is the reason why all pantheistic and monistic systems must conceive of finite things not as being given a true share in being, but rather as being given something of a different and lower order than being. Finite things within these systems stand in relation to their existence as something that they only have. In other words, each finite thing "has" existence in the form of being a temporary and non-substantial modification of the only one being that truly is—Spinoza's *deus sive natura*. It is not by chance then that finite things are conceived of within these systems as being originally in conflict with each other. Within these systems, the normal condition of the relation among finite things must be *polemos* because *omnis determinatio est negatio*.[67] But what is the root of this polemical, competitive metaphysics? Precisely the fact that being is neglected as a gift and is instead turned into a thing which is given as some "thing" simply "had." A finite thing must therefore act to secure its existence into being to make it its own, and this can only happen at the expense of the other finite things which are condemned to the same polemical and competitive destiny from the very beginning.

2.6.1. The problem of how to understand negation at this juncture may benefit from a brief analysis of Augusto Del Noce's reflection on modern rationalism. To use Hegel's phrase, "Everything depends here on

---

66. This raises the interesting question, that is, under what conditions I can truly give X as a gift when X is not being.

67. *Omnis determinatio est negatio* is wrong in two senses: First, because it takes a negative judgment ("This determination is not that determination") and builds it into the very nature of things; it is a confusion of metaphysics with logic. Second, because (piggybacking on the first point) it neglects that there is something more original than the *negatio*, that is, the relation. After all, even the apprehension of a mutual negation presupposes a comparison (which is still a judgment) and the comparison presupposes a relation. *Omnis determinatio est in relatione*. Many today want to go even further and affirm that *omnis determinatio est relatio*, but there does not seem to me to be a reason to go this far, even assuming that creatures are what they are because they are in a "constitutive relation" with God.

the correct understanding of the status and significance of negativity."[68] Following Del Noce, one might even say that the history and reception of the Hegelian thought itself depends on this very question, or that the different interpretations of Hegel's thought that were given coincide largely with the different answers given to this question.[69]

On the one hand, the theological interpretation of Hegel sees the finite as negation and thus God, the infinite, as the negation of the negation—where this negation of the negation must be understood not merely in light of a traditional Christian metaphysics of transcendence, as it is, for instance, in Meister Eckhart,[70] but rather as the real historical process in and through which spirit becomes itself. According to the well-known Hegelian interpretation of the Christian narrative, the immanent and the economic Trinity are collapsed, and both are speculatively reinterpreted and demythologized.[71]

On the other hand, the atheistic interpretation, which has in Marx and Kojève its clearest voices, also sees negativity as the inherent feature of the finite, but in this case the finite does not require a theological reconciliation. Rather, the finite must be sacrificed to the universal or, in concrete, individuals must give their life to the revolutionary process

68. Hegel, "Review of Jacobi's *Werke*," 8.

69. Also Charles Taylor's different but in many ways complementary genealogy of modernity stresses the pivotal role played by a new understanding of death in the "immanent revolt" of Romantic and post-Romantic philosophy. See his *A Secular Age*: "One of its major themes [i.e., of the Romantic and post-Romantic era] is a new understanding of the centrality of death, a kind of answer to the inability of mainstream exclusive humanism to cope with mortality. . . . Life properly understood also affirms death and destruction. To pretend otherwise is to try to restrict it, tame it, hem in it, deprive it of its highest manifestations, what makes it something you can say 'yes' to. (373) . . . The Nietzschean understanding of enhanced life, which can fully affirm itself, also in a sense takes us beyond life; and in this it is analogous with other, religious notions of enhanced life (like the New testament's 'eternal life'). But it takes us beyond by incorporating a fascination with the negation of life, with death and suffering" (374). Along the same lines, Taylor discusses the early twentieth-century fascination with war (416–19), proposed as the great antidote to the stagnation of civilization: the great revitalizer.

70. See Meister Eckhart: "The One is negation of the negation and privation of the privation" ("Unus Deus at Pater Omnium," 226).

71. See Jean Hyppolite: "Infinite spirit should not be thought through beyond finite spirit, beyond man acting and sinning, and yet infinite spirit itself is eager to participate in the human drama. Its true infinity, its concrete infinite, does not exist without this fall. . . . We must learn that this fall is part of the absolute itself, that it is a moment of total truth. Absolute self cannot be expressed without this negativity; it is an absolute 'yes' only through saying 'no' to a 'no,' only by overcoming a necessary negation" (*Genesis and Structure of Hegel's Phenomenology of Spirit*, quoted in Del Noce, *Problem of Atheism*, 292). For a critique of this interpretation of Hegel, see Roessiger, "Hegelian Nihilism."

and to the world to come at the end of the revolutionary process. God's negation of the negation becomes here revolution's liberating negation of the finite.

What underlies both interpretations, however, is the common trait which Del Noce calls the "ontologization of guilt," that is, the theoretical decision according to which mortality is assumed as an original and constitutive feature of finite being. Hegel famously reads the biblical account of the fall as a necessary moment in the self-development of spirit. According to Del Noce, the ontologization of guilt is the typical feature of modern rationalism, which finds its ancient remote roots in the thought of Anaximander and its most recent offshoots in revolutionary Marxism.[72] Del Noce writes:

> The rationalist attitude is simply the assumption, as a consequence of the initial rejection of the Fall, that man's current condition is his normal condition; it coincides with an original moral devalutation of miracles and of the supernatural in the broadest sense and, thus, with the negation of free creation and of the theme of sin in their biblical meaning. . . . But such assumption that man's fallen reality is his normal reality cannot but coincide with the assumption that the moral destiny of finite being is normal and, thus, with the affirmation of the negativity of the finite. These categories are clarified historically if we consider what is undoubtedly the most important chapter in the whole history of atheism—namely, the process of thought from Hegel to Marx. In Hegel alienation is surpassed through idealism as the dissolution into thought of the reality of the finite; by the absolutization of the type of the philosopher (i.e., of the man who achieves his freedom by taking the perspective of being considered in its totality). We know how in Marx this perspective is replaced by an entirely different one. But it is important

---

72. Del Noce, *Problem of Atheism*, 17–18. See also Alexandre Kojève: "Hegel est donc d'accord avec le Christianisme pour dire que l'Absolu' ou la Totalité de ce qui *est*, est non pas Identité, Être-donné, Substance ou Nature, mais Esprit, c'est-à-dire Être-révélé par la Parole ou par la Raison discursive (Logos). Mais, pour le Chrétien, cet Esprit 'absolu' est un Dieu transcendant, tandis que pour Hegel il est Homme-dans-le-Monde. Et cette différence radicale et irréductible se ramène en fin de compte à ceci, que l'Esprit chrétien est éternel et infini, tandis que l'Esprit qu'a en vue Hegel est essentiellement fini ou mortel. C'est en y introduisant l'idée de la mort qu'on transforme la théo-logie en anthropologie. Et c'est en prenant cette idée à la lettre, c'est-à-dire en supprimant les notions de survie et de résurrection, qu'on aboutit à l'anthropologie *vraie*, ou hégélienne" (*Lecture de Hegel*, 573; emphasis in original). "Ainsi, la philosophie 'dialectique' ou anthropologique de Hegel est, en dernière analyse, *une philosophie de la mort* (ou ce qui est la même chose: de l'athéisme)" (539; emphasis in original).

Material Kenosis

to notice that this replacement takes place based on the thesis of the mortality of the finite, viewed as the soul of dialectics.[73]

What is relevant here for our analysis is the following problem: What is the passage from *esse sequitur agere* to the ontologization of death typical of the rationalistic tradition and epitomized in Hegel and his legacy? I would answer by putting forth the following interpretation: once the I recognizes that the project of acting in order to secure its existence into being to make it its own is destined to failure (i.e., the "being" of the finite is either a totalizing original gift or it can never be acted into existence), the I turns that "internal negation" that it was trying to overcome while remaining itself an original and constitutive feature of itself, to the point that the overcoming or removal of the negation *means* the overcoming or the removal of the I itself.

According to the atheistic reading of Hegel which has undoubtedly prevailed, *the meaning of finite being is established as essentially self-sacrifice and self-removal*: embracing finitude means embracing mortality and embracing mortality means expropriating one's life-being, which is "nothing" in itself, as a finite moment of the historical process. A most representative expression of this view is summed up according to Del Noce in the words of Engels: "In accordance with all the rules of the Hegelian method of thought, the proposition of the rationality of everything which is real resolves itself into the other proposition: All that exists deserves to perish."[74]

Tracing the details of this history goes beyond the scope of this work, so I will not proceed further in this analysis. The main point, however, must be stressed: that, as Del Noce suggests, the ontologization of death—death turned into something original and constitutive of finite being—is the typical feature of that modern atheistic rationalism which through praxism leads to the legitimization of the annihilation of the individual. Del Noce sees in this process the chief example of the denial of the supernatural and the biblical meaning of the fall. His diagnosis agrees with and complements ours, in the sense that the ontologization of death corresponds to the forgetfulness of the Judeo-Christian idea of

---

73. Del Noce, *Problem of Atheism*, 290–91.

74. Friedrich Engels, *Ludwig Feuerbach and the Outcome of Classical German Philosophy*, quoted in Del Noce, *Problem of Atheism*, 293.

THE ANALOGY OF BEING AND THE NONBEING OF DEATH

creation and the meaning of *nihil* which is essential to it, as I will explain in greater detail in section 3.[75]

2.6.2. One final point must deal with Heidegger, even though a much longer discussion to the Heideggerian tradition will be provided in the final section of this chapter. For now, one brief comment will suffice to sketch out his place in this Delnocean retrieval of the problem of death vis-à-vis modern philosophy, even though Del Noce does not take Heidegger into consideration. As is well known, for Heidegger embracing finitude means embracing mortality (so, for him as well, death is original and constitutive, in line with the rationalist tradition) but embracing mortality in being toward death does not seem to imply, at least as such, any sacrifice of individuality. On the contrary, being toward death is the way in which Dasein's authenticity, wholeness, and individuality are instituted, although one should always read these remarks in light of Heidegger's utter repulsion for liberalism and his commitment to the view according to which historical Dasein is one with the German *Volk* and its salvific destiny.[76] The negation of death is not what must be overcome or removed but, on the contrary, what must be preserved precisely because it is original and constitutive. So, if Del Noce is correct, it would follow that it is in Heidegger, not Marx, that the true "coming into itself" of that

---

75. On the ultimate positivity of finitude in the context of creation, see Silvano Petrosino, "Is Creation a Negation?"

76. An adequate treatment of this point would of course require a discussion of the political dimension of Heidegger's thought. In particular, Heidegger's involvement with National Socialism (it doesn't really matter here whether of the "vulgar" or "spiritual" kind) should be discussed in relation to the problem of the political myth of death in the revolutionary right of the twentieth century. On this, see Fritsche, *Historical Destiny and National Socialism*; Wolin, *Heidegger in Ruins*, esp. the introduction and ch. 2. Wolin, based on his analysis of the *Black Notebooks*, shows how Heidegger came to think that the project of an "existential ontology" had to be deepened in the direction of a "metaphysics of German Dasein" and, more explicitly, as a "metapolitics of the historical [German] *Volk*" (*Heidegger in Ruins*, 57). Thus, if Wolin is correct in interpreting Heidegger's critique of "average, everyday being-in-the-world" and *das Man* as the critique of a reactionary modernist against the democratic massification of society, one could say that Heidegger's stress on the individuality of Dasein obtained through being toward death is not a defense of individuality per se, but rather the defense of the individual who belongs to the Germanic Volk as opposed to the individual of the democratic mass society. Accordingly, "Heidegger developed a form of spiritual nationalism that ... elevated the Volk to a metaphysical entity" (Göpffarth, "Rethinking the German Nation, 261). More specifically, it would be necessary to study Heidegger's embrace of the trope of the "self-obliteration of the earth and the disappearance of contemporary humanity" and "downfall" of the West as the way toward the "purification of Being" (Wolin, *Heidegger in Ruins*, 67–68).

rationalistic tradition according to which death is original and constitutive emerges. Or, in other words, Heidegger would articulate with greater coherence the path already opened by Marx and his heirs, according to which finitude means death and embracing finitude is, at once, the instituting moment of individuality and the relativization of individuality to that destiny to which individuality belongs entirely.

The moral of this story for the present chapter should be pretty clear at this point. Once this historical context of the problem of "negation" in recent times becomes clear, both in its Hegelian roots and its more recent developments, it should also become clearer that any attempt at reproposing the traditional Thomistic metaphysics of being by appealing to the constitutive role of dialectical negation for the intelligibility not only of the determinateness of the finite ("A is not non-A") but also of God's transcendence and infinite positivity (the "absolutely positive" of God manifested as the *negatio negationis*, à la Eckhart), should be extremely careful in distinguishing its own proposal from that of modern rationalism, of Hegel and of his successors.[77] More simply, any genuinely Christian metaphysics, even when it sees fit to ascribe to "dialectical" negation a constitutive function, should avoid at all costs reading into such a negation any trace of the negation of death, which is on the contrary typical of the line that goes from Hegel to Heidegger, who see a fundamental isomorphism between the negation constitutive of determination and the negation of death. Contrary to this line of thought, death is and

---

77. See Barzaghi, "Eternal Design-Mystery," esp. 229–31. Note that the description of God as *negatio negationis* can be helpful not only in order to unpack the notion of the infinite positivity of God while moving from the finite (*negatio negationis* = removal of the determination of the determinate), but also to unpack the way in which "God" is introduced through the proofs for his existence. In fact, the notion of the First Cause, Unmoved Mover, etc. is introduced always and only in order to remove the contradiction (*negatio*) of becoming which would ensue if the world subject to becoming were absolutized. To exemplify this point with respect to Thomas's first way, if the world subject to becoming were absolutized, the change of something A would be explained only by something else B in the world, which, by being itself still subject to change, would not constitute a sufficient and ultimate reason; in this sense, then, A would be at once explained and non-explained, which is contradictory. *Hic autem non est procedere in infinitum* because *procedere in infinitum* would mean remaining in a contradictory situation. Hence, the Unmoved Mover is introduced to remove (negate) the negation (the contradiction) of the world of change when this world of change is absolutized. Here, *negatio negationis* = God's removal of the contradiction of absolutized becoming. As we can see here again, however, the use of the dialectical negation to refer to the positive—or even to institute the positive in its meaning, dialectically!—has nothing to do with the genuine negation of death.

must remain metaphysically unanalogizable for any orthodox Christian metaphysics.[78]

3. THE ONTOLOGIZATION OF DEATH AND THE FORGETFULNESS OF CREATION

3.1. In a passage that is as insightful as it is unsettling, Mauro G. Lepori speaks of the internal link between death and life in our culture. It is worth quoting the passage in full:

> A contradiction engulfs our culture: *we fear death without loving life*. Our culture is suspended between the two poles of abortion and euthanasia. It is as if society were made of people who live only because they have not died yet, as if life were nothing else than the witness of death, the frame of death. The two extreme funerary poles of abortion and euthanasia, although often censured, invade our thought, our consciousness, our relationships, to such an extent that our consciousness can only be a consciousness of death. Life is nothing more than a temporary suspension of death, and happiness, if we ever experience it, is nothing more than a flash that passes through and vanishes, like the effect of a narcotic. This fear of death without love of life is a contradiction that penetrates everything and becomes culture, a way of living and thinking.[79]

What Lepori says, I believe, is not only representative of a major trend in our culture but also of the continental philosophical attitude toward life and death. Of course I am not saying that every continental philosopher "fears death without loving life." On the contrary, what I shall try to suggest through the analyses contained in this section is that continental philosophy manifests a *tendency to see life and death as coessential*.

This dialectical tradition, initiated by Hegel and exemplarily inherited and developed by Georg Simmel, Hans Jonas, Paul Tillich, and Vladimir Jankélévitch, tends to *ontologize the nonbeing of death and to make it an ontological condition of possibility of life-being* (admittedly

---

78. Even if we understand Christ as the "concrete *analogia entis*" (Balthasar, *Theology of History*, 74), this does not imply per se that death has any resemblance whatsoever with any kind of original or constitutive function for being we may want to ascribe to dialectical negation. As I have explained, Christ who is "slain from the foundation of the world," has always already freely assumed what is *toto coelo* different from being, life, and love, namely, the fallen and death-bound nature of man.

79. Lepori, *Si vive solo per morire?*, 14–15; emphasis in original.

in very different ways in each thinker). In turn, the tradition of hermeneutic phenomenology initiated by Heidegger, which I will discuss later in this chapter with special reference to Sartre, Gadamer, Vattimo, and some later Heideggerian thinkers, proposes, despite its many internal differences, a quasi-ontological concept of death by turning it into the ultimate horizon of meaning for Dasein. Although it would be not only uncharitable, but also absurd to ascribe to these thinkers a "lack of love for life," it is nevertheless true that they claim that life-being is either ontologically or phenomenologically *dependent and suspended on the nonbeing of death*. I leave it up to the reader whether this position eventually concludes in the widespread mentality of fear of death and lack of love for life that Lepori diagnoses. My conclusion in the final section of this chapter will be different, although complementary, to Lepori's. I shall claim that, through a very different path, the outcome of the engagement with death of continental philosophy is the same as the outcome of the analytic philosophy discussed in chapter 1, namely, the reduction of death to an ontic problem among other ontic problems, ultimately to be handled technologically.

3.2. The focus in this section will be on those authors in the largely-considered Hegelian tradition who propose an ontologization of the nonbeing of death and include it in their treatment of life-being. The authors with whom I shall deal in this section—Simmel, Jonas, Tillich, and Jankélévitch—have stressed the importance of recovering the sense of "nonbeing" in order to understand the genuine meaning of being. Their common metaphysical position has resurfaced both under the influence of philosophy of nature and theology, and one could almost see the former as the secularized version of the latter. The *ontologization of nonbeing* that we see at work in these philosophies coincides with the *ontologization of death*, in such a way that the couple nonbeing-death is seen as part of the very structure of reality. In the theological lineage, Hegel is the modern forerunner of the view that in recent years has had an explicit revival in various Protestant thinkers, most notably Paul Tillich.

From a general point of view, the ontologization of nonbeing-death should be considered the outcome of that tradition that posits the substantivization of nonbeing, together with the modern tendency to deny the biblical sense of the original sin (and its consequences) by an operation of ontologization of guilt and death, thus conceived as essential

THE ANALOGY OF BEING AND THE NONBEING OF DEATH

to finitude,[80] both championed and developed by Heidegger, for whom finitude must necessarily manifest itself in anguish. However, contrary to the tragic version of such a metaphysics, as we find for example in Schopenhauer, our authors, in this sense genuine heirs of Hegel, see in the ontologization of nonbeing-death the necessary condition of the glory of being, just as in Hegel the negation of the original sin is the necessary step of man toward the attainment of a final reconciliation: being-life is what it is precisely because it overcomes its opposite, nonbeing-death. In this sense, nonbeing-death is presupposed and necessary to being. This view not only produces the ontologization of the "nonbeing" of *creatio ex nihilo*, but also its undue identification with the "nonbeing" of death. The *nihil* of *creatio ex nihilo* ends up being identified with the negation of death, in such a way that not only the specificity of both senses of nonbeing is lost, but also the fact that death is "real" ("real," however, as mere negation or privation, as evil) results in providing (false) reasons for the ontologization of *nihil*.

Contrary to the modern reduction, one should remember that the *nihil* of *creatio ex nihilo* is a negation that has never been because it is the logical negation through which we make sense of the total gift of being by God;[81] it is the formulation of the radical creatureliness of the world, namely, its total and exclusive dependency on God, in whose generosity our participated being rejoices (it simply means that, without God, *nullum ens*); on the contrary, the negation of death has the reality of the negation or privation of evil, introduced into the world by the freedom of rational creatures as a rejection of the gift of being.

3.3. The ontologization of nonbeing-death results from a misunderstanding of the complex relation between *nihil* and death that I just

---

80. Del Noce sees in this precisely the sense of modern atheism, as a "recomprehension of Christianity within the interpretation of evil that had already been formulated in the fragment of Anaximander" (*Problem of Atheism*, 18).

81. Note also that, according to *creatio ex nihilo*, "passive potentiality" does not precede the creature temporally but is an abiding condition within the creature once the creature is created: "Notice that before an angel is made, we may say, in a certain manner of speaking, that the angel cannot be made, since no passive potentiality precedes its being, for an angel is not made from pre-existing matter.... Therefore, if we understand 'being made' or 'being caused' as implying the pre-existence of a passive potentiality, then it should to be conceded, according to faith, that something caused cannot always exist, for it would then follow that a passive potentiality has always existed, and this is heretical" (Aquinas, "On the Eternity," para. 4). See on this López, *Gift and the Unity*, 83–85, who claims that potency is not "'something' left behind" once a substance is created; rather, it is "the singular's ongoing availability to be confirmed in being."

explained. Nevertheless, the speculative appeal of this view lies, I believe, in the stress it makes on the *dynamism of being*. In fact, Simmel, Jonas, and Tillich all want to maintain that being is dynamic, not static. And if we ask what such dynamism does precisely, the answer that we get is: it essentially overcomes its opposite, nonbeing. The reason why "life" is taken then as the chief exemplification of this understanding of being is clear: in life's overcoming of death we have the highest and most exemplary manifestation of being's overcoming of nonbeing.

However, we should ask, is this view the only or best implication of the view of being as dynamic? I shall respond to the question negatively. As I will explain, the dynamism of being should be understood not as the consequence of its opposition to an ontologized nonbeing, but rather as the participation in the dynamism of the Origin of being. In other words, *the ontologization of nonbeing-death in order to account for the dynamism of being is the consequence of the forgetfulness of the Judeo-Christian notion of creation.*

3.4. Georg Simmel's and Hans Jonas's positions are the chief examples of the tendency to ontologize nonbeing in the context of the development of a philosophy of nature. Jonas's doctrine represents the accomplished synthesis of a "biologistic" tendency in understanding the negation of death as co-original to life and being, insofar as, as Jonas says, being as such is "recapitulated" in life because "organisms [are] the manner in which universal Being says yes to itself."[82] And while we can welcome a notion of life understood as the final creaturely recapitulation of being and nature as such through D. C. Schindler,[83] Simmel's and Jonas's ontologization of death must be rejected. Such a tendency has its origin in Bichat's famous claim that life is "an ensemble of functions that resist death."[84] In the same lineage, Simmel claims that "that very life which is becoming fuller and stronger must be seen in the overall context that is defined by death" and that death is what gives life its "form" and "shape."[85] In fact, "just as any automatic or voluntary movement can be interpreted

---

82. Jonas, "Burden and Blessing of Mortality," 36. Such claim reveals that Jonas's position is not merely a biological position but wants to be a claim on being as such.

83. "Interpreted according to an analogical concept of nature, the *reditio completa* shows itself to be the completion of the self-appropriation of forms that defines nature simply" (Schindler, "*Analogia Naturae*," 672).

84. Bichat, *Recherches physiologiques*, 1 (author's translation).

85. Simmel, "Metaphysics of Death," 74–75.

as a desire for life (and for more life), it can also be interpreted as a flight from death."[86]

In short, life and death are co-original insofar as life is nothing else than the self-assertiveness of being in its temporary holding ground against the nonbeing of death. For Simmel, our concrete existence is a Hegelian dialectic of life and death, in which the various syntheses constituting the temporal career of a being would not be possible without the antithesis-negation of death. Similarly, Jonas claims that "death is coextensive with life" and that "you cannot have the one without the other."[87] In light of this view, then, "life has become a task rather than a given state, a possibility ever to be realized anew in opposition to its ever-present contrary, not-being, which inevitably will engulf in the end."[88]

3.4.1. It is indisputable that Simmel and Jonas have made valuable contributions to our understanding of death. We find in them the appropriate stress on the idea that death cannot be reduced to an event placed at the end term of life.[89] Moreover, we find in them the correct valorization not only of the dynamism of being, which, in its dynamic self-cohesiveness, is "concern" about itself and "values" itself in wanting its continuing existence;[90] but also of its radical self-assertiveness, which goes hand in hand with its dynamism.

Nevertheless, the complete loss of the distinction between the two senses of nonbeing—the *nihil* of *creatio ex nihilo* and the negation of death—results into an identification of the affirmation of life with the escape from death. For this reason, all those operations which constitute

---

86. Simmel, "Metaphysics of Death," 75.

87. Jonas, "Burden and Blessing of Mortality," 34. See also Jonas, *The Phenomenon of Life*, 5: "That life is mortal may be its basic self-contradiction, but it belongs to its nature and cannot be separated from it even in thought: life carries death in itself, not in spite of, but because of, its being life."

88. Jonas, "Burden and Blessing of Mortality," 35.

89. Simmel, "Metaphysics of Death," 74. I have claimed that this is the correct way to also interpret St. Thomas's view, for whom death understood as substantial change can be fully appreciated only within the broader metaphysical context of a wounded (death-affected) hylomorphic unity of soul and body. I have also claimed that a Peircean, realistic metaphysics, contrary to the Wittgensteinian nominalistic metaphysics and view of death, allows for such "presence" of death in life.

90. "Life says yes to itself. By clinging to itself it declares that it values itself" (Jonas, "Burden and Blessing of Mortality," 36). One can see here a metaphysical framework similar to the one utilized by Thomas in grounding the transcendental "good" in relation to the notion of being's "inclination" to its proper operation according to its form, see *ST* 1-2, q. 94, a. 3, co.

the specific form of life of a being are at the same time the specific ways in which that being always again flees death. The negation of death and the positivity of being and life are both principles of the dialectical dynamism of reality.

Why do Simmel and Jonas think this way? Precisely because the sense of creation has been completely lost, and the positive self-affirmation of being is now thought on the backdrop of the negativity of death.[91] While Simmel criticizes the Christian view for having removed the "a priori significance from death,"[92] arguably due to its affirmation of an afterlife and its genealogy of death in original sin, it is precisely Simmel's loss of the sense of creation out of nothing, echoed by Jonas, that prevents him from seeing how the positivity of the gift of being can stand alone, and does so originally, apart from any genuine negation, let alone the negation of death.

However, if we adopt the vantage of creation, we see that the self-affirmation of being and life is, in fact, the affirming of itself "out of nothing," but only in the sense that such self-affirmation is the participation in the creative act, namely, in the act of the Origin of being, to whom nothing is presupposed beyond himself.

Thomistic being is act and power (*actus essendi* or *virtus essendi*), and as such, act and power of self-affirmation. We find therefore in Thomas the self-assertiveness of being stressed by Simmel and Jonas. But the *self*-affirmation of created being is always already displaced as self-*affirmation* through an active participation in the *self-giving affirmation*, or self-affirmation as self-giving, of God. In its essential sheer generosity, being does not need anything *against which* it can affirm itself.

Erich Przywara speaks of created being as at once "passive" and "positive" (or "active") potentiality."[93] Against the metaphysical tendency, which Przywara calls "theopanic," that would make created being as created equal to nothing and therefore a pure manifestation of the Creator, Przywara claims that because the potentiality of the creature lies "in God"

---

91. Note that Jonas's and Simmel's position would be correct if seen as a theological. In effect, as Speyr says, "life is inwardly informed by the resurrection principle," so that "life has become a life that is being raised from the dead." Needless to say, this does not seem to be the *suppositio* of Jonas's and Simmel's claims. I take this to be yet another instance of the importance for a Catholic philosopher to be a "guardian of metaphysics."

92. Simmel, "Metaphysics of Death," 74.

93. Przywara, *Analogia Entis*, 223, 228–29.

it is not simply a "powerless nothing."[94] It is an "active potentiality."[95] Since it proceeds from God, the creature "is already filled with the breadth of this positivity of the pure Is"; therefore, "by virtue of its abiding inner potentiality," the creature does not have an "orientation towards nothing," but rather "towards an ever new 'is.'"[96] It is for this reason that the creature can be said to be "transparent" to God,[97] or, in other words, to be through-and-through a reenactment of his creative act, summed up in the paradoxical idea of self-creation: "For so little does the activity of the divine Is . . . intend for the creature to sink back into nothingness that, on the contrary, *the (enduring) positivity of the creature mysteriously merges with God's own (eternal) positivity.*"[98] In its true sense then, the "utterly passive potentiality" of the creature is "a summons to action."[99] The creature is transparent to God *in its own participated* self-affirming positivity.

---

94. Przywara, *Analogia Entis*, 223.

95. "'Active' wholly and 'utterly' upon the basis of the 'negative' of the negative potentiality, but nevertheless in such a way that makes fully clear what the positive potentiality was meant to establish: namely, a sharp distinction from any 'fusion with God (in some passive theopanism). It becomes the active potentiality of an unlimited 'service to God'" (Przywara, *Analogia Entis*, 228–29; see also 235). For Thomas's defense of the secondary causes of creation, see, for instance, *ST* 1, q. 105, a. 5.

96. Przywara, *Analogia Entis*, 224. See also Antonin-Gilbert Sertillanges: "Thomas is so firmly convinced that creatures have an autonomy grounded in their creation itself that, unlike many other doctors, he stoutly refuses the position that creatures tend towards nothingness and require God's constant support to keep them from doing so. In this respect, Thomas would reject Descartes' *creatio continua*. . . . Created being not only does not tend towards nothingness, it positively tends towards the growth and perfection of its own being and, in this way, to be always more and better. . . . Inasmuch as the creature is autonomous thanks to God, inasmuch as it exists *in itself*, albeit not *per se*, the creature tends to be and to increase. This tendency is the primary property of its very being. . . . Concretely, the autonomy granted the creature by the very nature of its origin is prolonged in its consequences, which orient it towards the increase and betterment of its being according to the full measure of its power" (*Idée de creation*, 62; emphasis in original).

97. Przywara, *Analogia Entis*, 432.

98. Przywara, *Analogia Entis*, 224; emphasis added. See also Sertillanges: "The idea of creation has two main features . . . the creature is *per se* nothing, albeit not nothing *in itself*. . . . On the other hand, since creation is a pure relation, and a one-sided one at that . . . this condition gives the creature the most perfect autonomy in existence and action. Not, of course, from God or against God—but by God's will itself, since creation, according to our account, *gives created being a sort of priority with respect to its own creation*. It is as if the creature spontaneously tended towards the divine Source and, in so doing, constituted itself a kind of author of its own being" (*Idée de creation*, 59; emphasis in original).

99. Przywara, *Analogia Entis*, 229.

It would be hard to think of a stronger way to state the dynamic, self-affirming nature of being-life—what could be more radical than the understanding of it as self-creation, namely, as the analogous, participated, realization of God's creative act? In one formula: just as God's creative act does not presuppose anything beyond itself for the production of the world (that is why the nihil of *creatio ex nihilo* is best understood as the onto-logical negation of the created being once it is created, *nullum ens*), so created being, as the analogous participation of God's creativity, does not require an ontologized nonbeing for its dynamism. For this reason, that is, in virtue of the notion of creation out of nothing, the negation of death does not have any co-originality with the gift of being.

If it is true, in a derivative sense that needs to be made precise, that (the) being (or life) affirms itself against (the) nonbeing (of death), it remains nevertheless true that the self-affirmative dynamism of being is not originally correlated to or in any way dependent on the negation of death. One could appeal here to the fundamental speculative distinction between *beginning* and *origin*. Even if death had been present in created being from the *beginning* of time, it would still not be a principle of its *origin*.

3.5. We can find similar metaphysical shortcomings related to the ontologization of nonbeing-death in the thought of Paul Tillich. Tillich has pages in which he beautifully gives voice to a view similar to Simmel and Jonas: "If one is asked how non-being is related to being itself, one can only answer metaphorically: being 'embraces' itself and non-being. Being has non-being 'within' itself as that which is . . . present and . . . overcome."[100] Despite its seeming soundness, the problem with Tillich's position is not only that he introduces genuine negation into God in order to make sense of the divine "Life," but also that, when it comes to the "finitude" of creation, he does not seem to distinguish carefully the two meanings of nonbeing, namely, that of the finitude of created being and that of privation of being-good of evil.

This becomes evident when his discussion of nonbeing in man is immediately interpreted according to the figure of the human anxiety in the face of death:

> Anxiety is the existential awareness of non-being. "Existential" in this sentence means that it is not the abstract knowledge of non-being which produces anxiety but the awareness that

---

100. Tillich, *Courage to Be*, 47.

> non-being is part of one's own being. It is not the realization of universal transitoriness, not even the experience of the death of others, but the impression of these events on the always latent awareness of our own having to die, that produces anxiety. Anxiety is finitude, experienced as one's finitude. This is the natural anxiety of man as man, and in some way of all living beings. It is the anxiety of non-being, the awareness of one's finitude as finitude.[101]

As one can see, there is an ambiguity here that has nefarious consequences on the whole discussion. The problem with such statement is precisely the identification of finitude with the negation of death. But finitude is not necessarily so. If we take "finitude" to mean creatureliness—the constant, transcendental exposure to the *nihil* of *creatio ex nihilo*, not to the negation of death—then it is not clear why such exposure should inspire anxiety rather than prayerful gratitude. From the point of view presented in this chapter, finitude does not (some would even say, analytically!) imply end: the finite is not that which must "finish." What finitude implies, rather, is that what is called finite is not identical with the origin (creation) and that what is called finite has a beginning (in time). Anxiety results from the exposure to the nonbeing of death, the total negation of the gift of life "at work" in our being, despite us and yet because of us. We see at work in Tillich the Heideggerian legacy, which is in turn the result of that tendency of ontologization of nonbeing-guilt-death of which Del Noce speaks, as outlined in section 2. If death is definitive for our human condition, it is neither original nor constitutive.[102]

3.6. Vladimir Jankélévitch, himself a student of Henri Bergson and, indirectly, of Simmel, proposes what may be considered the subtlest form of the ontologization of the nonbeing of death. His works on death are endlessly rich and insightful and it would be impossible to recount them in all their detail. Thus, I will attempt something even more difficult and I will try to extract the structural aspects of his discourse on death. As I will try to show, the hinge of his entire treatment is the concept of the "organ-obstacle." Death is, at once and from the same point of view, what

---

101. Tillich, *Courage to Be*, 44.

102. The following verses by Henry Scott Holland are misguiding, both with respect to revelation and philosophy: "Death is nothing at all. / I have only slipped away to the next room. / . . . Life means all that it ever meant. / It is the same that it ever was. / There is absolute and unbroken continuity. / What is this death but a negligible accident?" (*Death Is Nothing at All*, unnumbered pages).

is *toto coelo* opposed to life and being and an *enabling condition of life and being*—the "lethal a priori" of finite life.

It would seem impossible at first to liken Jankélévitch's proposal to what Simmel and the others maintain. Jankélévitch writes in fact powerfully against the meaningfulness of death:

> It is not being that is defined on the backdrop of nonbeing, but is the nonbeing which, despite everything, appears as a suspension of being and is defined by rapport and in relation to being.[103]

Jankélévitch devotes many pages to explain that death is

> the flat nonsense of sense and the pure and simple nonbeing of being.[104]

> In what way would death ground the meaning of life? Death is so far from being a ground that it is the thing most in need of a justification! ... Death, far from giving becoming its ultimate meaning, subtracts from it that little meaning that it still has for a carefree mind. Death is, if you wish, the depth of life, but this truth is not an essential or central truth ... No! This truth is rather a nontruth, this "principle" is a counterprinciple that presides to the inscrutable absurdity of our annihilation.[105]

Death is the end that terminates the ends of life; it is neither direction nor telos; and so forth.

Despite all these provisos, Jankélévitch also believes that death and finitude coincide metaphysically:

> Life is paradoxically an allusion to that pernicious antithesis [death] which is the evil of finitude. ... Since it was necessary to choose between an existence steeped in limitation and the infinity of inexistence, and since the creature could not accumulate the incompossibles nor could it be someone without renouncing to be everyone, destiny has always already chosen, right from birth, the determination which is negation. As for the free choices of the empirical existence, they are decisions through which the creature confirms and ratifies her own unilaterality, adheres fully to its finitude, assumes the bane of the alternative instead of protesting desperately against it.[106]

---

103. Jankélévitch, *Mort*, 408.
104. Jankélévitch, *Mort*, 69.
105. Jankélévitch, *Mort*, 70.
106. Jankélévitch, *Mort*, 116.

It is on these grounds that Jankélévitch can affirm that death is an "organ-obstacle": death is that enabling condition of life which makes life what it is while at the same time undermining life by putting an end to it.[107]

Jankélévitch's treatment is enriched by a discussion of the dialectic or polarity between life and death. On the one hand, life and thought win over death by acknowledging "ironically" (i.e., with detachment) their transcendence over death. Life "comprehends" death in thought and recognizes that the logical principles by which it abides transcend time and space, finitude and death. Moreover, life's victory over death is the victory of "right," of the metaphysical superiority of the yes of being over the no of nonbeing. On the other hand, death wins over life by "deriding" the transcendence of life and thought in the simple act of destroying them forever: death, which is and remains "illegitimate and should not happen," is "the most real of facts."[108]

The dialectic of life and death, their mutual and never-resolved partial victories, "irony" and "derision," corresponds more to what Guardini calls a "polar opposition" rather than a proper dialectic. It is what Jankélévitch characterizes sometimes as a "contradictory reciprocity": no superior, transformative synthesis is ever possible, and taking life and death "seriously" may mean precisely living and dying in the wake of this irreducible polarity. Saying that death is the only victorious actor is not correct, not only because life and thought acknowledge their transcendence over death by embracing it in comprehension, but also because death cannot annihilate the fact that I have existed—even after I stopped existing (death destroys the *factum* but in the very same gesture immortalizes the *fecisse*). At the same time, however, life and love can be considered unilaterally victorious over death only poetically according to Jankélévitch: it is only a poetic metaphor to maintain that love makes life stronger than death. For him, in fact, death is not only constitutive (although paradoxically so), but also definitive and ultimate. The polar opposition between life and death is therefore a chief case of "omnipotence against omnipotence," because love, as the Song of Songs teaches us, is "as strong as death" and not stronger than death.

---

107. It is worth noting that Jankélévitch exemplifies the idea of "organ-obstacle" with the relationship that the body bears to the soul. The body would be for the soul analogous to what death is for life: the body enables the activities of the soul (no thinking without a brain) while at the same time hindering them (the distraction of the flesh and headaches—related or unrelated to the flesh—make thinking difficult).

108. Jankélévitch, *Mort*, 409.

For Jankélévitch, then, there is no actual contradiction, insofar as the respective victories of life and death are victories from different points of view. They are "radically asymmetrical": the victory of death over life is "physical" or, we may say, a matter of fact; the victory of life-thought over death is "ideal," a matter of right. Death is a motivating factor for man's initiative, for his "movement," but never in the sense of something that is transformed into something else by the initiative of life: life and the will affirm themselves in relation to death but always an only by distancing themselves from it and by establishing themselves in opposition to it. To use two images (not used by Jankélévitch), death is not like the mistake on the canvas that the painter turns into a part of the picture; it is rather the hole on the sidewalk which cannot be patched up and which therefore forces me to jump from one side to the other.

3.6.1. Now, two questions emerge with respect to this proposal. First, is Jankélévitch's idea of death truly coherent? It seems not. On the one hand, it could make sense to state that life distances itself from death understood as nonbeing and nonsense. But on the other hand, it seems contradictory to maintain that life affirms itself by distancing itself from finitude. Rather, finitude is the positive character of that living being that we are.

Second, what does it mean to make death one of the poles of human existence? It does not mean simply to acknowledge the unsurpassable and unavoidable presence of the negation of death in life, which is something that any sound philosophical treatment of death should do. More strongly but also more problematically, it means turning this presence, this negation, into something constitutive and ultimate for the human condition. The philosophical and one may even say spiritual challenge would be precisely to acknowledge death for what it is, a total negation (which Jankélévitch does, albeit partially), without turning it into a pole, a principle, a *sine qua non* of life. Jankélévitch resists this temptation as much as possible with his talk of death as a "nontruth," a "counterprinciple," etc., but he cannot avoid concluding that there is an identity between the negative limit of death and the positive limit of finitude.

Jankélévitch's thought on death pushes the paradox so far that it turns it into a contradiction. Jankélévitch's thought is itself a spirit of contradiction and should be read as such: it cannot not reject, based on a deeply sound metaphysical intuition about the positivity of life and the negativity of death, what he cannot not maintain, thus agreeing with the philosophical wisdom of his time according to which death and creaturely finitude are one. His philosophy of death is a witness to what he calls the "necessary impossible": it is necessary for him to state that death is nonbeing and nonsense, while it is also impossible (given the Zeitgeist?) to do so fully without falling back into the ontologization of the nonbeing of death as a constitutive polarity of human existence.

4. THE SCANDAL OF BECOMING NOTHING

4.1. In having become subject to death, our creatureliness has stopped being just a "condition" and has become a challenging metaphysical mystery, which puts the self into question and demands a response. One could say, somewhat imprecisely from a metaphysical standpoint, that because of death our "nothing" is not just "behind" us but lies "ahead" of us. In other words: man in his fallenness—i.e., man in his concrete situation—can take position with regard to his *contingency* only by taking position with regard to his *mortality* (despite the fact that contingency does not originally include mortality). More deeply, this means that embracing one's creatureliness requires embracing one's death, as Antonio López states:

> The positive intimations of death can be perceived if we realize that death, beyond its meaning of biological extinction and interruption of the original giving, reminds the person of the gift of his own existence. Death reminds the receiver of the constant being allowed to be. In this regard, death reveals anew the truth of birth: finite gift's ontogenetic dependence on the source that begets the human being at every moment. . . . Perhaps more forcefully than birth itself, death discloses that life is a gift that calls for further giving, but a giving that in reality, since it is a response to the presence that calls, coincides with permitting oneself to be taken. Our contemporary culture holds up sudden death as the ideal way to die. Yet, while in some cases death may occur abruptly, normally speaking one is called to receive it, that is, to learn to give oneself over to the origin of one's own existence. Through death, one is asked to give oneself over completely."[109]

109. López, *Gift and the Unity*, 34–35. See Claudel, *Tidings Brought to Mary*, 4.5.177–78: "Is the object of life only to live? Will the feet of God's children be fastened to this wretched earth? It is not to live, but to die, and not to hew the cross, but to mount upon it, and to give all that we have, laughing! There is joy, there is freedom, there is grace, there is eternal youth! . . . What is the worth of the world compared to life? And what is the worth of life if not to be given?" Luigi Giussani comments: "Human

Material Kenosis

One should be aware at this point of the *scandalous* nature of this statement: How can it be that embracing the gift of being-life as gift from Another—which is the meaning of genuine creatureliness—must occur through the embrace of what is originally opposed to the gift of being-life, i.e., death as the consequence of sin? How can it be that embracing that "nonbeing" which has a "priority of nature" as the reminder of the metaphysical generosity that we always again receive requires accepting that antagonistic movement to being and life—the "nonbeing" of the genuine force of negation, division, rejection of death?

There are two ways in Christianity to deal with this issue that might be unsatisfactory. A first tendency, which reaches its fulfillment with German idealism, is to consider the negation of death as a necessary and original moment in the dynamism of being and life—both in God and in the creatures. The other tendency, exemplified in the theology and metaphysics of Hans Urs von Balthasar and Ferdinand Ulrich, is to see the negation of death as prefigured in the very life of the Triune God, right from the kenosis of the Father into the generation of the Son. As far as I can see, however, both tendencies run the risk of a certain univocization of nonbeing: in the former case, a univocization of the nonbeing of finite determination-difference and of death; in the latter case, a univocization of the nonbeing of self-giving love and of death. In both cases, the attempt to make sense of death leads to a hiding of the fact that death is originally what is opposed to and therefore radically incompatible with being and life. One caveat: the few things I will have to say in this section on Balthasar and Ulrich do not come even close to a comprehensive and satisfactory study of their theology and philosophy, which far exceeds the scope of this work and the competence of its author. As someone indebted to their thought, however, I offer my critiques simply as a way to clarify my own position rather than as a systematic treatment of theirs.

4.2. The perspective introduced by material kenosis seems to suggest a different way to think about death. From a metaphysical and theological point of view, "becoming nothing in death" (I summarize with this expression everything about material kenosis that I have said so far) means realizing that in embracing the total negation of death one

---

existence is a consuming of oneself 'for' something" (*Origin of Christian Claim*, 93). This in turn echoes another passage from Claudel's work: "Be a man, Pierre! Be worthy of the flame which consumes you! And if one must be consumed, let it be like the Paschal-candle, flaming on its golden candelabrum in the midst of the choir for the glory of all the Church!" (43).

is assimilated not to death, which does not have the last word, but to the *nihil* of *creatio ex nihilo*, in which and out of which one can be regenerated. So, material kenosis attempts to deal with the unmanageable scandal of evil, especially the unavoidability of death, by showing that the total negation of death has *always already been relativized* to another nonbeing—the *nihil* of creation out of nothing.

This does not mean, however, that the negation of death has been defused, nor that we have been made immune to it. On the contrary, if on the one hand such relativization means that the negation of death cannot have priority, because the only "nonbeing" that has priority in the creature remains that of the *nihil* of *creatio ex nihilo* in virtue of God's act of creation, on the other hand, this relativization means that the negation of death confers an unheard-of intensity to the *nihil* of *creatio ex nihilo*, transforming it in something more radical. Because of our sin and because of death, what lies now at the heart of our being is, to speak paradoxically, *less than nonbeing*—i.e., less than the original *nihil* of *creatio ex nihilo*.[110] It is an open-wounded *nihil*. So, in becoming nothing by embracing the total negation of death, we are assimilated to the *nihil* of *creatio ex nihilo*, which in turn has been radically intensified precisely by the insertion into being of the negation of death. This means that, in material kenosis, the *Urpunkt* from which we experience our concrete creatureliness is a nonbeing that asks not for a confirmation of being, but for the *radical regeneration* in being. A nonbeing from which springs a desire not for *more* life, but for *radically new* life.

As one can see, material kenosis does not require any univocization of nonbeing (i.e., the nonbeing of the negation of death and of the *nihil* of *creatio ex nihilo*) because according to its creaturely metaphysics the antagonistic element of death is not reabsorbed into a superior dynamic—that of the self-unfolding of life or of the self-gift of love. At the same time, the antagonistic element of death is also preserved in the fact that, according to material kenosis, the embrace of death is the embrace of the

---

110. Pseudo-Dionysius interestingly distinguishes, within the created order, between a "nonbeing" that still in a sense participates in Good and Beauty by aspiring to it and the "nonbeing" of evil, which has nothing to do with Good, Beauty, and being. The first "nonbeing" must not be taken as a "thing." It could be considered as the unformed dimension of everything that is and aspires to its fulfillment—for instance, the "nonbeing" implicit in my writing this un-finished chapter that aspires to a final completion. But the "nonbeing" of evil and death is not subject to the same law, being precisely the disruption of such law. The "nonbeing" that participates in Good and Beauty stands to the "nonbeing" of evil and death just like the unformed is related to the deformed.

totalizing, though not annihilating, negation of one's being as an ultimately unexplainable, irreducible scandal. And finally, the way in which material kenosis deals with death is not by making it a necessary and original moment of the self-unfolding of life or the self-gift of love, but by turning it into a factor of intensification of the nonbeing of the creature, which manifests itself in a different kind of questioning, a deeper kind of desire, a cry for super-generating being.

From a theological point of view, one could say, with Balthasar and Ulrich, that the self-gift of the Father to the Son that "holds nothing back" is a foreshadowing of the kenosis of the Son in Christ and therefore also of his cross. One must also take at face value the claim that "the lamb is slain from the foundation of the world" (Rev 13:8). This does not mean, however, that there is any original need for death on the part of being-life, as the idealists say, nor that there is any analogical resemblance between death and love. On the contrary, it means that Love has always already assumed within himself, in order to redeem it, that which is *toto coelo* different from him, precisely the negation of death, the rejection of being-life. Analogously, giving one's life for the love of the other is eminently reasonable for a human being—in fact, the peak of reasonableness—not because there is a common logic to love and death (as if death could be domesticated by showing that there is such a logic, maybe already in being-life, maybe even in God), but because love willingly assumes what is totally other from it—the need to die introduced into the world by distrust, hatred, and pride—in order to make all things new. In accepting death for the love of the other, man imitates the Son of God, who assumes what is totally other from him—not only a finite, human nature, but a human nature marked by the radical antagonism to being-life of death—in order to make the will of the Father, who is Love.

The eternal idea of love is and remains that of a perfect communion in which no antagonism to being-life needs to be assumed and conquered. In other words, death is not part of the original plan for creation. The perfection of love manifested in Christ is precisely that of a love that is willing to freely assume such antagonism to being-life upon itself in order to redeem it. And this not because of a commonality of nature between death and love, but precisely because of the infinite distance of the latter from the former.

4.3. Let us take two remarks by Balthasar and Ulrich as exemplificative of the whole issue. While I think that Balthasar's and Ulrich's theology and metaphysics have accomplished much in deepening theologically the sense of God's suffering and death by treating it not merely "anthropologically" but "theocentrically and in trinitarian terms,"[111] I also feel that their position presents a radical misunderstanding regarding the role of "death" vis-à-vis God's love. Balthasar wonders: "Might it not be the case (as Ferdinand Ulrich has tried to show) that the mystery of the end—God's *kenosis* in Christ—is analogically prefigured in the mystery of the beginning, namely, being as the theme of metaphysics? Might it not be the case that being, whose luminous clearing is coextensive with its noughting, mediates the radiance of the divine only insofar as it is a kind of prophecy pointing ahead to the uttermost humility of the Cross?"[112]

Balthasar claims that the "total reciprocal self-giving" of the persons in the Trinity—"God's 'blood circulation'"—is the "basis for there being a 'death' in God."[113] Balthasar spells out what this "basis" is by appealing to two principles: first, there must be in God a metaphysical condition of possibility "corresponding to death" in order for death to be assumed and conquered; second, this "corresponding to death" means that the death in man analogously corresponds to a sort of death in God, which in turn is interpreted as the kenosis of the Son (incarnation and death of Jesus) foreshadowed in the kenotic reciprocal self-giving of the persons of the Trinity. Balthasar quotes approvingly two passages to this extent, one by Hein Schürmann and one from Ulrich. Here's Schürmann: "The 'death of God' actually takes place in him in the kenosis and tapeinosis of the love of God. . . . The ontic possibility for God's self-emptying in the Incarnation and death of Jesus lies in God's eternal self-emptying in the mutual self-surrender of the Persons of the Trinity."[114] And here's Ulrich: "It is only because pain and death are internal to God, as a fluid form of love, that God can conquer death and pain by his death and Resurrection. . . . Pain and death are superseded, not in virtue of some eternal indifference on the part of God's essence, but because, by his absolute free will, pain and death are eternally the language of his glory (and this applies even to

---

111. Balthasar, *Last Act*, 244.

112. This is the translation of the passage provided in Oster, "Thinking Love," 672. For the standard translation, see Balthasar: "And may it not be the case (as Ferdinand Ulrich tries to show) that the final mystery of the kenosis of God in Christ has an analogous structure in the metaphysical mystery of being, which shines forth as it destroys, which mediates the radiance of the divine only by pointing forward to the utter humility of the Cross?" (*Realm of Metaphysics in Antiquity*, 38).

113. Balthasar, *Last Act*, 245.

114. Balthasar, *Last Act*, 243.

the cry of death, the silence of death, and to *being* dead itself)."[115] We can clearly see in these two passages the two principles laid out above.

A first remark here would be that the question "What is the condition of possibility in God that allows him to take death upon himself?" should be rather understood as part of a broader question, namely, "How can God assume human nature?" And even granting the formulation of the question along the lines of Balthasar's position, the answer should be: God's unconditional love, mercy. The point would be hardly denied by Balthasar and Ulrich, of course. Nevertheless, saying this allows us to reframe the problem dealt with by Balthasar and Ulrich regarding what in God's love "corresponds" to human death.

Now, Ulrich writes: "By his absolute free will, pain and death are eternally the language of his glory." I think that Ulrich's insight here is illuminating and unveils a deep truth. God has always already accepted the need to die out of love for man, arguably already in the self-giving of the Father in the generation of the Son. What is unacceptable, I think, is to establish a sort of *isomorphism (no matter how analogically stretched out) between God's love and death based on the idea that God's love is total self-giving and, therefore, utter poverty, total self-emptying, etc.* None of this, in fact, includes or implies that negation of life and love that death is—death being the very opposite of life and love, an ultimate form of antagonism to being-life. It is for this reason that the Christian God, who assumes human nature and death out of love, is even more lovely and scandalous—a God who is so "capable of the other" to assume not only finite nature, but its fallenness.

In other words, if one wants to find a sort of metaphysical condition of possibility in God for assuming evil and death, the best candidate is precisely his *capacity for the totally other as other*. God is so capable of loving the other that he willingly assumes not only the other in his goodness (i.e., human nature), but also the other in his evil and fallenness (the consequences of sin and death). He is willing to follow his beloved "other" even there where this other has become "less than nothing," in that utmost distance from God that is death. There is nothing that "corresponds to death" in God beyond this unimaginable capacity for the other. The advantage of this position is that it resists the temptation to domesticate the utter, antagonistic negation of death by subsuming it somehow within the nonantagonistic self-negation, self-gift of love.

---

115. Balthasar, *Last Act*, 246; emphasis in original.

THE ANALOGY OF BEING AND THE NONBEING OF DEATH

Between the two negations there can only be *equivocity*, an equivocity of death vis-à-vis being, life, and love that neither the reciprocal self-giving of the persons of the Trinity nor the hypostatic union of Christ eliminate. That is why God's power over death can only be manifested in, through, and after death's power over God is manifested on the cross.

A reflection from Adrienne von Speyr that both Balthasar and Ulrich must have known can help us clarify the point further. She writes:

> We understand life as constant endeavor. But the poverty and need that are at the source of our striving are altogether foreign to eternal life. Life for us is an anxious affair, and we snatch what we can, whereas eternal life is free and open, all giving and receiving, accepting and granting, an undisturbed flow of riches; eternal life is love. . . . In another sense both life and death are images of God. Of course, one cannot say that death, as an end, is in any sense in God, since his eternal life is unending. But if death is understood to mean the sacrifice of life, then the original image of that sacrifice in God is the gift of life flowing between Father and Son in the Spirit. For the Father gives his whole life to the Son, the Son gives it back to the Father, and the Spirit is the outflowing gift of life. This "living death" is the absolute opposite of the death of sin in which man ceases giving. . . . Sinful death and sacrificial death are as fire and water, opposites that have nothing in common. The death of sin is annihilated by the death of Christ on the Cross.[116]

The "absolute opposition" between the sacrificial death of the "living death" of God and the "sinful death" of the human being means that between the two there must be onto-logical equivocity. No metaphysical analogical taming, based on the original meaning of love, being, and life, is available for the death introduced into the world by man. *Christ, understood as the "concrete analogy of being," spans the entire distance between God and nonbeing only by assuming the dis-analogy of the total negation*

---

116. Speyr, *Meditations on John 1–5*, 39, 42–43. See Bieler, "Cross of Christ as Trinitarian," 187–88. Elsewhere, however, Speyr is not careful enough to stress the "absolute opposition" (equivocity) of the two senses, e.g.: "By entering into time he becomes nothing, he renounces his heavenly life (without losing his vision of the Father): this is a death. Even his birth contains a premonition of the cross. And it is clear that those who wish to follow him must include in their self-dedication that renunciation which the Son performs at his birth. He undergoes a twofold death to redeem the world: he bids farewell to the Father and to his beloved heaven in order to address himself to the world's need, in order to cultivate his vision of the Father in a way which includes the perspectives of earth, and in order, finally, to die on the cross totally forsaken by the Father, presenting the perfect sacrifice of his life for sinners" (*Mystery of Death*, 108).

of death, the meaning and irreducibility of which is therefore indispensable even when we "philosophize in Christ" (as one should).

4.3.1. John Betz has stressed the importance of understanding that Balthasar's language is informed by the analogy of being: "Whatever Balthasar ascribes to the immanent Trinity on the basis of revelation—as when he speaks of the Son's eternal obedience or even of the father's self-sacrifice and 'death'—is ascribed not directly but according to the *analogia entis*."[117] However, this is precisely the *punctum dolens*: no metaphysical inclusion of death into being is possible.[118]

Nor is Betz's appeal to "paradox" more helpful here. He claims that the way to avoid any reductive account of God's nature is to have the "simple intuition of the paradoxical nature of divine simplicity in which majesty and humility, glory and kenosis, like mercy and justice, are inscrutably one."[119] "Majesty and humility" and "justice and mercy" are the paradoxical poles of God's simple nature. However, when it comes to "glory and kenosis," the issue is different because kenosis also includes death, which is precisely the element which makes the paradoxical paradigm put forth by Betz explode. In fact, with the first two polarities, we are "on the side of being," as it were; we are describing more carefully the internal articulation of being; but with the polarity "glory and kenosis," we are introducing an element which is not and cannot be originally associated with being, namely, death. The hypostatic union of Christ, thus, insofar as Christ assumes a fallen human nature, manifests the unity of what is and remains *toto coelo* different, that is, life and death, love and its contradictory. The cross does not reveal that there is some deeper unity of nature, graspable through the analogy of being, between life and death. It reveals that what is *toto coelo* different from being, love, and life has been assumed and conquered. Przywara is spot on when he calls the

---

117. Betz, *Christ, Logos of Creation*, 382.

118. Betz's later comments on Przywara and "the real contradiction of sin" seem hard to square with his claim that death is susceptible of an analogous (and not merely metaphorical) reading. "For the unity of the mediator is not simply a unity that includes multiplicity and apparent antithesis . . . but a unity that bears in itself—and overcomes in itself—the real contradiction of son. As Przywara puts it: 'The mediator appears not merely as a human being (rather than pure spirit), but as the expiation for sin. . . . Hence, what is meant by the concrete form that 'God-as-middle' assumes in the mediator is . . . a 'oneness' with (through the vicarious bearing of) the nothingness of sin'" (*Christ, Logos of Creation*, 397–98).

119. Betz, *Christ, Logos of Creation*, 391.

theological analogy of being a "blessed *contradiction*."[120] Love and death are linked, *Deo gratias*, not by an analogous tie manifesting itself to man in the form of a paradox; but by a union of equivocal terms manifesting itself in the form of a scandalous mercy.

Saying that there must be something "like death" in God's love to redeem human death and reading something like this death into the emptiness, poverty, or humility of the reciprocal self-giving of the persons sounds too much like that "philosophical logic of identity" that Balthasar and Ulrich correctly criticize at many points in their work. I cannot shake off the feeling that Balthasar, while rightly criticizing Hegel and the kenotic theologies stemming from his metaphysics, might have caught the idealist bug along the way, though maybe in a less fatal form than the great theologian from Stuttgart.[121] Or maybe more it should be said more correctly that Balthasar fails to maintain the right distinction between theology and metaphysics, thus collapsing the metaphysical analogy of being into the figure of Christ.

4.4. A similar risk can be found, I believe, in Ulrich's metaphysics of being.[122] Ulrich articulates a metaphysics of being (and a metaphysical anthropology based on it) which is the deepening of St. Thomas's claim that created being is *completum et simplex, sed non subsistens* (complete and simple, but not subsistent).[123] Common being, as the first perfection of creation and the *imago Divinae bonitatis* (image of divine goodness), is neither something different from the substances that are, nor something reducible to them. Insofar as common being subsists only in the various substances that are, it is a perfection that is always already given away in the most radical way. In this sense, the original meaning of being for

---

120. Przywara, *Analogia Entis*, 568; emphasis in original.

121. As a possible corrective to what I am saying, see Betz: "Balthasar's doctrine of kenosis was informed by a long-standing tradition of philosophical and theological reflection on this biblical trope. At the same time, as a Catholic theologian, he was by no means an unqualified assimilator of this tradition, as Cyril O'Regan has shown with respect to Hegel and Jennifer Newsome Martin has shown with respect to Soloviev and Bulgakov" (*Christ, Logos of Creation*, 370–71).

122. I am not in a position to compose an extensive analysis of Ulrich's position on death because his book on the subject, *Leben in der Einheit von Leben und Tod*, is not available in any translation, as far as I know, and I cannot read German. Nevertheless, the passage quoted from Balthasar's book, Ulrich's kenotic metaphysics of being, and Ulrich's remarks in "Unity of Life and Death" (the English translation of a section of *Leben in der Einheit*) seem to point in the direction of the same problem present in Balthasar's theology of death.

123. QDP, q. 1, a. 1.

Ulrich is *kenotic*. The fullness and wealth of common being lie in its utter poverty, in its refusal to cling to itself. It is always already self-expropriatedness and emptiness. In this sense, then, common being is "nothing" in itself, not only in the obvious sense that it is no-thing, but, more radically, in the sense that it is "fullness given away."[124]

Stefan Oster clarifies the origin and scope of Ulrich's metaphysics:

> Being is, in truth, love, love radically given away. Now, Ulrich is a Christian whose faith enables him to recognize the identity between the God who created the world good at the beginning and the God who redeemed it on the Cross. It is therefore fitting that his *philosophical* account of created being as love, while not derived from the theology of the Cross, should nonetheless fully display the radicalness of its implications in light of that theology.... There is an analogy, then, between being and the kenosis of Christ, insofar as the former reflects the character of the latter: Christ does not cling to his glory (wealth) as if it were something to be grasped at, but empties himself (poverty) in obedience to the point of death on the Cross (Phil 2:6–8). Ulrich explains this analogical mirroring by means of a speculative unfolding of the profound insight of Thomas that created being is "*completum at simplex, sed non subsistens.*" ... Being is wealth, unity, plenitude, light, life, goodness: pure, simple act..... Nevertheless, *as such* it is always given away radically. In this sense, it can be thought of as poverty, refusal to cling to self, expropriatedness, emptiness (the emptiness of love).... Given all of this, says Ulrich, then metaphysics, with its question about being, comes fully into its own precisely when it pursues its account of being in light of this radical Christological depth.[125]

Ulrich's metaphysics is nothing shy of being a uniquely exemplary instance of Catholic philosophy which "overcomes the baneful dualism between philosophy and theology, and it does so perhaps more successfully than ever before."[126] For this reason, one can simply hope to learn from the perspective opened by it. Nevertheless, one can also wonder whether Ulrich's interpretation of common being as kenotic and analogous to Christ is fully satisfactory. In fact, in order for the analogy to be

---

124. Ulrich, *Homo Abyssus*, 30. Ulrich's expands on this through the notion of "transnihilation" (*Durchnichtung*): being "gives itself up in transnihilation unreservedly" (*Homo Abyssus*, 30).

125. Oster, "Thinking Love," 672–73; emphasis in original.

126. Balthasar, letter, quoted in Oster, "Thinking Love," 660–61.

genuine, the kenosis of being must exhibit that same assumption of genuine negation that we find in Christ. And this is precisely what Ulrich's position cannot do consistently. On the one hand, in fact, Ulrich stresses repeatedly that the movement of "transnihilation" (*Durchnichtung*) of common being, which is one with its "movement into subsistence" (*Subsistenz-bewegung*), is not a genuine self-negation, precisely because any real negation (such as the negation of death) can occur only in and to a substance. More deeply, "transnihilation" and "movement into subsistence," far from carrying within themselves any trait of antagonism to being, life, and love, are precisely the inner dynamism of being, life, and love. Therefore, self-negation with respect to common being is said only metaphorically, in order to convey the idea of the original openness and utmost generosity of creation. On the other hand, however, Ulrich's position has the tendency to read death—which is, from our point of view, a genuine negation, as carrying within itself a true element of antagonism to being, life, and death—back into that metaphorical negation of kenotic being.[127] In this way, the genuine negativity of death is lost in its specificity, and the original sense of kenosis in being remains ambiguously suspended between a self-giving that is not identifiable with any genuine negation (let alone the negation of death) and a negation of death that is more or less systematically inserted into the original sense of being, life, and love.

4.5. All I have been trying to say, in short, is that the *utter loss of one's being* implied in one's total loving self-communication to the other or, which is the same, the loving embrace of and patient surrender to the *utter loss of one's being*, can only be loved, desired, and pursued per accidens. The idea of "accidens" points to two important truths, one metaphysical, the other eminently theological and Christian.

First, as I have repeatedly said, there is nothing in love itself that implies per se the self-negating, self-destructive dynamic proper of death, which is in fact an irreducible element of antagonism to being-life. There is nothing common, metaphysically speaking, between life and death, between being and the nonbeing of evil. Thus, it just so stubbornly "happens," with the necessity of a fact (maybe even an *eternal* fact!) but not of a law of being, that we must become "nothing" in order to give ourselves back to God. Similarly, it just so happens that love requires sacrifice to

---

127. See Bieler, "Introduction." Bieler analyzes Ulrich's unpublished work "Death in Knowledge and Love."

the point of death, to the point of "laying down one's life for one's friends" (John 15:13).

Second, the idea of "accidens" also stresses that the negation of death has been assumed into and redeemed by the love of God in an "accident," that is, in the unimaginable and undeducible "event" of the incarnation, passion, death, resurrection, and ascension of our Lord Jesus Christ. However, this does not mean necessarily, as Balthasar worries, that the sense of God's suffering and death is therefore treated merely "anthropologically" and not "theocentrically and in trinitarian terms." One can still accept, as I think one should, Balthasar's deep insight that the total self-giving of the Father to the Son is also originally kenotic and prefigures the kenosis of the Son in his incarnation and death. In doing so, however, one must stress that this means that God in his infinite love has always already accepted to deal with what is totally other from him. It does not mean, as it is sometimes claimed, that death is somehow already included in the very unfolding of love, as if death were not something essentially and irreducibly antagonistic to being-life. God has always already decided that not even sin and death—what is most distant from Life—can be an objection to his love, and has brought this to perfection in the event of Christ.[128] To use another important notion used by Ulrich,

---

128. C. S. Lewis offers profound reflections on this very point, and I believe that what I say here can also illuminate back what Lewis says: "If you ask God to take you back without it [death], you are really asking Him to let you go back without going back. It cannot happen. Very well, then, we must go through with it. But the same badness which makes us need it, makes us unable to do it. Can we do it if God helps us? ... Now if we had not fallen, that would be all plain sailing. But unfortunately we now need God's help in order to do something which God, in His own nature, never does at all—to surrender, to suffer, to submit, to die. Nothing in God's nature corresponds to this process at all. So that the one road for which we now need God's leadership most of all is a road God, in His own nature, has never really walked. God can share only what He has: this thing, in His own nature, He has not. But supposing God became man—suppose our human nature which can suffer and die was amalgamated with God's nature in one person—then that person could help us. He could surrender His will, and suffer and die, because He was man; and He could do it perfectly because He was God. You and I can go through this process only if God does it in us; but God can do it only if He becomes man. Our attempts at this dying will succeed only if we men share in God's dying, just as our thinking can succeed only because it is a drop out of the ocean of His intelligence: but we cannot share God's dying unless God dies; and He cannot die except by being a man. That is the sense in which He pays our debt, and suffers for us what He Himself need not suffer at all" (*Mere Christianity*, 57–58). Note how the sentence "He could surrender His will, and suffer and die, because He was man; and He could do it perfectly because He was God" shows that Lewis's position does not need to be understood anthropocentrically.

man's "obedience to being"[129] requires the humble and patient surrender to the genuine negation of death only by accident, as just explained.

The loving surrender to suffering and death is certainly the surrender in our life to the love of God who calls us back to him in a final, definitive way. But it is also, in the very same movement, a surrender to *what needed not to be* and has been from the very beginning *toto coelo* opposed to love, being, and life, namely, the negation of death. It is also the surrender to, in the embrace of, the God who, in his unconditional love and capacity for the other, has assumed out of love for his creature the same negation of death, that which is even more distant from his Love, Being, and Life than it is from us, if it is true, as Przywara has reminded us that, no matter how great a similarity, there is an always greater dissimilarity between God and man. Becoming nothing in death *in the God who has become nothing in death* is something scandalous indeed.

4.6. A note may be in place here regarding the language of "condition of possibility" used by Balthasarians to defend Balthasar's position. Two authors, Angela Franks and John Betz, have recently provided illuminating defenses of Balthasar's theology of the cross, especially by comparison to Thomas Joseph White's criticisms of Balthasar. This is not the place to unpack and discuss the many wonderful points treated by Franks, Betz, and White. In general, I do agree with Franks and Betz that Balthasar (but also John Paul II and Benedict XVI) has made clear that the locus of the redemption of the world on the cross is the actual "experience of 'the separation, the rejection by the Father,' that is proper to us sinners, not to the Son. But on the Cross, the Son takes on our experience, for the sake of his mission to save us."[130] While White defends the utter "dis-analogy"[131] between Jesus's redemptive suffering and the sinner's suffering, Franks and Betz, following Balthasar, are more correct, as far as I can see, in putting forth the interpretation according to which it is precisely the sinner's suffering, understood as the consequence of the separation from the Father due to sin, that Jesus experiences on the cross—that same Jesus who is sinless. As also Thomas and the tradition recognize, Jesus suffers the consequences of sin without being a sinner. The important point for our purposes however, as I have anticipated, is the language of the "condition of possibility" that Franks and Betz tend

---

129. Ulrich, *Homo Abyssus*, 23n4.
130. Franks, "Thomistic-Balthasarian Comments," 594.
131. White, *Lord Incarnate*, 318.

to use. For instance, Franks writes: "Balthasar is not arguing that the difference between moral evil and God is simply analogous to the difference between the divine Persons. Rather, his point is that the *possibility* of sin is derived from the Trinitarian difference";[132] "the distinction of the Persons of the Trinity provides the conditions of possibility for the Son to take on the sinner's separation from God."[133] Betz adopts a similar terminology when he speaks of the kenosis of the Father: "Following Bulgakov, he [Balthasar] also infers from the Son's self-sacrifice an eternal kenosis within the immanent Trinity as its transcendental condition—ultimately finding the archetype for the Son's kenosis in the eternal generation of the Son from the father, thereby making kenosis constitutive of God as God."[134] What I am interested in here is not to question the Ur-kenosis of the Father, but the language of the "transcendental conditions" that Balthasarian in general, and Betz in this case, adopt to explain the relation between the negation of difference and the negation of contradiction.

The claim that the difference among the persons is the condition of possibility (of the possibility) of evil can be understood in three ways. First, by giving the no used in both cases an analogous meaning—no matter how remote the second use may be from the first. So, the no intrinsic and constitutive of difference—the Father is not the Son, the Son is not the Father, the Spirit is neither the Father nor the Son—would be the condition of possibility of the no of the creature to the Creator. This seems hardly a viable option for Catholic theology, simply because the no of rejection (which is the opposite of love) is analogously identified with the no of difference (which is a condition, or essential ingredient, of love). Balthasar's rhetoric comes very close to something like this sometimes, as I have shown above, but it would be obviously uncharitable and wrong to interpret his overall position in this way.[135] It is not hard to find passages where Balthasar clearly rejects anything of this sort: "Diabolical contra-diction cannot be assimilated into God's logic."[136] It remains true however, it seems to me, that the analogous assimilation of kenotic,

---

132. Franks, "Thomistic-Balthasarian Comments," 590–59n38.

133. Franks, "Thomistic-Balthasarian Comments," 595.

134. Betz, *Christ, Logos of Creation*, 371.

135. This rhetoric has induced authors such as Brotherton to criticize Balthasar precisely for the assimilation of the "otherness" between sinner and God with the "otherness" of the distinction of the persons of the Trinity. See Brotherton, *One of the Trinity*, 218, 244–46.

136. Balthasar, *Theo-Logic* 2, quoted in Franks, "Thomistic-Balthasarian Comments," 591.

self-giving love and death must imply what Balthasar otherwise clearly denies.[137]

A more nuanced reading of the language of the "condition of possibility" could be the following. The difference or "distance" among the persons is an original "space of freedom" which metaphysically grounds and makes possible the "space of freedom opened up between the creature and God."[138] Accordingly, it is precisely this space of freedom that would constitute the condition of possibility of two things: first, of the positivity of the creature in its freedom-otherness from God; second, of the no of the creature to the Creator. To this statement, one could certainly consent, but, as one sees, an essential qualification would be in place. In fact, the element of continuity or similarity here between the Trinitarian Creator and the creature would be the yes of freedom, which is the fullness of being "dramatically" understood, not the no of rejection, which is the contradiction of that positive "drama" of love. The no of rejection happens as the *overall corruption or denial of freedom*, not as one of its possible implementations (unless one understands freedom as a superficial "freedom of choice," which seems very far from Balthasar's robust view of freedom).

Also in this second case, however, the language of the "condition of possibility" seems to introduce an element of confusion which tends to corrupt a metaphysical understanding of genuine negativity. For this reason, although according to this second interpretation the no of rejection is not per se treated as an ingredient of being and love, the unqualified statement that the Trinitarian space of freedom is the condition of possibility of the creaturely evil tends almost inevitably to make the nonbeing

---

137. A passage where Betz discusses the reservations that some Thomists have regarding Balthasar's language represents well my hesitation to endorse Balthasar's position without qualification: "Brotherton recognizes that things might 'on the surface' seem worse than they are and that if Balthasar speaks of a 'wound' in the divine nature, it is not a wound per se but only a wound 'of sorts,' namely, a 'wound' of love by which the Father is 'touched' by the Son's willingness to give himself up for the sake of the world's redemption. It is evident, in other words, that Balthasar is speaking metaphorically and perhaps never so much as when he speaks of the Father's generation of the Son as a kind of 'death.' Nevertheless, for Brotherton, following Kevin Duffy, no amount of scare quotes—or what he and Duffy call the 'metaphor defense'—is enough to save Balthasar's theology from (at the very least) incoherence. For what we see in Balthasar, in their view, is at the end of the day 'an undifferentiated amalgam of metaphor and analogy' whereby 'literal assertions such as 'There is super-change in God' are accorded quasi-metaphorical status that they [strictly speaking] do not possess" (*Christ, Logos of Creation*, 377).

138. Franks, "Thomistic-Balthasarian Comments," 598.

of evil *slide into the positivity of being*—one could safely say, against the intention of Balthasar and his followers. My sense is that this sliding is made possible precisely by the appeal to the notion of "condition of possibility." The notion of condition of possibility is not "dangerous" due to its Kantian and thus epistemologistic (and not ontological) ancestry, as some commentators claim.[139] On the contrary, the Kantian origin of the phrase, if taken seriously, would teach us something valuable on the point under consideration. What it can teach us is that the phrase "condition of possibility" usually makes sense as the device, typical of the transcendental method of doing philosophy, which connects a positive to another, more original or constitutive, positive, in order to explain it. So, in the Kantian system, the positive of the object of science, the *phenomenon*, is made possible by the a priori structures of human knowledge, which thus work as the original and implicit conditions of possibility of science as such. If this is true, it means that the use of the phrase "condition of possibility" to explain a negative—evil, the nonbeing of death, etc.—by relation to a positive is at least unorthodox, and a careful construction of this explanation should be aware of this unorthodoxy.

However, the real problem in my view does not even lie in the unorthodoxy of this use of the phrase "condition of possibility"—given that philosophical unorthodoxy is certainly not the mark of falsity—but rather in its viability as explanation. And this leads us to the third possible interpretation of the Balthasarian claim. According to this third interpretation, the difference among the persons would be the condition of possibility of the no of the creature in the same way that what is positive is the condition of possibility of what is negative. The point here would be very simple, and very classical indeed. There would be no blindness without an eyed person, no limping without a legged person, etc. Also in this case one could agree with this claim, but with two essential qualifications—qualifications which may turn the original claim into something very different, so that one may not be able to speak any longer of an "agreement." First, one should point out that, by saying that the positive is the condition of possibility of the negative, one should be aware of the risk of *explaining too much*. In fact, while in the case of a positive reduced to its positive conditions of possibility we have a proper explanation (see again the example of Kantian science), in the case of the negative reduced to its positive conditions of possibility we do not

---

139. For instance, Brotherton, *One of the Trinity*, 248.

have a proper explanation but, rather, the mere metaphysical clarification that the negative cannot be original and that it enjoys only a parasitical existence. In other words, evil and the nonbeing of death can be clarified in their metaphysical "nature" (that is, their non-nature), but cannot be explained, transcendentally or otherwise. Evil is, by definition, the absurd. Such an excess of explanation would then easily result (not necessarily, but easily, especially when the thinker's rhetoric is loaded in this direction) in the surreptitious insertion of an analogical continuity—no matter how remote—between *explanandum* and *explanans*, between negative and positive, with the ill-fated consequences which we have been discussing. Xavier Tilliette's words come to mind: "To answer this question [Why death?] is to deprive death of its sting, something that we cannot and should not do."[140]

Second, one should also point out that such a construction would be common to everything that is and everything that is not—the positivity of God is the condition of possibility of both participated beings as well as of the negations or privates which affect them—and, while Balthasar would certainly not say that God is the condition of possibility of both in the same way, the very structure of the argument would tend to hide the difference. Needless to say, caution in pointing out the difference would solve this issue, but, once we remove the risk of misunderstanding, what is left may be an explanation that, precisely because it works as an explanation of everything, might end up being an explanation of nothing. In other words: the problem of negation is a (metaphysical, philosophical, human) problem precisely because it seems to contradict being. Now, by saying that God, the absolutely positive, is the condition of possibility of the misuse of freedom and of its consequences, we adopt a kind of argument that can be applied to everything: God, the absolutely positive, is the condition of possibility of my headache now, of my bad sight now, of the bread being moldy, etc., which is, in a sense, true, but only insofar as these realities are participated beings, and not insofar as they are lacking in being. And third, if the point of the third interpretation is to simply affirm that the negative only enjoys a parasitical existence, then it is hard to see how the "explanation" of the nonbeing of death might have to inconvenience God instead of stopping at the level of that finite being which is affected by such negativity—in this case, the human being. Certainly, if the transitive property applies to this case, as it does, we can say that if

---

140. Tilliette, *Morte e sopravvivenza*, 405.

God is the condition of possibility of the existence of the human being, and the human being is the condition of possibility of the no of death, then we can also say that God is the condition of possibility of the no of death. But, as we have already said, we use the notion of condition of possibility in very different ways: in the first case, as per se; in the second case, as per accidens. And it is precisely the difference between this per se and this per accidens which constitutes the heart of the metaphysical issue at stake here. So again, by saying this, we either risk explaining too much or, which is even worse, we surreptitiously insert some kind of continuity between being and nonbeing.

5. THE PERSONAL ACT OF DEATH

5.1. In the context of their reflection on human death, some contemporary Catholic theologians and philosophers have stressed the "practical" and the "existential" moment of man's being confronted with death. Ladislaus Boros, Roger Troisfontaines, and especially Karl Rahner, in part under the influence of existentialism and Heidegger's existential analytic of Dasein, and in part summing up a long tradition of the Christian meditation on the preparation to death, have put forth the notion of death as an act.[141] According to Rahner, for instance, death in its fundamental meaning has to do with the *personal free act of self-decision vis-à-vis God* that man makes when confronted with the end. To use a paradoxical but accurate expression, one would have to say, following these authors, that we must "act death" in order to rescue death from being a merely objective, natural event and therefore in order to experience it as a properly personal phenomenon. In other words, the person does

---

141. Also Marcel speaks of the act of death: "Death must be an act, it must be felt as a positive mode of sharing in a certain good which is itself bound up with history" ("Value and Immortality," 137). For Marcel, however, this "act" is an "explicit refusal, a definite negation of death," namely, what corresponds to the claim "To love a being is to say you, you in particular, will never die" (140). It is that unconditional act of "fidelity" to the beloved which implies the negation of death, to the point that failing to deny death in such way would amount to an act of "betrayal" of the beloved. "Act" here means something very different from what Rahner and the others discuss, and Marcel helpfully points out that his position is directly opposed to Heidegger's (141). Marcel does not want to provide a "proof" of immortality along the lines of the traditional arguments for the indestructibility of the soul. Nevertheless, he maintains that love would contradict itself if he did not deny the death of the beloved, and that this is safe enough ground to put into question that death is the end of life: "To consent to the death of a being is in a sense to give him up to death" (140).

not undergo death as a merely objective or natural event "from without" but accomplishes it as the self-consummation of the subject "from within."[142] Jacques Derrida seems to point to something similar when he suggests that one must paradoxically "exist death."[143]

What I have to say in this section aspires to be an integration (and maybe a partial correction?) of the position put forth by Rahner and the other authors just mentioned. My proposal does not want to discount the positive or affirmative element present in the act of death understood as a personal act. After all, I agree with them that a certain self-transcendence—and thus, a certain transcendence of the negativity of death in the very act of personal decision—is coessential to the nature of the person. Nevertheless, I see in Rahner's and similar positions the risk of neglecting the negativity of death when it comes to the *personal* dimension of death. More specifically, it seems to me that a position such as Rahner's may end up reducing the negativity of death to the *extrinsic*

---

142. Rahner, *Theology of Death*, 38–39. See also Boros, *Mystery of Death*; Troisfontaines, *I Do Not Die*.

143. Derrida, *Aporias*, 68. Also Paul-Louis Landsberg comes close to this view when he writes: "Personal existence is not fatality; its task is to transform the fatality of death into liberty" (*Experience of Death*, 22). Nevertheless, Landsberg's treatment seems to me more balanced and subtler than Rahner's and the others because it stresses more convincingly the unnaturality of death and the incapacity of natural hope and freedom to overcome it successfully: "It is only in myth and dreams that the hero finds death as the culminating point of his perfection. From this fact we may already conclude death is not in its primitive sense an immanent possibility of personal existence, of the *Dasein* itself. Death comes from an alien sphere and is introduced as it were from outside into our existence. The spiritual appropriation of death is the supreme task of each human person, but the effort is an acknowledgment of the nature of this death which has to be transformed. . . . The acceptance of death transforms death, but this acceptance presupposes resistance. The human person is not, in its true essence, an *existence towards death*. Like every other existence, after its own fashion, it is a movement towards self-realisation and towards eternity. . . . It can only change its outer ontological aspect by turning death into the means of its own fulfilment. Metaphysics do not originate in the nothingness revealed by anguish but in the being which by its very nature participates in the philosophical Eros. Thus the ontological character of the person derived from a negative which the person can only *accept*. The special decision through which the person may, in fact, become existence towards death, is an intermediate state between this primary exteriority of death, and the hope of the spirit, which transcends death itself" (22–23; emphasis in original). Maurice Blondel even puts forth the idea that "death" ought to be the quintessence of action: "To be active even in dying, to make of each act a death and of death itself the act *par excellence*" (*Action*, 350). Despite the terminological similarity, the notion of the "act of death" plays in Blondel a different role than in the authors we are discussing in this section. What he means is the radical "abnegation" required by love. I will not deal with this issue here, as it would take us too far.

motivation or opportunity for the personal act of self-consummation from within, a motivation and an opportunity which coincide with the natural, "cosmic" event of the dissolution of the body. On the contrary, if death is truly the totalizing negation of man's being, as also Rahner maintains, the practical embrace of death must be considered in a much more scandalous way than Rahner can account for: it must be the embrace of a negativity that manifests itself also and primarily in the personal act of self-consummation from within.

When Rahner says that in death man experiences "the unmastering of the personal consummation in the emptiness of the bodily end,"[144] he would have then to explain how the utter negation of the "emptiness of the bodily end"—death "from without"—also manifests itself in the personal act of freedom and consummation, death "from within." If he fails to do so, the negativity of death risks being understood merely as the extrinsic occasion for the positive act of self-decision vis-à-vis God. To be clear: given that Rahner thinks the death is the negation of the totality of man, he must also think that death, understood as the personal act of the self-consummation from within, must not be exempt from a certain radical negativity, a theoretical desideratum which he expresses when he says, as I have just quoted, that death means "the unmastering of the personal." Nevertheless, and this is my point, his framework does not succeed in satisfying this desideratum because the entire negativity of death which the "person" suffers is on the side of "nature," on the side of the "emptiness of the bodily end."

Consistently with what I have tried to explain in chapter 2, the limit of Rahner's view may be the result of his inadequate understanding and use of Thomistic hylomorphism. According to Rahner, the account of death in terms of "separation of soul and body" falls short of grasping many aspects of the phenomenon of death, most importantly, the personal and active dimension. In order to stress this dimension, Rahner goes as far as stating that, despite all the disruption brought about by death, "death is also not only an act, but 'the act,' the act of freedom."[145] He clarifies this claim by stating that death is not just the instantaneous event that puts an end to our life, but rather the permanent attitude and act of "abandonment" and "last surrender"[146] to God which must characterize the entirety of our life as such. Death is here understood as the

---

144. Rahner, *Theology of Death*, 69.
145. Rahner, *Theology of Death*, 92.
146. Rahner, *Theology of Death*, 95.

radical self-decision of man vis-à-vis the eternal, in a way which is not too different from the thesis by Speyr according to which death determines the "birth" of the "moment." What I said about Speyr's thesis could be also said here in relation to Rahner. However, while Speyr stresses more the dimension of dramatic uniqueness and unrepeatability of the instant, Rahner stresses more the relation of death and freedom:

> Continually we narrow the possibilities of the freedom of life through our actual decisions and actual life until it is exhausted completely and we drive life into the straits of death; ... and because only then do we exist in a properly human manner, if we do die all through our life, therefore, that which we call death is actually the end of death, the death of death. Whether this death of death will be a second death or the killing of death and the victory of life, depends completely on us. Hence, because death is permanently present in the whole of human life, biologically and existentially, death is the act of freedom.[147]

A question imposes itself: How can we avoid reading into Rahner's proposal the same idea that we find in Sartre, namely, that death is a transcendental condition of possibility of freedom?[148] It seems contrary to Rahner's intentions to interpret "death" metaphorically or equivocally when he likens death to freedom. As a consequence, either Rahner is taking death according to its complete sense, which also includes the negative, and is turning it into a positive condition for human freedom (even more so, as "the act" of freedom itself!), or he is stressing only the positive dimension of death, that which coincides with the act of freedom (why should we call it "death" then?), but then it is hard to see how the negativity of death is present in the personal dimension of death besides being imported, so to speak, from the natural, cosmic dimension of death. Either way, Rahner's proposal does not seem satisfactory.

5.2. The personal and free act of death is the deed in which the different attitudes of man toward death emerge such as in a synthesis. If this is the case, it follows that what I have said so far—specifically, the fact that death is definitive but is neither original, nor constitutive, nor ultimate—must be represented and enacted, as it were, in the act of death. In other words, the act of death must affirm and "will" death as something definitive about our condition while, at the same time, rejecting that death is something original, constitutive, or ultimate for our condition,

---

147. Rahner, *Theology of Death*, 93.
148. See below sec. 6.

that is, rejecting that we may ever "make peace" with death. Accordingly, the act of death is always "difficult": *it must will death* (i.e., affirm its definitiveness and thus affirm death as an un-transcendable condition of life) *as that which can never be willed*, as that which can never be desired as such (therefore, rejecting death as original, constitutive, or ultimate).

As I will try to show, what the act of death accomplishes is not primarily a decision for the destiny of the person in the afterlife, but rather, in line with the this-worldly approach which I have championed throughout the book, a "transformation of our finitude," as Emmanuel Falque and Henry L. Novello put it[149]—a transformation, however, that is parasitical on our finitude (as every evil always is) and neither original to, nor ultimate for or constitutive of it.

5.3. Such a transformation of our finitude accomplished by the act of death is threefold, as far as I can see. First, freely enacting the definitiveness of death means accepting as definitive the negation-limitation of our practical-productive capabilities and, in light of this, it means reinstituting in oneself *the priority of the contemplative attitude over the practical-productive attitude*. It means bringing about a *willed stasis* as the fundamental attitude in life.

Second, freely enacting the definitiveness of death also means accepting as definitive the negation-limitation of our intellectual and volitional capabilities (in short, our powers to understand the truth and love the good), that is, *accepting meaninglessness and the incapacity to love as a possibility*, as an eventuality that may and will likely affect me.

Third, freely enacting the definitiveness of death means accepting that one will be turned into a lifeless object, a mere object devoid of all freedom, spontaneity, and grace. More precisely, it means apprehending one's life as already showing this process of objectification and metaphysical hardening. Enacting death and thus giving to this process of metaphysical hardening the stamp of definitiveness means knowing already that the power of self-transcendence of which I am capable ("I will change my life today!") must be reinterpreted already now in light of the inevitability of defeat—no matter how hard I try, the loss of freedom, spontaneity, and grace that I already witness in me cannot be overcome by me. In this case, then, enacting death amounts to the *total exposure of one's being in all its negativity*—a self-exposure in which the cry for mercy takes the place of excuses and projects of self-change.

---

149. Falque, "Suffering Death," 46; Novello, *Death as Transformation*.

THE ANALOGY OF BEING AND THE NONBEING OF DEATH

As one can see, none of these three dimensions of the act of death implies that one "makes peace" with death. The impossibility to make peace with death corresponds to the rejection, contained *in actu exercito* in the act of death, that death may be considered something original, constitutive, and ultimate for man. I will say more about this as I unpack the three dimensions of the act of death just mentioned.

5.4. Let us see, first, how what I have called the willed stasis is brought about in our life through the act of death. One crucial point to grasp is that when we talk about the act of death, we must also acknowledge that death is never, strictly speaking, a practical possibility. In order to see this, a brief reflection on Emmanuel Levinas's insight on the nature of death may prove useful. The essential point of Levinas's reflection on death is that for him death is never a possibility that can be assumed.[150] Accordingly, death is for Levinas one of the figures of the subject's passivity in relation to the totally other. On this point, Levinas clearly disagrees with Heidegger and agrees with Sartre.[151] His point is particularly interesting because it allows us to rethink the idea of death in the context of one's choices and acts. In fact, how could death be chosen if it is the negation of being and life? What do we really choose when we choose death? And what do we act upon, or with what intention, when we perform the act of death? How can we act or "exist" death while at the same time preserving the valuable intuition contained in the claim that death is not a possibility that can be assumed?

This tension within the notion of the "act of death" is particularly clear when we state, with Levinas and against Heidegger, that death is not the "possibility of the impossibility of any further possibility" (Heidegger)—thus, not a possibility which can be intentionally, deliberately, and existentially assumed—but rather the self-imposing "impossibility of every possibility."[152] For Levinas, death is an otherness which can only be passively received and suffered, without any possibility of intentional decision and self-projection. Nevertheless, as I have said, it seems also

---

150. See, e.g., Levinas: "I even wonder how the principal trait of our relationship with death could have escaped philosophers' attention. It is not with the nothingness of death, of which we precisely know nothing, that the analysis must begin, but with the situation where something absolutely unknowable appears. Absolutely unknowable means foreign to all light, rendering every assumption of possibility impossible, but where we ourselves are seized" (*Time and the Other*, 71).

151. However, as we will see, Sartre will change his mind in the *Notebooks*, reapproaching somehow the Heideggerian position.

152. Levinas, *Totality and Infinity*, 235.

necessary to say that death must become in some sense a personal, free act, and as such death must be assumed. How do we keep together these two seemingly contradictory truths, that, on the one hand, death must somehow become an act of the human being and, on the other hand, that death is never a possibility to be assumed? How do we keep together radical passivity (Levinas) and personal activity and self-transcendence (Rahner)? How can we act something that is a practical impossibility? How can we act or "exist" death (Derrida) without turning death into something constitutive (Hegel, Heidegger)?

One way to untangle this issue is to think of the act of death as essentially an *act of attention*.[153] Attentional acts are the fundamental acts that guide and reorient the spiritual energies of our person. One could say, using a more traditional terminology, that it is a purely spiritual act. The act of death, so understood, marks that point in which the *bonum operabile* turns into its contradictory; it marks the point in which man "assumes" practically that which cannot be done.[154] Insofar as it chooses a practical impossibility, this act is *willed stasis*; it is a willed condition in which man's capacity for action and production is bracketed. It is an active, attentional "confrontation with the impossible," as Derrida puts it.[155] And as Derrida also says elsewhere, "The impossible must be done."[156] In this sense, Derrida's formulations, in all their paradoxicality, may help us find a via media between the stress on activity and possibility present in Heidegger's and Rahner's view and the stress on sheer passivity in Levinas's approach. To play a bit on words, in light of these formulations, one

---

153. Much has been written recently on attention which still awaits to be fully assimilated, especially with respect to how attention plays a (the?) fundamental role in our spiritual and moral life. On this, see the work of Simone Weil and Iris Murdoch.

154. Remember that St. Thomas says that "choice is only of possible things" (*ST* 1–2, q. 13, a. 5 co.). Suicide would not be an act of death insofar as suicide turns death into something that we can do, into a *bonum operabile*, thus avoiding death as death, which is neither a *bonum* nor an *operabile*. This is also why "learning how to die" can never be understood as a "training for death," insofar as the idea of self-training makes sense only in relation to a *bonum operabile*.

155. Derrida understands the impossibility of death in quasi-Epicurean terms: "The one [the living] and the other [death] never arrive together at this rendezvous" (*Aporias*, 65). Despite the impossibility to experience death, death leaves a "trace" throughout life, obsesses life with the presence of its inevitable absence. We see here how Derrida's discourse on death mirrors his discourse on reality as such, which, according to him, is never given as such, always postponed and delayed in the givenness of its signs. Needless to say that this discourse may end up collapsing death into being and being into death.

156. Derrida, "Certain Possible Impossibility."

could perhaps define death neither as the possibility of impossibility, nor simply as the impossibility of possibility, but rather as the *impossibility enacted as possibility*, or as the *enactment of the definitive practical impossibility amounting to willed stasis*.

Insofar as it is willed stasis, the act of death is the act which contemplates its own demise. More deeply, this act acquires a more universal meaning for man's life as such. In this act, man contemplates the demise of man's being-active as such, of man's practical and productive capacities. To use Levinas's categories, it is an act "suffering" its own demise and, in this sense, it is intentional activity only insofar as it is "seized" by its own demise. It is a threshold of activity, where activity is stasis.

Another way to state the same idea is that the act of death, by choosing a practical impossibility, removes itself as act. It "erodes" from within its practical and productive aspirations and is left with a *pure act of contemplation of one's practical and productive demise*. To put it simply, what is left in our act when the act of death is performed and the negativity of death is assumed is its contemplative core. The attitude of willed stasis is a contemplative attitude. When our practical and productive capacities are negated, either in an actual condition of sickness or in the act of death which assumes death's negativity, the practical and the productive is relativized to the contemplative. The self-perception that the person has as a primarily practical and primarily productive being (as manifested typically in the fallen condition of an I that acts in order to secure his life into "being") is put into question, and the contemplative attitude emerges, at last, as what is primordial. The act of death is the act that enacts the original primacy of the contemplative.

Contrary to Levinas, then, the genuine experience of death, understood as that which does not let man's intentionality seize it but instead as something that seizes us, does not determine the overcoming of what he calls "ontological intentionality." Rather, the experience of death contained in the act of death brings to the surface that man's intentionality is originally and primarily contemplative rather than practical and productive. Adapting Falque's formula, we may speak here of a transformation of ontological intentionality as a rediscovery of its original nature rather than of its overcoming.

In the act of death which introduces us to a more fundamental attitude of contemplation, what is contemplated is not only the *definitiveness of death*, but also its *non-originality*, its *non-constitutiveness*, and its *non-ultimacy* for our condition. In fact, the reinstitution of the primacy of the contemplative over the practical-productive which occurs in the act of death comes at a cost which should not and could not have been paid—the cost of death. Man could and should have relativized his practical-productive capacities to the primacy of the contemplative-receptive without having to undergo and suffer death. The fact that it *so happens* that the primacy of the contemplative is reinstituted in and through the assumption of the negativity of death (i.e., in this context, the negation of man's practical-productive capacities) does not turn the negativity of death into something positive—into something helpful, or functional, or even something expressing an intrinsic dimension of the nature of being. On the contrary, the reinstitution of the primacy of the contemplative, which is a good, is experienced as occurring contextually to a genuine loss and a genuine privation.

The negation of one's being taking place in the fall from a logic of being to a logic of having (and the coessential absolutization of the action to turn life into "being") is one with the negation that eventually erodes from within of practical-productive capacities. Insofar as the fall initiates a dynamic of self-destruction, what comes later (the negation of the practical-productive capacities) removes what comes earlier (the absolutization of the practical-productive at the expense of the contemplative-receptive, that is, the negation of the primacy of the contemplative-receptive). However, two negations do not always annul themselves into a pure affirmation, into a resulting positive which leaves the negation(s) behind. In this case, the second negation is added to the first one instead of removing it. The positivity resulting in the act of death (for what we have said so far, the remaining positivity is the fundamental contemplative-receptive attitude of willed stasis, or the reinstatement of its primacy) is a *radically-wounded positivity*, that is, it carries within itself the emptiness of a negation—a double negation, to be precise!— which is not removed in any way, but must be *endured* in and through the act of death.

5.4.1. It may be helpful to briefly comment on a certain tendency which takes the negation of death as something that almost immediately "opens us up" to God. For instance, Simone Weil writes: "The irreducible character of suffering which makes it impossible for us not to have a horror of it at the moment when we are undergoing it is destined to bring the will to a standstill, just as absurdity brings the intelligence to a standstill, and absence of love, so that man, having come to the end of his human faculties, may stretch out his arms, stop, look up and wait."[157] Similarly, Fabrice Hadjadj asks rhetorically: "To acknowledge that one is a total failure, doesn't it mean perhaps opening oneself up to grace?"[158]

What Weil and Hadjadj suggest is not wrong. The act enacting its own demise and thus recognizing the priority of the contemplative-receptive and the prayerful is the final blessing on what has already appeared, the pure positivity of being within the midst of the negation of death. This is the "metaphysical atmosphere," so to speak, within which the act of death may reasonably open up the contemplative-receptive once again to God. However, Weil and Hadjadj may be moving too quickly from the experience of one's demise and failure to the openness of prayer, to the "looking up." In fact, how do we answer Sartre's objection that the "looking up" of prayer is just a self-delusional "optimism" emerging out of "desperation" and "cowardice"?[159] Accordingly, I think that it is necessary to recalibrate claims such as Weil's and Hadjadj's by acknowledging that, as I said, a double negation (the final fatal negation of our fallen, already negated, self) does not lead dialectically to an affirmation. In the contemplation of one's own demise, the act of death might even lead to a further negation—the final negation of despair, the claim that one's existential failure is the original, constitutive, and ultimate destiny of one's existence. What counts against this outcome and makes "betting" on being more reasonable than despairing of nonbeing is precisely the appearance of one's being in its absolute positivity—the positivity of the giftedness of being which is now more fully and fittingly received in the newly reinstated primacy of the contemplative-receptive. Thus, the vantage of material kenosis is, in its more complete sense, the vantage of the primacy of the contemplative-receptive brought about through the act of death.

Byung-Chul Han has recently reflected on the loss of contemplation in contemporary society and on the necessity of rediscovering the fact that "inactivity" is the originating center of human life.[160] Following Maurice Blanchot (his notion of "disoeuvrement"), he likens inactivity, contemplation, and death. His analysis however, though thought-provoking and timely, does not make explicit the internal relations and differences between positive inactivity and death, nor does it problematize

157. Weil, *Gravity and Grace*, 112.
158. Hadjadj, *Farcela con la morte*, 12.
159. Sartre, *Notebooks for an Ethics*, 228.
160. Han, *Vita Contemplativa*, 1–16.

the relation between act and death, so that, due to this lack, it risks becoming another contemporary celebration of the morbid. Despite this, Han has the merit to point out that "inactivity is not the opposite of activity," so much so that "it is the *proportion of inactivity in . . . activity* that makes possible the emergence of something *altogether different*."[161] Thus, the primacy of inactivity and contemplation does not imply a disavowal of the practical-productive as such, but of its primacy or absolutization resulting in fundamental restlessness. It coincides, concretely, with an acting and producing *contemplatively*[162]—both when we can still act and produce and when action and production are not available to us any longer because of illness and suffering.

5.4.2. One more point needs to be addressed in order to clarify this first dimension of the act of death. "Assuming" death in the act of death does not mean in any way "accepting" death. As I have already said, acknowledging the definitiveness of death for the human condition (and undergoing the corresponding transformation of finitude) must go hand in hand with a *rejection of death's originality, constitutiveness, and ultimacy*.[163] Thus, "assuming death" is much more a rejection than an acceptance of death. In the act of the assumption of death, death's negativity is not reabsorbed in any way into being.[164] This casts some doubts on those positions such as Rahner's in which the negativity of death seems lost when it comes to the personal act of death. If personal death is the subject's act of personal self-consumation "from within," what is left of the unabsorbable negativity of death?

5.5. We can now move to the second dimension of the act of death. I have said that in the act of death the negation of death, in the specific form of the negation of the practical-productive capacities of man (and thus, a negation of their absolutization and prioritization), is assumed. However, it would be of course naïve to stop here and suggest that what is negated in death is only the practical-productive. The *entire person is*

---

161. Han, *Vita Contemplativa*, 18; emphasis in original.

162. Han states that "immanence as life is *living in the mode of contemplation*" (*Vita Contemplativa*, 21; emphasis in original).

163. This is, in the end, one of the fundamental differences between my proposal and Heidegger's. Heidegger's purely phenomenological perspective cuts out of the picture all the other fundamental perspectives—the theological, the metaphysical, the assiological—without which death cannot be understood.

164. On this point, I find Emmanuel Levinas's reflections on the book of Job most enlightening; see his "Postface: Transcendence and Evil," in Nemo, *Job and Excess of Evil*, 165–82.

THE ANALOGY OF BEING AND THE NONBEING OF DEATH

negated in death and as a consequence also the contemplative-receptive dimension of the human being is negated. As I have said, in the act of death we do not simply enact the original priority of the contemplative-receptive over the practical. We enact the demise of all our being.

But what does this mean? It means that in the act of death we enact also the demise of our intellect, which is structurally made for receiving the truth in contemplation, and our will, which is structurally made for affirming the good in love.[165] Thus, assuming death as definitive of our condition and enacting our own demise means acknowledging as a more-than-likely possibility for me that I may go through life without understanding the truth of the world and without loving its goodness. It is, in other words, acknowledging the more-than-likely possibility of the experience of meaninglessness and error and incapacity for love. It is an interesting fact that every time we speak of the corruption of man's faculties due to his mortality we interpret such corruption merely ontically—man's becoming "senile." On the contrary, this corruption must be understood ontologically: it is the possibility of not finding meaning, of stopping to look for meaning, of becoming insensitive to the goodness and beauty of the world, etc. Of course, acknowledging this eventuality of ontological demise in the very act of death does not mean "accepting" it. Assuming, or even embracing, death implies a rejection of what death means. It means acknowledging that one ought not make peace with it.

A superficial perspective on this dimension of the act of death could oppose "believers" and "nonbelievers." According to this superficial take, Christians would be those who have found meaning in the encounter with Christ while nonbelievers would be those who must recognize the possibility of not understanding, not being capable of love, etc. In truth, it is exactly the opposite. It is precisely when *the* meaning, Christ, has been encountered, that one must face more dramatically the all-too-likely possibility of not understanding and not loving the Truth, Goodness, and Beauty that one has nevertheless received: "He came to what was his own, but his own people did not accept him" (John 1:11).

It seems to me that also at this level, the formula of the radical negation without annihilation proves very helpful: our capacity to know the truth and love the good are not annihilated, but they can certainly go astray; knowing the truth about oneself and loving the good of life must

---

165. Aquinas, *Disputed Questions on Truth*, q. 1, a. 1.

Material Kenosis

therefore face and endure the likelihood of the intellect's and the will's woundedness.

5.6. A satisfactory account of the act of death would not complete without discussing a third dimension, which has to do with the fact that in dying we are to some extent turned into objects. Now, Rahner explains that the personal act of death is the act in and through which man distances himself as spiritual from himself as a mere object of nature undergoing death. The personal act of death is the final realization of man's spiritual irreducibility to the order of natural organisms for which death can only be an event undergone from without, as we have already seen. However, it seems to me that, in a certain sense, the act of death must be the opposite of what Rahner envisions. In the act of death, *man wills his own being-turned into an object*—where "wills" means again, as stated earlier, the affirmation of the definitiveness of death and the concomitant rejection of its originality, constitutiveness, and ultimacy.

Sartre's analysis of death as the turning of the "for-itself" into an "in-itself" are illuminating on this point. According to Sartre, death puts an end to our capacity for self-transcendence and thus for reinterpretation of the meaning to give to our life ("for-itself") and reduces us to a purely objectivized and done-once-for-all meaning ("in-itself") at the mercy of those who survive and still perform their interpretative freedom.[166] "Assuming" this dynamic of objectification means assuming the

---

166. See, e.g., Sartre: "Death represents a total *dispossession*; . . . Thus the very existence of *death* alienates us wholly in our own life to the advantage of the Other. . . . The alienations which we studied there, in fact, were those which we could nihilate by transforming the Other into a transcendence-transcended, just as we could nihilate our *outside* by the absolute and subjective positing of our freedom. So long as I live I can escape what I *am* for the Other by revealing to myself by my freely posited ends that I *am* nothing and that I make myself be what I am; so long as I live, I can give the lie to what others discover in me, by projecting myself already toward other ends and in every instance by revealing that my dimension of being-for-myself is incommensurable with my dimension of being-for-others. Thus ceaselessly I escape my outside and ceaselessly I am reapprehended by the Other; and in this 'dubious battle' the definitive victory belongs to neither the one nor the other of these modes of being. But the *fact of death* without being precisely allied to either of the adversaries in this same combat gives the final victory to the point of view of the Other by transferring the combat and the prize to another level—that is, by suddenly suppressing one of the combatants. In this sense to die is to be condemned no matter what ephemeral victory one has one over the Other; . . . we must recognize that my *existence after death* is not the simple spectral survival "in the Other's consciousness" of simple representations (images, memories, etc.) concerning me. My being-for-others is a real being. . . . Thus not only does death disarm my *waiting* by definitively removing the waiting and by abandoning in indetermination the realization of the ends which make known to me

THE ANALOGY OF BEING AND THE NONBEING OF DEATH

fact that being mortal means being subject to a process of deprivation of the freedom and spontaneity which are the mark of life. Death is the metaphysical hardening and thus the loss of the vital spontaneity of life-being.

As far as I can see, it would not be far from the truth to say that acknowledging that death can be described in this way is the specifically modern contribution to a phenomenology and metaphysics of death. While the ancient and medieval man's reflection on death is oriented by his familiarity with the world of life as it is found in nature, the imagination of the modern and contemporary man is slowly absorbed by the omnipresence of the machine.[167] Thus, if death is classically conceptualized as a moving away from life, in the age of the machine, death is rather conceptualized as a moving toward the condition of an automaton. The organism's subjection to death is its slow loss of vital spontaneity, of its capacity to learn and adjust, of its flexibility and openness to the new. Its death is its metaphysical hardening into inflexible habits, a process which slowly unfolds throughout life and reaches its apex at the very moment of passing ("rigor mortis"). Socrates already characterized the "purification" of the soul as a "habituation" of the soul to collect herself all by herself and apart from the body.[168] In the modern consciousness, a full-fledged habituation stops being the mark of a spiritual life and becomes the sign of a lifeless death. If, on the one hand, death is the "specter of the amorphous,"[169] on the other hand, as we are stating here, it is also the curse of the inflexible shape. In a deathlike existence, "Nothing is new under the sun!" (Eccl 1:9).

Among the contemporary thinkers who have treated death in these terms one can name Charles S. Peirce,[170] Henri Bergson,[171] Max

---

what I am—but again it confers a meaning from the outside of everything which I live in subjectivity. Death reapprehends all this subjective which whole it 'lived' defended itself against exteriorization, and death deprives it of all subjective meaning in order to hand it over to any *objective* meaning which the Other is pleased to give it" (*Being and Nothingness*, 564–65; emphasis in original).

167. On the intertwinement of modern ontology and death, see Jonas, *The Phenomenon of Life*, 9–12; Pickstock, *After Writing*, ch. 3; a similar view is developed in Schmitz, *Recovery of Wonder*.

168. *Phaedo* 67c.

169. Jankélévitch, *Mort*, 93.

170. See Stango, "Mortality in Light of Synechism."

171. It seems to me that both Peirce's and Bergson's approaches can be traced back to a common Aristotelian root, variously developed by the idealistic philosophy of nature—especially Schelling—and by the French spiritualism of Félix Ravaisson.

Scheler,[172] and Charles Péguy. To exemplify this position, let's read Péguy's masterful presentation of this idea:

> The death of a being is its complete saturation by habit, its complete saturation memory, that is its complete saturation by ageing. And thus its complete saturation by sclerosis and hardening.... [Death occurs] when all matter of the being is *busy* with habit, memory, hardening, when there no longer remains one atom of matter for the new which is life.... Death is the limit of the filling up by memory, the limit of the filling up by habit, the limit of the filling up by hardening, ageing, amortization. When all matter is consecrated to memory, there is death.... And a dead soul is also a soul habituated to the extreme.[173]

---

172. Scheler, Morte e sopravvivenza, 43, 100. Here Scheler quotes Windelband and Bergson approvingly. Admittedly, Scheler's analysis has more to do with the phenomenology of time linked to the experience of aging than the notion of hardening of habits. But between his view and, say, Péguy's, there is a sort of family resemblance. Scheler's fundamental idea about death as an a priori of the consciousness of lived time is anticipated by Augustine (*City of God* 13.10).

173. Péguy, *Notes on Bergson and Descartes*, 94–95; emphasis in original. Péguy continues: "It is highly noteworthy that spiritual death, the death of the soul, is represented in the traditional language of the Church as the result (and we could say the limit) of a hardening. We must refrain from seeing this as a metaphor.... When one speaks of the final hardening and final impenitence, it is necessary to understand this as a real phenomenon of induration that renders the soul like dead wood. It is really a spiritual incrustation, a cladding of habit, which henceforth prevents the soul from being moistened by grace. All the spiritual matter, all the matter of the soul, is thus allotted to the cladding of habit, consecrated to the cladding of habit, devoured by habit in order to be, to become that cladding" (95). As noted above, Guardini's account of death could also be mentioned here, in the sense that the "cladding of habit" of which Péguy speaks could be likened to Guardini's notion of the limit case of the "pure realization" of the pole "form" over and against the pole "fullness." Needless to say, such understanding of death sheds much light on the always-possible misunderstanding of the idea of virtue in the ethical life. A genuine virtue can never be an inflexible, self-identical habit. Insofar as the concrete configuration of the good is different in the different situations, a genuine virtue will be the habit in which a maximum of stability and a maximum of flexibility coincide: the virtue of courage, for instance, will be to always pursue the same courageous actions according to the ever-changing demands of the different contexts in which the actions must be performed. Compare this to the seemingly opposite reading of "death" in Chesterton, *Orthodoxy*, 35–36. The tradition is not unaware of this point. Thomas, for instance, speaks of "hardening" and "freezing" to describe a lack of love, that is, a person's being "hard to pierce" by the beloved. He opposes "melting" to this as a consequence of proper love. Any metaphysics that sees love as the true meaning of being could profitably develop the concepts of "melting" and "being available to being pierced" as revelatory of what being-life is—as being's proper capacity for the mutual indwelling that characterizes the lover and the beloved—and consequently the concepts of "hardening" and "freezing" as metaphysical contraries to being, life, and love—the loss of the readiness "for the entrance of the beloved." See *ST*

Enacting death understood in this way means acknowledging that all the negativity already present in our life in the form of the hardening of our habits (both physical and spiritual) cannot be reabsorbed and thus 'turned into meaning' by us through later acts of self-transcendence. As Péguy says elsewhere, "When a man lies dying, he does not die from disease alone. He dies from his whole life."[174] At a certain level, the negativity present in our life cannot be redeemed by us, and the act of death is precisely the performative recognition of this fact. To put it more simply, this third dimension of the act of death simply means for man "being done" with the false attitude through which we excuse our flaws in light of what we may be able to do tomorrow, in light of the ways in which we think we may be able to change our life at a later time.[175] In the act of death, we acknowledge the definitiveness of a negativity—the vices, the insuperable distractions that have become a habit, the laziness, the lack of poverty of spirit, the pain inflicted on other people to which we have become insensitive, the pain inflicted on us by others that has remained without explanation, this very pain inflicted on us by others that we have turned into a justification to act unjustly, etc.—that will remain until the very end and on which we have no power.

This character of death is essentially linked to death understood in relation with time. Following Sartre and to some extent Scheler, Ernst Tugendhat has especially highlighted this point. He claims that the troubling character of death lies precisely in the fact that one must acknowledge that there is an unsurpassable residuum of negativity in our life which we cannot hope to change or overcome through subsequent acts. It is true that man is directed toward the end of his time in the future, but what that means for his now is manifested only by the fact that he looks at his past in the present.[176] One could appeal here to Paul Ricoeur's lapidary statement: "The work of memory is the work of mourning."[177]

Tugendhat's somewhat tragic view of death may be exemplified by Walter Benjamin's angel of history: as the angel of history is irresistibly propelled toward the future by a stormy wind while facing toward the

---

1–2, q. 28, a. 5, response to the objections.

174. Péguy, *Basic Verities*, 7.

175. One is reminded of Chesterton here: "Believing in himself is one of the commonest signs of a rotter" (*Orthodoxy*, 4).

176. See Tugendhat, *Über den Tod*.

177. Ricoeur, *Living Up to Death*, 39. He adds: "And both are a word of hope, torn from what is unspoken."

past and seeing in it a catastrophe he cannot change, so is man propelled toward his future end, which means that the negativity he sees in his past and his present will be left to some extent unredeemed by his acts.[178] To paraphrase Kierkegaard: once life cannot be "lived forward" any longer, one must turn "backwards" and stare at that which cannot be "understood."

Once again, such assumption does not imply a peaceful acceptance on our part. Recognizing that we, due to our weakness, do not have the power to overcome the negativity lying at the center of our life and unfolding as a metaphysical hardening, does not mean excusing it, nor does it invalidate the divine injunction "Harden not your hearts" (Heb 3:8). It is not a call for indifference to ethical and spiritual growth. Rather, it is a call to reframe in the right way all our attempts of self-cultivation, in order to see that, if left to its own resources, eudaimonism is hopeless. The injunction "Harden not your hearts" is more than an injunction: it is the expression of the deepest aspirations of our heart. Striving toward it means following what our heart truly and ultimately desires—it is a matter of self-consistency. But we must acknowledge that it does so happen that our heart is wounded by an invincible (to us) negativity, i.e., in this sense, a propensity to become hard.

Also at this level, the awareness and assumption of death implies a gap between being and nonbeing which cannot be eliminated. In the act of death, however, a certain transformation of finitude is produced. Someone who assumes the being-turned into an object is someone who *accepts to be fully exposed in his negativity*—fully exposed to oneself; potentially, to the other human beings; and actually, to God.[179] Such self-exposure is more perfect once the thought that one's negativity may be overcome by one's later acts of self-transcendence is overcome. In the metaphysical atmosphere provided by the apprehension of the purity of being in its giftedness and by the awareness that the insuppressible relation that the Origin of being has with us, the acknowledgment of an un-transcendable negativity in us becomes a cry for mercy addressed to ourselves (which amounts to a remaining open to mercy), to the others and, ultimately, to the Other.

---

178. See Benjamin, "Philosophy of History," 257–58.

179. One will recognize the affinity between this notion of self-exposure and Sartre's idea of death as "total dispossession" (*Being and Nothingness*, 564). However, while Sartre reads this total dispossession as radical "alienation," the religious consciousness can see in it the possibility of a surrender to God's grace.

6. FROM ONTOLOGICAL WHOLE TO ONTIC FRAGMENT: A GENEALOGY OF THE REDUCTION OF DEATH TO A TECHNOLOGICAL PROBLEM IN THE HEIDEGGERIAN TRADITION

6.1. The final part of my overall argument—i.e., trying to clarify all the ways in which death can and should not be turned into something positive—must address directly the Heideggerian and post-Heideggerian approach to the problem of death.[180] As I have mentioned in the introduction to this chapter, my aim here is not to provide a new and original interpretation of Heidegger's being toward death, of Sartre's objection's to Heidegger's position, etc. Rather, my aim is to provide an argument regarding the overall meaning of the Heideggerian and post-Heideggerian approach to death considered as a unitary episode of thought.

To state the argument clearly at the outset: for Heidegger death is not only something phenomenologically positive, but is what one might call an essential dimension of the very horizon of meaning of Dasein.[181] Death, in other words, plays a fundamental transcendental condition in the self-constitution of Dasein as Dasein. Nothing really new up to this point. The argument that I want to put forth, however, is the following: the very fact that death is conceived as playing the positive role of a transcendental condition of possibility for Dasein leads over a few generations of Heideggerian thought to a different stress with respect to the meaning of existence and the meaning of death as a whole. In fact, if existence is essentially understood as *radical finitude or mortality*, as it is in the Heideggerian tradition, that means that existence must be understood in terms of a radical fragmentation, a fragmentation of lawless, pure events without a unitary transcendental horizon. Thus, any unitary

---

180. Iain Thomson has a forthcoming book entitled *Rethinking Death in and After Heidegger*. Unfortunately, I was unable to consult this study before the present book went to print.

181. In this section I rely mostly on *Being and Time*, but Niederhauser has convincingly shown that death plays a key role in all four key phases of Heidegger's "question of being," the existential-ontological and transcendental analytic of Dasein; the thinking of *Ereignis*; the question of technology and the world as fourfold; language and poetry. See his *Heidegger on Death and Being*, "Introduction." His work proceeds along the lines of Singh, *Heidegger, World, and Death*. See Niederhauser's telling reading: "Our mortality, then, is not a source of meaninglessness, but a source of meaning" (*Heidegger on Death and Being*, xiv); "Heidegger's thought . . . is devoted to a thinking of death that is neither metaphysical nor technological" (xv); "Death co-constitutes Dasein's horizon of understanding" (xvi).

horizon of meaning and any transcendental condition of existence is rejected and reabsorbed into the lawless occurring of pure events.

But this means that death loses the "serious" meaning that it still had in Heidegger's philosophy. It loses its status of a horizon of meaning or transcendental condition and is demoted to the status of one of the several different ontic "problems" of the essentially-fragmented and radically contingent human existence. But—note—this happens not *in spite of* Heidegger's instituting death as a transcendental condition of meaning, but precisely *because* of this—as its logical unfolding, so to speak, even though as an exemplary case of heterogenesis of ends. The Heideggerian institution of death as a transcendental condition for Dasein initiates that episode of thought the logical conclusion of which is its opposite—the denial that death is anything constitutive, let alone something "serious" or more than ontic. Thus, the Heideggerian premise—that death is something constitutive in the form of a transcendental condition of possibility of Dasein—ends up "swallowing" itself and the philosophy that flows from it. Death, far from being understood as that without which existence cannot make sense, is now understood as one of the many ontic problems with which we ought to deal within a technoscientific framework. Despite its fundamental mistaken premise, the Heideggerian position still allowed for thinking of death as more than a mere ontic problem, and, in this sense, could be considered as an ally of other, though different, approaches, which saw in the mystery of death a privileged access to the great metaphysical questions of life—especially the Christian approach to death.[182] However, by removing itself, the Heideggerian philosophy of death also removes the metaphysical depth that was still granted to death.

Thus, we come full circle with the argument sketched in the introduction to the book and in chapter 1. What is the contemporary intellectual attitude toward death? Death is an ontic problem to be handled technoscientifically. One of the philosophical roots of this idea was found in the position of certain analytic philosophers to reduce death to a mere accident of our material existence: when we die, we still are, although we are of course dead. In this light, the aspiration of technoscience to solve the problem of death makes sense: technoscience can either prevent

---

182. As I have explained above, however, considering Heidegger's being toward death as a development of the Christian and humanistic tradition of the memento mori would be like saying that contemporary transhumanism is a continuation of Dante's *trasumanar*.

death from taking (its accidental) place or it can cure the accident of death, thus reverting man's existence to its living status. This is the naturalistic root of the contemporary technoscientific attitude toward death.

However, the whole story requires considering also the contribution of the continental, and especially Heideggerian, philosophy of death. If my argument on the Heideggerian approach to death is correct, it shows that, while moving from completely different premises, also the Heideggerian approach to death ends up, surprisingly and ironically, to the reduction of death to a mere problem, once death has lost its transcendental status and is wholly reabsorbed into existence understood as the purely contingent and lawless occurrence of fragmented events. Once death is so reduced, it becomes fair game to the technoscientistic mentality. As far as I can tell, nobody in the recent Heideggerian tradition has positively embraced the view of a technoscientific treatment of death. And the interpretation that I put forth here seems to me even more interesting given that, as Johannes Niederhauser stresses, for Heidegger "death harbours the distinct possibility to overcome [the technological] *Gestell*."[183] Despite this, my argument maintains that a technoscientific reduction of death is what must logically come out of the very premises of the Heideggerian position on death, and that signs going in this direction can already be found in the "weakening" of Dasein's existence, from something "whole," supported by a transcendental structure, to something essentially fragmented and made up of events which cannot be re-comprehended into a unitary framework.

The fact that both analytic philosophy (to be more precise, those voices in analytic philosophy that seem most relevant to understand what is culturally relevant) and continental philosophy seem to converge toward an identical result, or at least to provide the premises for the contemporary reduction of death to a technological problem, is as surprising as it is instructive.

6.2. *Heidegger*. Heidegger's main point in his treatment of death in *Being and Time* is the identification of Dasein's determinateness ("I am this and not that") with his finitude and mortality, understood ontologically as the "dying authentically" of "being toward death." The Dasein that I am is not an indefinite dispersion of possibilities. Instead, I am gathered into that Dasein that I am, into the "mineness" of my Dasein, only in being toward death. I am this "I can die any instant."

---

183. Niederhauser, *Heidegger on Death and Being*, xvi.

Material Kenosis

Dasein is essentially "care" and projectuality-possibility in time and thus what grounds the phenomenological consistency of Dasein as a "whole"—what gives Dasein his "own" possibility—is being toward death.[184] I am "authentic"—that is, I can be what I am, the Dasein that I am—only if I am at every instant a being toward death.[185] As Heidegger puts it early on, "*Sum moribundus, moribundus* not as someone gravely ill or wounded, but insofar as I am, I am *moribundus*. *The moribundus first gives the sum its sense.*"[186]

The horizon of possibilities that I am, which is in principle indefinite, becomes finite only in light of that archi-possibility that is being toward death. I am this whole of possibilities only if I grasp as properly mine the possibility of being toward death:

> We did assert that care is the totality of the structural whole of the constitution of being of Dasein. But have we not at the very beginning of our interpretation renounced the possibility of bringing Dasein as a whole to view? ... As long as Dasein exists, it must always, as such a potentiality, *not yet be* something? A being whose essence is made up of existence essentially opposes itself to the possibility of being comprehended as a whole being.... As long as Dasein is, something is always still outstanding.... But the "end" itself belongs to what is outstanding. The "end" of being-in-the-world is death. This end, belonging to the potentiality-of-being, that is, to existence, limits and defines the possible totality of Dasein. The being-at-an-end of Dasein in death, and thus its being a whole, can, however, be included in our discussion of the possible *being* whole in a phenomenally appropriate way only if an ontologically adequate, that is, an *existential* concept of death has been attained. But as far as Dasein goes, death *is* only in an existential *being toward death*. The

---

184. See already Heidegger: "Death is not a missing part of a whole taken as a composite. Rather it constitutes the totality of Dasein from the start" (*History of Concept of Time*, 313).

185. Heidegger, *Being and Time*, 252. See also Jalbert: "As fallen, *Dasein* 'awaits' death by fleeing from it, and when it flees in the face of death, it in effect ignores its individuality" ("Time, Death, and History," 269). Jalbert shows that the essential connection between death and individuality is already found in Simmel ("Time, Death, and History," 272–74), notwithstanding Heidegger's complaint that Simmel treats the "ontological-existential problematic" of death (being toward death) as a merely "biological-ontical" problematic.

186. Heidegger, *History of Concept of Time*, 317; emphasis in original.

existential structure of this being turns out to be the ontological constitution of the potentiality-for-being-whole of Dasein.[187]

As I have said other times in this chapter, for Heidegger death is a constitutive, if not original, dimension of Dasein; as we see now, it is an essential dimension of Dasein's transcendental horizon of meaning.[188]

6.2.1. It would be too easy to oppose Heidegger's purely phenomenological approach and a metaphysical assessment of death, so I will leave for later whatever I have to say on this point.[189] However, one could already question Heidegger's analysis of existence and death at the phenomenological level. The question is how do we account phenomenologically for Dasein's finitude, for his being a whole. So one may wonder: Why is the possibility of death that which turns me into that whole that I am? Sartre has already highlighted in a definitive way the flaws present in the Heideggerian position when he claims that (1) in order to be the possibility of *my* death, being toward death must presuppose a certain sense of subjectivity; (2) more radically, finitude is not given by mortality, but rather by the fact that the for-itself (the living man) has constituted himself as a unique being through his free choices.[190] Accordingly, finitude, namely, being a whole and, more deeply, being this whole and not that whole, is compatible in principle with an indefinitely open temporality.

---

187. Heidegger, *Being and Time*, 223–24; emphasis in original; see also 248. Paul Ricoeur's development of the Heideggerian position is telling: "It is to be noted that the will to live is reflected and even given cohesion only under the threat of death, therefore in and through anguish. The expression 'will to live' does not represent a simple or elementary 'instinct.' As a living being, I pursue goals which are disparate, heterogeneous, and, in the end, incoordinate: life, at least at the human stage, is a bundle of tendencies whose aims are neither clear nor concordant. Only in catastrophic situations, under the threat of the indetermined absolute—my death—does my life become determined as the totality of what is threatened. For the first time, I look upon myself as a threatened totality. The threat of death bestows upon life the greatest degree of simplicity of which it is capable" ("True and False Anguish," in Ricoeur, *History and Truth*, 291).

188. Nevertheless, Heidegger carefully distinguishes death phenomenologically understood from mere "perishing" (*Being and Time*, 232) and stresses that "ending" is in no way to be understood as "fulfilment" (235).

189. From a general point of view, I tend to agree with Theodore Adorno's assessment of Heidegger: "However close to experience Heidegger's pronouncements may seem, they simply do not connect with the reality of society. . . . Heidegger's tendency [is] to camouflage irresolvable contradictions, like those between timeless ontology and history, by ontologizing history itself as 'historicity' and turning the contradiction as such into a 'structure of Being'" (*Against Epistemology*, 187–88).

190. Sartre, *Being and Nothingness*, 554–55.

Material Kenosis

By extending the Sartrean view, one could put forth a different view of finitude. Why can't we explain finitude in terms of *the memory of a history that grows*? All the possibilities that come to me from the future and which in a sense already determine that being that I am are received by me in light of or according to my memory, that is, of my history. My history is a history that has had a precise beginning, which has grown, keeps on growing, and which is not contradictory to think of as never-ending or, at least, as not having to end in self-destruction.

The main point here is that a personal history so understood does not need to end in order to constitute itself as that whole that it is. The finitude and the determination of a history do not mean its being already determined by an inevitable end, but rather the fact that it has taken shape in a certain way, it has developed a certain historical "body" which cannot be undone (*factum infectum fieri nequit*). A love story is not what it is because it is destined to end. And one is not called to live it by anticipating its final demise, because otherwise it would become scattered and dissolved in the indefiniteness of indefinite possibilities. A love story is the love story that it is because it is born at a certain time and in a certain way and because it develops in a certain way, taking a certain shape. Not only its determinateness is compatible with its having no end; but one could also say that its desire to grow without an end—or to be definitely confirmed in its being without being negated—is the most characteristic feature of the true nature of a love story. Marcel is thus right when he claims that loving a person amounts to telling him, "You, you in particular, will never die."[191]

Thus, the fact that one's personal history has had a beginning, that it has taken a shape, and that it continues, is, so to speak, the ontic counterpart of creation—that is, of the fact that I have been given to myself at a certain point and that my history can continue to take shape because I keep being given to myself—I am created. Thus, my being is that whole that it is not because I anticipate the possibility of death in being toward death, but because I am the memory of a history that has begun and that keeps growing, that is, a history that grows deeper into the metaphysical memory not only of the beginning, but rather of the origin that accompanies my every step.

Heidegger of course is not unaware of the relevance of "birth" for the wholeness of Dasein. In fact, as he remarks, Dasein "*stretches along*

---

191. Marcel, "Value and Immortality," 140.

between birth and death" and in its historicity Dasein has to take upon itself its own past always again, a past with which Dasein is in a constant relation in its "being-toward-the-beginning,"[192] and with respect to which it remains nevertheless in a structural condition of "lateness." However, despite these remarks, given that Dasein is essentially care and temporality, birth—being given—seems to be an insufficient condition for wholeness, which instead essentially and necessarily requires being-toward-death.[193]

Despite Heidegger's claim of metaphysical neutrality and of absence of all presuppositions in the description of the existential structures of Dasein, it seems fair to say that one can find in Heidegger a certain option which establishes death as the only structure capable of guaranteeing Dasein his wholeness and determinateness. The phenomenology of being toward death developed in *Being and Time* and its constructive use to unpack what Dasein is are just the unfolding of a previous decision for the essential mutual implication of death and finitude.

One last element needs to be added to complete the picture. In fact, Heidegger goes as far as saying that Dasein's being toward death is the "performance" of the ontological difference between being and beings:[194]

192. Heidegger, *Being and Time*, 356; emphasis in original. Hannah Arendt will start from this undeveloped point in Heidegger's analytic in order to develop her famous reflections on "natality." See ch. 4, sec. 7.

193. "The assumption of its being assigned to something already given, which refers to the existential phenomenon of birth, demands, then, the freedom of an authentic ability-to-be supposing the assumption of mortality. It is only in terms of this future which will never become present, this absolute future which is death, that Dasein can assume the absolute past of its birth, and thus become *one* existence" (Dastur, *Death*, 72; emphasis in original). It is worth noting that two years before the publication of *Being and Time* (i.e., in 1925), Romano Guardini claimed that, as any other living being, the human being has a "center" and "lives from it and towards it" (*Opposizione polare*, 203). In other words, the human being is a whole not because he is being toward death, but because he is from and toward his center.

194. On temporality and the ontological difference, see Heidegger: "In the question as to what that which is, is *as* something that is—what a being is *as* a being—being is treated like a being. Nevertheless, although unsuitably interpreted, it is still made a problem. Somehow the Dasein knows about something like being. Since it exists, the Dasein understands being and comports itself toward beings. The distinction between being and beings *is there* [*ist da*], later in the Dasein and its existence, even if not in explicit awareness. The distinction *is there* [*ist da, i.e., exists*]; that is to say, it has the mode of being of the Dasein: it belongs to existence. Existence means, as it were, 'to be in the performance of this distinction.' Only a soul that can make this distinction has the aptitude, going beyond the animal's soul, to become the soul of a human being. The *distinction between being and beings is temporalized in the temporalizing of temporality*" (*Basic Problems of Phenomenology*, 319; emphasis in original).

man exceeds the world of ontic possibilities and actualities by being rooted in the ecstatic and temporal structure of care and, ultimately, in the impossibility of death, in that future without future which is "the possibility of the absolute impossibility of Dasein."[195] The horizontal transcendence of Dasein's existence coincides with the negativity of death. Here lies Heidegger's conclusive and fundamental move, which brings his reflection on Dasein's wholeness to completion: the more-than-ontic "openness" of Dasein, that which informs its ecstasis and care, is the impossibility of death.[196] Accordingly, anxiety understood as the fundamental *Stimmung* of Dasein, puts Dasein in front of that Nonbeing ("nobeing" and "no-thing") from which beings emerge, as Heidegger explains in "What Is Metaphysics?"[197]

Despite their superficial convergence, Heidegger's position and my proposal are radically opposed. For Heidegger, Nothing is the horizon of meaning within which Dasein acquires his phenomenological and ontological consistency and within which beings are manifested as such. According to my proposal, the nonbeing of death is the circumstance—definitive for the human condition even though accidental—within which the only possible horizon of meaning, that is, being in its absolute positivity, is affirmed once again.

6.3. *Sartre*. Sartre's engagement with Heidegger's position on death is known for the critique of the idea that death can ever be a possibility to grasp. Accordingly, it would seem that Sartre is immune to Heidegger's mistake, that of identifying death as a fundamental, transcendental condition of meaning for man. Sartre correctly states in *Being and Nothingness* that death cannot be considered as an "a priori of human reality" and that it is in this sense "absurd."[198]

According to Sartre, there are two ways to look at death insofar as death is a "boundary": the realist view, according to which death is the extrinsic limit of life which as such is never part of life; and the idealist view, according to which death is the intrinsic limit of life and thus a constitutive element of life, in the same way as the end term of a series "belongs" to the series itself and structures it internally. According to the latter view, death is "interiorized and humanized"; it is a "human phenomenon"; it becomes "the meaning of life as the resolved chord

---

195. Heidegger, *Being and Time*, 232.
196. See "Why Poets?," in Heidegger, *Off the Beaten Track*, 227.
197. "What Is Metaphysics?," in Heidegger, *Basic Writings*, 93–110.
198. Sartre, *Being and Nothingness*, 554.

THE ANALOGY OF BEING AND THE NONBEING OF DEATH

is the meaning of the melody."[199] Heidegger would be the philosopher who has given "philosophical form" to this "humanization of death." For Heidegger, as we have seen, being toward death is the very possibility that gives individuality and wholeness to Dasein. (Incidentally, Sartre's reading of Heidegger may be exaggerated on this point, for at least two reasons: first, while it is true that being toward death is constitutive of Dasein's wholeness and individuality, it seems hard to maintain that for Heidegger it is fully humanizing, insofar as Heidegger clearly distinguishes between "ending" and "being fulfilled"; second, not all interpretations of death as a phenomenon pertaining to life in a definitive way see death as either constitutive or original; my proposal in this book would be precisely of this kind.)

Now, we have anticipated something about the way in which Sartre sees Heidegger's view of death as flawed—a true "sleight of hand." To repeat, Sartre thinks, first, that being toward death cannot be an individualizing possibility insofar as in order for death to be "mine" a prereflexive sense of the cogito must be presupposed. In other words, Sartre sees a flawed circularity in Heidegger's argument.

Second, and more importantly, Sartre famously points out that, properly speaking, death can never be either "waited for" nor "expected" (or, which is the same, we must always relate to it as what remains essentially "unexpected," i.e., accidental, foreign, and external to our free projects) and thus it cannot be a constitutive possibility for the for-itself: "This perpetual appearance of chance at the heart of my projects can not be apprehended as *my* possibility but, on the contrary, as the nihilation of all my possibilities, a nihilation which *itself is no longer a part of my possibilities*. Thus death is not *my* possibility of no longer realizing a presence in the world but rather *an always possible nihilation of my possible which is outside my possibilities*."[200]

Third, Sartre explains the reasons why death cannot be considered as a transcendental condition of possibility of meaning for man and should rather be considered as the "absurd." He does so by relying upon his understanding of the very structure of life's meaning and the essential being-for-others that we always are. In short, the meaning of our past and present actions and experiences is always to be decided in the future, just as the meaning of the efforts and the enterprises of a preceding

---

199. Sartre, *Being and Nothingness*, 553.
200. Sartre, *Being and Nothingness*, 557–58; emphasis in original.

generation is decided by the men of the present generation. If this future-oriented structure of meaning is correct, it follows that death, by taking away the very possibility of the future, takes away also the very condition of possibility of meaning: "The for-itself is the being in whose being being is in question; since the for-itself is the being which always lays claim to an 'after,' there is no place for death in the being which is for-itself. What then could be the meaning of a waiting for death if it is not the waiting for an undetermined event which would reduce all waiting to the absurd, even including that of death itself."[201]

As long as man is alive, he can reinterpret the meaning of his past and in this way he can "keep at bay" any limiting interpretation of his life coming from others. But when man dies, he does not simply disappear. What happens on the contrary is that his past is absolutized; he is not a "for-itself" anymore—a free, self-interpreting subject; he has become an "in-itself"—a totalized, absolutized past without any possibility of new *self*-interpretation: man is "engulfed in the in-itself." His "whole life *is*."[202] The interpretation and reinterpretation of the meaning of his life is not closed as such; it is only closed for him. He is now at the mercy of those who survive him—the surviving "being-for-themselves" or the "Other": "Death represents a total *dispossession*; . . . Thus the very existence of *death* alienates us wholly in our own life to the advantage of the Other. To be dead is to be prey for the living."[203] The dead man is an in-itself, and the in-itself is absolutized being-for-others. Also for this reason, then, death can only be seen as the absurd.

6.3.1. Despite Sartre's lucid critique of Heidegger's view of death in *Being and Nothingness*, a later development in Sartre's philosophy seems to point in a different direction.[204] This later development, instead of leading to a view of death opposed to Heidegger's view, would seem to amount to a Sartrean appropriation and deepening of the position

---

201. Sartre, *Being and Nothingness*, 561.

202. Sartre, *Being and Nothingness*, 561; emphasis in original. Jankélévitch speaks interestingly about the absolutization of the past as if it meant a de-temporalization of life and becoming and thus a spatialization of time: "When becoming is deprived of its future, it purely and simply ceases to be becoming. A time made 'fully past' is also detemporalized. . . . Time fully spent from one extreme to the other is rather space!" (*Mort*, 199). One may suggest that, in this experience of death, it is as if one saw one's flaws statically laid out on a flat surface, without a possibility to modify them (because such modification would necessarily imply moving through space *and time*).

203. Sartre, *Being and Nothingness*, 564; emphasis in original.

204. See Schumacher, *Death and Mortality*, 106–7.

THE ANALOGY OF BEING AND THE NONBEING OF DEATH

formulated by Heidegger. We find this development in his late reflections on freedom. In fact, in the posthumous *Notebooks for an Ethics*, we read that "death is its limit but also a constitutive factor of freedom."[205] Freedom is what it is because every time it grasps one possibility and this determines that all the other possibilities which could have been grasped then are lost forever. In this light, if there were an infinite time, freedom could not constitute itself and man's individuality, which relies on freedom, would disappear.

We see then that the idea of finitude understood as a determinate history which grows indefinitely and in so doing indefinitely deepens its origin is not acceptable from Sartre's point of view. Personal history makes sense only as the free construction of one's individuality and, as we have seen, freedom can be what it is only under the condition of death, that is, of a finite time. It seems fair to say that also for Sartre death becomes a constitutive element, the transcendental horizon for the authentic exercise of freedom.

Accordingly, man's freedom must recognize and, in and through this recognizing, "realize," the final limit of death as its ultimate condition of meaning and exercise. Despite Sartre's objections to the Heideggerian view of death as a possibility, death becomes also for the Sartrean for-itself something like a possibility to be grasped, to be affirmed as the ultimate condition of meaning for authentic freedom: "The choice of possible implies death and death as contingency."[206] The view presented in the posthumous *Notebooks for an Ethics* is not fully new. In fact, already in *Being and Nothingness* Sartre writes the following: "It is true that death is coming to me if I consider very broadly that my life is limited.... To wait for [it] is to accept the fact that life is a *limited* enterprise; it is one way among others of choosing finitude and electing our ends on the foundation of finitude."[207] So, while death can never be a project, death is that possibility that, once recognized and affirmed, gives full meaning to any project freely pursued.

In other words, if for Heidegger the meaning of being consists in a self-giving—a miraculous and transitory subtraction to nonbeing—of

---

205. Sartre, *Notebooks for an Ethics*, 326–27.

206. Sartre, *Notebooks for an Ethics*, 326.

207. Sartre, *Being and Nothingness*, 557; emphasis in original. Here, however, Sartre maintains this view not without hesitation. Only a few pages later he seems to backtrack: "Since death does not appear on the foundation of our freedom, it can only *remove all meaning from life*" (559).

which man, understood as the "shepherd of being," must take care and "let be," for Sartre the meaning of being lies in the "tragic" and "risky" capacity that man, in virtue of his freedom, has to temporarily subtract being from nothingness, knowing however that all that is realized by human freedom is contingent (it could have not been, it will not be, it has been realized at the expense of possibilities that will never be, etc.) and that it is meaningful precisely because of its contingency. Thus, tragedy is the meaning of man's life, that is, having internalized the mutual implication of radical nonnecessity, contingency, and death (that is, being destined to the ultimate failure of death) as the condition of meaning of one's own freedom.

The importance of Sartre's shift in his treatment of death lies in the explicit affirmation that only the "contingent" (understood, ultimately, as what is destined to death and carries death within its own structure), has value and meaning. The Sartrean contribution marks a clear step for continental philosophy in the direction of the now-widespread claim that death is what gives meaning to life and being. As we have seen, this position, while already present in nuce in Heidegger, remains in Heidegger wrapped in ambiguity. However, the crucial point is that death is for both Heidegger and Sartre a transcendental condition, a paradoxical a priori of existence—even though an a priori which Dasein must anticipate as his "ownmost" possibility in order to be a whole (Heidegger) and which must be "realized" through the free act of the for-itself as the possibility of the inevitable demise which grounds any projectual possibility (Sartre).

In the economy of my argument, one should acknowledge this point—death understood as a transcendental condition of existence—in order to then appreciate what must happen along the same path opened by Heidegger and Sartre: if man is truly his finitude-death, then man is radically contingent; but the contingent, in order to be truly so, must free itself from *any transcendental structure* and must identify itself with its anarchic and lawless occurring, with the fragmentation of events which cannot be gathered under a common framework.

In short: it is precisely the affirmation of death as the ultimate condition of meaning that leads to the radical contingency of being, that is, to being understood as lawless and anarchic dispersion and dissemination of events; and this, in turn, leads to that radical fragmentation of experience which is incompatible with and thus expels from itself any transcendental condition, including the a priori of death. Precisely because it is posited as a transcendental, death ends up removing itself as transcendental and leaves existence to its mere anarchic occurring, which comprehends also death as one of its various and accidental problems. Thus, once experience is understood as a fragmented series of events, the problem of death disappears as philosophical question—let alone as metaphysical mystery, that is, as a totalizing problem that puts into question life in its totality. Death is thus subjected to what D. C. Schindler calls the misological mentality[208] and death's mystery gets neutralized in the generalized market of ideas and options, as Plato would put it.

The anxiety-filled titanism of Heidegger and the tragedism of Sartre are replaced by the ironic sense of contingency of Vattimo and Rorty as the fundamental *Stimmung* of existence. By itself, this does not lead to the technoscientism of our age. Rather, the new post-Heideggerian outcome of the reflection on death, exemplified, as we will see shortly, in Vattimo's "weak thought," leaves the room open to the invasion of the only animating force of our time, the force of technological science. The post-Heideggerian approach to death is the *pars destruens* of any residual transcendental element, so that death, reduced to a merely ontic matter, can be fully framed according to the gaze of technoscience.

6.4. *Gadamer*. Before turning to Vattimo, it might be worthwhile dwelling, although briefly, on Gadamer's contribution to the issue we are discussing. Gadamer's reflection on death is particularly relevant insofar as it shows a new synthesis which contains elements of continuity and, at the same time, radical elements of discontinuity with Heidegger's thought. In fact, while Gadamer agrees with Heidegger that death is given in the fundamental *Stimmung* of anxiety, in the economy of his thought death does not play that transcendental role that it still plays in Heidegger (and, as we have seen, in Sartre).

Gadamer contextualizes his reflection on death within the very problem of hermeneutics.[209] If, as August Böckh says, the hermeneutical effort consists in knowing what is known, how is death truly known, given that death seems to be constitutive of man as man (as constitutive of man as thought is!) and thus something always already present to man's consciousness? Gadamer's response seems to be that death, the radical nonbeing of man, must remain a "problem" and an "aporia"—it is truly known only when it is given as problem and as aporia. In other words, death is genuinely thought only when it is thought as "unintelligible."

---

208. Schindler, *Plato's Critique of Impure Reason*, 1–39.
209. Gadamer, "Death as a Question," 1:59. See also Nielsen, "Gadamer on Death's Unintelligibility."

So, on the one hand, the thought of death is for Gadamer a constitutive factor of the human condition—just like the burial rituals are usually considered essential evidence of the hominization process—but, on the other hand, such thought must recognize that death is unintelligible and unthinkable. Gadamer suggests that a "not-willing-to-admit death," that is, a lack of recognition that death can only be thought as unintelligible, underlies the Platonic treatment of death in light of the proofs for the immortality of the soul, as well as the Greek inclusion of death as a necessary moment in the cycle of reproduction of *zōē*. Also Christianity seems to be responsible of a similar flaw insofar as it thinks death only in the context of immortality and resurrection.

The caution that I have proposed in the previous sections regarding the risk of turning the negativity of death into a positive is certainly echoed in Gadamer's remarks. Nevertheless, when it comes to the argument I am trying to develop in this section, Gadamer's thought on death becomes important in a different way. In fact, Gadamer's thought is relevant as one of the steps in the direction of that de-transcendentalization of death which belongs to continental philosophy's general attitude in thinking the radical historicity of Dasein more and more rigorously. The crucial point seems to be the following. Gadamer's claim that death must be thought as "unintelligible" does not originate in a concern to preserve being-life and its divine origin from any original affection of the negative, but rather, it originates in the incompatibility between man's thinking self-projectuality (which includes technology) and the possibility of thinking oneself as nonexistent in the future. Gadamer draws his cues from Aeschylus's presentation of Prometheus, according to which Prometheus's infinite merit among human beings comes not only from his gift of fire, but, more radically, from his gift of the ignorance (of the moment) of their death. According to Gadamer, these two gifts must be read conjointly:

> The obvious question is: how do these two things belong together: veiling the knowledge of death and the new craftsmanship? One can hardly avoid thinking the two together. Aeschylus does not say anything about how Prometheus hid from human beings the certainty of their death and the hour of their death. Did that not happen precisely through the fact that he directed their thinking toward something distant in helping them create enduring works through their planned efforts? This would be the connection between knowing and not knowing and between

> thinking about death and the idea of progress. . . . What lies behind the curiously enigmatic mythical overcoming of the certainty of death through a belief in the future?[210]

He concludes: "The fact that we are thinking beings seems to be the ground for the unintelligibility of death and, at the same time, seems to include the knowledge of this unintelligibility."[211] In short: thought as projectuality (which Gadamer also calls, adapting a Simmelian expression, the "transcendence of life") not only makes death unintelligible, but also provides the ground for knowing why it is unintelligible.

We see here how the substance of the Heideggerian position has been abandoned. In Heidegger, being toward death is the condition of possibility for Dasein to be a whole. For Heidegger, Dasein's anticipatory resoluteness "comes into itself" only in being toward death. For Gadamer, on the contrary, the future-oriented projectuality of thought seems to make the thought of death impossible. Gadamer still appeals to Heidegger to suggest that, if death can be thought at all, it is thought only in and through the *Stimmung* of anxiety.[212] Nevertheless, death has lost for Gadamer the transcendental role it still played in Heidegger.

According to Gadamer's view, death may be described as the aporetic and anxiety-filled atmosphere within which thinking is deployed: unavoidable, but ultimately unintelligible because incompatible in principle with the self-projectuality of thinking. The road is now open to Vattimo's more radical version of a hermeneutics of historicity.

6.5. *Vattimo and some Heideggerian Epigones.* The interest in the philosophy of Vattimo for our purposes lies in the fact that Vattimo pushes Heidegger's hermeneutics beyond any residual attachment to a transcendental perspective, in a much more explicit and decisive way than Gadamer does. Thus, working out the tension still present in Gadamer between, on the one hand, the affirmation of absolute historicity of being and interpretation and, on the other hand, the appeal to a meta-hermeneutical, transcendental horizon of meaning as a condition of possibility for interpretation, Vattimo decidedly aims at establishing a radically historicist hermeneutics without transcendental protrusions. "There are no transcendental conditions of possibility for experience

---

210. Gadamer, "Death as a Question," 1:66.

211. Gadamer, "Death as a Question," 1:69. Gadamer's overall position does not seem to be essentially different in his *Enigma of Health*, esp. ch. 4, "The Experience of Death."

212. Gadamer, "Death as a Question," 1:69.

which might be attainable through some type of reduction or *epoché*, suspending our ties to historical-cultural, linguistic, and categorical horizons. The conditions of possibility for experience are always qualified, or, as Heidegger says, Dasein is a thrown project—thrown *time and time again*. The foundation, the setting out, the initial sending of our discourse cannot but be a hermeneutical foundation."[213] This is the main premise of what he calls the "nihilistic hermeneutics"[214] of the "death of God,"[215] or, more simply, the ontology of "weak thought."

According to weak thought and its ontology, "thinking being" amounts to the recollection of what has been handed down to us (the Heideggerian *Andenken*)—thus, also, and maybe especially, the metaphysical tradition of the West—in the spirit of the Heideggerian *Verwindung*, that is, in the spirit of a distortion which aims, in the very same gesture, at treating the past with *pietas* (*Denken* toward the metaphysical truth as a "monument") and at weakening whatever remaining trace of immutability, solidity, trans-historicity, universality, and presence, the idea of being might still carry with itself.[216]

What is crucial for our argument is the fact that Vattimo certainly puts at the heart of his understanding of interpretation and being the Heideggerian being toward death, but this notion loses in Vattimo the transcendental flair Heidegger still read into it.

> Thus the transcendental, or that which makes any experience of the world possible, is nothing less than transience [*caducità*]. That which constitutes the objectness of objects is not their standing across from us in resistant stability (*gegen-stand*) but their be-falling, that is, their consisting thanks solely to an openness constituted by the anticipatory resolve upon death, as expressed in the existential analytic of *Being and Time*. Befalling, or *Ereignis* (in the multiple senses Heidegger accords to the term), is what allows the metaphysical characteristics of Being to exist, perverting them through the exposition of their constitutive mortality and transience. To recall Being means to recall such transitoriness [*caducità*]. Thinking the truth does not mean "grounding," as even Kantian metaphysics maintains. It means rather revealing the waning and mortality which are

---

213. Vattimo, "Dialectics, Difference, Weak Thought," 40.
214. Vattimo, *Oltre l'interpretazione*, 68.
215. Vattimo, "Dialectics, Difference, Weak Thought," 46.
216. Vattimo, "Dialectics, Difference, Weak Thought," 47.

THE ANALOGY OF BEING AND THE NONBEING OF DEATH

properly what make up Being, thus effecting a breaking-through or de-grounding.[217]

Vattimo's thought thus supports the conclusion of my argument, namely, that being toward death assumed as a transcendental of Dasein must eventually *remove itself as transcendental* and leave Dasein and all the other beings to the pure contingency of the event: Being (each radically-historical horizon of meaning) "is" not but simply "befalls" or "occurs," and the beings which Being "lets be" also become, ipso facto, mere occurrences, ungrounded events destined to fragmentation.[218]

That this is so can be seen in the different roles that being toward death plays in Heidegger and Vattimo. As we have said multiple times, for Heidegger, being toward death is the ownmost possibility assuming and anticipating which Dasein can constitute himself as a whole. The transcendentality of being toward death shows its more traditional, Kantian or Husserlian sense precisely in the fact that it performs a constitutive function: it makes Dasein whole. On the contrary, being toward death as it is deployed by Vattimo means the absence of any constitutive transcendental structure besides the completely historical horizon of language. It is apparent that Vattimo radicalizes here the view of being as historical horizon of meaning of Heidegger and Gadamer, so that Nietzsche could finally prevail over Kant and Husserl and any appeal to the "true world" may be finally seen as a "fairy tale." Of course Vattimo is relying upon a tendency toward radical historicity already present in Heidegger and Gadamer, as he himself recognizes.[219] The importance of Vattimo's final push into radical contingency and finitude remains: being toward death is what deprives being and interpretation of any appeal to a meta-hermeneutical ground.

Thus, if for Heidegger being toward death is what makes Dasein whole, for Vattimo, being toward death is what deprives beings and their interpretation of any unifying framework besides the several and irreducible traditions from which our languages, categories, horizons of meanings, are inherited. Tradition must be understood always in the

---

217. Vattimo, "Dialectics, Difference, Weak Thought," 47–48.

218. A more thorough account of Vattimo's ontology would have to qualify this statement to show in what way, according to him, the replacement of the traditional metaphysics of presence with the hermeneutical ontology of the occurrence of the ontological difference does not amount to the institution of a "truer" ontology, an ontology "closer to the real structure of being" compared to the old one.

219. Vattimo, "Dialectics, Difference, Weak Thought," 44.

plural—it is unsurpassably "babelical"[220] and without "unity, principle, foundation."[221] While being toward death was in Heidegger the guarantee for a certain totality of meaning—at least that totality that is the Dasein understood as a whole—the same notion becomes in Vattimo the gateway for the denial of the very conceivability of a totality of meaning—the mark of being's and interpretations' radical equivocity.[222] Accordingly, the fragmentation of experience into absolutely-contingent events is the natural correlate of this view of tradition, language, and truth reduced to interpretation understood as rhetorical and distorting trans-mission of a received tradition.

6.5.1. As I have said, the post-Heideggerian philosophy of death comes here to its structural end—it completes its cycle with Vattimo. Many of the contemporary epigones of Heidegger do not seem to appreciate the closure to which the Heideggerian approach to death comes with Vattimo's nihilistic hermeneutics. Most of them re-propose views inspired to Heidegger, stating in particular that the meaning and value of life can only be found in its finitude and caducity, without, however, registering the tension between the two meanings that being toward death has assumed in the span that goes from Heidegger to Vattimo. For instance, Françoise Dastur, using a Heideggerian vocabulary, speaks of the necessity of "assuming" and "accepting" death as that which gives meaning to life, but her proposal shows no indication of either a renewed acceptance of a transcendental perspective, or the acceptance of a more radically historicist and anti-transcendental meaning of being toward death, with all which follows from such radical historicity for our thinking and experience of death.[223] The short circuit which her thought reaches can be pointed out by the disparate meanings which the notion of death assumes in the economy of her thought: first, death means that fundamental caducity of being which grants "gaiety and hilarity" to life;[224] second, death is absolute nonbeing and thus is in principle a nonphenomenon and, at the same time, it is more "present, insistent, and

---

220. Vattimo, *Oltre l'interpretazione*, 114.
221. Vattimo, *Oltre l'interpretazione*, 115.
222. See Vattimo, *Avventure della differenza*, 138.
223. See Dastur, *How Are We to Confront Death?*
224. "For one who is none other than time, there is gaiety or hilarity . . . only with regard to that which can be lost and which, exhausting itself in the instant, projects no infinite horizon of possible repetition" (Dastur, *Death*, 3).

THE ANALOGY OF BEING AND THE NONBEING OF DEATH

obsessive" than any other phenomenon, "continually present as a threat";[225] finally, death is not only a non-phenomenon that constantly and obsessively phenomenizes itself (!), but is also a quasi-transcendental horizon of manifestativity, giving everything that appears its "singular 'tenor' of finitude"[226] and, more deeply, allowing being as such to manifest.[227]

Vattimo does not go as far as saying explicitly that death has now become a purely ontic problem which should be treated in technological terms. His Marxist critique of techno-capitalism, informed by Heideggerian themes, would actually seem to suggest that he would be against the reduction of death to a mere prey of techno-scientism. Nevertheless, given the premises of his proposal, it is hard to see what could prevent the technoscientistic perspective from breaking in and bringing death into its own horizon of meaning.[228] In fact, Vattimo goes as far as proposing a reading of Heidegger according to which the fragmentation of modernity lamented by Heidegger himself could in principle be healed by the new, nonmechanistic technologies. For Vattimo, the "remembering of the meaning of Being" that Heidegger is after is the privileged way to overcome the fragmentation of meaning typical of the metaphysical-technological (i.e., manipulative and violent) history of the West and especially of modernity. This remembering, somewhat surprisingly, may

---

225. Dastur, *Death*, 41–42.

226. "Continually present as threat, death as this absolute absence must be accorded a paradoxical mode of appearing which is not the origin of any particular phenomenon, but confers upon phenomena as a whole their singular 'tenor' of finitude by having them stand out against the background of its black light.... It is because it is related to this nothing of death that the human being thinks, and also speaks, and laughs" (Dastur, *Death*, 42).

227. "The very *being* of things ... is neither their mere sensible singularity nor their pure abstract concept, but the *alterity* of their absence.... Being is therefore nothing other than the *gift* we are given by death in its omnipotence.... More than in the clearing itself, it is in the *heart* of this, in the *lēthē* of *alētheia*, that man truly belongs. Because it is only from a bottomless darkness that the clearing of the world can spread out—just as, as Heraclitus suggests, it is from the 'crypt' favoured by it that *physis* may emerge, since 'self-revealing not only never dispenses with concealing, but actually *needs* it, in order to obtain essentially in the way it obtains disclosing.' Death as shelter of being and nocturnal source of all light is thus acknowledged to have an immeasurable power" (Dastur, *Death*, 82–83; emphasis in original).

228. In fact, one does not have to search much in order to see where even Vattimo's approach may lead it: "The ruling concepts of metaphysics ... turn out to be means of discipline and reassurance that are no longer necessary in the context of our present-day organization capability of technology" ("Dialectics, Difference, Weak Thought," 43).

come to fruition not in a view of reality more fundamental than technology, but in a different understanding of technology. Vattimo suggests that this may have been Heidegger's, admittedly undeveloped, point of view:

> It is in the *Ge-Stell*, Heidegger thinks, that the aperture of Being that characterizes modernity is concentrated and becomes visible. In a passage from *Identity and Difference* . . . he says explicitly that in the *Ge-Stell*—in itself a source of extreme danger for the humanity of mankind—we can also perceive "a first flash of the *Ereignis*," the (new) event of being, that is, on which the possibility of an overcoming of metaphysics depends. . . . Heidegger . . . never escaped from a vision of technology dominated by the model of the motor and mechanical energy, so for [him] modern technology could do nothing except bring about a society subordinated to a central power dispatching commands to a purely passive periphery, as gear wheels are driven, whether these commands were mechanical impulses, political propaganda, or commercial advertising. Actually though, if we try to think clearly about how the *Ge-Stell* might offer us a chance of overcoming metaphysics through the dissolution of the subject-object relationship that distinguishes human existence in modernity, we see that the only apparent solution is a radical shift in our vision of technology.[229]

It does not really matter for our purposes that Vattimo sees this "emancipating" shift in technology as already on its way in the universal implementation of information and digital technologies.[230] What matters is that his endorsement of the new technologies is performed in the name of Heidegger. One only needs to connect the remaining dots to see how Vattimo's Heideggerian proposal may easily welcome technoscience as the only historical horizon of meaning for dealing with death. The fact that he would still resist the characterization of this view as a reduction of

---

229. Vattimo, "Postmodernism, Technology, Ontology," 14–15.

230. Vattimo continues: "The technology that does actually give us a glimpse of a possible dissolution of the rigid distinction between subject and object is not the mechanical technology of the motor, with its one-way flow from the center to the periphery, but it might very well be the technology of modern communications, the means by which information is gathered, ordered, and disseminated. To speak more plainly: the possibility of overcoming metaphysics, which Heidegger describes obscurely in the *Ge-Stell*, really opens up only when the technology—at any rate the socially hegemonic technology—ceases to be mechanical and becomes electronic: information and communication technology" ("Postmodernism, Technology, Ontology," 15).

death to a merely "ontic" problem amounts to little more than a linguistic idiosyncrasy.

The reader will rightly think that the conclusion of the argument proposed in this section does not leave much room for optimism. While this is partially true, it is also the case that the cycle of the Heideggerian philosophy of death brings about something good. In fact, by removing death as a transcendental, nihilistic hermeneutics also removes the wrong premise of Heidegger's position, namely, the preconception of death as something constitutive of human being's finitude. This becomes particularly clear in the transhumanist take on death. By aspiring to put an end to death and thus extend human life indefinitely, transhumanists think that either finitude is not constitutive of who they are (if "finitude" is taken as a synonym of "death"), or that mortality is not essential to their finitude. In both cases, however, death is not taken any more as constitutive of the human condition—which is the unjustified premise of Heidegger's proposal. This is definitely a positive outcome of the Heideggerian cycle, which opens up new possibilities of reflection on the nature of death without assuming uncritically that death is constitutive of who we are.

This said, it is also true that transhumanism, by hoping for a technological overcoming of death, overlooks the definitiveness of death, and by overlooking the definitiveness of death, may end up turning death into something ultimate—an unsurpassed negativity hiding under a superficial layer of controlling technology. To see why this may be the case, we turn now to the last chapter of the book.

CHAPTER FOUR

The Transhumanist Overcoming of Death and Human Desire

What the Experience of "For a Child Is Born to Us, a Son Is Given to Us" May Tell Us About a Possible Misunderstanding Characterizing Our Technological Civilization

> Despite these miseries, man wishes to be happy, and only wishes to be happy, and cannot wish not to be so. But now will he set about it? To be happy he would have to make himself immortal; but, not being able to do so, it has occurred to him to prevent himself from thinking of death.
>
> BLAISE PASCAL, *THOUGHTS*, 69N169

The anguish of death, and not only the pain of dying, would be incomprehensible if the fundamental structure of our being did not include the existential postulate of something beyond. Without this, death would simply be a future fact, painful enough, no doubt, but without any exceptional gravity and without any danger of a metaphysical character. This very anguish reveals that death and nothingness are opposed to the deepest and most ineradicable tendencies of our being. We are not speaking here of the instinct to duration, inherent in life in general, of Schopenhauer's will to live.... If human nature has need of a belief in survival, this is neither egoism nor eccentricity nor some form of historical atavism. The very need itself is witness to a fundamental state of being: consciousness imitates the depth of being. If there were no real possibility to correspond with this tendency, the whole of human existence would perish in the abyss.

PAUL-LOUIS LANDSBERG, *THE EXPERIENCE OF DEATH*, 23–24

1. INTRODUCTION: MODERN TECHNOLOGY, TRANSHUMANISM, AND DESIRE

1.1. IT WOULD BE impossible to conclude the present study on the metaphysics of death without a direct engagement with the way in which technology bears upon the experience of our mortality. It is almost trivial to state that our civilization is chiefly characterized by the phenomenon of modern technology. It may be less trivial to reflect on the fact that our technological civilization expresses itself today in the form of the philosophical movements known as "transhumanism" and "posthumanism," for which the technological overcoming of death is an essential feature.[1] The system of technological solutions extends from the "how" and "when" to the "that" of death. In relation to this, it may be instructive to point out a focal shift over the past decades. An important book by Georg Scherer, dating back to 1971, exemplifies this fact. The first chapter of the book, titled "The Problem of Death in the Age of Science," presents the view according to which the "undoing of the idea of death" (Scheler) and the reduction of death to the idea of "natural death" (corresponding to a denial of any metaphysical treatment of death) are the product of a science-dominated theoretical and practical attitude in which absolute control over life and nature and complete self-determination are the fundamental values.[2] The interesting fact of which to take notice is that this tendency to absolute control and self-determination is exemplarily

---

1. The terms "transhumanism" and "posthumanism" have in the extant literature diverse and ever-changing meanings. Nevertheless, it seems possible to state that "transhumanism" is the philosophical movement supporting the process of transition (trans-) of the human being out of his "human" condition, into a condition in which humanity (as it has been known so far) is finally left behind (post-). For a discussion of this terminology in historical perspective, see Bostrom: "History of Transhumanist Thought"; *Transhumanist FAQ*. I found More and Vita-More, *Transhumanist Reader*, very helpful. For simplicity's sake, I will only use the term "transhumanism" to designate the overall technological attitude toward death which is under consideration in this chapter.

2. See Scherer, *Problema della morte*, 19–54.

illustrated according to Scherer by the phenomena of euthanasia and suicide, through which man decides how and when to die. It seems that today the spirit of science and technology is inviting us to a different kind of discussion—without of course eliminating the immense bioethical problem of euthanasia: not how and when we want to die, but *whether we want to die*.

To anticipate what I will have to say in this final chapter, the vantage from which I will address the issue of transhumanism will be that of *human desire*. What is human desire and how is it related to the transhumanist project of overcoming human death? How is our mortality related to human desire? And is it possible to rely on the nature and object of human desire in order to establish whether transhumanism is in fact a reasonable and desirable attitude toward death and life?

As it will become evident in due course, this chapter presents a critique of the transhumanist approach to death. Nevertheless, even more so than in the case of the previous chapters, the argumentative style followed here has nothing to do with the ideal of putting forth knock-down arguments. Nothing seems more foreign to the discussion of issues related to the nature and place of death in our life than the aspiration to see no value and no reasons in the view which we are about to criticize. More specifically, we are sympathetic not only with the inventiveness and creativity that modern technology reveals about the human being, but also with the desire for life and for overcoming the given limits that transhumanism seems to champion. To a large extent, in fact, we believe that the limits are given to the human being so that he may overcome them creatively: "The Lord God then took the man and settled him in the garden of Eden, to cultivate and care for it" (Gen 2:15). "Cultivation" is always, one way or another, an overcoming of a given limit, a creative transformation. That the human being is created "in the image and likeness of God" (Gen 1:26) means, at least in part, that the human being is called to be a co-creator, that what is given to him is given so that he may do something new with it: "So the Lord God formed out of the ground all the wild animals and all the birds of the air, and he brought them to the man to see what he would call them; whatever the man called each living creature was then its name" (Gen 2:19).[3] And as we shall see shortly, human desire itself is precisely at the origin of the specifically human

---

3. On this, see Stango, "Culture: Techne and Contemplation." This article also explains the relevant distinction between ancient techne and modern technology, which I presuppose in what I have to say here.

dynamism of limit-overcoming. Nevertheless, what I will suggest is that, in desiring to overcome the limit of death technologically, *the transhumanist does not desire adequately*. To put it roughly, he does not desire strongly enough; more correctly, *he desires too conservatively*.

As I was saying, the considerations entrusted to this chapter do not belong to that part of philosophy whose conclusions can be established apodictically. Here, the ideal of incontrovertible proofs must make room for a more patient and tentative *hermeneutics of the human condition*. I do not think that for this reason the ideas put forth here are less true. However, I do think that fewer people will be immediately drawn to endorse them without resistance. The persuasiveness of these ideas results more from the fact that they belong to an overall attractive and convincing picture of human life than from their merely logical cogency.

Once again we should ask: Is it possible to acknowledge the presence of death in our life without turning it into something positive? And is it possible to truly remain faithful to the nature of our desire, in such a way that death is acknowledged for what it is, namely, something definitive for us and yet neither original, nor constitutive, nor ultimate? It seems fair to say here that to the truth of death corresponds a difficult existential stance—a *desiring existence* which neither desires death nor desires in abstraction from death. Nietzsche's words come to mind: "The strength of a spirit would be proportionate to how much of the 'truth' he could withstand—or, to put it more clearly, to what extent he needs it to be thinned out, veiled over, sweetened up, dumbed down, and lied about."[4] And if it is correct to claim, with Nietzsche, that "no one would consider a doctrine to be true just because it makes people happy or virtuous,"[5] it seems also correct to state, this time against Nietzsche, that there has to be a truth about human desire and happiness, and that this truth may shed light on the various projects that claim authority on the meaning of life and death. Today, one such project is certainly transhumanism.

The centrality of the issue of human desire may lead some readers well-versed in Catholic philosophy to think of the work of Maurice Blondel. This would be apropos, and in fact I will draw significantly from Blondel's philosophy in what follows. Blondel's whole question in *Action* (1983) is to determine the object and nature of human desire through a phenomenology of the dialectic between what he calls "the willing will"

---

4. Nietzsche, *Beyond Good and Evil*, 37.
5. Nietzsche, *Beyond Good and Evil*, 37.

(corresponding roughly to what Thomas calls *voluntas ut natura*) and "the willed will" (corresponding roughly to what Thomas calls *voluntas ut ratio*).[6] Blondel also engages directly and insightfully with the problem of technology, showing that a correct understanding of the origin of the phenomenon of technology (the limit-overcoming desire for the infinite) brings with itself also an understanding of why technology cannot be the answer to what Blondel calls "the problem of life"—and, we may add, the problem of death.

1.2. Before we move forward, it seems important to clarify what we mean by *technology*, since the transhumanist attitude toward death falls precisely within the broader phenomenon of modern technology. For the purposes of this chapter, it is sufficient and relevant to reflect on the connection between modern technology and human desire. It is for this reason that Blondel's thought is immediately relevant. For Blondel, in fact, technology is first and foremost a *spiritual phenomenon*. More precisely, technology is that form of "spiritualization" of nature through which the human activity grows and tries to find the suitable and sufficient means for its full expansion—the means to equate in action (the "willed will") the desire that animates, secretly but stubbornly, everything that the human being does (the "willing will").[7] Thus, the technological transformation of the world corresponds to and is the expression of a deep-seated and legitimate desire in man—the desire for expansion and conquest, that is, man's conquest not of the world per se, but of himself through the world and through the introduction into the world of what in the world is not given at first.

Too often this aspect of the phenomenon of technology is neglected, and the genius of Blondel's approach is precisely that of proposing a non-naïve view of the human act as a key to interpret our technological civilization. The *technological expansion is to some extent necessary* because it *connaturally flows* from the need for self-*expansion* and self-*seeking* of the will in and through the world. In turn, this *self*-expansion and *self*-seeking are manifested in the self-serving goal inscribed in technology. In fact, no matter how "sustainable," technoscience is essentially a form

---

6. *ST* 3, q. 18, a. 3, co.

7. "Through them [the positive sciences and technology] the world of phenomena is submitted to man; it is penetrated by the spirit; it is opened up to the circulation of the interior life. . . . And spontaneously the forces of nature seem to have become an organ of the will: such is the beauty of scientific civilization!" (Blondel, *Action*, 203; see also 210, 214–15).

of self-serving use of the world, and it corresponds to the need that the human will has to try to equate itself (its secret final end) with action. Technology establishes the world (as much of the world it can "take in") as a controlled system of "co-acting" forces *for* human action—the logic here is the logic of "assimilation" for the sake of growth and expansion. Despite all the discussions on this point in the literature, there is ultimately no essential difference between technology-as-tool and technology-as-environment: technology is environment only because the entire world is subjected to the will's pursuit of self-realization. The technological transformation of the world is analogous to the will's subjection of the organism to the pursuit of the will's expansion and self-realization. Accordingly, the world is encountered along the same path as the organism—as a complex of docile-and-resistant powers that the will takes up and reshapes, and to which the will gives itself, in order to pursue the sought-after equation between desire ("willing will") and action ("willed will").[8]

Now, the most relevant point for our inquiry is the following. If death—that which puts an end to any growth, any expansion, any intention, any coaction—is one of the greatest stumbling blocks, if not the greatest stumbling block, for the self-expansion of the will in pursuing its equation with action, it will follow that death must become one of the chief targets of the conquering aspirations of modern technology. The dis-equation, the gap, between the willing will and action, which manifests itself in many and varied ways in Blondel's analyses, is ultimately faced with the problem of death. Thus, the *intrinsic logic* of the desire-powered expansion of human action brings about the *convergence of technology and death*: On what other limit will technology focus if not on the ultimate limit of death?

1.2.1. Some authors have recently pointed out that it would be impossible to understand the phenomenon of modern technology apart from the concept of "death." For instance, both Kenneth L. Schmitz and Catherine Pickstock see modern technology as the triumph of "death," taking "death" in the metaphorical sense of the "death of things" metaphysically understood: the outlook of modern technology implies a reduction of the nature of things to "raw material" available to unrestrained human manipulation.[9] A similar view was championed by Romano Guardini and has been recently confirmed magisterially by Pope

---

8. Blondel, *Action*, 215.

9. See Schmitz, *Recovery of Wonder*, esp. ch. 3; Catherine Pickstock, *After Writing*, esp. ch. 3.

Francis.[10] Along the same lines, Jeffrey Bishop has gone as far as saying that the modern technology ensuing in transhumanism is a form of what Heidegger calls "onto-theology": for the transhumanist, natural evolution is nothing else than a process governed by blind power ("power" as the ontology of evolutionism), up to the point when the human will, which is a product of the same blind process, assumes the evolutionary process and directs it deliberately toward the technological production of a post-human outcome (the human will as the "theological" element of the modern power ontology, hence transhumanism as onto-theology).[11] An essential dimension of the realization of this post-human condition is precisely the technological overcoming of death, where technology comes to play the soteriological role ("defeating death") that belonged to the Christian God.

The contribution of these positions is not only that of highlighting the essential connection between technology and death, but also that of spelling out what is "modern" about technology, namely, the new ontology, metaphysics, and philosophical theology, without which the true meaning of technology would wholly escape us. At the same time, Blondel's interpretation of the technological transformation of the world as a necessary stage in the self-expansion of action allows us to appreciate the fact that it is human desire itself that is ultimately responsible for technology to be what it is. The willing will is the animating force behind the aspiration to overcome any given limit technologically.

As it is often the case, any attempt to define the "essence" of a phenomenon runs the risk of providing a caricature of the phenomenon in question at best, or of putting forth a violent and ideological interpretation of the same phenomenon, at worst. Nevertheless, pace Galileo, *tentar le essenze* is necessary to the human mind, if the human mind wants to understand anything at all. For this reason, by way of integration to the positions of the authors just mentioned, I would like to propose the following way to look at modern technology in its difference from ancient techne. While ancient techne focuses on the *positivity of being*, modern technology is chiefly concerned with the *negativity of nonbeing*—what I have just called, following Blondel, the dis-equation or the gap between the willing will and the willed will. Following this path, modern technology must ultimately take death as its main concern and the overcoming

---

10. Francis, *Laudato Si'* §§102–14; see also Hanby: "Homo Faber and/or Homo Adorans"; "Gospel of Creation."

11. See Bishop, "Transhumanism, Metaphysics."

of death as its chief goal, both because death is the negativity of nonbeing and because death seems to represent the chief stumbling block to desire's aspiration to fulfillment.

Thus, both techne and technology are concerned with overcoming the given limits, but the relevant limits and the overall horizon encompassing the overcoming of the respective limits are different. Take, for instance, the case of medicine. The restorative role of medicine typical of the premodern times turns into the bioengineering's project of indefinite enhancement of the human being, to the point of freeing human life from death. This transhumanist outcome was already foreshadowed in the beginning of the development of modern physics. As it is well known, according to Francis Bacon, the new science's aim is a moral one, that is, "to ease and improve the human condition."[12] For him, the prolongation of life had to become the noblest of the defining goals of the physician.[13] More explicitly, René Descartes argues that one of the main outcomes of the new physics would be a renovated medical art through which "it would be possible to be free of innumerable illnesses of both body and mind, and perhaps even the decline of old age, if we knew enough about their causes and the remedies with which nature has provided us."[14] Contemporary transhumanism is the clearest actualization of this potentiality intrinsic to modern technology.

In order to avoid misunderstandings, let me stress once again, following Blondel, that not only is modern technology truly wondrous in some of its aspects, both for its concrete achievements and as a form of "spiritualization" of nature; and that not only does it correspond to a necessary and to some extent inevitable expression of the human will in the journey to find what may correspond to its secret aspiration; but also that, given this internal logic of technology, it is almost inevitable that technology ends up focusing on the removal of the negative, of the gap, and so, chiefly, of death, as its main target. If one disagrees, as I disagree, with this project, one must also recognize that the internal logic of this

---

12. Bacon, *New Organon*, 60. The phrase is used in the context of a scathing critique of Greek philosophy, which has not shown any tangible fruits. Despite "all sciences we have come from the Greeks," "the wisdom of the Greeks was rhetorical and prone to disputation." Hence, for Bacon, "the term 'Sophists,' which was rejected by those who wanted to be regarded as philosophers and applied with contempt to the orators—Gorgias, Protagoras, Hippias, Polus—is also applicable to the whole tribe—Plato, Aristotle, Zeno, Epicurus, Theophrastus and their successors" (58–59).

13. See Haycock, "Living Forever."

14. Descartes, *Discourse on the Method*, 52.

process corresponds to *something natural in us*—the desire to remove that obstacle that prevents the self-equation of the will with itself in action or, to put it more simply, the *desire to overcome the unnatural limit of death*.

This also makes sense when seen historically. The ancient form of techne grew within a religious and cosmological context in which death was considered part of the order of nature. Modern technology, on the contrary, is the product of a Christian mentality, in which death is the wage of sin. It thus makes sense that the removal of the negativity of death becomes, one way or another, the goal of modern technology and today one of the main concerns of the transhumanist project. Thus, there is some truth in the claim that the attempt to overcome death through technology cannot be reduced to an interpretation of modern technology as a gnostic phenomenon, which we find for example in Eric Voegelin and Augusto Del Noce.[15] What technology aims at directly would be *not* the manipulation of nature in order to flee what of nature is perceived as evil, but the overcoming of what is *toto coelo* opposed to nature, that is, the nonbeing of death. Thus modernity, to simplify things somewhat, presents a twofold attitude toward the limit of death: on the one hand, modernity shows the attitude typical of rationalistic philosophy, which, as Del Noce explains, tends to ontologize death by interpreting it as an original and constitutive trait of finite being (coessential to finite being's "ontologization of guilt"); on the other hand, modernity also manifests the scientific-technological aspiration to overcome death. It is this second soul of modernity that transhumanism embodies and brings to new heights.

1.3. The presence of death in life is an obvious challenge to all those who love life. Not surprisingly, transhumanism presents itself as a hymn to life, and understandably so. It does so by often conceiving of itself as a missionary movement, in which the spirit and the force of the humanitarian ideal coexists, somewhat contradictorily, with an equally strong posthuman attitude. For Aubrey de Grey, for instance, transhumanism's ideal of service to humanity (in order to bring about a new post-humanity) is best understood in opposition to what he calls the "suffocating deathism" of the humanist.[16] There is something epoch-changing and epic in the aspirations of the transhumanist, an aspect on which I will return below.

---

15. See Voegelin, *New Science of Politics*; Voegelin, *Science, Politics & Gnosticism*; Del Noce, "Violence and Modern Gnosticism"; Del Noce, "Eric Voegelin."

16. De Grey, "Suffocating Deathism." This article is interesting because it epitomizes

THE TRANSHUMANIST OVERCOMING OF DEATH & HUMAN DESIRE

Doesn't the presence of death in our life most reasonably evoke in us the desire for *survival*—a survival in the form of *more life*, what Ray Kurzweil calls an "extension" and "expansion" of life?[17] This "hunger for more life" is assumed as a defining identity by most transhumanists. Just to mention one anecdote which bears exemplary value, the transhumanist Nancie Clark, after marrying the transhumanist Max More (born Max O'Connor), changed her name into Natasha Vita-More, which means literally "Natasha More Life."[18] My argument in the following sections will try to show that, in an important sense, the transhumanist desire for extensive and expansive survival turns against its goal by bringing about the opposite of what it aims to, namely, an insidious *immortalization of death*. Moreover, I will suggest that, contrary to all appearances, the transhumanist interpretation of the human desire for life turns such desire into a subtle form of masochistic and sadistic *love of death*. I take this to be a most striking case of "heterogenesis of ends." After having established this, we will have to explore what our desire may actually be about, given that the transhumanist interpretation of the human desire turns out to be contradictory. In other words, in what sense can we say that, in the face of death, what we mostly desire is *life*, without being caught in the pitfalls of the transhumanist desire for life's extensive and expansive survival? Let us ask, with François Jullien, "What distinction shall we make, then, between the minimal being alive and having life in oneself? What separation shall we introduce within life, this most elementary of terms, so that it can rise from mere condition to vocation,

---

the moral and humanitarian nature of the transhumanist ideal against the "idiotic arguments" of the humanist: "And that, dear reader, has got to stop, because it is slowing us down and costing lives." See also De Grey and Rae, *Ending Aging*.

17. These expressions are recurring throughout Kurzweil, *Singularity Is Near*. Sometimes even the great Henri Bergson seems to suggest a similar idea: "As the smallest grain of dust is bound up with our entire solar system, drawn along with it in that undivided movement of descent which is materiality itself, so all organized beings, from the humblest to the highest, from the first origins of life to the time in which we are, and in all places as in all times, do but evidence a single impulsion, the inverse of the movement of matter, and in itself indivisible. All the living hold together, and all yield to the same tremendous push. The animal takes its stand on the plant, man bestrides animality, and the whole of humanity, in space and in time, is one immense army galloping beside and before and behind each of us in an overwhelming charge able to beat down every resistance and clear the most formidable obstacles, perhaps even death" (*Creative Evolution*, 295).

18. Giesen, "Transhumanism as Dominant Ideology," 190. Giesen convincingly points out that "transhumanism has now reached the stage where it has become a major political project involving mass ideological dissemination" (202).

and even the ultimate vocation?"[19] What, beyond mere extensive and expansive survival, constitutes the actual object of our innermost desire for life?

1.4. Vladimir Jankélévitch has a subtle and deep insight concerning this very point. According to him, each human being is a "mortal eternal verity."[20] While death is the irreversible, destructive negation of our being, death cannot do as if we had never existed: death "can take my being away materially, but it cannot annihilate my having-been," and it is precisely death, according to Jankélévitch, which seals the eternity of this metaphysical truth in the very same act of destroying a life.[21] Could this theory teach us something about how our desire for life may be different from a desire for an extensive and expansive survival? Should we not say, expanding on Jankélévitch, that our desire for life is, in its depth, a *desire for having-been*? There is much truth in this piece of wisdom by Jankélévitch, especially if one makes explicit the role played by the "memory" of the past as the dwelling of the immemorable origin (a connection that Jankélévitch does not draw explicitly, as far as I can tell).[22] How beautiful is to leave one's life knowing that one has truly lived at least once—at least one day, one hour, one minute. And how beautiful to think of the ends of one's days as the seal that completes and fulfills a definite story, one's story, which can now be entrusted to other people, so that these people can receive and protect its irreducible mystery? And yet, isn't this a desire already tamed by death? Should the desire for eternity and immortality be interpreted exclusively as a desire for having-been? Isn't this interpretation of desire one that ends up turning death into a pseudo-metaphysical, inevitable "happy ending"? Doesn't the rebellious and antagonistic dimension of desire vis-à-vis death get swept under the rug by Jankélévitch's philosophical move?

1.5. One last introductory note. It is not uncommon to find philosophers who dismiss the transhumanist project of overcoming death technologically on the grounds that according to them this project is simply unrealizable, mere science fiction. Now, despite the triumphant rhetoric often surrounding the transhumanist literature, it seems fair to

---

19. Jullien, *Resources of Christianity*, 40.
20. Jankélévitch, *Mort*, 409.
21. Jankélévitch, *Mort*, 465.
22. This line of thought is developed in Tilliette, *Morte e immortalità*, esp. chs. 1–3, with reference chiefly to Augustine, Schelling, and Bergson. While silent on this point, Jankélévitch may have come close to it, especially given his closeness to Bergson.

THE TRANSHUMANIST OVERCOMING OF DEATH & HUMAN DESIRE

say that the actual prospect of defeating death through the resources of technology is scant, to say the least. A rapid review of the transhumanist strategies to tackle death is sufficient to clarify this point. For instance, Eric Steinhart, a philosopher-transhumanist, distinguishes four "technological soteriologies": the medical curing of all diseases, the indefinite replacement of failing organs with artificial parts, cryonics, and mind-uploading.[23] Even Steinhart agrees that these four strategies are "at present . . . all science fiction."[24]

Nevertheless, it seems to me that the point of a philosophical discussion of the transhumanist aspiration to the definitive conquest of aging and death is not to ascertain whether the transhumanist project can achieve what it promises, but rather to acknowledge the way in which this project *already shapes* our view of the world, life, and death. Heidegger has rightly noted that the "essence of technology" cannot be reduced to the total sum of the technological practices in which we engage and of the devices which we use—and, we may add, to the problem of whether such practices and devices are successful or not. In this sense, the "essence of technology" is different from technology. According to him, such essence is rather a way of disclosing the totality of being as a bottomless and nature-less resource for unrestrained manipulation, which contextually hides other ways of disclosing being.[25]

Something similar applies to transhumanism. By disclosing the world, life, and death in a certain way, transhumanism systematically covers up other ways to understand reality. One of the most important aspects of this fact is that *death is immediately framed as an ontic problem to be addressed technologically rather than as a metaphysical mystery*. Max Scheler has imputed to the "structure of the experience" of the "European-Western modern man" the "pathological" "undoing of death" which characterizes our scientific and technological civilization:

> For the average modern man "to think" simply means "to calculate."[26]

> According to an "axiom" of modern medicine formulated a few years ago by a famous Parisian scientist, there is no natural

---

23. Steinhart, "Naturalistic Theories," 150–51.
24. Steinhart, "Naturalistic Theories," 151.
25. "The Question Concerning Technology," in Heidegger, *Basic Writings*, 311–41. See also "The Age of the World Picture," in Heidegger, *Off the Beaten Track*, 57–85.
26. Scheler, *Morte e sopravvivenza*, 61.

limit to life that medical science and technology, together with clinical praxis, could not differ indefinitely! . . . The fact that human beings still die will be blamed on the lack of "progress" of the extant medicine, if not even on the "idleness" of researchers and doctors, who for this reason will be considered morally guilty. . . . If this "axiom" already dominates the entire outlook of science, and if the meaning of science . . . is not that of showing the *true world*, but only that of articulating a "plan" to dominate and rule over it, then science itself *cannot* be capable of seeing death. It cannot help but denying its ultimate existence. If can only be blind in front of it, even more so given that it is born of the typically modern tendency to close its eyes in front of death, to remove it through the instinct of work.[27]

Michel Foucault makes a similar point quite powerfully in his account of the birth of "positive medicine" and the new "visibility of death" that is integral to it:

> This structure, in which space, language, and death are articulated—what is known, in fact, as the anatomo-clinical method—constitutes the historical condition of a medicine that is given and accepted as positive. Positive here should be taken in the strong sense. Disease breaks away from the metaphysic of evil, to which it had been related for centuries; and it finds in the visibility of death the full form in which its content appears in positive terms. Conceived in relation to nature, disease was the nonassignable negative of which the causes, forms, and manifestations were offered only indirectly and against an ever-receding background; seen in relation to death, disease becomes exhaustively legible, open without remainder to the sovereign dissection of language and of the gaze.[28]

The stall which transhumanism brings about is conjointly practical because this world-shaping outlook of technology-transhumanism becomes the *principle of organization* of our energies, forces, resources, etc. To use the classical Aristotelian terminology, if transhumanism is extremely weak as an efficient cause, it is at the same time extremely powerful as a final cause, as a moving ideal. And if on the one hand

---

27. Scheler, *Morte e sopravvivenza*, 71–72; emphasis in original.
28. Foucault, *Birth of the Clinic*, 243. Foucault's eminently epistemological study can be read in tandem with now-classical historical and sociological studies on the changing image of death from antiquity to our time in the West, such as Ariès, *Western Attitudes Toward Death*.

its prospected outcomes may be unfeasible, transhumanism is on the other hand already realized precisely as a driving and organizing force in our civilization. Thus, the transhumanist ideal of conquering aging and death is already real, precisely as the ideal that already governs the actual allocation of our theoretical and practical resources. It thus calls for a philosophical critique precisely as that *possibility* shaping our individual and collective experience. A society shaped according to the trans- and posthumanist ideal realizes in a radicalized way that twofold attitude towards death that, according to Edgar Morin, modern society in general always tends to produce:[29] on the one hand, the stress put on individuality (today in the form of a technologically-informed consumeristic individualism) produces an enhanced concern about one's own death and a feeling of "maladjustment" to one's mortality (in conformity with the anthropological law according to which the sense of and aversion to death grows together with the affirmation of individuation); on the other hand, the stress put on the superindividual collectivity (today in the form of the finally-liberated trans- and post-human technological civilization) produces a condition of radical "adjustment" to the thought of death, precisely in the form of the ideal of the technological overcoming of death, which Morin calls "amortality."[30] When it comes to the transhumanist approach to death, it is correct to say that technology is the practical application of that same device which, in the symbolic world, has always been known as "myth"[31] (myth and technology as two species of the genus "device for the self-immunization against the trauma of death"); in turn, however, technology performs its function only by turning into a new myth.

2. IMMORTALIZING DEATH

2.1. The merit of Heidegger's discussion of death is certainly to point out that the reality of death for the human being lies, in an important sense, not in the future event of perishing, but in the always-present and phenomenologically-dense mode of being-toward-death. For Heidegger death is "more real" now, in the form of an abiding and always-impending

---

29. Morin, *Uomo e la morte*, 79.
30. Morin, *Uomo e la morte*, 313–14.
31. Morin, *Uomo e la morte*, 317–19.

possibility, than as an actual event taking place at some point in the future.[32]

Now, this Heideggerian framework proves to be extremely helpful to assess the transhumanist project. In fact, according to transhumanism, the "definitive" conquest of aging and death can never occur as a once-and-for-all achievement. Concretely, it would mean that technology has achieved a point in which the *future event of death can be indefinitely controlled, contained, and thus deferred*.[33] The conquest of death would mean, more concretely, an indefinitely-prolonged cheating of death. Let us ask, then, what would happen to the human condition under the hypothesis that the future event of death was finally removed, that is, under the hypothesis that perishing was indefinitely controlled, contained, and deferred through the resources of technology. It seems to me that according to this scenario the transhumanist solution to the ontic problem of death would end up establishing death, understood as a possibility, invincibly at the heart of the human condition. While trying to provide a solution to the problem of death (understood as the future event of perishing), transhumanism would bring about the *immortalization of death* (understood as the Heideggerian being-toward-death). The cheating of death would turn into a being cheated by death. If successful, the transhumanist project would contradict itself: it would establish death as an *unsurpassable possibility*.

One may glimpse at this juncture another unexpected and surprising convergence between Heideggerian thought and technological

---

32. See ch. 3, sec. 6.

33. This corresponds to the "indefinite advancement" typical of the Enlightenment idea of "progress," as championed, for instance, by Condorcet: "It is manifest that the improvement of the practice of medicine, become more efficacious in consequence of the progress of reason and the social order, must in the end put a period to transmissible or contagious disorders, as well to those general maladies resulting from climate, aliments, and the nature of certain occupations. Nor would it be difficult to prove that this hope might be extended to almost every other malady, of which it is probable we shall hereafter discover the most remote causes. Would it even be absurd to suppose this quality of amelioration in the human species as susceptible of an indefinite advancement; to suppose that a period must one day arrive when death will be nothing more than the effect either of extraordinary accidents, or of the flow and gradual decay of the vital powers; and that the duration of the middle space, of the interval between birth of man and this decay, will itself have no assignable limit? Certainly man will not become immortal; but may not the distance between the moment in which he draws his first breadth, and the common term when, in the course of nature, without malady, without accident, he finds it impossible any longer to exist, be necessarily protracted?" (Condorcet, *Progress of Human Mind*, 367–68).

transhumanism. In fact, if being-toward-death is a fundamental trait of the authenticity of Dasein, and if the success of the transhumanist project results in the immortalization of death as an always-impending possibility, isn't transhumanism the ideal outcome of the Heideggerian account of Dasein in *Being and Time*? Wouldn't a transhumanist world be the ideal context for a radicalization of Dasein's being-toward-death? It can certainly be argued that at the time of *Being and Time* Heidegger had not yet tackled in a mature way the problem of technology and that his critical stance toward technology is incompatible with a celebration of transhumanism. However, it does not seem correct or even possible to oppose the transhumanist pursuit of "immortality" by relying on the resources of the existential analytic that Heidegger develops in his 1927 masterpiece, for the simple reason that the transhumanist pursuit of immortality ends up immortalizing death as a possibility, as I have explained.[34]

2.2. What would happen then to Dasein under the hypothesis that, to the indefinite deferral of the future event of perishing, would correspond a radicalization of being-toward-death, of death as a real possibility? It seems to me that Hegel's master-slave dialectic may prove illuminating on this point. Admittedly, the relationship between the life-and-death fight for recognition between two self-consciousnesses described by Hegel, ensuing into the master-slave dialectic, on the one hand, and the fight of human life against death in the transhumanist project, on the other hand, is only analogous, even just for the fundamental fact that what is at stake here is not the destiny of one self-consciousness versus another, but that of human life and self-consciousness as such against its opposite, the negativity of death. At the same time, however, death has been rightfully called "the last enemy to be destroyed" (1 Cor 15:26), and the overlapping analogies between Hegel's master-slave dialectic and the transhumanist project seem to me too many and too enlightening to overlook them. The reader is thus warned that what I have to say in the following paragraphs devoted to Hegel is only an analogous adaptation of Hegel's famous dialectic to the case of transhumanism rather than a

---

34. It seems to me that Iain Thomson and James Bodington make precisely this mistake in their essay "Against Immortality." Something similar, although not with reference to Heidegger, could be said about the beautiful book by Zygmunt Bauman, *Mortality, Immortality*. Bauman spends much of his book criticizing the modern and postmodern transhumanist project of conquering immortality, and yet for him death is "the ultimate condition of cultural creativity" and "transcendence," both in the forms of bringing about human "survival" (resisting death) and "immortality" (surviving beyond death) (5–7). Given his premise, wouldn't transhumanism be the highest form of culture?

perfect, point-by-point rewriting. As it is always the case, the usefulness of analogies is directly proportional to their potentially misleading power.

The master-slave dialectic in *The Phenomenology of Spirit* represents a key moment in "the drama of man as self-consciousness,"[35] which is the overarching theme of Hegel's work. The unfolding of spirit from "consciousness" to "Absolute Knowledge" is nothing else than man's self-consciousness coming into itself and finally being realized as mutual recognition within a community. By way of contextualization, we should remember that the reflection on the lord/master and the bondsman/slave is found at the beginning of the treatment of man as "self-consciousness." Let me provide a brief sketch of how Hegel gets to this point.[36] For Hegel, self-consciousness is "desire itself," namely, it is fundamentally *desire seeking its own truth and affirmation*.[37] Self-consciousness affirms itself as an absolute—"I am myself!"—but this self-affirmation cannot remain abstract, that is, limited to the inwardness of a self-identity ("I = I") removed from and opposed to the other, to the world. It must come into its truth and become concrete in mediating itself by mediating the other to itself. In other words, it must find and affirm itself through a definitively victorious engagement with the world. As it becomes clear, albeit slowly, through Hegel's book, what desire ultimately aspires to is recognition by another self-consciousness. Self-consciousness's aspiration, however, must face, first, the temptation to affirm itself by simply negating, i.e., destroying, killing, the other self-consciousness. This is the beginning of the "life-and-death struggle" for recognition.[38] However, it becomes clear very soon that by destroying the other self-consciousness, the recognition that I seek is made impossible: I undermine the very conditions of possibility to be recognized by the other. As a consequence, I realize that I must subjugate the other self-consciousness (in this sense, I have to turn it into a "thing") while at the same time keeping it alive, so that I may be recognized by it. At the same time, the other self-consciousness, faced with the fear of being killed, gives in to my claim to mastery and lordship, renounces its condition of equality with my self-consciousness, and thus

---

35. Kalkavage, *Logic of Desire*, 110.

36. I focus here on Hegel, *Phenomenology of Spirit*, "A. Independence and Dependence of Self-Consciousness: Lordship and Bondage," §§178–96.

37. See Pippin, *Hegel on Self-Consciousness*, ch. 1.

38. Hegel, *Phenomenology of Spirit*, 114.

subjugates itself to my self-consciousness. The other self-consciousness has become a slave, and I have become its master.

Similarly to one of the self-consciousnesses found in Hegel's dialectic, the transhumanist's aims to fulfill his desire for life in a definitive way. In order to do so, he must affirm his absoluteness, not by appealing to introspection, but rather by transforming the world in such a way that his enemy, namely, death, is defeated once and for all. Some fundamental differences between the transhumanist project and Hegel's master-slave dialectic emerge already here. For instance, the transhumanist does not seek the recognition from death, the one he is trying to subject to his power. Nevertheless, it is true that his self-affirmation as absolute—the boundless affirmation of human life against and beyond that which opposes it, i.e., death—must be obtained by the transhumanist through the subjugation of death and thus, in this sense, through death and not in abstraction from it. Death is that other against which the transhumanist has to engage, literally, in a life-and-death struggle. Another important difference here is that the transhumanist, the want-to-be master, does not realize that he should not eliminate his enemy, without which, as we have said, he could not obtain the self-recognition which he seeks. Contrary to the violent fight leading to the physical death or elimination of one of the two consciousnesses described by Hegel, the transhumanist, as I have explained by appealing to Heidegger, *cannot eliminate death*. By controlling, containing, and indefinitely deferring the event of perishing through technological means, the transhumanist immortalizes death as an always-impending possibility. Thus, the point here is that, both the victorious self-consciousness in Hegel's master-slave dialectic and the transhumanist realize that the only way forward for them in order to fulfill their desire is to *become masters and subjugate the other*, i.e., respectively, the other self-consciousness, and death. They do so, however, for different reasons: in the first case, the victorious self-consciousness in Hegel's master-slave dialectic realizes that it needs the other self-consciousness alive; in the second case, the transhumanist acknowledges that the only way for him to "defeat" death is to keep it indefinitely under check; he cannot eliminate death once and for all. Despite this major difference, however, the outcome in the two cases is similar, and the drama can continue for both only by introducing the figures of the master and the slave.

According to Hegel's account, the situation in which the slave has become a slave and the master has become a master is apparently stable

Material Kenosis

at first. The slave is nothing but a slave, defined by and subject to his master's command and defined by and subject to the work he is called to do on the "thing," on the world ("thinghood" is the "essence" of the slave). The slave lacks all independence, is "for other," namely, for his master, and moreover he depends for his work on the "thing," the world on which he works and keeps on working and which thus maintains with respect to him a certain degree of independence: the world remains "other" vis-à-vis the slave, who, precisely for this reason, is called to keep working it. On the contrary, the master is "for itself," free, self-affirming, and independent from the "other," insofar as he has subjugated the other self-consciousness and insofar as he does not have to work the "thing," the world, but he can enjoy the world freely as shaped by the slave's work. Thus, the master is in a relation of lordship vis-à-vis the world and the other self-consciousness: not only the other self-consciousness has been enslaved, but also the "thing," the world, is now dependent on him insofar as he has successfully negated its independence through the mediation of the work of the slave. The master "enjoys" the fruits of the slave's work, and this is his relation to the world. The master's desire seems to be satisfied in the subjugation of the slave and in the fulfillment of his any material needs through what the slave produces.[39]

As it is well known, however, according to Hegel, the relationship between the master and the slave is far from stable. On the contrary, this relationship is a dialectic precisely because it reveals an inevitable inversion or reversal.[40] The master turns out to be a sort of slave and the slave turns out to be a sort of master or, in other words, the slave turns out to be, compared to the master, the self-consciousness which is truly on its way to the fulfillment of its desire. How so? For our purpose, the relevant reasons are at least two. First, insofar as the slave has renounced his self-consciousness and in this sense has been reduced to a thing, he cannot grant the master the recognition that the master seeks. The slave is not dead, but he is not an equal to the master either, and only an equal (or superior) self-consciousness can grant my self-consciousness the recognition which I desire: I do not want to be obeyed simply, like an inanimate tool obeys the commands of my actions; as Kant would put it, I want to be valued beyond any value, I want my dignity to be acknowledged, and for this to take place, I need an equally dignified self-consciousness, a

---

39. Hegel, *Phenomenology of Spirit*, 116.
40. Hegel, *Phenomenology of Spirit*, 117.

self-consciousness capable of the same dignity. Second, the fulfillment of the master's desire has been drained of all its spiritual dimension. The situation has reduced the master to the condition of a mere consumer, someone who "enjoys" the world without work and without thinking and who has put to sleep the epic aspirations that had initially guided his life-and-death struggle for self-affirmation. Having become a consumer, the master consumes the world and is consumed by his consuming. Theres is nothing essential to the relationship that the master is or does, and his lordship over the slave turns out to be a condition of dependency on the slave for what he is and does. The master is still formally and externally the master, but his self-consciousness has not made any real progress in the attainment of genuine fulfillment of his desire.

On his end, the slave remains a slave, fully subjected to the master's will, but his subjection to the master turns out to be a positive condition for a first approaching to the realization of himself as self-consciousness. In fact, it is the slave who exercises a certain power over the master. The slave works the world according to the will of the master and does not keep for himself any of the products of such work—he can't enjoy any of them. But it is precisely this work that sets the slave on the way of his liberation. It is the slave that imposes on the world his own form through his work. The world bears the traces of his labor, not his master's. In this sense, *the world in which the master lives has the face of the slave.*[41]

If we read the transhumanist project through the lens of this dialectic, we can learn, I think, something truly important about the inner logic that underlies the attempt to defeat death technologically. At first, the hypothetical scenario of a successful trans- and post-humanist world looks like the situation in which the master has successfully subjugated the slave. As in the case of the Hegelian dialectic, also in the case of the transhumanist project, the subjugation of the enemy is mediated by the "thing," by the world. Here the thing subject to reworking is the world as such transformed technologically. This is precisely the main point of transhumanism: it is technology, i.e., the technological transformation of the world, that which mediates and enables the victory over and subjugation of death. One could object to this point that, in the case of the transhumanist project, the subject at work is not the slave, i.e., death, but the master, i.e., the transhumanist. The slave is not enslaved through its work but by the master's (technological) work. This is certainly true, and not

---

41. Hegel, *Phenomenology of Spirit*, 118.

unsurprisingly this is another major difference between the master-slave dialectic and the case of transhumanism. At the same time, however, the analogies with the Hegelian dialectic remain enlightening also on this point. For one, the "thinghood," which, according to Hegel, is the essence of the slave, is also the "essence" of death in the case of transhumanism. This means that, as I have explained earlier drawing from Heidegger, the technological mindset becomes the only way in which death becomes disclosed. Death becomes a problem to be solved or, in the case of the success of transhumanism, a solved problem, that is, a problem which requires to be actually re-solved over and over again, in the form of the indefinitely prolonged technological control, containment, and deferral of the event of perishing. As in the case of the Hegelian dialectic, this aspect, which at first seems to suggest the victorious affirmation of the master over the slave, turns out to be, in truth, a defeat for the alleged master. In the case of the transhumanist project, the defeat consists in the fact that the transhumanist puts himself in the position of not being capable of apprehending death as something different from the problem that the technological problem-solving apparatus keeps in check. The transhumanist has condemned himself to seeing death only as an ontic problem and has given up the possibility to apprehend it as a metaphysical mystery. Within this scenario, his own death, that is, he himself as mortal, is just another instantiation of the ontic problematicity that goes hand in hand with the technological horizon of his understanding of the world. His own dignity and the mysterious nature of his death belong together (insofar as the former is the condition of the latter). But the thinghood to which death has been reduced kicks back onto the transhumanist, who is thus made blind to both his dignity and to the ontological mysteriousness of his own death. The transhumanist affirms his life against death, but at the coast of reducing his life to a thing wholly manipulable through the resources of technology.

Along the same lines, the transhumanist's desire tends to become victim of its own success and to accept the standards of a merely naturalistic interpretation of desire, in the form of an exclusive "enjoyment" of the world. Similarly to the master in Hegel's master-slave dialectic, the transhumanist envisions the technological overcoming of death as a condition in which man's extended and expanded life will be able to freely enjoy any desired pursuit, in a world made docile to man's will by the transformative power of technology. In Hegel, the master condemns himself to the condition of a mere consumer. Isn't it even too easy to see here an analogy with the fact that our technological age is one with what has been called consumer capitalism? Ivan Illich states that contemporary man is a "standard consumer of medical care," for whom death, now reduced to "clinical death," is nothing more than what resists the wealth of medical treatments understood as commodities.[42] Doesn't the transhumanist project represent the next step in this process of medicalization and marketization of life and death?

If this is true, it would follow that the success of the transhumanist project would likely coincide with an extension and expansion of the same consumer capitalistic system and with the consumeristic interpretation of human life that this system implies. We would exhaust ourselves in consuming the world and we would in a certain sense be consumed by our own consuming.[43] This point is particularly relevant to our discussion also because it attenuates an element of dis-analogy between Hegel's master-slave dialectic and the transhumanist project. I said earlier in this section that one point of divergence between Hegel's master-slave dialectic and its application to the transhumanist project is that, in the former, the work is the work of the subjugated slave, while in the latter, the work is the work of the subjugating master. While this difference is not fully overcome, it is also true that, according to a realistic projection of what the success of the transhumanist project may look like, the majority of humanity would be not the subject of the technological control, containment, and deferral of the event of perishing, but rather the subject of "enjoyment" of the products of the technological work of a scant minority. A confirmation of this point lies in the fact that most of the discussion over the state of humanity once death has been defeated has to do with the problem whether an indefinitely prolonged "enjoyment" of life is actually sustainable, that is, whether it can actually bring about true happiness in the long run. Some, the transhumanists, usually answer positively; other answer negatively.[44] The relevant point is that, in either case, the post-human condition freed from death is represented as, essentially, a condition of enjoyment and not a condition of work.

One final point can bring our Hegelian reflections to a close for the moment. It is true that, contrary to the case of the slave in Hegel's account, in the case of the transhumanist project, death is not an active energy that transforms the world with its work. Nevertheless, it seems to

---

42. Illich, *Limits to Medicine*, esp. chs. 2, 5.
43. See Cavanaugh, *Being Consumed*.
44. Famously, Bernard Williams, "Makropulos Case."

me that, even on this final and extreme point, one could learn an important lesson from the master-slave dialectic. In fact, while death is not an active agent, it *works indirectly and vicariously on the world*, as it were, by monopolizing the intellectual, emotional, and practical energies of the transhumanist. Even though death cannot act on the world, it must transform the world more and more and impart its shape (that is, a non-shape, a non-form, the shape and form of a nonbeing) on it, insofar as the transhumanist, in order to always again hold death in check, must keep the control of death at the very top of his concerns. A "culture of death" is shaped underneath the vitalistic world of the transhumanist project.[45] According to the unfolding of this logic, then, the enjoyment of the world would be accompanied by a *totalizing concern for the control over death*, the ingredients of which would be, among others, a constant fear of losing control or making mistakes and the imperative of safety at all costs and thus the inability to take risks and grant freedom. Death would become "the consequence of personal neglect or untoward accident."[46] It is in this way that death, without being itself an active energy of transformation, imparts indirectly its form/non-form on the world and thus exercises a genuine power over the alleged master, the transhumanist, who is thus indefinitely held in check by that which he thinks he has subjugated.[47]

It has been noted, for instance, by Zygmunt Bauman, that the replacement of the "existential worry" about death with the "daily bustle about *health*" brings about also the replacement of the paralyzing "angst" for death, which can never be overcome, with the technological hope in the possibility of conquering illness, a hope which "does not paralyze but

---

45. I borrow the expression from John Paul II, *Evangelium Vitae* §12.

46. Fulton, *Death and Identity*, 4.

47. "The big carcass of mortality has been sliced from head to tail into thin rashers of fearful, yet curable (or potentially curable) afflictions; they can be now fit neatly into every nook and cranny of life. Death does not come now at the end of life: it is there from the start, calling for constant surveillance and forbidding even a momentary relaxation of vigil. Death is watching (and is to be watched) when we work, eat, love, rest. Through its many deputies, death presides over life. Fighting death may stay meaningless, but fighting the *causes* of dying turns into the meaning of life. . . . The life-giving promise rebounds in a life-poisoning threat. Now the whole of life serves the purpose of war against 'causes of death.' The permanent horror can only be dispelled in the bustle of 'doing something about it,' in near-hysterical busyness and incessant sniffing for cloak-and-dagger conspirators. . . . Eschatology has been successfully dissolved in technology. . . . The price for exchanging *immortality* for *health* is life lived in the shadow of death" (Cf. Bauman, *Mortality, Immortality*, 141–43; emphasis in original).

spurs into action."⁴⁸ While this is true, I think that the most striking *Stimmung* of the therapeutic paradigm would lie elsewhere and that it would hide, as it were, a much darker side. The most fundamental *Stimmung* of the transhumanist-master in such death-shaped world would be, I think, the coexistence of *resentment and elation* with respect to death, together with a *hygienistic phobia* about those who disagree with the transhumanist project or cannot have access to its death-conquering resources.⁴⁹ The resentment would be due to the fact that, despite all efforts, death cannot be truly overcome, and the alleged power of the transhumanist master is revealed for what it is, a tragic powerlessness that can only immortalize death in the form of an always impending possibility. Moreover, the transhumanist-master would be resentful toward death because his mastery over death turns out to be a form of being held in check by it. In turn, however, the wondrous achievement of being capable of controlling, containing, and indefinitely deferring the event of perishing would be at the origin of an uncontrollable elation. Who would not indulge in such a feeling, in such unimaginable sense of power, even at the cost of losing one's wits? In the first case, leading to resentment, the relation to death cannot be avoided; in the second case, the relation to death is happily, albeit secretly, maintained, insofar as the elation of power is fed, kept alive, and affirmed only if death remains there to be overcome always again through the post-human technological mastery. The purity of that anxiety that, according to Heidegger, sets the tone of the Dasein who is authentically toward-death, is contaminated here by a strange enjoyment towards death: the always-impending possibility of death is received in the fundamental mood of a *wicked thrill*—the thrill that comes from *indulging in inflicting a violent control upon a fierce enemy*. Accordingly, the transhumanist must entertain toward death a complex *Stimmung*, in which the *thanatophobia* animating his entire enterprise must turn into a subtly contradictory form of *thanatophilia*. It is as if the pursuit of absolute control were doomed to turn into violence and as if violence could not produce anything other than greater violence and destruction, *even when addressed to the absolute negativity of death*. This seems to

---

48. Bauman, *Mortality, Immortality,* 142; emphasis in original. See also 153: "Modernity . . . reinterpreted the chimera of final victory over death as the long chain of temporary triumphs over its currently most publicized causes. . . . All in all, it 'demetaphysicized' mortality. Death under modern conditions was no more 'tamed'; but it has been *rationalized* instead" (emphasis in original).

49. See the discussion on hygiene and racism in Bauman, *Mortality, Immortality,* 156–60.

be the destiny of any human attempt that prefers the establishment of universal conditions allegedly capable of getting rid of negativity once and for all to the drama of human freedom dealing with the limit and negativity present in life. The gospel may be referring to this in the parable of the wheat and the chaff: "When the crop grew and bore fruit, the weeds appeared as well. The slaves of the householder came to him and said, 'Master, did you not sow good seed in your field? Where have the weeds come from?' He answered, 'An enemy has done this.' His slaves said to him, 'Do you want us to go and pull them up?' He replied, 'No, if you pull up the weeds you might uproot the wheat along with them. Let them grow together until harvest" (Matt 13:26–30). In other words, the presence of the "chaff" in life is not a justification for *any* attempt at universal control, which would inevitably metamorphize into one sort or another of violent and (self-)destructive project, thus extending and expanding the presence of the chaff.

Of course, there will be individual transhumanists who will show neither signs of thanatophilia nor signs of thanatophobia, although this last case seems extremely unlikely. But this does not seem to contradict the fact that the transhumanist as such, according to the intrinsic logic of his project, must be both. Human incoherence is not an argument against the truth.

3. DIVERSION AND DEATH AS ABSOLUTE POSSIBILITY

3.1. But maybe the Hegel-inspired dialectic between the transhumanist and death that we have just explored gets the meaning of the human lordship over death wrong. That dialectic, in fact, presupposes that the transhumanist project can be actually brought to a successful conclusion. However, as we have seen, some transhumanists deem the technological conquest of death only a remote possibility. Does this mean that the transhumanist attitude vis-à-vis death will remain ineffective until it has proven its value by showing the evidence of its success? Not at all. As in the case of any other utopias or dystopias, the success of transhumanism precedes its actual success; it does not need to be experimentally verified in order to be validated because its validation lies elsewhere, not in the success of the experiment. Even before becoming the actual master of death, the transhumanist already feels like the king of nature, thus extending his perceived *kingship over life and death*. In what does his kingship consist?

It is Pascal who has explained most insightfully where the power of a worldly king truly lies. According to Pascal, the condition of the fallen human being is one of inescapable misery—he knows his weakness, his impotence, his mortality. There are only two ways to deal with his own misery. One is supernatural and coincides with Christianity. The other is natural and is that specific psychological and spiritual strategy which Pascal calls "diversion." Man cannot think of his life without acknowledging his mortality and he cannot acknowledge his mortality without being utterly miserable. Thus, giving oneself to a diversion is the most promising natural remedy to an otherwise unbearable condition. He writes: "Man wishes to be happy, and only wishes to be happy, and cannot wish not to be so. But now will he set about it? To be happy he would have to make himself immortal; but, not being able to do so, it has occurred to him to prevent himself from thinking of death."[50] That diversion truly works up to a point by appeasing our misery is, paradoxically, a further sign of our invincible misery: the fact that the only successful natural resource to cope with our misery is some form of distraction and self-deception deepens our sense of misery at the same time that it works to ease it.[51]

In Pascal's argument, the figure of the king represents man's power in his fallen condition. In what does the king's power truly consist? Why does the king appear to be happy and why are his position and title enviable? According to Pascal, the king has the resources to surround himself of people all the time and immerse himself in constant distractions so that he may be spared from thinking about himself and his mortality.[52] This is that in which the king's power ultimately consists. The true natural power of the fallen human creature is, according to Pascal, the power of self-diversion. That is why his position is envied.

50. Pascal, *Thoughts*, 64n169.

51. "*Misery.*—The only thing which consoles us for our miseries is diversion, and yet this is the greatest of our miseries. For it is this which principally hinders us from reflecting upon ourselves, and which makes us insensibly ruin ourselves. Without this we should be in a state of weariness, and this weariness would spur us to seek a more solid means of escaping from it. But diversion amuses us, and leads us unconsciously to death" (Pascal, *Thoughts*, 64n171).

52. "Hence it comes that men so much love noise and stir. . . . And it is in fact the greatest source of happiness in the condition of kings, that men try incessantly to divert them, and to procure for them all kinds of pleasures. The king is surrounded by persons whose only thought is to divert the king, and to prevent his thinking of self. For he is unhappy, king though he be, if the think of himself" (Pascal, *Thoughts*, 53n139).

Pascal's account of diversion would not be complete, however, if we did not add that what grants man the temporary bliss of a truly efficacious diversion is his "excitement" for the *possibility* of obtaining the object of his pursuit. As Pascal puts it, "It is the chase, and not the quarry, which they [i.e., human beings] seek."[53] In other words, the source of diversion and of its life-boosting "excitement" is not the obtainment of the object of pursuit (since the obtainment would show the dissatisfactory nature of the object to lift man from his misery) but the pursuit itself, which is sustained by the mere possibility of the attainment of the object.[54]

Accordingly, diversion feeds off possibility and not actuality. The diversion device corresponds to an ontology in which possibility has priority over actuality. The miser's attitude may be helpful to exemplify this point. The miser, in fact, accumulates money and keeps it jealously because he finds enjoyment and excitement not in the actual act of spending, but rather in the mere idea or possibility of spending. The greater his patrimony, the greater the possibility he has to spend money; and the greater the possibility to spend money, the greater his sense of immunization from and control over the bad luck that may be in store for him in the future. Hence, his enjoyment and excitement for the mere possibility of spending. Notice that the actualization of the spending would actually be perceived as a fatal blow against what sustains the enjoyment/excitement and therefore the diversion of the miser, namely, the possibility of spending. In the soul of the miser, who is never a daring investor, the act of spending money always corresponds to a diminishing of his patrimony, that is, of the breadth of the possibility represented by his patrimony.

---

53. Pascal, *Thoughts*, 54n139. The passage continues: "The hare in itself would not screen us from the sight of death and calamities; but the chase which turns away our attention from these, does screen us."

54. Pascal, *Thoughts*, 47n109. "So we are wrong in blaming them. Their error does not lie in seeking excitement, if they seek it only as a diversion; the evil is that they seek it as if the possession of the objects of their quest would make them really happy. In this respect it is right to call their quest a vain one. . . . And thus, when we take the exception against them, that what they seek with such fervor cannot satisfy them, if they replied—as they should do if they considered the matter thoroughly—that they sought in it only a violent and impetuous occupation which turned their thoughts from self, and that they therefore chose an attractive object to charm and ardently attract them, because they do not know themselves. They do not know that it is the chase, and not the quarry, which they seek. . . . They imagine that if they obtained such a post, they would then rest with pleasure, and are insensible of the insatiable nature of their desire. They think they are truly seeking quiet, and they are only seeking excitement. . . . Thus passes away all man's life. Men seek rest in a struggle against difficulties; and when they have conquered these, rest becomes insufferable" (54n139).

3.2. I think that also in this case we can draw a valuable lesson from Pascal's insights. In a sense, in fact, the transhumanist project works precisely insofar as *it does not become actual*. Its efficaciousness lies in the fact that it is a constant promise of a possible future, the future when technology will have conquered death. It does not matter whether the extant technology is in fact on its way to actualize the promises of transhumanism. It is sufficient that technology grants the post-human scenario of a life without death the status of a genuine possibility. Actual technology "possibilizes" for us a future of technological overcoming of death which would be otherwise perceived as mere nonsense, as pure science fiction. On the contrary, the extant technology grants credibility to what transhumanism envisions and empowers it, in the form of a possibility, to direct our resources and energies in the present, without even having to actualize what the transhumanist project promises.

The parallel with Pascal's account of diversion should be clear: the transhumanist project feeds off the possibility of its realization (instead of its actual realization) and its entire reality is drawn from the priority of such possibility (its center of gravity, so to speak, is the possibility of its actualization, rather than the actualization of its possibility); while promising to overcome death technologically, it reduces death to an ontic problem soon-to-be-solved and thus frees us from the miserable experience of having to think of ourselves as mortal, where death is a metaphysical mystery and the "wage of sin" rather than a fact of nature like any other now put under our control; in this way, *the transhumanist's insistence on death works as a most powerful device of diversion from death*. Nothing else can match the enjoyment and the excitement ensuing from the pursuit, the "mission," of bringing about "the death of death."[55]

We discover at work here another metaphysical trait of modernity, namely, the primacy of possibility over actuality. This fundamental trait of modern ontology is also a constitutive factor of the ontology implicit in the techno-scientific paradigm.[56] The transhumanist project is imbued with this ontology. In a sense, what gives consistency to the actual life of the transhumanist is the possibility of overcoming death technologically. Along the same lines, the enjoyment and excitement that underlie the transhumanist project is an enjoyment not in the actual, but in the merely possible.

55. See Cordeiro and Wood, *Death of Death*.
56. Many interpreters of modernity have evidenced this point. For a recent discussion, see Schindler, *Freedom from Reality*, 242–52.

Material Kenosis

Among the many points that could be derived from this Pascalian critique of the transhumanist project, one seems to me of particular interest to understand the contemporary scene. In fact, it seems fitting that, if the transhumanist project feeds off the mere possibility of its actualization, an essential dimension of the phenomenon of transhumanism must be, to put it simply, *self-promotion and publicity*. One may go as far as saying that the technologies which allow the transhumanist project to hype its goals and results and to establish a compelling and appealing narrative about the technological conquest of death are as essential to the phenomenon of transhumanism as those medical, bioengineering, and digital technologies which are developed to actually extent and expand human life. The latter would not be efficacious without the former. Actual technology must enhance itself by presenting itself as a variety of magic in order to establish itself as the ultimate paradigm of life and understanding. Any project that relies upon mere possibility must equally rely on some form of propaganda. For this reason, it is not uncommon to hear transhumanists make grand claims about the imminent discovery of the method to stop aging, the technology to grant digital immortality, and the like. It is such claims that give substance to the possibility of the transhumanist project, and not the other way around.

Accordingly, the possibility of overcoming death technologically can be said to be even "more possible" because, on the one hand, it can never be truly actualized, and because, on the other hand, its credibility is supported by the extant wonders of technology. It is wholly and only a possibility; in this sense, it is an *absolute possibility* (i.e., a possibility without relation to its actualization, the essence of ideological utopia; impossibility universally lived as the possible guiding goal of life and, in this sense, irreducible to a mere impossibility). Thus, we could say that the absolute possibility of the technological overcoming of death is the other component of the enjoyment and excitement characteristic of the transhumanist project: the enjoyment of/excitement for death as *possibly defeated* (i.e., the thanatophilic element present in the thanatophobia of transhumanism) is fulfilled in the enjoyment for the *absolute possibility of the defeat* of death.

4. A DESIRE FOR NEW LIFE

4.1. A complementary way to try to characterize the attitude of the transhumanist would be to consider it as a specific form of *nihilism*, taking "nihilism," as Blondel teaches, in the specific sense of a theoretical and practical attitude in which life is affirmed in order to be negated. Blondel's *Action* opens with a discussion of the two spiritual-philosophical attitudes which would put an end to the search for the mystery present at the heart of the will, "the problem of life," even before this search could begin.[57] The first attitude is that of the aesthete, whose way to deal with the problem of life is to deflate its meaning: there is no actual problem of life to be addressed. The second attitude is that of the one we might call the positivist-pessimist, namely, the scientistically-minded materialist who thinks that "nothing" is at the very heart of all there is, including himself (he is "nothing" insofar as he is only the temporary, random aggregation of particles, energy, etc.), and who thus wills that nothing as his ideal destiny. The positivist-pessimist gives the problem of life the negative answer of his *noluntas* and thus precludes any actual search for a positive and adequate telos of human action.

Now, the nihilism so described seems to be in sharp contradiction with the attitude of the transhumanist. While also the transhumanist usually thinks that he is nothing else or nothing more than an aggregate of material particles, contrary to the positivist-pessimist, he is eminently attached to this nothing which he calls his own life. He does not aspire to abolish it through his *noluntas*, but rather to extend and expand it through the resources of technology. How is it possible to liken the two attitudes as similarly nihilistic?

The answer lies in the inevitable dialectic that we have discussed above. Blondel criticizes the attitude of the positivist-pessimist on the grounds that his desire for annihilation cannot be original. This is so not only because for him, not differently from Bergson after him, the "thinking of nothing" and the "willing of nothing" are always parasitical on the thought and will of something—the thought of nothing is always the thought of something which is thought so that it may be negated and the will of nothing follows the same grammar; but also because, once studied in its transcendental conditions of possibility, the desire for annihilation turns out to rely on a deeper desire-love for a fullness of life that

---

57. Blondel, *Action*, 16–50.

is constantly frustrated.[58] According to Blondel, the positivist-pessimist must bear the characters of a devout lover who has been betrayed:

> Hence the will that tends toward the annihilation of the human person is founded, whether it knows it itself or not, on a singular esteem and an absolute love for being.[59]

> From the phenomenon [i.e., the experience of the finitude of the world] he [the positivist-pessimist] argues against being, even though he senses the insufficiency of the phenomenon only because he is first penetrated with the greatness of being: he affirms it before denying it and in order to deny it.[60]

Thus, even though he does not acknowledge this fact, the positivist-pessimist must affirm life and being (at the level of his willing will) in order to deny them (at the level of his willed will). In this sense, the attitude of the positivist-pessimist is essentially *self-contradictory*. This is why the transhumanist shares with the positivist-pessimist an analogous nihilistic attitude. The self-contradiction is for the transhumanist at the level of his willed will: he wills more life, namely, an extended and expanded survival, but he ends up immortalizing death, negativity, at the heart of his action.

The category of nihilism also applies, albeit in an analogous way, to the attitude of the aesthete. The aesthete also, in fact, pushes self-destruction and death into the center of his being through his own actions. Blondel in fact brings up the case of the aesthete while considering one of the possible meanings of nihilism:

> To will and to experience nothingness, what does that mean ordinarily? It means unscrupulous passion for pleasures, attachment to the life of the senses, an ardent search for well-being, levity in seriousness and gravity in the frivolous, contempt for man and exaltation of myself. One wills nothingness, and one enjoys everything possible: a forced will, a fictitious experience, a lie. Does one realize what this desire harbors, shameful because of its self-interest? A disordered love of being and well-being.[61]

---

58. Blondel, *Action*, 41. See also ch. 3, sec. 2.
59. Blondel, *Action*, 46.
60. Blondel, *Action*, 45.
61. Blondel, *Action*, 45.

The aesthete, insofar as he is "always busy at moving and fragmenting himself,"[62] is doomed to the same outcome of the transhumanist: while he wants to cultivate life, he harvests death.

Now, it would be not only wrong, but also unfair, to submit that all transhumanists must be aesthetes and hedonists in the way Blondel describes. Nevertheless, it seems hard to deny that at the heart of the transhumanist view of life there is an individualistic and pleasure-based concept of "well-being," the same category used by Blondel. If we replace the idea of a crass and purely sensual hedonism with a more sophisticated idea of the pursuit of one's own emotional, psychological, and physical wellbeing, chiefly understood, as in Epicurus, as absence of suffering, don't we get something similar to what Blondel is describing, one might call it the attitude of the "scientifically informed, responsible, and conscientious aesthete"?[63]

This conclusion seems even more plausible if, expanding on Byung-Chul Han's reflections,[64] we reflect on the fact that the system of capitalism is one with the technologies without which the transhumanist project would be unintelligible (that's why some rightly talk of "techno-capitalism") and that some of the most characteristic things that the capitalist first world enjoys are the easy access to the consume of goods (hence "consumerism") and the omnipresence of entertainment, especially as it is evidenced in the digital era. If we add to this fact that, by denying a unitary and teleologically-oriented view of the human being, the transhumanist usually concedes to the postmodern view of human existence as essentially fragmented (for instance, in the way Vattimo champions it, as explained in the previous chapter), one is led to see that the likening of the transhumanist to Blondel's aesthete is not so preposterous after all. What transhumanism envisions is an indefinitely-prolonged, extended, and expanded existence in which each human being can freely pursue his own desired version of emotional, psychological, and physical well-being, and in which radical changes of all sorts and thus fragmentation is not only tolerated but rather actively promoted—of course, with the blessings of the same capitalists who control the market and sustain the entire technological transhumanist enterprise.

4.2. What could the self-contradiction revealed at the heart of the transhumanist's attitude teach us, and what could it teach him? I think

---

62. Blondel, *Action*, 22.
63. See, for instance, "The Hedonistic Imperative" (https://www.hedweb.com).
64. Han, *Capitalism and the Death Drive*.

that the contradiction of the transhumanist is revelatory in at least two ways.

4.2.1. First, such contradiction could enable the transhumanist to revise his beliefs about the object of his desire and about the object of human desire in general. If his interpretation of the human desire is flawed (in fact, the desire for an extended and expanded survival through technological necessarily leads to its demise), it may be the case that a different interpretation is possible. In other words, the perceived contradiction could lead the transhumanist to raise the ultimate questions: "What is my desire for life truly about?" "Is it possible that death may be something other than a mere ontic problem seeking a technological solution?" Through these *questions*, the ontological mysteriousness of death would already be making a first breach through the barrier of the transhumanist. The transhumanist would thus be faced with a dilemma: either to follow the mysterious insight present in the putting into question his interpretation of desire and pointing beyond the temptation of a definitive technological solution; or to fall back into a self-contradictory pursuit of the technological mastering of death, which would require this time a more resolute and more dogmatic approach than before.

Incidentally, it also seems possible to say that this renewed attitude of "attention" to the phenomenon of death in its irreducibility to an ontic problem would constitute the inchoative moment toward a genuine destruction of death (the nature of which must be described below), if is true, as Weil suggests, that "every time we really concentrate our attention, we destroy the evil in ourselves."[65] Such attention would be, as it were, the speculative heart of the intentional movement of incarnation in which material kenosis consists (more on this below as well).

4.2.1.1. But what could be the desire for life other than the desire for an extended and expanded survival? What could "happiness" consist in if not in such indefinite extension and expansion? St. Thomas explains at different points in his work that the object of the human will is the "universal good," to be fulfilled in that to which each human being ultimately aspires, namely, the "beatific vision of God."[66] Thomas also explains that the human being naturally aspires to "perpetual existence."[67] Now, is it possible to rethink these different aspects of the Thomistic understanding of human desire in relation to the problem of man's mortality? What

---

65. Weil, *Waiting for God*, 111.
66. *ST* 1–2, qq. 1–3.
67. Aquinas, *Disputed Questions on the Soul*, q. 14, co.

concrete shape does the desire for life take in light of the negativity of death?

In order to address this question, I propose here to exploit the Thomistic notion of "mode of existence" more daringly than it has been traditionally done. In discussing the way in which the soul knows once it is separated from the body, Thomas explains that the soul has "one mode of existence [and action] when in the body, and another when apart from it, its nature remaining always the same."[68] Thomas immediately clarifies that, despite this distinction of modes, the soul's nature remains that of a substantial form which is essentially and not accidentally united to the body. He then explains that the soul has two different ways of knowing following from its two different modes of existing, when it informs a body (corresponding to the "fullness" of the specific nature of man) or when it is separated from the body (corresponding to an unnatural mode of existing).

Now, if the reading of St. Thomas presented in chapter 2 is correct, our present mode of existence may be considered a strange midway between the two modes of existence described by Thomas: being subjected to death is already a certain imperfect union, and thus, in this sense, an inchoative separation, of soul and body. The ambiguity of the Platonic *meletē thanatou* resides precisely in its incapacity to distinguish a first meaning of separation, identified with the positive transcendence of the soul vis-à-vis the body, and a second meaning of separation, that of mortality and the inchoative separation of soul and body in life. On the contrary, exploiting Thomas's account of the modes of existing of the soul allows us to point out this difference with clarity. Accordingly, just as for Thomas the separate soul "desires" to be reunited to the body in order for the human being to receive the grace of God according to the fullness of his nature (which essentially requires the body), what we truly desire can neither be life extension nor life expansion, but rather a radical *metamorphosis of life*, that is, a radical change in the very mode of our existence.[69] What we truly desire, in other words, is to remain who we are,

---

68. *ST* 1, q. 81, a. 1, co.

69. I take this notion from Emmanuel Falque, who has recently developed a systematic treatment of death and resurrection in terms of "metamorphosis of finitude." The notion is Pauline: "'Listen, I will tell you a mystery! We will not die, but we will be changed, in a moment, in the twinkling of an eye, at the last trumpet' (1 Cor 15:51–52). To die or to be transformed, or rather for *everyone to be transformed* whether already dead or not, since only the last trumpet sounds here, is the universal *metamorphosis* proposed by St. Paul as a definition, no less, of the resurrection" (*Metamorphosis of Finitude*, 1; emphasis in original).

both individually and specifically, but *in a wholly new way*—in a way in which negativity, and primarily the negativity of evil and death, has been wholly overcome. We do not desire another kind of life, we desire our life, as it is (again, as it is in its numerical and specific identity) but made wholly other, wholly new. The sense of *radical incompleteness* that always accompanies human desire is not due to the lack of another "piece" of me; it is due to the fact that the metamorphosis of my total being has not taken place yet.

This is the meaning of the expression "desire for *new life,*" where the adjective "new" means neither "of a different kind" nor "enhanced." In the Christian tradition, we talk about the final "liberation" of human life and the "resurrection of the body." The Christian tradition speaks of the resurrection precisely as that which gives definition and reality to the vague aspiration of desire. And yet, despite its vagueness and its unknowing, the human desire discovers in Christ's promise of personal resurrection, with surprise and joy, the most corresponding and most fitting response to its teleology.

One could make a Blondelian point here. As I have explained above, Blondel points out that the condition of possibility of the positivist-pessimist's desire to annihilate himself is the apprehension of contingent being as inadequate; in turn, such apprehension is made possible only on the condition that a different kind of being, the fullness and eternity of being, is secretly and implicitly apprehended.[70] Something similar could be said about the attempt to extend and expand our life indefinitely in the very mode of existence in which we find ourselves. For instance, our desire to replace our biological bodies with different technological supports relies upon a love of our biological condition and a disappointment with its endless failures, chiefly the final failure of death. Technology tries to solve the issue by aspiring to replace that which has disappointed our expectation of lovers of our (biological) life, the body. But would it not be more fitting and more faithful to human experience to cultivate *a desire which is also coherent with the secret love of our biological condition as it is*? Isn't the desire to "save" (in the two senses of "preserving the integrity of" and "redeeming") our biological constitution and the experience of the world

---

70. Pascal, among others, had made the same point earlier: "The greatness of man is so evident, that it is even proved by his wretchedness. For what in animals is nature we call in man wretchedness; by which we recognize that, his nature being now like that of animals, he has fallen from a better nature which once was his. For who is unhappy at not being a king, except a deposed king?" (*Thoughts*, 132n409).

it enables, i.e., both "body" and "flesh," simply more desirable?[71] Should it not our desire be a desire for a fully metamorphosed *biological* life?[72]

As the technological pursuit of immortality proves with its talk about the replacement of the material biological condition of human life with different types of supports, digital or otherwise, technology can only work by replacing what requires to be fixed. If the biological body is the problem, then we should push it out of the way piece by piece and finally replace it. On the contrary, the ideal object of our desire would be to have our biological condition metamorphosed in such a way that the mysterious "cause" of this metamorphosis would be capable of both keeping and letting our biological condition be what it is, according to its nature, and, at the very same time, renovating it wholly—as I said, "new life."

While aiming at preserving the human nature, the Christian desire also aims, in the same movement, to a radical change of its mode of existence—not of its natural specific identity, nor of its numerical identity, but of its mode of being. A desire for such a "cause" and such an "effect" do not seem to be compatible with the transhumanist technological project. To appeal again to Blondel, we could say that the object of human desire is not even commensurate to the entire universe. Not in the sense that the human desire aspires to an object that is "greater" than the entire universe—if it were so, technological transformation would be in a sense fully adequate to the human desire insofar as it brings about those imaginary scenarios through which our thought constantly overcomes the

---

71. "True corporality, today as yesterday, before as after death, is not in our corporeal and biological substance—important though that is in our *incorporation*—but in the *way* we live, accept, and receive this in our own *incarnation*. The *experience of our bodies* is what makes our *flesh*. And our *flesh* is how we truly appear to ourselves and to other people. This lived experience is really what constitutes us *today* 'in a truly ego-logical way' (Husserl) and, in Christianity, what will be resurrected *tomorrow* ('resurrection of the *flesh*'). 'What resurrects in me, precisely what starts to resurrect after death itself, is *my rebirth to others and to the world*,' says Fr. Varillon, speaking more pastorally but nonetheless appropriately. 'It is for man, in his *body and soul*, a *new way of existing*. Certainly in *his body*, because it is *through the body* that man has his relation to others and to the world'" (Falque, *Metamorphosis of Finitude*, 138; emphasis in original). Unfortunately, it is still possible to find in Falque a certain distrust toward the body understood as biology; such distrust seems unnecessary. For a study on the "flesh" as a medieval and Christian model of subjectivity, see Brague, "Flesh."

72. The essential importance of the body for a Christian anthropology against the dematerialization typical of transhumanism (obtaining "substrate independence" for the human mind) is stressed, among others, by Eberl, "Enhancing the *Imago Dei*"; and Smith, *From Here to Eternity*, 27–58. On the generalized dematerializing materialism (!) of our time, see Breton, *Adieu au corps*.

limitedness of the given universe. It is not commensurate to the entire universe because it is of a *different order*. One may say that desire does not need to travel to the borders of the universe to test itself and discover what it is made for. The limited milieu of one's life is, at once, sufficient and insufficient. It is sufficient because it can give me the opportunity to realize what I truly desire; it is insufficient because by itself does not constitute the object of my desire. What I desire is the metamorphosis of my life, or, to use Thomas's phrase, a new mode of existing.

4.2.2. We said above that the contradiction of the transhumanist's attitude could be revelatory in at least two ways. I have introduced the first insight that may come to the transhumanist and to us, namely, that the desire for life may be a desire for a wholly metamorphosed life rather than a desire for an extended and expanded survival. I will have more to say on this point in the remainder of this chapter. But there is also a second revelation which the contradiction may bring about, and this has to do with the very strange case of death. If the scenario of the total mastery over death turns into its opposite (a dependence on death and even a thanatophilia), may it not be the case that a complete, patient surrender to death, to the very point of perishing, is the only way toward a liberation? We will come back to this point later when discussing death in relation to the problem of freedom.

4.3. The case of transhumanism is particularly relevant from the philosophical point of view because it allows to make a further distinction, which is not always appreciated, within the phenomenon of human *suffering*. Suffering is in fact a fundamental human experience. While a description of the various aspects of suffering is impossible here, it suffices to point out two fundamental traits of suffering, which will allow us to draw an important conclusion with respect to the relation among suffering, desire, and death. The first point is that suffering is an *original* trait of the human being precisely because the human being is an animal capable of desire. As we said, human desire is always accompanied by a sense of radical incompleteness: the presence of happiness as absent, or the absence of happiness as present. Experience testifies to the seemingly unsurpassable disproportion between the completeness or fulfillment to which the desire aspires and that which the given, "limited," conditions of human existence seem to grant. Bringing together these different aspects, Francesco Botturi defines suffering as "the memory of the incompleteness and disproportion of desire."⁷³ This point is correctly grasped by the Buddhist wisdom, according to which desire is intrinsically tied to suffering insofar as desire is the origin of suffering (hence the Buddhist injunction to end desire in order to end suffering); but also by the Romantic philosophical movement, which sees in desire a never-satisfied and thus perpetually suffering dynamism. Thus, desire and suffering always already coexist insofar as the human being is a desiring animal on his way to his fulfillment—insofar as he is a historical being having to deal with the finite resources of a spatiotemporal existence (*homo viator*). A "suffering" (to stay underneath in order to bear something) freely assumed in its truth would thus be the virtue of bearing through one's historical journey the weight of the incompleteness and disproportion of desire, namely, patience. One can thus see that original suffering (the suffering tied to desire) and the corresponding virtue of patience (the assumption of the suffering resulting from the burden of desiring through time) exhibit formal traits that we have previously recognized in death: death as a present-absence or absent-presence. This formal overlapping has induced many to confuse death as an original ingredient of suffering and thus as an essential element of desire. Nothing further from the truth.

A second point is that suffering, just as desire, reason, etc., is a notion that has to do with the human being in his *totality*. Desiring and suffering are not specific experiences of the human being. Rather, human experience is, as such, desiring and suffering. Human pain, either psychological or physical, is always regional, namely, it has always to do with a part of the human being. We often confuse suffering and pain because, in the lived unity of human experience, pain is always "taken up" into human suffering, and more often than not, it constitutes a paradoxically privileged moment to enter into the mystery of suffering.

In light of what we just said, it follows that the human desire, as the desire for a metamorphosis of life, is contextually also a *desire for the overcoming of suffering*. But the overcoming of suffering to which desire aspires includes the overcoming of two different kinds of "limit": on the one hand, the original and positive limit of a history in the making, and on the other hand, the negative and "accidental" (yet totalizing and definitive) limit of death. The "impatience of the limits"⁷⁴ of the human condition manifests this ambiguity. Two kinds of wound inhabit

---

73. Botturi, "Uomo di fronte alla sofferenza."
74. The title of a book by Stanislas Fumet: *Impatience des limites*.

human experience, the *positive lack* of the unfinished work of love and the *negative wound* of the fatal blow of death.[75] Profound claims such as Léon Bloy's, according to which "suffering is the helper of creation," must be received and meditated without ever forgetting the irreducible ambiguity of the term "suffering."[76] Man would have suffered and would have sought the overcoming of his structural suffering—would have "desired"—even without the irruption of evil and death into his life. Many in the Western tradition forget this important point and tend to speak of death as the origin and positive source of man's finitude, historical drama, suffering, aspiration, and even philosophical questioning, etc.[77] While it is undeniably true that mortality imposes on our metaphysical questioning a certain tone from its beginning, it can never be taken to be its originating force. The transhumanist project inherits this tendency by bringing it under the gaze of the technological mindset of modernity. Transhumanists aspire to overcoming death technologically and to put an end to human suffering, thus overcoming that historical condition or mode of existence in which suffering and death are still so stubbornly and dramatically present (post-humanism).

Accordingly, the transhumanist's misunderstanding of human desire is also a mystification of human suffering, and this for at least two reasons. First, because it blurs the line of separation between the positive limit of history and the negative limit of death. Second, because, by reducing death to an ontic problem to be solved technologically, it tends to interpret suffering as a mere extension or expansion, a mere intensification, of psychological and physical pain. This is also why the transhumanist project is destined to fail. What technology can operate on is always and only parts or pieces of nature. The transhumanist must intervene technologically on those parts of his physical constitution that have proven to be insufficient or unreliable, i.e., that have caused or may cause psychological and physical pain. Technology cannot intervene on the whole, on the totality of the human experience. If human desire and

---

75. Derrida, for instance, systematically confuses the two.
76. Bloy, *Pilgrim of the Absolute*, 253.
77. See, for example, the famous opening line of Franz Rosenzweig's *Star of Redemption*: "From death, it is from the fear of death that all cognition of the All begins" (11). Claims such as this abound in the tradition from Plato onward. When adopting these claims (see ch. 1), one should always be aware of their ambiguity and one should read them cautiously, in light of the distinction I am proposing here.

suffering are figures of the totality of the human being, it seems fair to say that transhumanism must fall short of its project once again.

4.4. Emmanuel Falque has recently developed systematically the idea that the object of the human desire is in fact a metamorphosis of its given existing conditions, what he calls, quite insightfully, a "metamorphosis of finitude" (to be opposed to a false understanding of metamorphosis as fleeing from finitude). Following his and Claude Romano's insights, we may ask, What is the internal form of this desire for metamorphosis? Drawing from Romano, Falque opposes the traditional form-formula "Become what you are" with the more correct (according to him) form-formula "Be what you become."[78] Now, according to Romano and Falque, "Become what you are" would be an inadequate formula to express the inner form of the desire for metamorphosis because in it the "what" represents the burdensome weight of a metaphysics of "essences," whose conservative spirit seems incompatible with the radically transformative promise speaking from within the human experience of desire. So Romano, approvingly quoted by Falque:

> The formula that will most closely correspond to [the believer, or to the one who desires properly] is not "Become what you are" (Pindar) but rather "Be what you become." Against the formula of an odyssey that is a return to the self, of mediation and totalization, we need to set that of a "oneway ticket" (Benjamin), of the simple outward journey, of simply-going, to where time is no longer the reliquary of the being but a freeing oneself with regard to all "essence" and the disburdening oneself of all "property."[79]

Contrary to what Romano and Falque seem to suggest, there is no contradiction between the two formulas. On the contrary, the two formulas can be taken as mutually enriching. On the one hand, by stressing the fundamental role of a given essence or nature ("Become *what you are*"), the first formula emphasizes the point that the metamorphosis that one desires cannot come at the cost of a destruction or alteration of what one is according to his specific nature. Neglecting man's specific nature

---

78. The formula, originally from Pindar and also used by Nietzsche and Heidegger, has been most recently appealed to by Przywara in order to express the teleology of created being as informed by the *analogia entis*. For a recent appropriation and development of this notion in the spirit of Przywara, see Betz, "Mere Metaphysics," 698–700.

79. Claude Romano, *Événement et le temps*, quoted in Falque, *Metamorphosis of Finitude*, 108.

would in fact mean to undermine a genuine understanding of metamorphosis, because the idea of a genuine metamorphosis relies upon the abiding concern for *what* we are. Against Romano, the "essence" is not a burden from which one must free oneself or be freed by another, but the stable condition of sense of any desire of liberation. Falque is appealing to Romano's formula in order to describe what resurrection may mean, but also in this case, we should remember, with Thomas, that grace presupposes and perfects nature rather than destroying it.

On the other hand, also the formula "Be *what you become*" is insightful insofar as it stresses the eschatological moment of our desire of metamorphosis. We desire to be what we become, what we are metamorphosed into, without, however, knowing precisely that in which such metamorphosis may even consist. What we know, however, as it is foreshadowed in our desiring, suffering, and mortal experience, is that such metamorphosis must be the reception, the gift, of a radically new mode of existing.

4.5. While aiming at preserving the human nature, the Christian desire also aims, in the same movement, to a radical change of its mode of existence. Accordingly, Christian desire has both *a radically conservative* side and a *radically revolutionary* side: the preservation of human nature as totally changed. Also the desire underlying the transhumanistic project is at once conservative and revolutionary, but in a different and less radical way. It wants to preserve human life as it is (namely, it cannot conceive or trust the desire for a wholly different mode of existence), and thus it is radically conservative. However, insofar as it realizes that life as it is is not enough, it aims at extending and expanding it indefinitely in a way which substitutes in substantial ways life as it is. But the stress here is on the *conservative* side: the transhumanist wants to change everything about the human condition so that everything may remain the same, that is, so that any order "other" than that of human making is precluded. Metamorphosis ends up being nothing else than an indefinite variation of the same.

On the contrary, when it comes to the Christian desire, the stress is on revolution, metamorphosis: the human nature must be preserved *so that man may be wholly transformed and thus liberated to what he truly is beyond any evil and nonbeing.*[80] A Christian anthropology and

---

80. It may be interesting to note here that Nietzsche's alternative to Christian resurrection in the metamorphosis of the Übermensch preserves the need for continuity of specific and numerical identity (not a different life, but the same life) but substitutes to

a Christian humanism can only be "eschatological," and thus they must relativize and transform all the images that man crafts for himself in light of the radical metamorphosis engendered in and by the resurrected Jesus Christ.[81]

Given the topic of this chapter, it may be worth noting that transhumanists such as Steinhart who reflect on the possibility of "naturalizing" resurrection fall very short of grasping the basic meaning of resurrection in the Christian tradition. For Steinhart, for instance, "resurrection" means the "reassembly" of the dead person based on the pattern ("patternism") that the dead person's body used to have when alive. Such pattern would be the "program" identical to the soul, the form of the body. Between the once-alive person and the resurrected person there is no causal continuity; there is also no biological continuity—death has happened; there is, however, informational-computational continuity. The resurrected would be the "replica" of the old person-body, with either equal or enhanced computational capacities, implemented in a new synthetic substratum. Insofar as multiple replicas are possible, the computational continuity does not allow for the preservation of the actual personal identity after death, unless we are willing to say that the original career of the person has "split" into multiple careers, thus producing a "tree of lives."[82] Needless to say, what Steinhart is speaking of is not an analogate of Christian resurrection, and in his discourse the "naturalization" of resurrection ends up meaning pure equivocation of the meaning of the Christian tradition. This fundamental misunderstanding, however, brings much clarity, by way of contrast, to the nature of human desire: Is the human desire for "eternal life" a desire for "reassembly" through an ongoing replacement of parts? Or is it rather that desire for a totalizing metamorphosis, for a radically different mode of existing of who we are?[83]

---

the radical change of the mode of life the radical change of the will—eternally willing one's life. Or to put it differently, the change not of life, but of its mode, is brought about by the willing will "biting into the snake." As if a true metamorphosis could be brought about by this; as if the will were "outside" that death-struck existence that needs to be resurrected. See on this the references and discussions in Falque, *Metamorphosis of Finitude*, 49.

81. See on this Brague, *Après l'humanisme*.

82. See Steinhart: "Naturalistic Theories," 151–52; "Digital Theology."

83. See on this the insightful remark by Falque: "The impossibility of believing, nowadays even more than previously, in the 'resurrection of the body' ('I believe in the resurrection of the body and life everlasting' [Apostles' Creed]), derives very probably from the lack of a *contemporary anthropology* that would fit a body capable of being transformed" (*Metamorphosis of Finitude*, 136; emphasis in original).

The answer is that the interpretation of desire implied in the transhumanist project is in fact *too conservative*. The transhumanist interprets his desire according to an immanent logic of extension and expansion, of enhancing replacement of parts, in which what replaces and what is replaced belong to the same order. However, as we have seen, this interpretation of desire and the ensuing transhumanist project, instead of overcoming death, ends up spreading death out into an indefinitely prolonged dying. It is itself a *self-mortification* of human desire. Neither the extension/expansion of survival nor the replacement of parts belong to the same order of that metamorphosis of our mode of existence which we truly desire. In short, the transhumanist does not desire boldly, nor does he think of the object of his desire in a daring fashion. Aristotle speaks of the "credible impossible" to describe the object of good poetry,[84] and it seems fitting to borrow his phrase to characterize the object of human desire: man aspires to what seems wholly beyond reach ("impossible" to him) and yet what would be unreasonable not to seek as the adequate object of desire ("believable"). On the contrary, the transhumanist desires only the "incredible possible," namely, a mere science fiction obtained by a projection of our finitude. C. S. Lewis and Jacques Lacan seem to converge, somewhat surprisingly, on the importance of remaining faithful to the depth and breadth of one's desire for one's life to succeed in the eyes of the Truth: "Our Lord finds our desires not too strong, but too weak";[85] "Have you acted in conformity with the desire that is in you?"[86]

5. *L'CHAIM?*

5.1. The religious approach to life is not necessarily opposed to and incompatible with the transhumanist project, or at least this seems to be

---

84. *Poetics* 25, 1461 b12.

85. Lewis, *Weight of Glory*, 26. He explains: "We are half-hearted creatures, fooling about with drink and sex and ambition when infinite joy is offered us, like an ignorant child who wants to go on making mud pies in a slum because he cannot imagine what is meant by the offer of a holiday at the sea. We are far too easily pleased."

86. Lacan, *Ethics of Psychoanalysis*, 314. This question is what Lacan calls the "Last Judgment." He continues: "In the last analysis, what a subject really feels guilty about when he manifests guilt at bottom always has to do with—whether or not it is admissible for a director of conscience—the extent to which he has given ground relative to his desire" (319). Needless to say, I am not stating that Lacan is a Thomist, nor that his idea of desire is identical to the Christian view. I am just stressing the fact that, in his discourse as in ours, the faithfulness to the truth of desire comes to play an essential role in determining the truth of a life and of a culture.

the belief of some religious thinkers. In his article "*L'Chaim* and Its Limits: Why Not Immortality?," Leon R. Kass, himself a strong opposer of the transhumanist project, provides an interesting account of why some Jewish thinkers are in fact in favor of transhumanism. As he recounts, "In the debates taking place in the United States, Jewish commentators on these and related medical ethical topics [such as enhancement and transhumanism] nearly always come down strongly in favor of medical progress and on the side of life—more life, longer life, new life. They treat the cure of disease, the prevention of death, and the prolongation of life as near-absolute values.... At a meeting in March 2000 on 'Extended Life, Eternal Life,' scientists and theologians were invited to discuss the desirability of increasing the maximum human life span and, more radically, of treating death itself as a disease to be conquered. The major Jewish speaker, a professor at a leading rabbinical seminary, embraced the project—you should excuse me—whole hog. Gently needling his Christian colleagues by asserting that, for Jews, God is Life, rather than Love, he used this principle to justify any and all life-preserving and life-extending technologies, including those that might yield massive increases in the maximum human life expectancy. When I pressed him in discussion to see if he had any objections to the biomedical pursuit of immortality, he responded that Judaism would only welcome such a project."[87]

While the phenomenon of Jewish voices favorable to transhumanism is interesting by its own right, my concern with Kass's article has to do less with his account of those voices and more with his own reasons to oppose the transhumanist project of overcoming death technologically, especially when this project seems to receive the blessings of the believer. Motivated by the view of his Jewish contenders, Kass rightly wants to deconstruct the facile idea that, since "life is good and death is bad," no limit should ever be set to the human attempt to overcome death technologically. Moreover, Kass has the merit to go to the philosophical heart of the matter, while the most common criticism of transhumanism, still subject to the paradigm of the utilitarian calculus, takes usually two forms: "Predictions of bad social consequences and complaints about distributive justice." His central argument hinges upon the centrality of virtue for human flourishing, and his main point is that removing death

---

87. Kass, "*L'Chaim* and Its Limits," paras. 6, 8. While being from 2001, the article still seems relevant today, if not to describe the sociology of the Jewish community (on which I have no expertise), at least to point out an interesting take on transhumanism from the point of view of a religiously motivated love for life.

from life would mean removing something essential to human life, i.e., its constitutive finitude, thus depriving the human being of the opportunity to cultivate and prove his virtue according to its properly human, i.e., finite and mortal, shape and measure.[88] Kass's view is representative of the view of other religious thinkers, including Catholic thinkers. He writes: "I wish to make the case for the virtues of mortality. Against my own strong love of life, and against my even stronger wish that no more of my loved ones should die, I aspire to speak truth to my desires by showing that the finitude of human life is a blessing for every human individual, whether he knows it or not. . . . This is a question in which our very humanity is at stake. . . . For to argue that human life would be better without death is, I submit, to argue that human life would be better being something other than human." According to Kass, "virtue and moral excellence" become impossible without death. He explains: "To be mortal means that it is possible to give one's life, not only in one moment, say, on the field of battle, but also in the many other ways in which we are able in action to rise above attachment to survival." Kass names "moral courage, endurance, greatness of soul, generosity, devotion to justice," but it is clear that he is thinking of virtue and moral excellence as such. It seems fair to say, then, that for Kass death is the finite measure and occasioning condition for a truly human flourishing. A confirmation of this interpretation comes from the fact that Kass mentions repeatedly the Homeric and Greek wisdom of Ulysses, who decides to remain faithful to his human condition by refusing the gift of immortality offered to him by the nymph Calypso. In light of these considerations, Kass rightly explains that the human desire is made for a fulfillment that transcends an indefinitely-prolonged attachment to survival, and that the fullness of "life" to which we all aspire implies a devotion for "wisdom" and "justice" so fundamental that even the desire to stay alive may be sacrificed to it.

Despite the many points of agreement with Kass's view, what I am trying to articulate in this study differs in subtle but fundamental ways from what Kass proposes. For one, his identification of finitude and the human measure with mortality cannot be accepted. Not only does this tendency lead to the many short circuits of the contemporary

---

88. Kass speaks of the possibility to cultivate virtue as only one of the reasons to oppose the transhumanist project. The other reasons are: death is at the origin of a genuine "interest and engagement" with life; death motivates real "seriousness and aspiration"; death is essential to "beauty" and "love." Thus, Kass turns death into something constitutive of the human condition. I have discussed the limits of this philosophical tendency in ch. 3.

philosophical engagement with death that I have discussed in ch. 3, but it is also contrary to that biblical wisdom to which Kass appeals. In fact, it seems to me that the problem of man's faithfulness to his own finitude and human measure—we could say, more explicitly, to the goodness of his creatureliness—is prior to and in this sense independent from his mortality. In truth, his mortality, in the sense of the negation of his life, is the consequence of his ill-fated decision not to be faithful to the goodness of his creatureliness. The snake in Genesis plays precisely on this weakness of man, leading him to the unfaithful aspiration to be other than himself: "Now the snake was the most cunning of all the wild animals that the Lord God had made. He asked the woman, 'Did God really say, 'You shall not eat from any of the trees in the garden?... God knows well that when you eat of it ["the tree in the middle of the garden"] your eyes will be opened and you will be like gods, who know good and evil" (Gen 3:1–5).

If this first point is correct and death is not the measure of human finitude but is instead "the wages of sin," it also follows that death cannot be an essential condition of human flourishing. We discover here, once again, the helpful distinction that I have proposed earlier among four different aspects of death which are usually confused: death as original, constitutive, definitive, and ultimate. Without explaining again the different senses of these terms, it seems fair to say that Kass sees death, if not as original and ultimate, at least as constitutive and definitive. On the contrary, according to the Catholic view that I have tried to articulate, death is certainly definitive of the human condition but not constitutive. The measure of the human being is identical to his creatureliness.[89] The constitutive "limit" of the human being is thus that of *not* being God, which is the false negativity hiding the treasure of a sheer positivity, that of being in relation with God, a relation which is, as we have discussed in chapter 3, the most fundamental metaphysical meaning of creation.

Insofar as death has entered the human condition, and even more so given that death is a totalizing negativity of human life already at work while man is still alive and not just a partial aspect of man's existence (it is "definitive"), it becomes of course true that the cultivation of virtue on the part of the concrete, historical man will have to deal with the presence of death in his life. In Aristotle's favorite example, "courage" is precisely the virtue which allows us to endure the fear of death on the battlefield,

---

89. St. Thomas uses the notion of "measure" to speak of the essences of things; see, e.g., Aquinas, *Disputed Questions on Truth*, q. 1, a. 2.

but his narrow definition of courage could be certainly extended to mean "fortitude" and thus to include, among many other things, also the capacity to face the fear of death in all aspects of life.[90] However, the point is, of course, what does it mean, concretely, to face the fear of death? How will we stare at death in the face? Will we look at it as an essential trait of human creatureliness? Will we welcome it as a constitutive, unconditional "blessing" and as the very condition of the specific measure of human flourishing? Contrary to Kass, my answer to these questions would be more cautiously negative. Kass relies on an all-too-Greek identification of human finitude and mortality which seems untenable.

5.2. The historical drama of human life, which originally and constitutively implies a desirous suffering, the riskiness of doing the good that is "up to us" to do, and the freedom of self-giving love to others, does not share its essence with death, even though it is true that, once death has entered the world, "No one has greater love than this, to lay down one's life for one's friends" (John 15:13), because *unconditional* love surpasses *all* limits. Self-giving love is self-giving love, not death, nor is death the specific measure of human love and virtue. Note again: we agree with Kass that facing death through the dramatic cultivation of virtue is correct, and certainly more correct than trying to conquer death technologically, thus succumbing to the idolatry of universal automatism. This seems true also in a Christian perspective: "So by the ineffable mercy of God even the penalty of man's offence is turned into an instrument of virtue."[91] What we cannot grant is that this is so because death is *one in essence* with human finitude.

What we said above about the immortalization of death and about diversion and technology should have provided some grounds to tentatively conclude, with fear and trembling, that *one should "welcome" the negative limit of death while at the same time resisting the temptation to see in death a constitutive blessing for the human condition.* Accordingly, the correct stance toward death may be expressed by the following words of one of Victor Hugo's characters: "I am not prepared, but I am ready": I am ready to welcome that for which I could never be prepared.[92] The challenge of transhumanism makes this truth even more apparent: welcoming death

---

90. "Courage consists in acting and reacting in the face of death and the risk of death. A being who cannot take that risk cannot have that virtue" (Nussbaum, *Therapy of Desire*, 224).

91. Augustine, *City of God* 13.4.

92. Hugo, *Dernier jour d'un condamné*, 454.

may be the only wise thing to do, not because we cannot do otherwise, but precisely *because we could do otherwise*, because we could chose the transhumanist option (and note: one could be a transhumanist at heart even before or without having access to the transhumanist technology).

Are there additional reasons that may point in the same direction, that is, in the direction of a welcoming of the negative limit of death? To address these questions we will have to navigate the fine line separating philosophy from Christian theology. The issue, as I will try to show in the following section, requires a conjoined reflection on the nature of creation and freedom.

6. FREEDOM, CREATION, INCARNATION

6.1. It may be said that the final philosophical word on the metaphysics of human death has to do with the mystery of freedom and the meaning of creation and redemption. However, when philosophy reaches this point, it is not so sure anymore that it is walking a purely "natural" path. Here philosophy must open itself up to the revelation of God in Christ and, if not theology, it must become Christian philosophy explicitly.[93]

The question "Are we free, or are we rather determined in our actions by unescapable psychological and physical cause-and-effect series?" is the question that is usually raised in contemporary debates when addressing the problem of freedom. This question—freedom versus determinism—while not central to the phenomenon of freedom, is nevertheless helpful to bring to light what freedom is truly about.[94] In

---

93. "We shall not examine the questions pertaining to the proofs and to the integration of the facts on which Christian religion is grounded and what is called positive theology. Nor is our role to organize the ensemble of truths to be believed in, nor to go over in the least into the field of dogmatic theology. Our task is altogether different. It must consist in justifying the formula according to which human meditation and the philosophical study of naturally inaccessible mysteries is nevertheless fruitful, very illuminating, quite appropriate for showing the conveniences as well as the speculative and practical coherences of the faith. This is the rational task that calls for intelligence, having recourse as well to the experience built up through the exercise of moral and religious life, as to the concatenation of truths that support one another and call for one another. This is indeed the ensemble, made of nuances and of clarity, of spiritual tact and of intellectual ordinance, that we can call the Christian spirit" (Blondel, *Philosophical Exigencies of Christian Religion*, 11).

94. I abstract here from the discussion on whether a strict Laplacian determinism is still tenable according to contemporary physics (it is not). My only assumption here is that some form of cause-and-effect determinism must be granted to nature in order to explain its works.

fact, following Blondel once again, it seems necessary to state that the challenge of determinism can be overcome if one tries to think the relation between freedom and the determinism of nature in analogy with the relation between God the Creator, understood as the First Cause of the world, and the world itself, i.e., creation.[95]

It may be said, in fact, that freedom is the essence of the relation of creation. According to St. Thomas, the First Cause creates by letting be or "freeing" creatures to their own being and their proper operation, thus instituting them as substances and efficacious secondary causes.[96] Similarly, man's rational nature, his freedom, by informing the body, lets the natural determinism of the body be, that is, it frees it to its proper nature and operation. If we accept this view, the determinism of nature, working at the level of man's psyche and body, is not the final nail on the coffin of freedom, because freedom is the origin of such determinism and in a sense requires it in order to exercise its nondeterministic causal power.[97] Thus, man's freedom implies natural determinism, just like God's creative act implies the power of the creature.

However, how can God creatively let be and free a creature who has turned against her own being and against the Creator? How can God still give to the one who has turned against the gift of being and its Giver? He can do so by freeing this creature again, by freeing her in an unprecedented and radical way, in a supernatural way. When thinking about evil and death, God's creative freedom—i.e., creation as freeing the creature to herself and to her operation—is confronted with the greatest and unsurpassable limit to his liberality, with a no. In this sense, once the creature has embraced nothing, there is almost "no-thing" left to be freed. It is "as if" man's no had made God's creation impotent. And it is precisely this the reason why God becomes incarnate to free our nothing. God, remaining identical to his infinite mercy and faithful to his creature, remains faithfully bound—willingly bound, but bound nevertheless—to this strange impotence, to this limit, that man's no has forced upon him. God's re-creation of a fallen world is not a magical act which wipes away this impotence, this negative limit introduced into the world by man's disobedience. Instead, in virtue of the faithfulness described above, God's re-creation takes the form of the acceptance and assumption upon

---

95. See Spencer, "Divine Causality and Created Freedom."
96. *ST* 1, q. 105, a. 5.
97. Blondel, *Action*, 160–61.

himself of this impotence and limitation. He becomes man by assuming a mortal human nature.

If one sees the issue in this way, one can speculate that the position of the soul vis-à-vis the body is analogous to the position of God vis-à-vis his creation. The decision of God vis-à-vis a fallen creation is analogous to the position of the soul vis-à-vis its own fallen and dying bodily life. God becomes incarnate and assumes a fallen human nature, marked by suffering and sin. Similarly, the soul, which is always already embodied, must become *truly and fully incarnate*, i.e., incarnate as in the incarnation of our Lord Jesus. The human being has thus the opportunity of becoming cruciform and it is in this cruciform, free assumption of death that it becomes truly incarnate. Thus, the vocation of the soul is not, as Plato would have it, to avoid as much as possible "consorting with the body and communing with it,"[98] but rather that of a *"surplus" of embodiment in the form of a cruciform, Christlike incarnation* by intentional information, or obedient assumption, of a bodily dying life. This is, one might say, the deepest level of the anthropological meaning of the idea of material kenosis. This is the metaphysical and Christological structure corresponding to the decision and experience of *freely suffering death patiently*. Freely suffering death patiently *is* the meaning of leading a fully Christlike, *incarnate* life when it comes to death.[99] Only in this imitation

---

98. *Phaedo* 67a. It may be, however, that Plato's deepest insight on the soul and the negativity of death is found not in the *Phaedo* but elsewhere. In other words, it may be that Plato expressed the deeper sense of the *meletē thanatou* in Socrates's decision to "go down" (*katabasis*), which opens and organizes the drama of the *Republic*.

99. It follows, incidentally, that refusing to do so results into the enactment in life of a de facto soul-body dualism of the worst sort. Jankélévitch seems to go in this direction when he writes: "Even if the secret of biological rejuvenation was found, I would age anyway; even if the aging of the organs was slowed down or restrained, the weight of the years and of the memories would cause our aging; . . . . In fact, what makes us age is time in its pure state, that is, a satiety, the exhaustion of all freshness" (*Mort*, 189–90). The soul, become old and carrying the weight of its own time, would thus see itself informing an always-young body which is off time and thus out of touch with her, and she with it; the soul, thus marked by the death-bound weight of time, would carry around this youthful and healthy body very much as a dead body. Plotinus stated that the body is the portrait that the soul makes of herself with the colors (the materials) she finds available. In this case, it would be as if the soul intentionally sought colors and materials which would systematically prevent her from painting a portrait in which she could recognize herself. Thus, a soul-body dualism, but neither of the Platonic type (where the soul transcends the body because she is "like" and "communes with" the ideas), nor of the Cartesian type (where the "cogito" is characterized by the thinking experience of and capacity for the infinite), but of a new type, in which the soul condemns itself to a condition of melancholic "obsolescence" constantly reminded to her by an ever self-perfecting body.

of Christ—an imitation of Christ whose triumphalism must always coincide with his cruciform life—can we get a glimpse, already in this life, of what a genuine liberation from death, or the victory over death, may mean. Even when it comes to death, the Christian attitude is a creative one; "decreation" is not an option;[100] a creative stance lets death be in its nonbeing and thus inaugurates the re-creative liberation from death. The Christlike decision and experience of freely suffering death patiently has nothing thanatophilic, masochistic, or morbid to it; on the contrary, it is a gesture of creative love. The Socratic victory over death is rooted in the experience of one's *pneumatic distance* from death; while what characterizes Christ is precisely a *creative and re-creative nearness* to death. Socrates's pneumatic self-immunization from death is accompanied by an *agnostic detachment*; Christ's creative and re-creative attitude is perfectly manifested in the *agonic embrace* of death. From a Greek point of view, Christ's death may be perceived as overly dramatic, especially if compared to Socrates's; in fact, however, it is the perfect manifestation of the infinite, creative and re-creative power of God. This may be one of the meanings of the infinitely rich statement that we find in the gospel: "For whoever wishes to save his life will lose it, but whoever loses his life for my sake will save it" (Luke 9:24). Death as material kenosis is, ultimately, the agonic embrace of the nonbeing of death in virtue of a participation in the infinite creative and re-creative nearness to death of the God become man.[101] It is precisely in this agonic embrace and creative and re-creative nearness that lies the victory over death. While the attitude of the Christian may look to a superficial gaze one of resignation, it is actually the expression of a creative and re-creative attitude towards that to which one cannot resign himself.

---

100. "Decreation: to make something created pass into the uncreated.... Our existence is made up only of his [God's] waiting for our acceptance not to exist.... In a sense God renounces being everything. We should renounce being something. That is our only good" (Weil, *Gravity and Grace*, 32–33).

101. It seems to me that the perspective of creation here adopted deepens and grounds metaphysically the astonishing insights by Ricoeur: "I therefore discover that my will to live evades anguish only when my reasons for living are placed above my life itself, when concrete values, which form the meaning of my happiness and my honor, transcend the very opposition between my life and my death. It stands to reason that this act of transcendence is achieved only within the comportment of sacrifice. Thus my life is at one and the same time threatened and transcended, threatened by death in the catastrophic situation, and transcended by its own reasons for living which have become reasons for dying. But in this matter, it is easier to speak than to live" ("True and False Anguish," in Ricoeur, *History and Truth*, 391).

If the act of creation consists in the freeing of being to itself and its own operation, how can God "free" that being which has become radical self-denial, nonbeing? *He lets nonbeing be.* He "allows" evil in the sense that, even in the case of evil, the logic of the act of creation is not subverted. He lets everything be—he does not impose or superimpose his own power, because *his power is to empower and to free whatever is created*—and so, he also lets be that nonbeing that the rational creature has chosen for herself. This of course should not be taken in the sense that God creates evil, but in the sense that his treatment of the nonbeing introduced by man's rebellious act remains consistent with the logic of creation, with his letting the other be. Wiping evil out with an act of power would have been contrary to and infinitely inadequate with respect to his almighty power and his creative letting be. Instead, to speak analogously, he *empowered nonbeing*—the very nonbeing of death—by willingly subjecting himself to the "power of death." John states as much in his gospel: "No one takes it [my life] from me, but I lay it down of my own accord" (John 10:18); "You would have no power over me if it had not been given to you from above" (John 19:11).[102]

Without God's creative willingness, death would have had no power over him. In other words, if God, *per impossibile*, had not been all-powerful, death would have had no power over him. Thus, precisely because his almightiness is manifested also in his creative act, he lets death be and in a sense empowers it, so that his almighty power over it may be realized in his willingly undergoing its effects, in his passion and death. If Jesus truly is God (which is something that only faith can establish), then we can see the "fittingness" of the metaphysical view according to which the Almighty Creator of the world, the one who lets things be, manifests and fulfills his almightiness, his pure activity, in a fallen world, by *being utterly passive*. At each spit, at each atrocious physical and spiritual injury *passively* received by Jesus, God's *creative act* of *empowering nonbeing* becomes more manifest, his *most active* almightiness evidenced and fulfilled in his *most passive* undergoing pain, suffering, and finally death. "Power is made perfect in weakness" (2 Cor 12:9). Christ's passive

---

102. Complementarily: "God raised him up, having freed him from death, because it was impossible for him to be held in its power" (Acts 2:22); "Jesus summoned them and said to them, 'You know that those who are recognized as rulers over the Gentiles lord it over them, and their great ones make their authority over them felt. But it shall not be so among you. Rather, whoever wishes to be great among you will be your servant; whoever wishes to be first among you will be the slave of all. For the Son of Man did not come to be served but to serve and to give his life as a ransom for many'" (Mark 10:42–45).

suffering is the way in which the Son does the will of the Father Almighty, with whom he is one in substance: "Son though he was, he learned obedience from what he suffered" (Heb 5:8). This is why *precisely Jesus's death* may become a powerful evidence of his divinity: "Truly, this was the Son of God" (Matt 27:54).

This account of the incarnation and passion of Jesus also shows why the passion and death of Christ are *sufficient* for the redemption of the world. God's "new creation" of the world is the cross of Jesus. His re-creative power is realized in the empowering of nonbeing so that he may be passively victorious over that death which he nevertheless suffered as true God and true man. Resurrection, as we know, is the fruit of the redemption already accomplished on the cross. The *Ars Moriendi* is thus very precise in exhorting the dying person "to commit himself entirely to the Passion of Christ [and not immediately to his resurrection!], holding fast to it and meditating on it."[103]

Jesus's death shows a victory over death that bears no signs of thanatophilia, no signs of masochism and sadism, and no signs of violent control over being or even over what opposes being. Thanatophilia, masochism and sadism, violence and control prove to be the marks of a finite, limited, fallen power. God's almightiness manifests itself in the perfect passivity of the Lamb who is slain, even before the resurrection.

The attitude grasped by the concept of material kenosis does not mean the *resigned acceptance* of death corresponding to impotent human immanence and according to which death *must* and therefore *can* be accepted. Rather, it is the *hopeful nonacceptance* of death corresponding to the fact that human impotence is "taken up" by divine creative and re-creative omnipotence, a position from which death is precisely *that which cannot be accepted (the "unacceptable" par excellence)* and thus that which must let be (in its totalizing nonbeing) so that it may be patiently and nonviolently conquered. Just as for Blondel "the one thing necessary" (the "life" of God) is the "impossible" (to reach, to attain) for man, so in this case, "the one thing *un*necessary" (death) is also the "impossible" (to accept) for man. But "what is impossible for human beings is possible for God" (Luke 18:27). In Christ, what is impossible for man

---

103. Thomas, *Art of Dying*, 40. As I have remarked in the introduction of this book, the medieval *ars moriendi* seems to be different in essence from a modern art of dying à la Montaigne, for instance. In fact, the former consists in learning how to avoid the vices which are likely to accompany the experience of dying (the devil's temptations: loss of faith, despair, impatience, vainglory, and avarice), while the latter is an invitation to assimilate oneself to death so that death may lose its pernicious advantage on us.

becomes real, namely, the self-communication of God to man and, in the very same event, the unaccepting but creative and re-creative embrace of man's death by God.

6.2. St. Bernard of Clairvaux states that "while God cannot suffer, it is not impossible that He suffers with."[104] In other words, God's suffering love for man has the nature of *compassion*. In the incarnation of the Son in Jesus, God assumes in him and upon him the suffering of man in such a way that he "suffers with." It seems possible to me to draw from this point a crucial anthropological implication, which brings us, finally, to the very heart of material kenosis. Insofar as the human being is created "to the image and likeness of God" (Gen 1:26), man is also created to the image and likeness of God's compassion. Thus, the decision and experience of freely suffering death patiently is the decision and experience of freely becoming what one already is, namely, *compassion*.[105] If unpacking the idea of death as the separation of soul and body within the hylomorphic framework required introducing the notion of material kenosis,[106] the notion of material kenosis requires, in turn, to be completed in light of the notions of creation and incarnation. In material kenosis, man is revealed for what he truly is in his godlike, fallen, redeemed, metaphysical, and historical constitution: *freely assumed subsistent compassion*.

This metaphysical anthropology of compassion, in which we find the heart of material kenosis, can be likened to a circle, which does not change its essence no matter how small or large its radius becomes. Accordingly, compassion can be detected at different levels of human life. Let us assume that the hylomorphic structure of man corresponds to the narrowest instantiation of this circle. The compassion of which I am speaking can already be discovered in the very hylomorphic relation of the soul to the body after the first sin. If one allows a "theologization" of this metaphysical structure, one could say, somewhat daringly, that the soul, though it was in the form of a likeness to God due to its spiritual nature,[107] did not regard its similarity to God something to be grasped; rather, it emptied itself, taking the form of a slave, that is, taking man's

---

104. Bernard of Clairvaux, *Sermones in Cantica* 26.5 (PL 183:906c).

105. The reflections presented here have been inspired by the profound meditation on the conjoined experiences of "com-passion," "com-motion," and "con-solation" put forth in Barzaghi, *Sguardo della sofferenza*. I am not in a position to say how much of my development Barzaghi would be willing to accept.

106. This was developed in ch. 2.

107. See Augustine, *City of God* 13.24.

Material Kenosis

bodily mortal life as its own life, and humbled itself, becoming obedient to death—an obedience describable according to the formulas presented in chapter 2 (self-negation and self-emptying, radical negation without annihilation). The way in which death casts light on the hylomorphic relation of soul and body is susceptible of an even greater theological illumination. In its very core, the hylomorphic involvement of the soul with the body corresponds to a dynamism of compassion: the soul "suffers with" the body having made the life of dying body its own life, and it is in this "suffering with" that the secret of its metaphysical structure and its historical condition is revealed.

The circle could be expanded to include also man's experience without changing its essence. The experience corresponding to material kenosis (the experience of death, of dying!) is, ultimately, an experience of compassion. I am always already in relation with: in relation with myself and in relation with others. It is not necessary to try to find out whether a metaphysical priority should be granted to "myself" or to the "others." If the "I am" must be always understood as the abridged version of "I am in relation with," the essential point is already established, namely, that there is never for me a "before" or "outside" of the "relation with." Accordingly, in material kenosis I "suffer with"—both "with myself" and "with others." The enormous philosophical literature devoted to the puzzle of the origin of the experience of death—Do I experience death in myself and then "read it" into the life of others? Or do I experience death only in the other and then "introject" it into myself?[108]—melts into insignificance once critically assessed in light of the structure of the "I am in relation with" and the experience of compassion for oneself-as-another and for the other-as-oneself. The compassion for myself, if it is true *compassion*, is never selfish or egotistical—it is always already an open space where others, known or unknown, are present; and the compassion for others, if it is genuine, never leaves out the one who suffers as, at once, the subject and the *object* of such compassion. The circle of our compassion is always social; the center of my being is, at once, a wounded center in which my wound and the wounds of others recognize themselves and seek shelter conjointly.[109] Despite the superficial differ-

---

108. Scheler has an interesting insight when he says that the belief that one's death can be known only inductively relies upon the "pathological" loss of the knowledge of one's death as an a priori of the consciousness of lived time typical of the "Modern European man" (*Morte e sopravvivenza*, 64).

109. See the deep insight of Elias Canetti: "The one who truly knew what binds men

ence, I do not think that this position is at odds with Gabriel Marcel's claim that "what matters is the death of those we love."[110] Insofar as *compassion* is always already relational, the experience of death encapsulated in the concept of material kenosis is, from the very start, a figure of what Marcel calls the "open," i.e., the space of intersubjectivity;[111] it is from the start a form of "grief" remaining faithful to the beloved against all temptations of "betrayal."[112]

Finally, the radius of the circle can even become infinite and, when this happens, its center can be found everywhere, namely, everywhere each one of us is, while its circumference is found nowhere, namely, in no singular, precise, place—nowhere we can point to. The circumference stops being the radial projection of a center; the center becomes embraced by a circumference which remains hidden, invisible, given and yet beyond reach. The experience of compassion, this "suffering with," becomes the threshold of God's compassion and "suffering with," and, as such, it offers itself as the privileged locus of a mysterious *consolation. Consolation is the perfection of compassion and "suffering with."* Note that the consolation does not remove fully the negativity of death; rather,

---

together would also be able to rescue them from death. The enigma of existence is a social enigma" (*Libro contro la morte*, 106) See also Augustine's account of his suffering after the death of his friend Nebridius, *Confessions* (Chadwick): "I was surprised that any other mortal was still alive, since he whom I had loved as if he would never die was dead. I was even more surprised that when he was dead I was still alive, for he was 'my other self'" (59); "The lost life of those who die becomes the death of those still living" (61).

110. Marcel, *Presence and Immortality*, 231.

111. Marcel, "Death and Immortality." For Marcel, it is the death of those we love—the other person's death—which (1) is the death that truly counts and (2) enables me to actually know about mortality (there is no other empirical access to my own death apart from the death of the other). This is a widespread position in contemporary philosophy. For instance, Ricoeur writes: "Death is an external threat in the sense that it is not necessarily implied by life; on the whole, life could be immortal. I learn of the necessity of my death empirically by witnessing the death of others. . . . The death of another pierces me as an injury to our communal existence" ("True and False Anguish," in Ricoeur, *History and Truth*, 289). Also Melchiorre has stressed that the death of the other is the origin of the experience of my own death. I turn into the contradiction of death because the dead one lives in me: "The tragedy of the survivor is here: the one struck by death seems to continue to live in him, the survivor carries within himself this contradiction, he is this contradiction" (Melchiorre, *Sul senso della morte*, 290). Compare to Scheler, for whom the *"spiritual* feelings" are characterized by the fact that they are, originally, an "experiencing *together* the *same* feeling with respect to the same value" (*Morte e sopravvivenza*, 93–94; emphasis in original).

112. By way of ideal integration to Marcel's point, Landsberg insightfully points out that the experience of the death of the beloved is always accompanied to some extend by a feeling of "tragic infidelity" on the part of the departed (*Experience of Death*, 32).

it embraces it in the experience of compassion.[113] When experience is transfigured by grace, our compassion and "suffering with" are fulfilled, that is, they are made perfect. In becoming wholly compassion, in this mysterious encounter of freedom and grace, I suffer with myself and with the others, but in this suffering, I discover with the others that Another suffers with me and with us; accordingly, I suffer with this Other who has preceded me in his suffering with us and for us; I suffer for this Other and the others, because I am the cause of their suffering; I am consoled, because no suffering—neither mine, nor the other's—is left out in my suffering with the One who suffers with and for me and the others. "Now I rejoice in my sufferings for your sake, and in my flesh I am filling up what is lacking in the afflictions of Christ on behalf of his body, which is the church" (Col 1:24).

6.3. The child who patiently accepts to go to sleep at the established time does so with an obedience to the parents which is not devoid of a bursting, antagonistic desire to stay up. Out of love he accepts and does what remains nevertheless foreign to his ways. It seems to me that the welcoming of the limit of death on the part of the Christian resembles

---

113. "Let us recall the warning the Church gives the faithful on Ash Wednesday when the priest marks our forehead with a cross of ashes: 'Remember, man, you are dust and unto dust you shall return!' This dramatically shows the Church's insistence that although the Christian view of death (which indeed is death's only true estimate) must be the definitive perspective for us, nonetheless the natural view with all its dread should not disappear totally from our consciousness" (Hildebrand, *Jaws of Death*, 93). Hildebrand continues: "All Christians must strive to succeed in the great task of having this victorious aspect of death outshine the natural aspect of death's fearful inevitability. This latter view is a threat to death's glorious mission to allow the marriage of the soul with the Bridegroom. As we strive to make our own this supernatural view of death, our constant prayer must be: 'May God grant us this grace—to be led by death to the Bridegroom!'" (103); "The character of the Cross *as cross* should not be eliminated from Christian life. Certainly we can endure joyfully a physical suffering for the sake of Christ, but the suffering does not thereby cease to cause pain; it is not changed into a sense of physical well-being. There is a constant temptation here. We are human. Our transformation in Christ should not mean that we somehow cease to be human. The purely human, natural aspects of life must be faced and experienced even as we must transcend and outgrow them. We give a woefully incomplete response to the death of a beloved person, therefore, if we only rejoice; it may be that the dead person was like a saint and thus may confidently be expected to be enjoying eternal bliss. Even so, the human heart cries out with Virgil, 'Here, tears are called for!'" (112; emphasis in original); "Yes, death continues to be painful and should remain so. But the deep sorrow of all concerned is transfigured through the light of Christ. A new dimension in our human relationship mysteriously emerges alongside the sorry realities of death" (127). This mysterious insistent presence of the negativity of death in and through its supernatural transfiguration corresponds, experientially, to the ineffable nature of the hypostatic union.

more this child than the old Stoic sage who has mastered a self-possession of his inner life, especially by having turned death into something familiar, that is, by having turned himself into something deathlike.[114] The tears on the face of the child trying to fall asleep in his little bed are closer to the "virtue of death" than the ironic or impassible face of the old sage on his deathbed. Having heard the Word made flesh and resurrected from the dead (*ob-oedientia*) and having been transformed by this Word, we welcome, regenerated in hope, faith, and charity by this Word's love, what cannot be welcomed, we accept the limit of death, as a child goes through the struggle of falling asleep filled with the thought of the love received and the love still to be received. I cannot at this point not cite at length the conclusive remarks in one of Xavier Tilliette's essays on death:

> The couple death-resurrection takes place eminently and perfectly in the case of Christ, and it is above all the glorious Christ who attracts the attention of the theologian of the afterlife. But the real eschatological archetype is the Christ on the cross: it is from him that emanates that obscure light that illuminates every man that leaves this world. For the Christian the light of death is the death of Christ. In his unique solitude, it gathers all those who die.... The dying Christian descends into the abyss dug by the cry of the dying Redeemer. To die with Christ means, in the perspective of faith, to be subtracted to the power of death. The agony is communion. But also the communion is agony; to be united to the death of Christ means to assume the burden, which is the weight of sin, it means to taste the bitterness, to drink from that sponge of vinegar which is suffering. Between the wage of sin and the gain of death, St. Paul has penetrated more deeply into the mystery of Christ. But when he writes: Where, O Death, is your sting?, he does so in view of an anticipation, when there will be neither death nor time. Theology is not the beatific life, and even less so than philosophy can she undo the sting of death.[115]

---

114. See again the attitude of Montaigne; a subtler reading of ancient Stoicism could reveal a difference between, say, Epictetus and Seneca, the latter showing an abiding "despair" due to death even within the most perfect *virtus moriendi*. Landsberg discusses this; see in particular his illuminating comment: "The Stoic decision is not an escape as with the Epicureans; it is an attack which includes an element of despair. However, the stoic attitude seems to me to be the noblest that can be achieved if we do not accept that man participates in an order of existence which transcends death" (*Experience of Death*, 44).

115. Tilliette, *Morte e sopravvivenza*, 46–47.

6.4. Only the gift of faith can enable us to recognize the resurrection of Christ as the object of our desire. The resurrection is not a theorem that we can deduce, a principle that we can discover, or a philosophical scenario that we can envision with enough imagination. Nevertheless, a philosophical reflection on human desire may lead us to the point of acknowledging, as I have explained, that what we desire is a new mode of existing—radically identical to what we are *and at the same time* wholly new.

Despite all the distraction and the strategies of diversion that we ourselves put in place, experience and reflection let this mysterious object of desire emerge to our consciousness, almost like a dream, almost like a voice that barely speaks, something in relation to which doubting and misinterpreting are all too normal and common, especially if we try to define it more thoroughly and remove it from its condition of obscurity. It is the almost dreamlike consciousness of the object of desire that enable people to take seriously the imagined, truly oniric project of transhumanism.[116] The object of desire is "general and vague" and ought to remain so at the level of the natural light of reason; it is the natural potential matter to which supernatural revelation gives its form. Even more than simply doubtful and hard to interpret, isn't the object of desire so described a plain contradiction? What could it possibly mean that we desire a life that is, at once, wholly identical to itself and wholly new? Isn't this thought, aiming at a most vague, obscure, and seemingly contradictory object, a thought about nothing and therefore a nothing of thought? Isn't this desire a desire of nothing and therefore a nothing of desire? A life wholly identical to itself and wholly new? How can this be? Doesn't this idea bear the mark of the contradictory impossible? Shall we not say instead, with the transhumanist, that our thirst for life is the thirst for an extensive and expansive survival, which is now on its way thanks to the wondrous resources of technology?

And yet, the voice of desire does not stop calling those who have ears to listen to it; a desire whose obscure nature is matched only by the light of its insistence. One must open oneself to this strange object of desire, to its persuasiveness, *due to* its stubborn insistence and anthropological convenience, which inexorably asks us to receive and accept as believable that which cannot be fully subjected to the clarity of comprehension, that

---

116. A sentence from Blondel applies here beautifully: "The will exhausts everything, invents everything, admits everything, even the impossible, in order to be self-sufficient and to content itself; it does not succeed at it; and this very ambition is contrary to its most intimate wish" (*Action*, 233).

which seems to defy the laws of thought, that which seems impossible. Despite its seeming impossibility, one must believe this object of desire because *desiring boldly and daringly beyond reason* seems to be *the only reasonable thing to do*. Here is where the ancient Greek wisdom reaches its peak; here is where Plato's "poor wealth" or "wealthy poverty" of eros and Aristotle's "believable impossible" meet. Here, at the heart of human desire, we discover the hidden presence of the true end of human life, which is "equally inaccessible and infinitely desirable."[117]

7. "FOR A CHILD IS BORN TO US, A SON IS GIVEN TO US"

7.1. One last section in this tentative hermeneutics of the human condition must confront the further challenge regarding whether there is anything in human experience realizing analogically and symbolically that to which the desire for resurrection aspires transcendentally. In fact, if it is true, contrary to the positivistic, historicistic, and postmodern interpretations of human life, that it is both possible and necessary to speak of human experience as such, it is also true that the vice of philosophy is often that of neglecting the specificity of concrete human experiences and the bearing that they have on human experience in its totality. In order to talk about human experience, philosophy ends up forgetting that human experience only subsists in human experiences.[118] While human experience has one unitary structure, not all experiences are the same; and while any experience can bear a unique and life-changing meaning for some, some experiences are more pregnant of meaning than others for all. Thus, the opportunity offered by the postmodern disintegration of human experience could be the following: that by valuing the fragment against the whole, postmodernism may allow us to rediscover the fragment as that through which the whole shines. In a very paradoxical sense, as it has been shown by Balthasar's treatment of the smile of the mother for the child, it is some specific experiences that turn out to be conditions of possibility for experience as such.[119]

---

117. Blondel, *Philosophical Exigencies of Christian Religion*, 84.

118. A philosopher should always be aware of that philosophical vice that Elias Canetti calls "the *emptying* process of thinking" (*Human Province*, 126; emphasis in original).

119. See, e.g., Balthasar, "Resumé of My Thought," 470–71.

Material Kenosis

Even more so than the previous sections, the proposal in this last section is little more than a sketch, and I am fully aware that such a sketch may be painfully insufficient for the reader, especially when the ideas put forth seem to defy commonsense and the received wisdom of our time. But all I have said in this book up to now would be not only incomplete, but also easily misunderstood, if I did not include this last bit. In a sense, what this section clarifies regarding the nature of human desire is the point from which everything else must be interpreted. In my defense, however, the only thing I will say is that the fact that this last part is only developed over few pages should not surprise the reader too much. After all, the fulcrum of a lever is always much smaller than that which it allows to lift.

Now, the idea that I would like to explore here is that the natural analogate and symbol of the desire for the resurrection is the *desire emerging in parenthood*. More precisely: it is the loving desire that is reawakened, clarified, and fulfilled by the birth of a child. The experience of being a parent means, not exclusively but essentially, having one's human desire reawakened and clarified in a radically surprising way by the birth of the child. The desire for the resurrection, for the resurrected I, is in fact the desire for something that is, at once and paradoxically, wholly identical to what and who I am (continuity of nature and numerical identity) and wholly different (a wholly new "mode of existence," to repeat Thomas's language).

Following an intuition of Levinas, we find an analogous and symbolical realization of this structure in the phenomenon of paternity or, more precisely, in the love-desire for one's child:

> Paternity is a relationship with a stranger who, entirely while being Other, is me. It is the relationship of the ego with a selfsame ego who is nonetheless a stranger to the ego. The son in fact is not simply my work, like a poem or manufactured object, neither is he my property. Neither the categories of power nor those of having can indicate the relationship with a child. Neither the notion of cause nor the notion of ownership permit grasping the fact of fecundity. I do not have my child, I *am* in some way my child. Only the words "I am" here have a signification different from the Eleatic or Platonic significance. . . . Paternity is not simply a renewal of the father in the son and

his confusion with him. It is also the exteriority of the father in relation to the son. It is a pluralist existing.[120]

Neither Levinas nor I want to suggest, of course, that there is a proper numerical identity between father and son. At the same time, however, Levinas does suggest, and I follow him, that describing father and son as merely specifically identical is radically insufficient, as it is insufficient to simply conceptualize the father as the "cause" and the son as the "effect" (*omnis agens agit simile sibi*). My child *is* I, but he is I as *wholly new* and thus *wholly different* from me. We may say that between me and my child there is consubstantiality—where "consubstantiality" means more than mere specific identity and less than proper numerical identity.

If the meaning of being is truly love, if being is love in its deepest sense, then we have to remember that love is a unitive power, but a unitive power that *the more deeply it unites, the more strongly it frees to their own being those who are in love*. Genuine love is not a *unity of fusion* but, if we can say it this way, it is a *unity of relation*, which is a deeper and more unitary union than any unity of fusion.[121] This is the "pluralist existing" of which Levinas speaks. In generative love, love is at its most powerful, and as such it is at its most unitive: my beloved son, the one who is generated, truly is myself. And yet, for the very same reason for which it is at its most unitive, fruitful love is also at its most distancing and liberating: my child truly is wholly other. In generation, the new life that is generated out of love is wholly new, a new beginning. Thus, in receiving a child, in becoming father, in always again receiving one's child, one receives *oneself* as *totally other from oneself* and as *totally new*, and the son can do so precisely because he is wholly other from me while being consubstantial with me.

The awareness of one's failures, one's sins, one's nonbeing, one's impending end—one's death-likeness, if you will—is infinitely deepened by the birth of a child. And at the same time, the child, who is unwittingly, in his infant flesh, the harshest judge, is also the source of hope and liberation, that wholly new mode of being that comes to me from someone

---

120. Levinas, *Time and the Other*, 91; emphasis in original. Also quoted and discussed in Levinas, *Ethics and Infinity*, 71–72. A similar, though undeveloped, insight is found in Aristotle, *Nicomachean Ethics*, 1161b27–29: "Parents, then, love children as themselves (for things that come from themselves, by being separated, are a sort of other selves)."

121. I originally came across the helpful distinction between "union of fusion" and "union of relation" in a lecture by Fabrice Hadjadj.

who is wholly other than me. My judge is the same as the source of the liberation to which I aim, because being judged by the truth (*veritas redarguens*) is the same as being put in the condition of acknowledging how short I fall, when left to my own resources, of that truth that wants to free me and that is already freeing me (*veritas lucens*).[122] Thus, if I can put it this way, I am analogically and symbolically resurrected *by* my son and *in* my son *through the perfect assimilation to* the *radically novel otherness* of my son, from whom I nevertheless remain *completely distinct*.

Note how different the present interpretation of the phenomenon of paternity is from other, more common interpretations. The desire for the son underlying the relationship of paternity is not the desire to perpetuate oneself in someone else beyond the limits of one's biological existence, along the lines of the way in which the ancient Greek heroes wanted to immortalize themselves through their gestures and thus "cheat" the inevitable oblivion of death, or to the way in which artists want to become immortal through their work.[123] On the contrary, the desire-love for the son, understood according to the three features described above—(1) maximal union—identity; (2) maximal separation—otherness; (3) newness, radically new beginning within a generative continuity—reveals to me that of which this desire-love is the image, i.e., the desire for the resurrection. It is by going more deeply into this experience that the love for the son opens to what lies beyond it, that which the love of the son anticipates analogously and symbolically, namely, that love-desire for oneself as totally other, that love-desire for one's metamorphosis and for what may be capable of engendering it.

7.2. Maybe unsurprisingly, the meaninglessness of the negation of death is clarified in light of the positive meaningfulness of life, but the positive meaningfulness of a life carrying the wound of the meaninglessness of death is clarified in light of the redeeming meaningfulness of birth. Whose birth? Surprisingly, not ours, or not directly ours, but the birth of one's child. In the birth of another, the child, we experience that rebirth of our I which is, at one and the same time, the reawakening and clarification of the true nature of desire, which is, as I have explained, desire for the resurrection. Falque has developed the same theme in a

---

122. For the two notions of *veritas lucens* and *veritas redarguens*, see Augustine, *Confessions* (Chadwick), 200.

123. It is impossible not to be reminded here of Woody Allen's wisdom: "I don't want to achieve immortality through my work . . . I want to achieve it through not dying" (Ratcliffe, *Oxford Essential Quotations*, quote 8).

masterful way, by showing that the New Testament presents the "resurrection" as a "rebirth." By appealing to a Heideggerian terminology, he shows that "resurrection" is not a mere "ontic" fact taking place "in the world" but rather an "ontological event" transforming the "world" and our "being-in-the-world." The main contribution of his work is to show that one cannot understand what resurrection means without approaching it through the lens of "the act of rebirth," which, in turn, must be approached in light of "the act of birth," "outside which ... the term *resurrection* remains only an 'empty word,' a *flatus vocis*, lacking a veritable existential situation to describe."[124]

Despite its insightfulness, it seems to me that Falque's treatment does not describe deeply enough the "veritable existential situation" in which the experience of birth and rebirth is truly granted. As I have claimed, the experience of one's rebirth is given to us in the birth of a child, and it is in this very experience that the desire for the resurrection-metamorphosis is reawakened and clarified and awaits to be fulfilled. Like in many of the most important things in life, also this phenomenon follows an *indirect, roundabout path*: we discover, as if by chance, the true love-desire for the fulfillment of our being in the gratuitous love-desire for another being.

It is in this light that we can assess, albeit briefly, the way in which the notions of "birth" and "natality" have been brought back to the center of the broader philosophical discourse by Hannah Arendt. As it is well known, Hannah Arendt has put forth an articulate political anthropology of natality, according to which man is essentially characterized by his capacity for genuine novelty, freedom, and action, three conjoined phenomena that Arendt sees archetypically contained in and originating from "the fact of natality" (which is, for this very reason, much more than a simple "fact"). For Arendt, natality is the "source" or "root" of our "capacity to begin."[125]

> [The freedom of man] is identical with the fact that men are being born and that therefore each of them is a new beginning, begins, in a sense, the world anew.... The very source of freedom is given with the fact of the birth of man and resides in his capacity to make a new beginning.[126]

124. Falque, *Metamorphosis of Finitude*, 129.

125. Arendt, *Human Condition*, 247. For a helpful discussion of these themes, see Totschnig, "Arendt's Notion of Natality; Bowen-Moore, *Hannah Arendt's Philosophy of Natality*.

126. Arendt, *Origins of Totalitarianism*, 466.

> Beginning, before it becomes a historical event, is the supreme capacity of man; politically, it is identical with man's freedom. *Initium ut esset homo creatus est*—"that a beginning be made man was created" said Augustine. This beginning is guaranteed by each new birth; it is indeed every man.[127]

> The miracle that saves the world, the realm of human affairs, from its "natural" ruin is ultimately the fact of natality, in which the faculty of action is ontologically rooted.[128]

> Philosophically speaking, to act is the human answer to the condition of natality. Since we all come into the world by virtue of birth, as newcomers and beginnings, we are able to start something anew; without the fact of birth we would not even know what novelty us, all "action" would be either mere behavior or preservation.[129]

Arendt's merit is undoubtedly that of having asserted with clarity that natality and the human capacity for radically new beginnings belong together. However, there seems to be a limitation in Arendt's analysis, resulting from the fact that for her the first experiential analogate of our being-from-birth is the subject's free action. What is lacking in Arendt, as it is lacking in Falque, is a more concrete reflection on the phenomenon of parenthood as the first experiential analogate of birth and natality. Note: what I am claiming is that also the sense of *my own capacity* for new beginnings, freedom, and action is given to me in and through the experience of parenthood. Or, which is the same, that the sense of my own birth and natality would not be ultimately true if it remained independent from the love-desire for resurrection that is reawakened and clarified in the love-desire for the child. To put it simply, there is no genuine sense of one's freedom apart from a desire that such freedom may be liberated from what impairs it and thus may be liberated to what it aspires to be.

In fact, we may ask, is Arendt's proposal ultimately satisfactory when seen in relation to death? Is the meaning of birth something that can be identified with myself as the originating origin of novelty? It seems to me that my action cannot be the chief experiential symbol of

---

127. Arendt, *Origins of Totalitarianism*, 479.
128. Arendt, *Human Condition*, 247.
129. Arendt, *Crises of the Republic*, 179.

natality (i.e., that which recapitulates the meaning of being-from-birth) because the agent's action, no matter how great his capacity for transcendence and novelty, does not and cannot transcend the ultimate passivity of death.[130] In fact, the origin of my action is at the same time the place in which the disintegration of death is mysteriously nestled. As Blondel explains in detail, following St. Paul, there is a lawlike disintegration in our members which fight "from within," as it were, the aspirations of our action.[131] If the love-desire awakened and clarified in us by birth is the natural analogate of the desire for resurrection (i.e., that common experience in which the desire for resurrection is given a sort of natural simulacrum), the birth at stake here is not primarily mine, but my child's. As I said, one gets to one's being only indirectly and in a roundabout way. Thus, my "faculty of action" can be "ontologically rooted" in my birth only because it is eschatologically rooted in the birth of my son, from whom I receive myself *anew*, in the hope of the resurrection (cf. 1 Thess 4:13–18). A fourth and essential element emerges, namely, (4) the fact that the true novelty that the human being desires is something received, gifted. The sense of the *child's giftedness to us* as the fundamental trait of the novelty and birth that "saves the world" is what is ultimately lacking in Arendt's analysis. "For a child is born to us, a son is *given* to us" (Isa 9:5; emphasis added).

7.3. The suffering self-emptying in which death consists for each one of us, a true total negation without annihilation, is never meaningful per se, and we should always guard ourselves, I believe, against the temptation of turning evil and lack of being into an excuse and temptation for a compensatory enjoyment. Understanding Christianity as that mode of life in which "everything works, including death," would amount precisely to conceptualize Christianity through the same technological logic by which transhumanism abides: the ideal would be that of a perfect automatism in which everything works more or less smoothly. Instead, as Silvano Petrosino maintains, the existential dilemma becomes for us whether "to look at life from the point of view of death," so that "life comes toward us as death"; or "to look at death from the point of view of life," an attitude which manages "to keep death from turning into the whole of life."[132] In Christ, life is revealed to be unconditionally meaningful and worth living, even though "nothing works, especially death." In

---

130. See ch. 3.

131. See Blondel, *Action*, 161.

132. Petrosino, "Perire, morire," 7.

Christ, the possibility of looking at death from the point of view of life has become real, concrete, and definitive, it has become a person. Jesus of Nazareth *is* this looking at death from the point of view of life; this radically novel point of view has become real in his suffering and resurrected flesh. The Christian knows, by the gift of faith, that it is his resurrection that which he ultimately desires for himself and for everybody: our metaphysical desire is the desire for the resurrection, as explained. However, everybody can have a premonition of what desire truly aspires to, albeit vaguely and in a somewhat confused way, in the experience of the desire-love for the child that we receive as a gift. The child comes to us as a radical novelty, the radical novelty for me and for everybody in the world: "My child comes to the world not as one being among many beings, but rather as the renewal of the entire world for me."[133] As a consequence, looking at death from the point of view of life means, naturally, to make this love-desire awakened by a child become the guiding and orienting principle of our life.

7.4. Falque devotes many beautiful pages to the different ways in which Nicodemus and Mary wonder about the supernatural action of God in their life. As Falque rightly points out, Nicodemus's questioning response to Jesus is an accurate one. To Jesus's claim, "Amen, amen, I say to you, no one can see the kingdom of God without being born from above," Nicodemus responds by asking: "How can a person be born again? Surely he cannot reenter his mother's womb and be born again, can he?" (John 3:3–4). Nicodemus in fact wonders about the conditions of possibility of something which he deems to be impossible and thus unrealizable.

On the contrary, to the annunciation of the angel Gabriel, "Behold, you will conceive in your womb and bear a son, and you shall name him Jesus," Mary responds by asking: "How can this be, since I have no relations with a man?" Mary's question, though similar, is radically different from Nicodemus's, insofar as she does not question the possibility of the taking place of what the angel announces but instead wonders about the modality of realization of the grace of God which is already actually operating in her.[134]

Falque describes Mary as the "anti-Nicodemus," but both questions are necessary in order to gauge the infinite distance that needs to

---

133. Hadjadj, "Pourquoi donner la vie," 91.
134. See Falque, *Metamorphosis of Finitude*, 132–35.

be crossed so that our nature may be in fact transformed by grace, the infinite distance that lies between the "believable impossible" of a metamorphosis which we desire vaguely and confusedly and the resurrection of the flesh "possible to God" that has been accomplished in Jesus and that is promised to all: "For the human beings this is impossible, but for God all things are possible" (Matt 19:26). As I have explained, the desire awakened by the child is what gives exemplary experiential denseness to this desire for the impossible, the desire for being born again. We may add to what we have already said that this desire is also a desire to be made *omnipotent*. "Omnipotence" should not be understood in the sense of an enhanced corporality, such as the corporality envisioned by transhumanism and posthumanism, but rather in the sense of a toti-potentiality: a flesh, a lived body, an embodied life, *made fully and completely available to receive the good, i.e., a perfection that one lacks and can only receive from another*. The child is the analogate and the symbol of this toti-potentiality—the child, precisely in what we call lack of psycho-physiological organization, is truly omnipotent in the sense of toti-potent, truly unburdened by the weight of deadly habits blocking the road to the irruption into life of novelty, of grace, as Péguy would put it. He is the analogate and the symbol, one may say, the exemplary rule, of a truly metamorphosed life: "Amen, I say to you, unless you turn and become like children, you will not enter the kingdom of heaven" (Matt 18:3).[135] In trusting our desire for the omnipotence and toti-potentiality reawakened and clarified in us by the love-desire for the child, we come to wonder in what way (Mary) the impossibility of a new life (Nicodemus) may actually be realized in us and all by the one to whom nothing is impossible.

7.5. There is one last, simple, but truly fundamental way in which it is the child that reawakens in us and clarifies for us the true object of our desire. The son awakens in me the desire to give, to love, *to subsist in giving myself*, in loving the child; to be wholly self-giving and loving. Even the experience of the resistance to love and to give to the child, which can reach the extreme point of the refusal to recognize one's child, presupposes the "call" to love and give to the child, simply because a "resistance" is what it is only in relation to a prior "call." Isn't an essential dimension of desire, then, the aspiration to live up to this call? Accordingly,

---

135. See Gilles Deleuze, *Pure Immanence*, 30: "Small children, through all their suffering and weakness, are infused with an immanent life that is pure power and even bliss." For a metaphysical exploration of this topic, see Ferdinand Ulrich, "Man in the Beginning: Toward a Philosophical Anthropology of Childhood."

my desire for the resurrection is revealed at this level in the desire *to be wholly metamorphosed into self-giving and love,* and perhaps the desire for such metamorphosis is greater where one experiences one's selfish resistance to actually loving and actually giving. The resurrected body is the metamorphosis of a flesh wholly made for the other. Falque shows that self-giving love is in fact one of the chief traits of the resurrected flesh of Jesus: "The invitation to 'come and have breakfast' (John 21:12) is not that of a *hungry body*, which, after all, one could not really see as belonging to a resurrected being. It is that of *flesh transfigured*, which recalls that it was expressly made to *give*: Jesus came and 'took the bread and gave it to them, and did the same with the fish' (John 21:13)."[136] Note that, also in this case, the indirect and roundabout path that we have encountered earlier is essential to describe this aspect of the phenomenon of desire. The focus of my desire is not *on me*, and in this sense it can be claimed that I do not desire directly that my being is metamorphosed into perfect love for the other; rather, the focus of my desire is wholly and fully on the other. What I truly desire is to become capable of losing myself in the one I love, namely, of identifying myself with the one I love so perfectly that I may forget about my own happiness; that is, that *the perfect happiness of the beloved may become for me the reward that I do not seek and the rebirth that I have forgotten.* In conclusion, the desire for my resurrection may ultimately coincide with the totalizing desire for the resurrection of the child.

---

136. Falque, *Metamorphosis of Finitude*, 147; emphasis in original.

Conclusion

If this book has achieved anything at all, its contribution may be summed up in the idea that the negativity of death must be metaphysically guarded against all those philosophical pretensions that tend to cover up its burdensome, scandalous weight. Psychological and even spiritual distraction from the thought of death is too widely practiced and its value too evident to anyone to require being pointed out once again. However, after our philosophical intransigence has been humbled and made less pure by the simple recognition of this fact, we are still left wondering up to what point will we be willing to devise metaphysical systems, ingenious thanatologies, in which death is given "a human face."

According to Heidegger, "Higher than actuality stands *possibility*."[1] That for him "death is the possibility of the absolute impossibility of Dasein"[2] means precisely that death *is* for Dasein never as an objective presence, i.e., the actualization of a possibility, but rather precisely as an ultimate impossibility. In being toward death, Dasein relates to the world of ontically actualizable possibilities and to itself through the mediation of the impossible, of death. It is this specific form of the impossible that gives shape to Dasein, its care, its being-in-the-world, etc. Most importantly, it is the impossibility of death the vantage from which Dasein is rescued from getting lost in a world of purely ontic possibilities. Its temporal ecstasis must be ultimately rooted in a future that is the removal of any future, that is, the always "imminent" possibility of the impossibility of life. But here lies Heidegger's fundamental thesis: in being toward death, Dasein enacts its being "more" than any and all the ontic possibilities that could ever be turned into actuality. It is through death that

1. Heidegger, *Being and Time*, 34; emphasis in original.
2. Heidegger, *Being and Time*, 232.

Dasein "exists" its ontological excess with respect to beings; the being of beings is given as Dasein's embrace of its own impossibility. Heidegger's nihilism reaches here one of its defining points (a point which will never be rejected later on, but only deepened, expanded, and articulated in different directions): the impossibility of death possibilized in being toward death is the ecstatic and existential realization of the ontological difference.[3] It does not seem unfair to state that, for Heidegger, the glory of Dasein is the dying man.

As a consequence, as some commentators have acutely remarked, while it remains true that for Heidegger higher than actuality stands possibility, it is even truer that for him "higher than possibility stands impossibility."[4] The impossibility of death plays in Heidegger's thought the role of a constitutive condition of possibility of Dasein. Since according to him impossibility is essentially identified with death, the positivity of being and the negativity of nonbeing collapse into each other. Man can truly be who he is only by becoming one with his own death. The "shepherd of being" can love his sheep only by loving death more.

The notion of impossibility offers itself, it seems to me, as an ideal point of reflection to conclude this work—a conclusion which cannot be other than a beginning for further and hopefully renewed thinking. In fact, the meaning of impossibility changes radically depending on the framework within which it is considered. For Heidegger, whose hermeneutical phenomenology remains faithful to a methodological atheism, the impossibility of death is what Dasein is called to possibilize in being toward death. For the transhumanist, who is generally committed to a naturalistic worldview, the impossibility of death is possibilized by being immortalized through the technoscientific indefinite control, containment, and deferral of perishing. The extended and expanded life of the transhumanist vision turns the Heideggerian Dasein into something very different from what Heidegger envisioned, but not so different that a hidden, fundamental commonality between the two views cannot be noticed: for Heidegger, death must be kept at the center of care for man to be who he is; for the transhumanist, death must be kept at the center of the concern of civilization for technoscience to unleash its full potential; in both cases, nihilism requires that the impossibility of death is possibilized as a key resource.

3. Heidegger, *Basic Problems of Phenomenology*, 319.
4. Esposito, "Impossibilità come trascendentale," 310.

CONCLUSION

However, for a thought that is at least open to the possibility of Christian revelation and grace, impossibility acquires a different meaning by presenting a twofold nature. In this context, impossibility is, at once, the mark of that radical negativity of death which cannot be embraced by man and, simultaneously, the identifying feature of the object of human desire; the desire for that credible impossible, i.e., the resurrection of the flesh in the resurrected God made man, to which it would be unreasonable not to consent. It is this specific form of the impossible that ought to give shape to the philosophical life. And that which is unreasonable not to embrace in the depth of one's desire may be super-rationally confirmed in faith for those who believe, because "what is impossible for human beings is possible for God" (Luke 18:27). For those who are given the gift of faith, impossibility stands higher than possibility, neither in the sense of Heidegger's ontological nihilism, nor in the sense of the transhumanist's technoscientific utopia, but because the inexhaustible actuality of the event of Christ embraces and transfigures them both, so that man may "hope against hope" (Rom 4:18).

Man's excess beyond himself and the world is not explained by his living in the possibilized impossibility of death. A more modest, but also more sound, philosophy must recognize that the negativity of death is an evil of privation and not, for lack of better phrase, a negativity of excess. Man is a sign, to himself and to the world, of a mysterious but radical positivity that exceeds himself and the world, a positivity that shines the more in the midst of the perceived scandalous contradiction of a dying life.

Bibliography

Adorno, Theodor W. *Against Epistemology: A Metacritique*. Translated by Willis Domingo. Cambridge, MA: MIT Press, 1986.
Agazzi, Evandro, and Anna-Teresa Tymieniecka. "The Complex Phenomenon of Illness." In *Life—Interpretation and the Sense of Illness Within the Human Condition: Medicine and Philosophy in Dialogue*, edited by Evandro Agazzi and Anna-Teresa Tymieniecka, xi–xiii. Analecta Husserliana 72. Dordrecht: Springer, 2001.
Amerini, Fabrizio. *Aquinas on the Beginning and End of Human Life*. Cambridge, MA: Harvard University Press, 2013.
Aquinas, Thomas. *Commentary on Metaphysics*. Translated by John P. Rowan. Latin-English Opera Omnia 50–51. Steubenville, OH: Emmaus Academic, 2020.
———. *Commentary on Philippians*. Aquinas, n.d. https://aquinas.cc/la/en/~Philip.
———. *Commentary on the Book of Causes*. Translated by Vincent A. Guagliardo et al. Washington DC: Catholic University of America Press, 1996.
———. *Disputed Questions on the Power of God*. Translated by Lawrence Shapcote. Latin-English Opera Omnia 25. Steubenville, OH: Emmaus Academic, 2023.
———. *Disputed Questions on the Soul*. Aquinas, n.d. https://aquinas.cc/la/en/~QDeAn.
———. *Disputed Questions on Truth*. Aquinas, n.d. https://aquinas.cc/la/en/~QDeVer.
———. *The Division and Methods of the Sciences: Questions V and VI of His Commentary on the "De Trinitate" of Boethius*. Translated by Armand Maurer. Toronto: Pontifical Institute of Medieval Studies, 1963.
———. "On the Eternity of the World." Aquinas, n.d. https://aquinas.cc/la/en/~DeAeternit.
———. *Sentences Commentary*. Aquinas, n.d. https://aquinas.cc/la/en/~Sent.I.
———. *Summa Contra Gentiles*. Aquinas, n.d. https://aquinas.cc/la/en/~SCG1.
Arendt, Hannah. *Crises of the Republic*. New York: Harcourt, Brace Jovanovich, 1972.
———. *The Human Condition*. Chicago: University of Chicago Press, 1958.
———. *Origins of Totalitarianism*. New York: Harcourt, Brace and World, 1966.
Ariès, Philippe. *The Hour of Our Death*. Translated by Helen Weaver. New York: First Vintage, 1981.
———. *Western Attitudes Toward Death: From the Middle Ages to the Present*. Translated by Patricia M. Ranum. Baltimore: Johns Hopkins University Press, 1975.
Aristotle. *Metaphysics*. Translated by C. D. C. Reeve. Indianapolis: Hackett, 2016.
———. *Nicomachean Ethics*. Translated by Joe Sachs. Focus Philosophical Library Series. Indianapolis: Focus, 2002.

BIBLIOGRAPHY

———. *On the Soul*. In *The Basic Works of Aristotle*, edited by Richard McKeon, 533–603. Modern Library Classics. New York: Modern Library, 2001.

———. *Rhetoric; Poetics*. Translated by W. Rhys Roberts and Ingram Bywater. Modern Library 246. New York: Modern Library, 1954.

Augustine. *City of God*. Translated by Henry Bettenson. Penguin Classics. London: Penguin, 2003.

———. *Confessions*. Translated by Henry Chadwick. Oxford World's Classics. New York: Oxford University Press, 2008.

———. *Confessions*. Edited and revised by Mark Vessey. Translated by Albert C. Outler. Barnes & Noble Classics Series. New York: Barnes and Noble, 2007.

Bacon, Francis. *The New Organon*. Edited by Lisa Jardine and Michael Silverthorne. Cambridge Texts in the History of Philosophy. New York: Cambridge University Press, 2003.

Baker, Lynne Rudder. *Persons and Bodies: A Constitution View*. Cambridge Studies in Philosophy. Cambridge: Cambridge University Press, 2000.

Balthasar, Hans Urs, von. *The Action*. Translated by Graham Harrison. Vol. 4 of *Theo-Drama: Theological Dramatic Theory*. San Francisco: Ignatius, 1994.

———. *The Christian and Anxiety*. Translated by Dennis D. Martin and Michael J. Miller. San Francisco: Ignatius, 2000.

———. "The Descent into Hell." In *Explorations in Theology*, translated by Edward T. Oakes, 4:401–14. San Francisco: Ignatius, 1995.

———. *The Last Act*. Translated by Graham Harrison. Vol. 5 of *Theo-Drama: Theological Dramatic Theory*. San Francisco: Ignatius, 1998.

———. "Movement Toward God." In *Explorations in Theology*, translated by Brian McNeil, 3:15–55. San Francisco: Ignatius, 1993.

———. *The Realm of Metaphysics in Antiquity*. Translated by Brian McNeil et al. Vol. 4 of *The Glory of the Lord: A Theological Aesthetics*. San Francisco: Ignatius, 1989.

———. *The Realm of Metaphysics in the Modern Age*. Translated by Oliver Davies et al. Vol. 5 of *The Glory of the Lord: A Theological Aesthetics*. San Francisco: Ignatius, 1991.

———. "A Resumé of My Thought." *Comm* 15 (1988) 468–73.

———. *A Theology of History*. San Francisco: Ignatius, 1994.

Balthasar, Hans Urs von, and Joseph Ratzinger. *Mary: The Church at the Source*. Translated by Adrian Walker. San Francisco: Ignatius, 2005.

Balthasar, Hans Urs von, and Adrienne von Speyr. *To the Heart of the Mystery of Redemption*. San Francisco: Ignatius, 2010.

Barzaghi, Giuseppe. "Eternal Design-Mystery: The Simultaneity of Inspection." *DivThom* 126 (2023) 221–42.

———. *Lo sguardo della sofferenza*. Bologna: ESD, 2011.

Bauman, Zygmunt. *Mortality, Immortality, and Other Life Strategies*. Cambridge, UK: Polity, 1992.

Becker, Lawrence C. "Human Being: The Boundaries of the Concept." *Philosophy & Public Affairs* 4 (1975) 334–59.

Benjamin, Walter. "Theses on the Philosophy of History." In *Illuminations: Essays and Reflections*, translated by Harry Zohn, 253–64. New York: Schocken, 2007.

Bergson, Henri. *Creative Evolution*. Translated by Arthur Mitchel. New York: Random House, 1944.

BIBLIOGRAPHY

Bernanos, George. "Dialogues of the Carmelites." Translated by Michael Legat. In *The Heroic Face of Innocence: Three Stories*, 39–150. Grand Rapids: Eerdmans, 1999.

Betz, John R. *Christ, the Logos of Creation: An Essay in Analogical Metaphysics*. Renewal Within Tradition. Steubenville, OH: Emmaus Academic, 2023.

———. "Mere Metaphysics: An Ecumenical Proposal." *Modern Theology* 35 (2019) 683–705.

Bichat, Xavier. *Recherches physiologiques sur la vie et la mort*. 3rd ed. Paris: Brosson/Gabon, 1805. https://archive.org/details/recherchesphysiooobich/page/n7/mode/2up.

Bieler, Martin. "The Cross of Christ as a Trinitarian Act." *Ang* 98 (2021) 151–88.

———. "Introduction." In *Homo Abyssus: The Drama of the Question of Being*, by Ferdinand Ulrich, translated by D. C. Schindler, xlix–li. Washington, DC: Humanum Academic, 2018.

Bishop, Jeffrey P. "Transhumanism, Metaphysics, and the Posthuman God." *Journal of Medicine and Philosophy* 35 (2010) 700–720.

Bloch, Ernst. *The Principle of Hope*. Translated by Neville Plaice et al. 3 vols. Cambridge, MA: MIT Press, 1986.

Blondel, Maurice. *Action (1893): Essay on a Critique of Life and a Science of Practice*. Translated by Oliva Blanchette. Notre Dame, IN: University of Notre Dame Press, 2007.

———. *Philosophical Exigencies of Christian Religion*. Translated by Oliva Blanchette. Notre Dame, IN: University of Notre Dame Press, 2021.

Bloy, Léon. *The Pilgrim of the Absolute*. Edited by Raissa Maritain. Translated by John Coleman and Harry L. Binsse. Tacoma: Cluny, 2017.

Boethius, Anicius Manlius Severinus. *The Consolation of Philosophy*. Translated by P. G. Walsh. Oxford World's Classics. New York: Oxford University Press, 2008.

Boros, Ladislaus. *The Mystery of Death*. New York: Herder and Herder, 1965.

Bostrom, Nick. "A History of Transhumanist Thought." *Journal of Evolution and Technology* 14 (2005) 1–25.

———. *The Transhumanist FAQ: A General Introduction*. Nick Bostrom, 2003. Version 2.1. https://nickbostrom.com/views/transhumanist.pdf.

Botturi, Francesco. "L'uomo di fronte alla sofferenza." *DivThom* 106 (2003) 196–203.

Bowen-Moore, Patricia. *Hannah Arendt's Philosophy of Natality*. New York: St. Martin's Press, 1989.

Bradley, Ben, et al., eds. *The Oxford Handbook of Philosophy of Death*. Oxford Handbooks. New York: Oxford University Press, 2013.

Brague, Rémi. *Anchors in the Heavens: The Metaphysical Infrastructure of Human Life*. Translated by Brian Lapsa. South Bend, IN: St. Augustine's, 2019.

———. *Après l'humanisme: L'image chrétienne de l'homme*. Paris: Salvator, 2022.

———. "The Flesh: A Medieval Model of Subjectivity." In *The Legend of the Middle Ages: Philosophical Explorations of Medieval Christianity, Judaism, and Islam*, translated by Lydia G. Cochrane, 91–106. Chicago: University of Chicago Press, 2009.

Brand, Dennis J., trans. *The Book of Causes (Liber de Causis)*. Milwaukee: Marquette University Press, 2014.

Braun, David. "Indexicals." *Stanford Encyclopedia of Philosophy*, Sept. 14, 2001; revised Jan. 16, 2015. Edited by Edward N. Zalta. https://plato.stanford.edu/entries/indexicals/.

Brook, Angus. "Thomas Aquinas on the Effects of Original Sin: A Philosophical Analysis." *HeyJ* 59 (2018) 721–32.

Brotherton, Joshua R. *One of the Trinity Has Suffered: Balthasar's Theology of Divine Suffering in Dialogue*. Renewal Within Tradition. Steubenville, OH: Emmaus Academic, 2019.

Brown, Deborah J., and Calvin G. Normore. "Automata." In *Descartes and the Ontology of Everyday Life*, 63–93. New York: Oxford University Press, 2019.

Buber, Martin. *Il problema dell'uomo*. Translated by Fabio Sante Pignagnoli and Irene Kajon. Genoa: Marietti, 2004.

Canetti, Elias. *Il libro contro la morte*. Translated by Renata Colorni et al. Milan: Adelphi, 2017.

———. *The Human Province*. Translated by Joachim Neugroschel. New York: Seabury, 1978.

Carel, Havi. *Phenomenology of Illness*. Oxford: Oxford University Press, 2016.

Carrasco, María A., and Luca Valera. "Diagnosing Death: The 'Fuzzy Area' Between Life and Decomposition." *Theoretical Medicine and Bioethics* 42 (2021) 1–24.

Carter, W. R. "Will I Be a Dead Person?" *Philosophy and Phenomenological Research* 59 (1999) 167–71.

Cavanaugh, William T. *Being Consumed: Economics and Christian Desire*. Grand Rapids: Eerdmans, 2008.

Chesterton, G. K. *Orthodoxy*. N.p.: Snow Ball Classics, 2015.

Cioran, Emile M. *Un apolide metafisico: Conversazioni*. Milan: Adelphi, 2004.

Clarke, W. Norris. *The One and the Many: A Contemporary Thomistic Metaphysics*. Notre Dame, IN: University of Notre Dame Press, 2001.

Claudel, Paul. *The Tidings Brought to Mary*. Translated by Louise Morgan Sill. N.p.: Human Adventure, 2009.

Condorcet, Antoine-Nicholas de. *Outlines of an Historical View of the Progress of the Human Mind*. London: Johnson, 1795.

Cordeiro, José Luis, and David Wood. *The Death of Death: The Scientific Possibility of Physical Immortality and Its Moral Defense*. Copernicus Books. Cham, Switz.: Springer, 2018.

Corte, Marcel de. *Fenomenologia dell'autodistruttore: Saggio sull'uomo occidentale contemporaneo*. Translated by Roberto Antonetto. Torino: Borla, 1967.

Cullman, Oscar. *Immortality of the Soul or Resurrection of the Dead? The Witness of the New Testament*. Eugene, OR: Wipf & Stock, 2000.

Cunningham, Conor. *Genealogy of Nihilism: Philosophies of Nothing and the Difference of Theology*. Routledge Radical Orthodox. New York: Routledge, 2002.

Dante Alighieri. *La divina commedia*. Torino: UTET, 2003.

Dastur, Françoise. *Death: An Essay on Finitude*. Translated by John Llewelyn. London: Athlone, 1996.

———. *How Are We to Confront Death? An Introduction to Philosophy*. Translated by Robert Vallier. Perspectives in Continental Philosophy. New York: Fordham University Press, 2012.

De Grey, Aubrey D. N. J. "Suffocating Deathism: We have Given It the Oxygen of Publicity for Long Enough." *Rejuvenation Research* 23 (2020) 365–66.

De Grey, Aubrey, and Michael Rae. *Ending Aging: The Rejuvenation Breakthroughs That Could Reverse Human Aging in Our Lifetime*. New York: St. Martin's, 2007.

BIBLIOGRAPHY

De Haan, Daniel D., and Brandon Dahm. "After Survivalism and Corruptionism: Separated Souls as Incomplete Persons." *Quaestiones Disputatae* 10 (2020) 161–76.

Deleuze, Gilles. *Pure Immanence: Essays on A Life*. Translated by Anne Boyman. New York: Urzone, 2002.

Del Noce, Augusto. "Eric Voegelin and the Critique of the Idea of Modernity." In *The Crisis of Modernity*, edited and translated by Carlo Lancellotti, 287–306. McGill-Queen's Studies in the History of Ideas Series 64. Montreal: McGill-Queen's University Press, 2014.

———. *The Problem of Atheism*. Edited and translated by Carlo Lancellotti. McGill-Queen's Studies in the History of Ideas Series 84. Montreal: McGill-Queen's University Press, 2021.

———. "Violence and Modern Gnosticism." In *The Crisis of Modernity*, edited and translated by Carlo Lancellotti, 19–48. McGill-Queen's Studies in the History of Ideas Series 64. Montreal: McGill-Queen's University Press, 2014.

DeLorenzo, Leonard J. *Work of Love: A Theological Reconstruction of the Communion of Saints*. Notre Dame, IN: University of Notre Dame Press, 2017.

Derrida, Jacques. *Aporias*. Translated by Thomas Dutoit. Meridian: Crossing Aesthetics. Stanford, CA: Stanford University Press, 1993.

———. "A Certain Possible Impossibility of Saying the Event." *Critical Inquiry* 2 (2007) 441–61.

Descartes, René. *A Discourse on the Method of Correctly Conducting One's Reason and Seeking Truth in the Sciences*. Translated by Ian Maclean. Oxford World's Classics. New York: Oxford University Press, 2006.

Desmond, William. *Desire, Dialectic, and Otherness: An Essay on Origins*. 2nd ed. Eugene, OR: Cascade, 2014.

Dubilet, Alex. *The Self-Emptying Subject: Kenosis and Immanence, Medieval to Modern*. New York: Fordham University Press, 2018.

Eberl, Jason T. "Do Human Persons Persist Between Death and Resurrection?" In *Metaphysics and God: Essays in Honor of Eleonore Stump*, edited by Kevin Timpe, 188–205. Routledge Studies in the Philosophy of Religion. New York: Routledge, 2009.

———. "Enhancing the *Imago Dei*: Can a Christian Be a Transhumanist?" *Christian Bioethics* 28 (2022) 76–93.

———. *The Nature of Human Persons: Metaphysics and Bioethics*. Notre Dame Studies in Medical Ethics and Bioethics. Notre Dame, IN: University of Notre Dame Press, 2020.

———. "A Thomistic Understanding of Human Death." *Bioethics* 19 (2005) 29–48.

Eckhart, Meister. "Unus Deus at Pater Omnium." In *I sermoni*, Translated by Marco Vannini, 224–29. Milan: Paoline, 2002.

Epicurus. "Letter to Menoeceus." In *The Stoic and Epicurean Philosophers: The Complete Extant Writings of Epicurus, Epictetus, Lucretius and Marcus Aurelius*, edited Whitney J. Oates, 30–34. Translated by Cyril Bailey. Modern Library Giant. New York: Modern Library, 1940.

Esposito, Costantino. "L'impossibilità come trascendentale: Per una storia del concetto di impossibile da Suárez a Heidegger." *Archivio di Filosofia* 78 (2010) 297–313.

Faller, Adolf. "Biologisches von Sterben und Tod." *Anima* 11 (1956) 260–68.

Falque, Emmanuel. *The Guide to Gethsemane: Anxiety, Suffering, Death.* Translated by George Hughes. Perspectives in Continental Philosophy. New York: Fordham University Press, 2019.

———. *The Metamorphosis of Finitude: An Essay on Birth and Resurrection.* Translated by George Hughes. Perspectives in Continental Philosophy. New York: Fordham University Press, 2012.

———. "Suffering Death." In *The Role of Death in Life: A Multidisciplinary Examination of the Relationship Between Life and Death,* edited by John Behr and Conor Cunningham, 45–55. Cambridge: Clarke & Co., 2015.

Feldman, Fred. *Confrontations with the Reaper: A Philosophical Study of the Nature and Value of Death.* New York: Oxford University Press, 1992.

———. "The Termination Thesis." *Midwest Studies in Philosophy* 24 (2000) 98–115.

Feser, Edward. "Aquinas on the Human Soul." In *The Blackwell Companion to Substance Dualism,* edited by Jonathan J. Loose et al., 88–101. Blackwell Companions to Philosophy. Oxford: Wiley-Blackwell, 2018.

Feuerbach, Ludwig. *The Essence of Christianity.* Translated by George Eliot. Dover Philosophical Classics. Mineola, NY: Dover, 2008.

Flannery, Kevin L. "Defining Death with Aristotle and Aquinas." In *Contemporary Controversies in Catholic Bioethics,* edited by Jason T. Eberl, 389–403. Philosophy and Medicine 127. Cham, Switz.: Springer, 2017.

Foucault, Michel. *The Birth of the Clinic: An Archaeology of Medical Perception.* Translated by A. M. Sheridan. 3rd ed. Routledge Classics. London: Routledge, 2003.

Francescotti, Robert. "Surviving Death: How to Refute Termination Theses." *Inquiry* 61 (2018) 178–97.

Francis of Assisi. "The Canticle of the Sun." Franciscan Friars, 1225. https://franciscanfriarscresson.org/the-canticle-of-the-sun/.

Francis, Pope. "*Laudato Si'*: On Care for Our Common Home." Vatican, May 24, 2015. https://www.vatican.va/content/francesco/en/encyclicals/documents/papa-francesco_20150524_enciclica-laudato-si.html.

Franks, Angela. "Thomistic-Balthasarian Comments on Thomas Joseph White's *The Incarnate Lord.*" *NV* 20 (2022) 575–600.

Freud, Sigmund. *On the History of the Psycho-Analytic Movement; Papers on Metapsychology and Other Works.* Edited and translated by James Strachey. Vol. 14 of *The Standard Edition of the Complete Psychological Works of Sigmund Freud.* London: Hogarth and the Institute of Psycho-Analysis Press, 1957.

Fritsche, Johannes. *Historical Destiny and National Socialism in Heidegger's* Being and Time. Berkeley: University of California Press, 1999.

Fulton, Robert. *Death and Identity.* New York: Wiley, 1965.

Fumet, Stanislas. *L'impatience des limites: Petit traité du firmament.* Freiburg, Switz.: Librairie de l'Université, 1942.

Gadamer, Hans-Georg. "Death as a Question (1975)." In *Hermeneutics Between History and Philosophy: The Selected Writings of Hans-Georg Gadamer,* edited and translated by Pol Vandevelde and Arun Iyer, 1:59–70. London: Bloomsbury, 2019.

———. *The Enigma of Health: The Art of Healing in a Scientific Age.* Translated by Jason Gaiger and Nicholas Walker. Stanford, CA: Stanford University Press, 1996.

Geach, Peter. "Good and Evil." *Analysis* 17 (1956) 33–42.

Giesen, Klaus-Gerd. "Transhumanism as the Dominant Ideology of the Fourth Industrial Revolution." *Journal international de bioéthique et d'éthique des sciences* 29 (2018) 189–203.
Gilson, Étienne. *Being and Some Philosophers*. Toronto: Pontifical Institute of Medieval Studies, 1952.
———. *Christian Philosophy: An Introduction*. Toronto: Pontifical Institute of Medieval Studies, 1993.
Giussani, Luigi. *At the Origin of the Christian Claim*. Translated by Viviane Hewitt. Montreal: McGill-Queen's University Press, 1998.
Gonzales, Philip John Paul. *Reimagining the* Analogia Entis: *The Future of Erich Przywara's Christian Vision*. Interventions. Grand Rapids: Eerdmans, 2019.
Göpffarth, Julian. "Rethinking the German Nation as German Dasein: Intellectuals and Heidegger's Philosophy in Contemporary German New Right Nationalism." *Journal of Political Ideologies* 25 (2020) 248–73.
Gorer, Geoffrey. "The Pornography of Death." *Encounter* 5 (1955) 49–52.
Gorman, Michael. "Personhood, Potentiality, and Normativity." *American Catholic Philosophical Quarterly* 85 (2011) 483–98.
Granados, José. "The Suffering Body, Hope, and the Disclosure of the Future." *Comm* 36 (2009) 652–72.
———. "Toward a Theology of the Suffering Body." *Comm* 33 (2006) 540–63.
Guardini, Romano. *Diario: Appunti e testi dal 1942 al 1964*. Translated by Nerea Ponzanelli. Brescia: Morcelliana, 1983.
———. *The Last Things: Concerning Death, Purification After Death, Resurrection, Judgment, and Eternity*. Translated by Charlotte E. Forsyth and Grace B. Branham. Notre Dame, IN: University of Notre Dame Press, 1965.
———. *Lettere teologiche ad un amico: Intuizioni al limite della vita*. Milan: Vita e Pensiero, 1979.
———. *L'opposizione polare: Saggio per una filosofia del concreto vivente*. Translated by Giulio Colombi. Brescia: Morcelliana, 2022.
Hadjadj, Fabrice. *A moi la gloire*. Paris: Salvator, 2018.
———. *Farcela con la morte: Anti-metodo per vivere*. Translated by Anna Rita Vignati. Assisi, It.: Cittadella, 2009.
———. "Pourquoi donner la vie à un mortel? À propos d'une vulnérabilité radicale." In *L'éthique de la dépendance face au corps vulnérable*, edited by Bernard N. Schumacher, 71–94. Toulouse: Érès, 2019.
———. *The Resurrection: Experience Life in the Risen Christ*. Translated by Michael J. Miller. New York: Magnificat, 2016.
———. *Réussir sa mort: Anti-méthode pour vivre*. Paris: Renaissance, 2005.
Hadot, Pierre. *What Is Ancient Philosophy?* Translated by Michael Chase. Cambridge, MA: Harvard University Press, 2004.
Han, Byung-Chul. *Capitalism and the Death Drive*. Translated by Daniel Steuer. Cambridge, UK: Polity, 2021.
———. *Vita Contemplativa*. Translated by Daniel Steuer. Hoboken, NJ: Polity, 2024.
Hanby, Michael. "The Gospel of Creation and the Technocratic Paradigm: Reflections on a Central Teaching of *Laudato Si'*." *Comm* 42 (2015) 724–47.
———. "Homo Faber and/or Homo Adorans: On the Place of Human Making in a Sacramental Cosmos." *Comm* 38 (2011) 198–236.

Hart, David Bentley. "The Devil's March: *Creatio ex Nihilo*, the Problem of Evil, and a Few Dostoyevskian Meditations." In *Theological Territories: A David Bentley Hart Digest*, 77–97. Notre Dame, IN: University of Notre Dame Press, 2020.

Haycock, David Boyd. "Living Forever in Early Modern Europe: Sir Francis Bacon and the Project of Immortality." In *The Age of Projects*, edited by Maximillian E. Novak, 166–84. UCLA Clark Memorial Library. Toronto: University of Toronto Press, 2008.

Hayen, André. *L'intentionnel selon Saint Thomas*. Paris: Desclée de Brouwer, 1954.

Hegel, G. W. F. *Phenomenology of Spirit*. Translated by A. V. Miller. New York: Oxford University Press, 1977.

———. "Review of Jacobi's *Werke* (1816)." In *Heidelberg Writings: Journal Publications*, translated by Brady Bowman and Allen Speight, 3–31. Cambridge Hegel Translations. Cambridge: Cambridge University Press, 2009.

———. *Science of Logic*. Translated by George di Giovanni. New York: Cambridge University Press, 2010.

Heidegger, Martin. *The Basic Problems of Phenomenology*. Translated by Albert Hofstadter. Bloomington: Indiana University Press, 1982.

———. *Basic Writings*. Edited by David F. Krell. New York: Harper Collins, 2013.

———. *Being and Time*. Translated by Joan Stambauch. Revised by Dennis J. Schmidt. SUNY Series in Contemporary Continental Philosophy. Albany: SUNY Press, 1996.

———. *History of the Concept of Time: Prolegomena*. Translated by Theodore Kisiel. Bloomington: Indiana University Press, 1985.

———. *Off the Beaten Track*. Translated by Julian Young and Kenneth Haynes. Cambridge, UK: Cambridge University Press, 2002.

Hershenov, David. "Do Dead Bodies Pose a Problem for Biological Approaches to Personal Identity?" *Mind* 114 (2005) 31–59.

Hildebrand, Dietrich, von. *Jaws of Death: Gate of Heaven*. Translated by Alice von Hildebrand. Manchester, NH: Sophia Institute, 1991.

Hinshaw, Daniel. "The Kenosis of the Dying: An Invitation to Healing." In *The Role of Death in Life*, edited by John Behr and Conor Cunningham, 155–63. Cambridge: James Clarke & Co., 2015.

Holland, Henry Scott. *Death Is Nothing at All*. London: Souvenir, 2007.

Howsare, Rodney A. *Balthasar: A Guide for the Perplexed*. Guides for the Perplexed. London: T&T Clark, 2009.

Hugo, Victor. *Dernier jour d'un condamné*. In *Oeuvres completes: Roman*, 399–487. Paris: Laffont, 1985.

Illich, Ivan. *Limits to Medicine: Medical Nemesis; The Expropriation of Health*. London: Boyars, 1976.

Jalbert, John E. "Time, Death, and History in Simmel and Heidegger." *Human Studies* 26 (2003) 259–83.

Jankélévitch, Vladimir. *La mort*. Paris: Flammarion, 1977.

———. *Quelque part dans l'inachevé*. Paris: Gallimard, 1979.

John Paul II, Pope. "Address of the Holy Father John Paul II to the 18th International Congress of the Transplantation Society." Vatican, Aug. 29, 2000. https://www.vatican.va/content/john-paul-ii/en/speeches/2000/jul-sep/documents/hf_jp-ii_spe_20000829_transplants.html.

———. "*Evangelium Vitae*: On the Value and Inviolability of Human Life." Vatican, Mar. 25, 1995. https://www.vatican.va/content/john-paul-ii/en/encyclicals/documents/hf_jp-ii_enc_25031995_evangelium-vitae.html.

———. "*Fides et Ratio*: On the Relationship Between Faith and Reason." Vatican, Sept. 14, 1998. https://www.vatican.va/content/john-paul-ii/en/encyclicals/documents/hf_jp-ii_enc_14091998_fides-et-ratio.html.

———. "*Novo Millennio Ineunte*: At the Close of the Great Jubilee of the Year 2000." Vatican, Jan. 6, 2001. https://www.vatican.va/content/john-paul-ii/en/apost_letters/2001/documents/hf_jp-ii_apl_20010106_novo-millennio-ineunte.html.

Johnson, Mark. "Augustine and Aquinas on Original Sin: Doctrine, Authority, and Pedagogy." In *Aquinas the Augustinian*, edited by Michael Dauphinais et al., 145–58. Washington, DC: Catholic University of America, 2012.

Jonas, Hans. "The Burden and Blessing of Mortality." *Hastings Center Report* 22 (1992) 34–40.

———. *The Phenomenon of Life: Toward a Philosophical Biology*. Evanston, IL: Northwestern University Press, 2001.

Jones, David A. *Approaching the End: A Theological Exploration of Death and Dying*. Oxford Studies in Theological Ethics. Oxford: Oxford University Press, 2007.

Journet, Charles. *The Meaning of Evil*. Translated by Michael Barry. London: Chapman, 1963.

Jullien, François. *Resources of Christianity*. Translated by Pedro Rodriguez. Cambridge, UK: Polity, 2021.

Kagan, Shelly. *Death*. Open Yale Courses Series. New Haven, CT: Yale University Press, 2012.

Kalkavage, Peter. *The Logic of Desire: An Introduction to Hegel's Phenomenology of Spirit*. Philadelphia: Dry, 2007.

———. "Plato's *Phaedo* and the Care of Death." *Teaching Great Books* 2 (2000). http://seaver-faculty.pepperdine.edu/mgose/GBQuarterly/winter00/journal2.html.

Kamm, F. M. *Almost Over: Aging, Dying, Dead*. New York: Oxford University Press, 2020.

Kass, Leon R. "*L'Chaim* and Its Limits: Why Not Immortality?" *First Things*, May 2001. https://www.firstthings.com/article/2001/05/lchaim-and-its-limits-why-not-immortality.

Kierkegaard, Søren. *The Sickness unto Death*. Translated by Bruce H. Kirmmse. New York: Liveright, 2023.

Klima, Gyula. "The Semantic Principles Underlying Saint Thomas Aquinas's Metaphysics of Being." *Medieval Philosophy and Theology* 5 (1996) 87–141.

Knepper, Steven. "Gabriel Marcel: Mystery in an Age of Problems." In *Critics of Enlightenment Rationalism*, edited by Gene Callahan and Kenneth B. McIntyre, 125–37. Palgrave Studies in Classical Liberalism. Cham, Switz.: Palgrave MacMillan, 2020.

Kojève, Alexandre. *Introduction à la lecture de Hegel*. Paris: Gallimard, 1947.

Kripke, Saul A. "The First Person." In *Collected Papers*, 1:292–321. New York: Oxford University Press, 2011.

Kurzweil, Ray. *The Singularity Is Near: When Humans Transcend Biology*. London: Duckworth Overlook, 2008.

Lacan, Jacques. *The Ethics of Psychoanalysis: 1959–1960*. Edited by Jacques-Alain Miller. Translated by Dennis Porter. Seminar of Jacques Lacan 7. New York: Norton & Company, 1997.

———. *"The Triumph of Religion," Preceded by "Discourse to Catholics."* Translated by Bruce Fink. Cambridge, UK: Polity, 2013.

LaCocque, André. *The Trial of Innocence: Adam, Eve, and the Yahwist*. Eugene, OR: Cascade, 2006.

Lacoste, Jean-Yves. "Toward a Kenotic Treatment of the Question of Man." In *Experience and the Absolute: Disputed Questions on the Humanity of Man*, translated by Mark Raftery-Skehan, 168–94. Perspectives in Continental Philosophy. New York: Fordham University Press, 2004.

Landsberg, Paul-Louis. *The Experience of Death; The Moral Problem of Suicide*. Translated by Cynthia Rowland. New York: Philosophical Library, 1953.

Le Breton, David. *L'adieu au corps*. Paris: Métaillé, 2013.

Leget, Carlo. *Living with God: Thomas Aquinas on the Relation Between Life on Earth and "Life" After Death*. Thomas Instituut Utrecht. Leuven: Peeters, 1997.

Lepori, Mauro Giuseppe. *Si vive solo per morire?* Siena, It.: Cantagalli, 2016.

Levinas, Emmanuel. *Ethics and Infinity: Conversations with Phillippe Nemo*. Translated by Richard A. Cohen. Pittsburgh: Duquesne University Press, 1985.

———. *"Time and the Other" and Additional Essays*. Translated by Richard A. Cohen. Pittsburgh: Duquesne University Press, 1987.

———. *Totality and Infinity: An Essay on Exteriority*. Translated by Alphonso Lingis. Pittsburgh: Duquesne University Press, 1961.

Lewis, C. S. *Mere Christianity*. New York: Harper Collins, 2001.

———. *"The Weight of Glory" and Other Addresses*. New York: HarperOne, 2001.

Long, A. G. *Death and Immortality in Ancient Philosophy*. Cambridge: Cambridge University Press, 2019.

López, Antonio. *Gift and the Unity of Being*. Veritas. Eugene, OR: Cascade, 2014.

———. *Spirit's Gift: The Metaphysical Insight of Claude Bruaire*. Washington, DC: Catholic University of America Press, 2006.

Lucretius, Titus. *De rerum natura*. Translated by William H. D. Rouse. Revised by Martin F. Smith. LCL 181. Cambridge, MA: Harvard University Press, 1959.

Macdonald, Paul A. "In Defense of Aquinas's Adam: Original Justice, the Fall, and Evolution." *Zygon* 56 (2021) 454–66.

Mackie, David. "Personal Identity and Dead People." *Philosophical Studies* 95 (1999) 219–42.

Marcel, Gabriel. *Being and Having: An Existential Diary*. New York: Harper & Row, 1965.

———. "Death and Immortality." In *Homo Viator*, translated by Emma Craufurd and Paul Seaton, 282–96. South Bend, IN: St. Augustine's, 2010.

———. "On the Ontological Mystery." In *The Philosophy of Existentialism*, translated by Manya Harari, 9–46. New York: Citadel, 1970.

———. *Presence and Immortality*. Translated by Michael A. Machado. Pittsburgh: Duquesne University Press, 1967.

———. "Value and Immortality." In *Homo Viator*, translated by Emma Craufurd and Paul Seaton, 128–47. South Bend, IN: St. Augustine's, 2010.

Maritain, Jacques. *Integral Humanism: Temporal and Spiritual Problems of a New Christendom*. Translated by Joseph W. Evans. Notre Dame, IN: University of Notre Dame Press, 1973.

———. *A Preface to Metaphysics: Seven Lectures on Being.* New York: Mentor Omega, 1962.

McFarland, Ian. "The Fall and Sin." In *The Oxford Handbook of Systematic Theology*, edited by John Webster et al., 140–59. Oxford Handbooks. Oxford: Oxford University Press, 2007.

McMahan, Jeff. "Death and the Value of Life." In *The Metaphysics of Death*, edited by John Martin Fischer, 233–66. Stanford Series in Philosophy. Stanford, CA: Stanford University Press, 1993.

Melchiorre, Virgilio. *Sul senso della morte.* Brescia: Morcelliana, 1964.

Monsó, Susana. *Playing Possum: How Animals Understand Death.* Princeton, NJ: Princeton University Press, 2024.

Montaigne, Michel, de. *The Complete Essays.* Translated by M. A. Screech. Penguin Classics. London: Penguin, 1991.

More, Max, and Natasha Vita-More, eds. *The Transhumanist Reader: Classical and Contemporary Essays on the Science, Technology, and Philosophy of the Human Future.* Oxford: Wiley-Blackwell, 2013.

Morin, Edgar. *L'uomo e la morte.* Translated by Riccardo Mazzeo. Trento: Erickson, 2014.

Mothersill, Mary. "Death." In *Life and Meaning: A Philosophical Reader*, edited by Oswald Hanfling, 83–92. Oxford: Blackwell, 1989.

Murphy, Jeffrie G. "Rationality and the Fear of Death." In *The Metaphysics of Death*, edited by John Martin Fischer, 43–58. Stanford Series in Philosophy. Stanford, CA: Stanford University Press, 1993.

Nagel, Thomas. *Analytic Philosophy and Human Life.* New York: Oxford University Press, 2023.

———. "Death." In *Mortal Questions*, 1–10. New York: Cambridge University Press, 1979.

Nemo, Philippe. *Job and the Excess of Evil.* Translated by Michael Kigel. Pittsburgh: Duquesne University Press, 1998.

Niederhauser, Johannes A. *Heidegger on Death and Being: An Answer to the Seinsfrage.* Cham, Switz.: Springer Nature, 2021.

Nielsen, Cynthia R. "Gadamer on Death's Unintelligibility and the Overflow of Life." *Analecta Hermeneutica* 14 (2022) 1–15.

Nietzsche, Friedrich. *Beyond Good and Evil: Prelude to a Philosophy of the Future.* Edited by Rolf-Peter Horstmann and Judith Norman. Cambridge Texts in the History of Philosophy. New York: Cambridge University Press, 2002.

———. *On the Genealogy of Morality.* Translated by Maudemarie Clark and Alan. J. Swensen. Indianapolis: Hackett, 1998.

———. *Thus Spoke Zarathustra: A Book for All and None.* Translated by Thomas Common. New York: Random House, 1917.

Novello, Henry L. *Death as Transformation: A Contemporary Theology of Death.* Surrey: Ashgate, 2011.

Nussbaum, Martha C. *The Therapy of Desire: Theory and Practice in Hellenistic Ethics.* Princeton Classics. Princeton, NJ: Princeton University Press, 1994.

Oakes, Edward T. "The Internal Logic of Holy Saturday in the Theology of Hans Urs von Balthasar." *International Journal of Systematic Theology* 9 (2007) 184–99.

Oderberg, David S. *Real Essentialism.* Routledge Studies in Contemporary Philosophy. New York: Routledge, 2007.

BIBLIOGRAPHY

Olson, Eric T. *The Human Animal: Personal Identity Without Psychology.* Philosophy of Mind. New York: Oxford University Press, 1997.

O'Regan, Cyril. "Changing the Subject to Christ." *Church Life Journal*, Nov. 5, 2020. https://churchlifejournal.nd.edu/articles/changing-the-subject-to-christ/.

Oster, Stefan. "Thinking Love at the Heart of Things: The Metaphysics of Being as Love in the Work of Ferdinand Ulrich." *Comm* 37 (2010) 660–700.

Pascal, Blaise. *Thoughts.* Translated by W. F. Trotter. New York: Collier & Son, 1910.

Pasnau, Robert. *Thomas Aquinas on Human Nature: A Philosophical Study of "Summa Theologiae," 1a 75–89.* Cambridge: Cambridge University Press, 2004.

Pattison, George. *Heidegger on Death: A Critical Theological Essay.* Farnham, UK: Ashgate, 2013.

Paul VI, Pope. "*Gaudium et Spes*: Pastoral Constitution on the Church in the Modern World." Vatican, Dec. 7, 1965, https://www.vatican.va/archive/hist_councils/ii_vatican_council/documents/vat-ii_const_19651207_gaudium-et-spes_en.html.

Pegis, Anton. "The Separated Soul and Its Nature in St. Thomas." In *St Thomas Aquinas, 1274–1974: Commemorative Studies*, edited by Étienne Gilson et al., 131–58. Toronto: Pontifical Institute of Medieval Studies, 1974.

Péguy, Charles. *Basic Verities: Poetry and Prose.* Edited and translated by Julian Green. Providence: Cluny, 2019.

———. *Notes on Bergson and Descartes: Philosophy, Christianity, and Modernity in Contestation.* Translated by Bruce K. Ward. Veritas. Eugene, OR: Cascade, 2019.

Peirce, Charles S. "Evolutionary Love." In *The Essential Peirce*, edited by Nathan Houser and Christian Kloesel, 1:352–71. Indianapolis: Indiana University Press, 1992.

Petrosino, Silvano. "Is Creation a Negation?" *Comm* 28 (2001) 311–23.

———. "Perire, morire, appartenere alla morte." Unpublished manuscript, last modified October 20, 2024. Microsoft Word file.

Pickstock, Catherine. *After Writing: On the Liturgical Consummation of Philosophy.* Oxford: Blackwell, 1998.

Pieper, Josef. *The Concept of Sin.* Translated by Edward T. Oakes. South Bend, IN: St. Augustine's, 2001.

———. *Death and Immortality.* Translated by Richard Winston and Clara Winston. New York: Herder and Herder, 1969.

———. "*Leisure: The Basis of Culture*"; *Including "The Philosophical Act."* Translated by Alexander Dru. San Francisco: Ignatius, 2009.

Pippin, Robert B. *Hegel on Self-Consciousness: Desire and Death in the "Phenomenology of Spirit."* Princeton Monographs in Philosophy. Princeton, NJ: Princeton University Press, 2011.

Plato. *Phaedo.* Translated by Eva Brann et al. Indianapolis: Focus, 1998.

———. *Phaedrus.* In "*The Collected Dialogues*"; *Including the "Letters,"* edited by Edith Hamilton and Huntington Cairns, 475–525. Bollingen Series. Princeton, NJ: Princeton University Press, 2009.

Przywara, Erich. *Analogia Entis: Metaphysics; Original Structure and Universal Rhythm.* Translated by John R. Betz and David Bentley Hart. Ressourcement: Retrieval and Renewal in Catholic Thought. Grand Rapids: Eerdmans, 2014.

Pseudo-Dionysius. *The Complete Works.* Translated by Colm Luibheid. Classics of Western Spirituality. New York: Paulist, 1987.

Purtill, Richard. "The Intelligibility of Disembodied Survival." *Christian Scholar's Review* 5 (1975) 3–22.

BIBLIOGRAPHY

Quevedo, Francisco, de. *Los sueños II*. Edited by Julio Cejador y Frauca. Madrid: Lectura, 1916. https://babel.hathitrust.org/cgi/pt?id=mdp.39015004272392&seq=7.

Quine, W. V. O. "On What There Is." In *From a Logical Point of View: Nine Logico-Philosophical Essays*, 1–19. New York: Harper and Row, 1963.

Rachels, James. *The End of Life: Euthanasia and Morality*. Studies in Bioethics. Oxford: Oxford University Press, 1986.

Rahner, Karl. *On the Theology of Death*. Translated by Charles H. Hankey. New York: Herder and Herder, 1961.

Ratcliffe, Susan, ed. *Oxford Essential Quotations*. Oxford: Oxford University Press, 2016.

Ratzinger, Joseph (Benedict XVI). *The Divine Project: Reflections on Creation and the Church*. Translated by Chase Faucheux. San Francisco: Ignatius, 2022.

———. *Eschatology: Death and Eternal Life*. Translated by Michael Waldstein and Aidan Nichols. Vol. 9 of *Dogmatic Theology*. Washington, DC: Catholic University of America Press, 1988.

Reichlin, Massimo. "The Experience of Illness and the Meaning of Death." In *Life—Interpretation and the Sense of Illness Within the Human Condition: Medicine and Philosophy in Dialogue*, edited by Evandro Agazzi and Anna-Teresa Tymieniecka, 81–95. Analecta Husserliana 72. Dordrecht: Springer, 2001.

Remenyi, Matthias. "Death as the Limit to Life and Thought: A Thanatological Outline." *HeyJ* 55 (2014) 94–109.

Ricoeur, Paul. *History and Truth*. Translated by Charles A. Kelbley. Evanston, IL: Northwestern University Press, 1965.

———. *Living Up to Death*. Translated by David Pellauer. Chicago: University of Chicago Press, 2009.

Robinette, Brian D. *Grammars of Resurrection: A Christian Theology of Presence and Absence*. New York: Herder and Herder, 2009.

Roessiger, Ursula L. "Hegelian Nihilism and the Christian Narrative: On Slavoj Žižek and John Milbank's Readings of Hegel's Philosophy of Religion." *HeyJ* 60 (2019) 244–59.

Romano, Claude. *L'événement et le temps*. Paris: PUF, 1999.

Rosenbaum, Stephen E. "How to Be Dead and Not Care: A Defense of Epicurus." In *The Metaphysics of Death*, edited by John Martin Fischer, 119–34. Stanford Series in Philosophy. Stanford, CA: Stanford University Press, 1993.

Rosenzweig, Franz. *The Star of Redemption*. Translated by Barbara Galli. Modern Jewish Philosophy and Religion: Translations and Critical Studies. Madison: University of Wisconsin Press, 2005.

Rousseau, Mary F. "Elements of a Thomistic Philosophy of Death." *Thomist* 43 (1979) 581–602.

Sadler, Gregory B., ed. and trans. *Reason Fulfilled by Revelation: The 1930s Christian Philosophy Debates in France*. Washington, DC: Catholic University of America Press, 2011.

Sànchez Sorondo, Marcelo, ed. "Why the Concept of Brain Death Is Valid as a Definition of Death: Statement by the Pontifical Academy of Sciences and Response to Objections." Special issue, Pontifical Academy of Sciences Extra Series 31 (2008). https://www.pas.va/content/dam/casinapioiv/pas/pdf-volumi/extra-series/es31pas.pdf.

Sartre, Jean-Paul. *Being and Nothingness: An Essay on Phenomenological Ontology.* Translated by Hazel B. Barnes. London: Routledge, 2003.

———. *Notebooks for an Ethics.* Translated by David Pellauer. Chicago: University of Chicago Press, 1992.

Scheler, Max. *Morte e sopravvivenza.* Translated by Edoardo Simonotti. Brescia: Morcelliana, 2012.

Scherer, Georg. *Il problema della morte nella filosofia.* Translated by Giuliano Sansonetti. Brescia: Queriniana, 1995.

Schindler, D. C. "*Analogia Naturae*: What Does Inanimate Matter Contribute to the Meaning of Life?" *Comm* 38 (2011) 657–80.

———. *Freedom from Reality: The Diabolical Character of Modern Liberty.* Catholic Ideas for a Secular World. Notre Dame, IN: University of Notre Dame Press, 2017.

———. "'Guardians of Metaphysics': The Task of Christian Philosophy in the Twenty-First Century." In *Restoring Ancient Beauty: The Revival of Thomistic Theology,* edited by James F. Keating, 167–80. Washington, DC: Catholic University of America Press, 2023.

———. "Metaphysics as Prayer: Introducing Ferdinand Ulrich." *Modern Theology* 40 (2023) 172–93.

———. *Plato's Critique of Impure Reason: On Goodness and Truth in the "Republic."* Washington, DC: Catholic University of America Press, 2008.

Schmitz, Kenneth L. *The Gift: Creation.* Aquinas Lecture, 1982. Milwaukee: Marquette University Press, 1982.

———. *The Recovery of Wonder: The New Freedom and the Asceticism of Power.* McGill-Queen's Studies in the History of Ideas 39. Montreal: McGill-Queen's University Press, 2005.

Schumacher, Bernard N. *Death and Mortality in Contemporary Philosophy.* Translated by Michael J. Miller. New York: Cambridge University Press, 2011.

Sertillanges, Antonin-Gilbert. *L'idée de création et ses retentissments en philosophie.* Paris: Aubier, 1945.

Simmel, Georg. "The Metaphysics of Death." *Theory, Culture & Society* 24 (2007) 72–77. https://doi.org/10.1177/0263276407084474.

Singh, Raj R. *Heidegger, World, and Death.* Lanham, MD: Lexington, 2013.

Smith, Randall B. *From Here to Eternity: Reflections on Death, Immortality, and the Resurrection of the Body.* Steubenville, OH: Emmaus Road, 2022.

Smith Gilson, Caitlin. "Heaven and the Transcendental Meaning of Death." *Church Life Journal,* Dec. 12, 2022. https://churchlifejournal.nd.edu/articles/heaven-and-the-transcendental-meaning-of-death/.

Snowdon, Paul. "Animalism and the Lives of Human Animals." *Southern Journal of Philosophy* 52 (2014) 171–84.

Spaemann, Robert. "Is Brain Death the Death of a Human Person?" *Comm* 38 (2011) 326–40.

Spencer, Mark K. "Aristotelian Substance and Personalistic Subjectivity." *International Philosophical Quarterly* 55 (2015) 145–64.

———. "Divine Causality and Created Freedom: A Thomistic Personalist View." *NV* 14 (2016) 919–63.

———. *The Irreducibility of the Human Person: A Catholic Synthesis.* Washington, DC: Catholic University of America Press, 2022.

———. "A Reexamination of the Hylomorphic Theory of Death." *Review of Metaphysics* 63 (2010) 843–70.

Speyr, Adrienne, von. *Meditations on John 1–5*. Translated by Lucia Wiedenhöver and Alexander Dru. Vol. 1 of *The Word Becomes Flesh*. San Francisco: Ignatius, 1994.

———. *The Mystery of Death*. Translated by Graham Harrison. San Francisco: Ignatius, 1988.

Stango, Marco. "Culture: Techne and Contemplation." *Logos* 26 (2023) 105–18.

———. "A Modern Genealogy of the Metaphysics of Information." *Comm* 50 (2023) 553–86.

———. "Mortality in the Light of Synechism: A Peircean Approach to Death." *Transactions of the Charles S. Peirce Society* 55 (2019) 387–407.

———. "Understanding Hylomorphic Dualism." *Proceedings of the American Catholic Philosophical Association* 91 (2019) 145–58.

———. "Wittgenstein, Peirce, and Death." *Idealistic Studies* 49 (2019) 45–63.

Stein, Edith. *Finite and Eternal Being: An Attempt at an Ascent to the Meaning of Being*. Translated by Walter Redmond. The Complete Works, Critical English Edition. Washington, DC: ICS, 2023.

Steinhart, Eric C. "Digital Theology: Is the Resurrection Virtual?" In *A Philosophical Exploration of New and Alternative Religious Movements*, edited by Morgan Luck, 133–52. Farnham, UK: Ashgate, 2012.

———. "Naturalism." In *A Companion to Atheism and Philosophy*, edited by Graham Oppy, 152–65. Blackwell Companions to Philosophy. Hoboken: Wiley-Blackwell, 2019.

———. "Naturalistic Theories of Life After Death." *Philosophy Compass* 10 (2015) 145–58.

———. "Spiritual Naturalism." In *The Philosophy of Spirituality: Analytic, Continental, and Multicultural Approaches to a New Field of Philosophy*, edited by Heather Salazar and Roderick Nicholis, 312–38. Value Inquiry. Leiden: Brill-Rodopi, 2018.

———. *Your Digital Afterlives: Computational Theories of Life After Death*. Basingstoke: Palgrave MacMillan, 2014.

Strawson, Galen. "I Have No Future." In *Things That Bother Me: Death, Freedom, the Self, Etc.*, 71–91. New York: New York Review of Books, 2018.

Sumner, L. W. "A Matter of Life and Death." *Noûs* 10 (1976) 145–71.

Tabaczek, Mariusz. "Is Pain Metaphysically Evil (*Malum Simpliciter*)? Some Thoughts from a Thomistic Perspective." *Scientia et Fides* 12 (2024) 143–62.

Taylor, Charles. *A Secular Age*. Cambridge, MA: Belknap, 2007.

Thomas, Columba, ed. and trans. *The Art of Dying: A New Annotated Translation*. Philadelphia: National Catholic Bioethics Center, 2021.

Thomson, Iain, and James Bodington. "Against Immortality: Why Death Is Better Than the Alternative." In *Intelligence Unbound: The Future of Uploaded and Machine Minds*, edited by Russell Blackford and Damien Broderick, 248–62. Newark: Wiley, 2014.

Thornton, Allison K. "Disembodied Animals." *American Philosophical Quarterly* (2019) 203–17.

Tillich, Paul. *The Courage to Be*. London: Collins, 1965.

Tilliette, Xavier. *Morte e immortalità*. Translated by Giuliano Sansonetti. Brescia: Morcelliana, 2011.

---. *Morte e sopravvivenza: In dialogo con Xavier Tilliette*, edited by Giuseppe Lorizio. Rome: AVE, 1995.
Tolstoy, Leo. "*The Death of Ivan Ilyitch*"; *And Other Stories*. Translated by Constance Garnett. London: Heinemann, 1902.
Toner, Patrick. "Hylemorphic Animalism." *Philosophical Studies* 155 (2011) 65–81.
---. "Personhood and Death in St. Thomas Aquinas." *History of Philosophy Quarterly* (2009) 121–38.
---. "St. Thomas Aquinas on Death and the Separated Soul." *Pacific Philosophical Quarterly* 91 (2010) 587–99.
Tonti-Filippini, Nicholas. "'Bodily Integration': A Response to Robert Spaemann." *Comm* 39 (2012) 413–21.
Totschnig, Wolfhart. "Arendt's Notion of Natality: An Attempt at Clarification." *Ideas y Valores* 66 (2017) 327–46.
Troisfontaines, Roger. *I Do Not Die*. Translated by Francis E. Albert. New York: Desclee Co., 1963.
Tugendhat, Ernst. *Über den Tod*. Frankfurt am Main: Suhrkamp, 2006.
Ulrich, Ferdinand. *Gebet als geschöpflicher Grundakt*. Einsiedeln, Switz.: Johannes, 1974.
---. *Homo Abyssus: The Drama of the Question of Being*. Translated by D. C. Schindler. Washington, DC: Humanum Academic, 2018.
---. "Man in the Beginning: Toward a Philosophical Anthropology of Childhood." In *Three Short Works*. Translated by Robert Van Alstyne, Andrew Shivone, and D. C. Schindler. Washington, DC: Humanum Academic, 2024, 55–172.
---. "The Unity of Life and Death in the Word of Life." *Comm* 28 (2001) 99–111.
Van Inwagen, Peter. *Material Beings*. Ithaca: Cornell University Press, 1991.
Vatican. "Catechism of the Catholic Church." Vatican, Nov. 4, 2003. From *Catechism of the Catholic Church* (Vatican City: Libreria Editrice Vaticana, 1993). https://www.vatican.va/archive/ENG0015/_INDEX.HTM#fonte.
Vattimo, Gianni. *Le avventure della differenza*. Milan: Garzanti, 1980.
---. "Dialectics, Difference, Weak Thought." In *Weak Thought*, edited by Gianni Vattimo and Pier Aldo Rovatti, translated by Peter Carravetta, 39–52. Contemporary Italian Philosophy. Albany: SUNY Press, 2012.
---. *Oltre l'interpretazione: Il significato dell'ermeneutica per la filosofia*. Rome: Laterza, 1994.
---. "Postmodernism, Technology, Ontology." In *Nihilism and Emancipation: Ethics, Politics, and Law*, edited by Santiago Zabala, translated by William McCuaig, 3–20. European Perspectives: A Series in Social Thought and Cultural Criticism. New York: Columbia University Press, 2004.
Velde, Rudi A. te. "Evil, Sin, and Death: Thomas Aquinas on Original Sin." In *The Theology of Thomas Aquinas*, edited by Rik van Nieuwenhove and Joseph Wawrykow, 143–66. Notre Dame, IN: University of Notre Dame Press, 2005.
Voegelin, Eric. *The New Science of Politics: An Introduction*. Walgreen Foundation Lectures. Chicago: University of Chicago Press, 1987.
---. *Science, Politics & Gnosticism*. Wilmington, DE: ISI, 2004.
Weil, Simone. *Gravity and Grace*. Translated by Emma Crawford and Mario von der Ruhr. London: Routledge, 2002.
---. *Waiting for God*. Translated by Emma Crawford. New York: Harper & Row, 1973.

BIBLIOGRAPHY

Weinandy, Thomas G. *In the Likeness of Sinful Flesh: An Essay on the Humanity of Christ*. Edinburgh: T&T Clark, 1993.

Welte, Bernhard. *Morire: La prova decisiva della speranza*. Translated by Sandro Gorgone. Brescia: Queriniana, 2008.

——. "Search and Find: An Address on the Occasion of Martin Heidegger's Funeral." *Universitas* 19 (1977) 301–5.

White, Thomas Joseph. *Lord Incarnate: A Thomistic Study in Christology*. Thomistic Ressourcement Series. Washington, DC: Catholic University of America Press, 2015.

Wiggins, David. *Identity and Spatio-Temporal Continuity*. Oxford: Blackwell, 1967.

Williams, Bernard. "The Makropulos Case: Reflections on the Tedium of Immortality." In *Problems of the Self: Philosophical Papers 1956–1972*, 82–100. New York: Cambridge University Press, 1999.

Wittgenstein, Ludwig. *Philosophical Investigations*. Translated by G. E. M. Anscombe et al. Revised by P. M. S. Hacker and Joachim Schulte. 4th ed. Oxford: Wiley-Blackwell, 2009.

——. *Tractatus Logico-Philosophicus*. Translated by D. F. Pears and B. F. McGuinness. Routledge Classics. Repr., London: Routledge, 2006.

Wojtyła, Karol. "Subjectivity and the Irreducible in the Human Being." In *Person and Community: Selected Essays*, translated by Theresa Sandok, 209–17. Catholic Thought from Lublin. New York: Lang, 1993.

——. "Thomistic Personalism." In *Person and Community: Selected Essays*, translated by Theresa Sandok, 165–75. Catholic Thought from Lublin. New York: Lang, 1993.

Wolin, Richard. *Heidegger in Ruins: Between Philosophy and Ideology*. New Haven, CT: Yale University Press, 2022.

Yourgrau, Palle. *Death and Nonexistence*. New York: Oxford University Press, 2019.

Index

Adorno, Theodor W., 209n189
Agazzi, Evandro, 100n91
Alighieri, Dante, 117
Amerini, Fabrizio, 66n3
Aquinas, Thomas, 5, 9n18, 13–14,
    18–19, 22, 26–27, 39n41,
    40, 42n48, 44, 52–55, 57,
    60–63, 65–80, 83–84, 87–94,
    99, 104–7, 110–12, 115–17,
    126, 138–139, 149, 158, 161,
    163n90, 164, 179, 183, 185, 190,
    194n154, 199n165, 202n173,
    230, 258–59, 271n89, 274
Arendt, Hannah, 211n192, 289–91
Ariès, Philippe, 30, 238n28
Aristotle, 7, 13, 16, 26–27, 38, 40, 53,
    57n76, 68, 71–72, 91, 117, 119,
    201n171, 238, 268, 285, 287
Augustine of Hippo, 10n19, 12–13, 78,
    82, 83n52, 111, 116, 126, 129–
    30, 143n44, 145n46, 150n62,
    202n172, 236n22, 272n91,
    279n107, 281n109, 288n122
Aurelius, Marcus, 34

Bacon, Francis, 233
Baker, Lynne Rudder, 41n45
Balthasar, Hans Urs von, ix, 6, 67n8,
    95n82, 107, 109–11, 115n131,
    127, 137, 143n43, 159n78, 172,
    174–80, 182–87, 285
Barth, Karl, 109
Barzaghi, Giuseppe, 158n77, 279n105

Bauman, Zygmunt, 241n34, 248–49
Becker, Lawrence C., 41n45
Benedict XVI, Pope, 183
Benjamin, Walter, 203–204
Bergson, Henri, 167, 201–2, 235n17,
    236n22, 255
Bernanos, George, 132
Bernard of Clairvaux, 279
Betz, John R., 178, 179n121, 183–85,
    265n78
Bichat, Xavier, 162
Bieler, Martin, 177n116, 181n127
Bishop, Jeffrey P., 232
Blanchot, Maurice, 197
Bloch, Ernst, 145n47
Blondel, Maurice, ix, 140, 151n63,
    189n143, 229–33, 255–57, 260–
    61, 273n93, 274, 278, 284n116,
    285n117, 291
Bloy, Léon, 264
Böckh, August, 217
Bodington, James, 241n34
Boethius, Anicius Manlius Severinus,
    130
Bonaventure of Bagnoregio, 111n118,
    146
Boros, Ladislaus, 188
Bostrom, Nick, 227n1
Botturi, Francesco, 262–63
Bowen-Moore, Patricia, 289n125
Bradley, Ben, 25n12
Brague, Rémi, 14n32, 125n2, 261n71,
    267n81

INDEX

Brand, Dennis J., 115n130
Braun, David, 57n76
Brook, Angus, 82n50
Brotherton, Joshua R., 184n135, 185n137, 186n139
Brown, Deborah J., 39n41
Bruaire, Claude, 113n123
Buber, Martin, xii, 145n46
Bulgakov, Sergius, xii
Butler, Judith, 145n47

Canetti, Elias, 280n109, 285n118
Carel, Havi, 101n92
Carrasco, María A., 46n56
Carter, W. R., 41n45, 56n75
Cavanaugh, William T., 247n43
Chesterton, G. K., 17n35, 131, 149n59, 202n173, 203n175
Cioran, Emile M., 140n34
Clarke, W. Norris, 19, 148n57
Claudel, Paul, 64, 171n109, 172n109
Condorcet, Antoine-Nicholas de, 240
Cordeiro, José Luis, 253n33
Corte, Marcel de, 124
Cullman, Oscar, 112n120
Cunningham, Conor, 125n1

Dahm, Brandon, 62n80
Dastur, Françoise, 6-9, 211n193, 222-23
De Grey, Aubrey D. N. J., 234-35
De Haan, Daniel D., 62n80
De Lubac, Henri, ix
Deleuze, Gilles, 71n17, 293
Del Noce, Augusto, 153-57, 161, 167, 234
DeLorenzo, Leonard J., 108-10
Derrida, Jacques, 189, 194, 264n75
Descartes, René, 20, 39n41, 74 note, 233, 275n99
Desmond, William, 114n126, 150
Dostoevsky, Fyodor, 81
Dubilet, Alex, 71n17

Eberl, Jason T., 26n16, 61n80, 66n3, 83n54, 261n72
Eckhart, Meister, 71n17, 154, 158
Engels, Friedrich, 156

Epictetus, 283n114
Epicurus, 23-26, 29, 34, 194, 257, 283n114
Esposito, Costantino, 296n4

Faller, Adolf, 91n76
Falque, Emmanuel, 3n5, 71n17, 75-76, 78-81, 192, 195, 259, 261n71, 265-67, 288-90, 292, 294
Feldman, Fred, 41n45, 45, 47n57, 48n61, 56
Feser, Edward, 99n90
Feuerbach, Ludwig, 113n121,
Flannery, Kevin L., 66n3
Foucault, Michel, 238
Francescotti, Robert, 41n45, 43n49, 48n58
Francis of Assisi, 127
Francis, Pope, 232
Franks, Angela, 183, 184-85
Freud, Sigmund, 30n22, 103n97, 135n24
Fritsche, Johannes, 157n76
Fulton, Robert, 248n46
Fumet, Stanislas, 263n74

Gadamer, Hans-Georg, 136-37, 160, 217-19, 221
Geach, Peter, 44
Giesen, Klaus-Gerd, 235n18
Gilson, Étienne, 52, 146-47
Giussani, Luigi, 171n109
Gonzales, Philip John Paul, 107n103
Göpffarth, Julian, 157n76
Gorer, Geoffrey, 10n21
Gorman, Michael, 99n90
Granados, José, 96-97
Guardini, Romano, 107, 126, 129n11, 169, 202n173, 211n193, 231

Hadjadj, Fabrice, 14, 17n35, 107n106, 146 n48 and 49, 197, 287n121, 292n133
Hadot, Pierre, 26n15
Han, Byung-Chul, 197-98, 257
Hanby, Michael, 232n10
Hart, David Bentley, 81
Haycock, David Boyd, 233n13
Hayen, André, 65

INDEX

Hegel, G. W. F., x, 7–8, 31, 136, 146, 152–56, 158–61, 163, 179, 194, 241–47, 250
Heidegger, Martin, x, 6, 9n18, 19, 27, 55n73, 67n7, 71, 80, 101, 113–15, 119, 136–37, 144–45, 147, 150, 157–58, 160, 167, 188, 193–94, 198n163, 205–17, 219–25, 232, 237, 239–41, 243, 246, 249, 265, 289, 295
Hershenov, David, 47n57, 48, 54n71
Hildebrand, Dietrich, von, xii, 282n113
Hinshaw, Daniel, 71
Holland, Henry Scott, 167n102
Hugo, Victor, 272
Husserl, Edmund, 221
Hyppolite, Jean, 154n71

Illich, Ivan, 247

Jalbert, John E., 208n185
Jankélévitch, Vladimir, 1–2, 8–10, 12, 14, 103, 136–37, 159–60, 167–170, 201n169, 236, 275
John Paul II, Pope, xiii, 2n4, 50n66, 129n11, 183, 248n45
Johnson, Mark, 84n57
Jonas, Hans, 136–37, 159–60, 162–64, 166, 201n167
Jones, David A., 69n3
Journet, Charles, 17n35
Jullien, François, 235–36

Kagan, Shelly, 28, 41n46
Kalkavage, Peter, 71n18, 72n21, 242n35
Kamm, F. M., 21–22
Kant, Immanuel, 40, 52–53, 55, 186, 221, 244
Kass, Leon R., 269–72
Kierkegaard, Søren, 5, 150n62, 204
Klima, Gyula, 53n70
Knepper, Steven, 12
Kojève, Alexandre, 136, 154–55
Kripke, Saul A., 20
Kurzweil, Ray, 235

Lacan, Jacques, 135–36, 268
LaCocque, André, 80n44

Lacoste, Jean-Yves, 70, 71n16
Landsberg, Paul-Louis, 13–14, 17 note, 189n143, 227, 281n112
Le Breton, David, 261n72
Leget, Carlo, 88n64
Leibniz, Gottfried W., 16
Lepori, Mauro Giuseppe, 159–60
Levinas, Emmanuel, 119n142, 193–95, 198n164, 286–97
Lewis, C. S., 182n128, 268
Long, A. G., 24n10
López, Antonio, 113n123 and n124, 138, 161n81, 171
Lowe, E. J., 54n71
Lucretius, Titus, 23–25, 29, 34
Luther, Martin, 145n46, 150n62

Macdonald, Paul A., 76, 77n36 and 37, 80n46
Mackie, David, 41n45, 42n47, 45, 46n55, 47n57, 48n58, 51n67, 54n71 and n72
Marcel, Gabriel, x–xi, 11–14, 35, 103, 138–40, 188n141, 210n191, 281
Maritain, Jacques, 109, 148
Martelet, Gustave, 81n48
Marx, Karl, 135n24, 145n47, 154–55, 157–58, 223
McFarland, Ian, 76
McMahan, Jeff, 21–22
Melchiorre, Virgilio, 14, 55n73, 281n111
Monsó, Susana, 101n94
Montaigne, Michel, de, 30, 278n103, 283n114
More, Max, 227n1, 235
Morin, Edgar, 10n20, 135n24, 239
Mothersill, Mary, 25n14
Murdoch, Iris, 194n153
Murphy, Jeffrie G., 61

Nagel, Thomas, 21n1, 23, 32n23
Nemo, Philippe, 198n164
Niederhauser, Johannes A., 150n62, 205n181, 207
Nielsen, Cynthia R., 217n209

319

INDEX

Nietzsche, Friedrich, ix, 20, 125n2, 135n24, 143, 221, 229, 265n78, 266n80
Normore, Calvin G., 39n41
Novello, Henry L., 69n12, n13 and n14, 192
Nussbaum, Martha C., 272n90

Oakes, Edward T., 129
Oderberg, David S., 26n16, 48–50
Olson, Eric T., 48–50, 54n71
O'Regan, Cyril, 130
Oster, Stefan, 107n102, 175n112, 180

Pascal, Blaise, 4, 29–30, 35, 74, 111, 140, 142–44, 150n62, 226, 251–54, 260n70
Pasnau, Robert, 84n59, 93n81
Pattison, George, 150n62
Paul VI, Pope, 4n8, 128n8, 129n10
Pegis, Anton, 84n59, 93n81
Péguy, Charles, 17, 18, 202–3, 293
Peirce, Charles S., 16, 17n34, 29n19, 163n89, 201
Petrosino, Silvano, 157n75, 291
Pickstock, Catherine, 201n167, 231
Pieper, Josef, ix, 14, 67n9, 72n21, 74, 91n76, 138, 142
Pippin, Robert B., 242n37
Plato, ix, 7, 26, 71–72, 74n26, 95, 152, 217, 259, 264n77, 275, 285
Plotinus, 275n99
Przywara, Erich, ix, 73, 82n50, 106–7, 109–23, 164–65, 178, 179n20, 183, 265n78
Pseudo-Dionysius, 124, 152, 173
Purtill, Richard, 99n90

Quevedo, Francisco, de, 64
Quine, W. V. O., 3

Rachels, James, 23n8
Rae, Michael, 235n16
Rahner, Karl, 66–69, 89n70, 95n83, 97n89, 101n92, 128n8, 188–191, 194, 198, 200
Ratcliffe, Susan, 288n123

Ratzinger, Joseph, 10–11, 17n35, 69n13, 74n27, 80n44, 143,
Ravaisson, Félix, 201n171
Reichlin, Massimo, 68
Remenyi, Matthias, 62n80
Ricoeur, Paul, 90n72, 203, 209, 276n101, 281n111
Robinette, Brian D., 108
Roessiger, Ursula L., 154n71
Romano, Claude, 265–66
Rorty, Richard, 217
Rosenbaum, Stephen E., 62
Rosenzweig, Franz, 264n77
Rousseau, Mary F., 82n50

Sadler, Gregory B., 2n3
Sànchez Sorondo, Marcelo, 66n3
Sartre, Jean-Paul, 136–37, 143, 150n62, 160, 191, 193, 197, 200, 203–5, 209–10, 213–17
Scheler, Max, xii, 133n22, 202–3, 227, 237–38, 280n108, 281n111
Schelling, Friedrich W. J. von, 201n171, 236n22
Scherer, Georg, 227–28
Schindler, D. C., 138, 141, 162, 217, 253n56
Schmitz, Kenneth L., 116n133, 138, 142n40, 201n167, 231
Schopenhauer, Arthur, 140, 161
Schumacher, Bernard N., 22–23, 25n13, 101n92, 102n95, 214n204
Seneca, Lucius Annaeus, 283n114
Sertillanges, Antonin-Gilbert, 165n96 and 98
Servais, Jacques, 127n7
Simmel, Georg, 136–37, 159–60, 162–64, 166–68, 208n185, 219
Singh, Raj R., 205n181
Smith, Randall B., 261n72
Smith Gilson, Caitlin, 130
Snowdon, Paul, 41, 47n57, 48n59, n60 and n62, 54n72, 55n74
Socrates, ix, 43, 71n20, 72n21, 150n62, 201, 275n98, 276
Spaemann, Robert, 51n66

INDEX

Spencer, Mark K., 66n3, 68n11, 90n73, 274n95
Speyr, Adrienne von, ix, 6, 127n7, 131–34, 164n91, 177, 191
Spinoza, Baruch, 116, 153
Stango, Marco, ix–xiii, 29n19, 36n32, 90n73, 201n170, 228n3
Stein, Edith, ix, 73, 139n31, 152
Steinhart, Eric C., 36n31, n32 and n34, 37–38, 40, 60, 237, 267
Strawson, Galen, 18, 28, 31–35, 38, 41
Sumner, L. W., 48n63

Tabaczek, Mariusz, 80n46
Taylor, Charles, 154n69
Thomas, Columba, 278n103
Thomson, Iain, 205n180, 241n34
Thornton, Allison K., 44n52, 54n71
Tillich, Paul, 136–37, 159–60, 162, 166n100, 167
Tilliette, Xavier, 1–2, 14, 17n35, 64, 187, 236n115, 283
Tolstoy, Leo, 102
Toner, Patrick, 44n50, 48n63, 61n80
Tonti-Filippini, Nicholas, 51n66
Totschnig, Wolfhart, 289n125
Troisfontaines, Roger, 188
Tugendhat, Ernst, 203

Tymieniecka, Anna-Teresa, 100n91

Ulrich, Ferdinand, ix, 137–38, 141, 153, 172, 174–77, 179–82, 293

Van Inwagen, Peter, 48
Valera, Luca, 46n56
Vattimo, Gianni, x, 136–37, 150, 217, 219–24, 257
Velde, Rudi A. te, 82n50
Vita-More, Natasha, 227n1, 235
Voegelin, Eric, 234

Weil, Simone, 125, 140n35, 194n153, 196–97, 258n65, 276n100
Weinandy, Thomas G., 65n1
Welte, Bernhard, 99n90, 150n62
White, Thomas Joseph, 183
Wiener, Norbert, 37
Wiggins, David, 86n62
Williams, Bernard, 247n44
Wittgenstein, Ludwig, 29, 59, 163n89
Wojtyła, Karol, xii, 68–69
Wolin, Richard, 157n76
Wood, David, 253n55

Yourgrau, Palle, 72n20

www.ingramcontent.com/pod-product-compliance
Lightning Source LLC
Chambersburg PA
CBHW052145300426
44115CB00011B/1532